Learning and Teaching from Experience

Learning and Teaching from Experience

Perspectives on Nonnative English-Speaking Professionals

Edited by Lía D. Kamhi-Stein

THE UNIVERSITY OF MICHIGAN PRESS
ANN ARBOR

Copyright © by the University of Michigan 2004
All rights reserved
Published in the United States of America by
The University of Michigan Press
Manufactured in the United States of America
∞ Printed on acid-free paper

2007   2006   2005   2004   4   3   2   1

A CIP catalog record for this book is available from the British Library.

ISBN 0-472-08998-6

Acknowledgments

There are a number of people to whom I am indebted for helping me complete this project. First, I would like to express my deepest appreciation to all the contributors to this volume. Their willingness to share their ideas and their commitment to the project made the process of producing the book an extraordinary experience.

Second, I would like to acknowledge Donna M. Brinton and Robby Ching, past co-editors of the *CATESOL Journal,* who in 1999 invited me to serve as guest editor of a special theme section on nonnative English-speaking (NNES) professionals. The theme section, published in 2001, gave me the opportunity to explore ideas regarding the role of NNES professionals and was the foundation for this book. I am grateful to Donna and Robby for their support and continuous guidance in the completion of the *CATESOL Journal* theme section.

Third, I am extremely grateful to John Evenhuis, David Ifergan, Troy Parr, and Damian Wyman, graduate assistants in the MA in teaching English to speakers of other languages (TESOL) program at California State University, Los Angeles (CSULA), who checked references, assisted with the indexes, and completed valuable editorial work. My appreciation also goes to the students in the MA in TESOL program at CSULA, who have been helpful in shaping my thinking about issues related to NNES professionals. To my NNES students, I owe my admiration and respect for their strength and perseverance.

Fourth, I want to acknowledge George Braine, Jun Liu, Rosie Maum, Luciana C. de Oliveira, Elis Lee, and all of my friends and colleagues in the Nonnative English Speakers in TESOL (NNEST) Caucus for their ongoing support and for their efforts to provide a voice and visibility to NNES professionals.

Fifth, I want to thank CSULA for providing me with grants that have enabled me to fulfill this project. Sixth, I am especially thankful to the two anonymous reviewers who provided valuable and constructive feedback.

Seventh, I would like to express my heartfelt appreciation to Kelly Sippell, my editor at the University of Michigan Press, for embracing the project. Kelly's tremendous patience, enthusiasm, encouragement, and acumen were invaluable in making this project a reality. I am also grateful to the staff of the University of Michigan Press for their invaluable editorial work on this volume.

Finally, I would like to express my deepest thanks to my husband, Alan, who has been a willing "weekend widower" for the duration of this project (and many other projects!). He is my cheerleader and biggest supporter. ¡Gracias por ayudarme a mantenerme en el camino!

Grateful acknowledgment is made to the following journal for permission to reprint previously published materials.

CATESOL Journal, volume 13, number 1, © 2001 CATESOL Journal for the following articles:

"Autonomy and Collaboration in Teacher Education: Journal Sharing among Native and Nonnative English-Speaking Teachers" by Aya Matsuda and Paul Kei Matsuda

"Confessions of a Nonnative English-Speaking Professional" by Jun Liu

"Teaching in Kindergarten through Grade 12 Programs: Perceptions of Native and Nonnative English-Speaking Practitioners" by Lía D. Kamhi-Stein et al.

"Collaboration between Native and Nonnative English-Speaking Educators" by Luciana C. de Oliveira and Sally Richardson

"Nativism, the Native Speaker Construct, and Minority Immigrant Women Teachers of English as a Second Language" by Nuzhat Amin

Every effort has been made to contact the copyright holders for permissions to reprint borrowed material. We regret any oversights that may have occurred and will rectify them in future printings of this book.

Contents

Introduction

Lía D. Kamhi-Stein

I immigrated to the United States in 1990. Prior to coming to the United States, I received two bachelor's degrees, one as a certified public translator and the other as a teacher of English to speakers of other languages in Argentina, the country where I was born and raised. In Argentina, I had worked as an English as a foreign language (EFL) teacher, a college professor, and a program administrator with the Binational Center (BNC) in Buenos Aires. As an administrator with the BNC, I had the opportunity to study at the 1986 Teachers of English to Speakers of Other Languages (TESOL) Summer Institute in Hawaii and to present at several annual TESOL conventions.

Shortly after my arrival in the United States, I attended a language teachers' conference in California. After reviewing the conference program book, I decided to attend a session featuring administrators from several intensive English programs (IEPs). After an interesting presentation in which the administrators discussed a variety of topics (including differences in students' profiles, materials development, etc.), it was time for questions and answers. A member of the audience, then, asked the panelists whether they had nonnative English-speaking (NNES) professionals on their staffs. At that point, my attention, which I have to admit was drifting, perked up. The panel members, as if in unison, all agreed and gave a response that is still engrained in my memory. They said something analogous to: Why would we consider hiring NNES professionals? Students come from abroad to be taught by native English speakers.

While this is a sad anecdote, 14 years later, it now has a happy ending. As Ahmar Mahboob shows in a chapter in this book, students enrolled in IEPs do not buy into the notion that only native speakers

can be good language teachers (Phillipson, 1992). Had research like
the one described by Mahboob (in this volume) been available in
1990, I, as an NNES professional, could have provided the administrators with a data-driven response. However, the paucity of literature
available in 1990 did not allow me to refute the negative perceptions
of the administrators. Nor did the limited, if any, available literature
about NNES professionals allow me to draw solace from viewpoints
that opposed the narrow ones expressed by the administrators.

In the early 1990s, there was some interest in the notion of the native speaker and NNES professionals (for discussions on the topics,
see Davies, 1991; Medgyes, 1994). However, it was not until the 30th
annual TESOL convention in 1996 when a NNES professionals' movement began. At the 1996 TESOL convention, George Braine organized
a colloquium titled "In Their Own Voices: Nonnative Speaker Professionals in TESOL" (see Braine, this volume, for a complete description of the colloquium) featuring the struggles and triumphs of NNES
educators.

As explained by Braine (this volume), the colloquium proved groundbreaking since it prompted the establishment of the Nonnative English
Speakers in TESOL (NNEST) Caucus that has given NNES professionals
both a voice and visibility in the professional community. Moreover,
issues related to NNES professionals have become a legitimate topic
of interest. For example, since 1996, interest in NNES professionals has
been reflected in the establishment of NNEST Caucuses at the TESOL
affiliate level and in the growing number of related presentations at
annual TESOL (and TESOL-affiliate) conventions. Since 1996, interest in issues related to NNES professionals has also been reflected in
the publication of more than 50 refereed articles and a twice-a-year
NNEST Caucus Newsletter; the writing of over four dissertations and
five master's theses; and the publication of two volumes focusing on
the topic (Belcher & Connor, 2001; Braine, 1999).

*Learning and Teaching from Experience: Perspectives on Nonna-
tive English-Speaking Professionals* reflects this current and growing
interest in NNES professionals and the issues that are of concern to
them. This volume consists of 16 chapters in which, writing from their
unique vantage points, both native and nonnative English-speaking
professionals focus on theory and research related to NNES professionals, examine a wide range of issues related to the professional
preparation of NNES teachers, and discuss implications for classroom
practice. In editing this book, one of my objectives was to widen the
range of voices available in the literature about NNES professionals
by including contributions not only by NNES but also by native English-speaking (NES) professionals. While it is critical that the voices
of NNES professionals continue to be heard through the nonnative

English speakers themselves, I believe that there is a need to integrate into the discussion the perspective of NES professionals who have contributed to strengthening the professional preparation of pre-service and in-service NNES professionals and to increasing the professional opportunities available to them.

This book does not seek to define the terms *native speaker* and *nonnative speaker*. As already noted in Braine (1999), this topic is well covered by Davies (1991) in his book titled *The Native Speaker in Applied Linguistics* and in his most recent book, *The Native Speaker: Myth and Reality* (2003). In the English language teaching (ELT) field, several researchers have questioned the validity of the native speaker construct and, by extension, challenged the notion that the native speaker is the ideal English teacher. For example, Kramsch (1998) argues that the "native speaker" is an abstraction "based on arbitrarily selected features of pronunciation, grammar, lexicon, as well as on stereotypical features of appearances and demeanor" (pp. 79–80) and relies on the assumption that native speakers are monolingual and monocultural and only speak a standard variety of the language of which they are native speakers. However, this assumption is not supported by reality since most people speak more than one language or varieties of a language and participate in more than one culture and subculture (Kramsch, 1998). Kaplan (1999) questions the validity of the "native speaker" construct on similar grounds. According to him, the construct "creates an impression that linguistic unity exists, when global reality reflects vast linguistic diversity" (p. 5), and terms such as *native speakers* or *nonnative speakers* only serve the purpose of separating people into different camps.

Several of the chapters in this book criticize the native speaker versus the nonnative English speaker dichotomy since it is "overly simplistic" (a point made by Pasternak and Bailey, this volume) and docs not capture the complexities involved in being a NNES professional. Rather than looking at the two groups of professionals as having discrete skills and competencies, several chapters in this book suggest that NES and NNES professionals *share* complementary skills and competencies. This idea is best explained by Pasternak and Bailey, who argue that language proficiency and professional development should be viewed "as continua rather than as categorical absolutes" (this volume).

I would like to think that this volume represents the "state of the art" in issues related to NNES professionals at the present time. The book is organized into four sections. **Section 1, Theoretical Underpinnings,** presents three chapters designed to provide an introduction and background information to the issues discussed in this book. Emphasis in this section is placed on contextualizing the NNES professionals' movement and identifying emerging research related to the topic of NNES professionals. This section also presents two personal narratives designed to promote a better understanding of the professional development process of two different types of NNES professionals: visible and invisible minorities—that is, minorities who come from white or non-white ethnic groups (Hansen, this volume).

Section 2, Focus on Research, presents four studies exploring issues related to NNES professionals from different perspectives. The first chapter in this section deals with the interaction of language, race, and gender and how such interaction affects students' perceptions of immigrant women instructors teaching adult English as a second language (ESL) classes in Canada. The next chapter focuses on kindergarten through grade 12 (K–12) teachers from a native and a nonnative English-speaking background and issues of professionalism, including perceptions about job satisfaction and professional preparation. The subsequent chapter focuses on a topic that has not received much, if any, attention in the literature: the hiring criteria implemented by U.S.-based intensive English program (IEP) administrators. The final chapter in the section presents the results of research focusing on another topic that has also received only limited attention in the literature: students' attitudes toward native and nonnative English-speaking professionals teaching in IEPs in the United States.

Section 3, Focus on Teacher Preparation, presents five chapters supporting the notion that it is the responsibility of teacher education programs to create conditions in which all teachers, regardless of language status, succeed. The first chapter in the section breaks new ground by articulating the idea that language proficiency is not the same as nativeness and that language proficiency and professional development should be viewed "as continua rather than as categorical absolutes" (Pastenak & Bailey, this volume). The next two chapters examine the dialogue journal entries of student teachers enrolled in practicum courses. The following chapter describes how a practicum course in the United States has been redesigned to address the cross-cultural needs of NNES student teachers. The last chapter in the section describes a variety of strategies used by a NNES teacher educator designed to empower nonnative English-speaking teachers for EFL teaching.

Section 4, Focus on the Classroom, discusses the implications of theory and research on NNES professionals for ESL and EFL classrooms. In the first chapter, a teacher educator and a U.S.-trained EFL professional reflect on their reconstructed views about EFL education and teacher preparation and offer suggestions for adapting Western instructional practices to the realities of an EFL setting. The next chapter focuses on a notion that has not been widely discussed in the literature—the figure of the "intercultural speaker"—and describes a variety of classroom projects designed to help EFL students become intercultural speakers. The final two chapters in the section emphasize the value of native and nonnative English speaker collaboration. There has been much talk about the value of native and nonnative English speaker collaboration, but to my knowledge, very few examples of collaborative projects have been published. The first of the final two chapters in Section 4 describes the history of the authors' collaborative relationship and discusses how their individual differences and similarities have contributed to their enhanced understanding of the teaching and learning process and to their shared growth as professionals. The last chapter in the book describes the lessons learned from and the steps followed in completing a project in which both native and nonnative English-speaking professionals collaborated to produce standards for EFL teachers, in-service teacher trainers, educational leaders, and in-service training courses in Egypt. Each of the four sections in the book concludes with Questions for Reflection, which provide readers with issues to consider regarding the chapters in each section. The questions also require readers to synthesize information from the different chapters in the section.

In this book, the notion that collaboration brings clear benefits to TESOL professionals is not limited to the chapters that describe collaborative projects between native and nonnative English-speaking professionals. Several other chapters in the book emphasize the importance of professional collaboration in that they have been co-authored by native and nonnative English speakers. In writing these chapters, the authors have engaged in a partnership characterized by their mutual respect for one another's ideas and experiences.

The chapters in the book vary as to their foci. Some chapters have been written with a North American/British/Australian audience in mind, and others have been specifically written with an EFL audience in mind. The chapters also differ in terms of the setting on which they focus (ESL or EFL) and the level of instruction with which they deal (K–12 programs, IEPs, adult ESL programs, ESL and EFL teacher preparation programs, etc). However, central to these chapters is the notion that the practices described for one setting or level may well be applicable to a different setting or level.

The contributors to this book come from diverse backgrounds. While all but one of the contributors have completed, at least in part, their studies in the United States, many of them are NNES professionals who have taught in EFL and ESL settings and who eventually became teacher educators in the United States and in other countries. Other contributors are NES professionals who have shown great interest in the NNES professionals' movement as well as in the NNEST

Caucus. (In fact, one of these contributors, Kathleen M. Bailey, was the president of the TESOL organization at the time the organization approved the establishment of the NNEST Caucus.) Other authors are practitioners from native and nonnative English-speaking backgrounds who teach at different levels (kindergarten through college) in ESL and EFL contexts.

It is my hope that the readers of this book—including teachers-in-preparation and practitioners from native and nonnative English-speaking backgrounds, teacher educators, and researchers interested in issues related to NNES professionals—will find the contributions insightful and meaningful to their professional lives. Issues of professional credibility, language proficiency, and job opportunities are of concern primarily to NNES professionals. On the other hand, issues of classroom management, teacher preparation, and the role of collaboration in professional development are of common concern to both native and nonnative English speakers alike. Whether the issues are common to both NES and NNES professionals or unique to one group or the other, this book seeks to develop a better understanding of the complexities involved in being a NNES professional and to identify strategies that will allow NES and NNES professionals to draw on their strengths and bridge their differences toward a common goal, the teaching of English.

Given the large numbers of NNES professionals worldwide, it is my hope that *Learning and Teaching from Experience: Perspectives on Nonnative English-Speaking Professionals* will increase the understanding about this group of professionals, who have only recently become more vocal and visible. I hope that the path that native and nonnative English-speaking professionals share is made wider by this book.

References

Belcher, D., & Connor, U. (Eds.). (2001). *Reflections on multiliterate lives.* Clevedon, England: Multilingual Matters.

Braine, G. (1999). *Non-native educators in English language teaching.* Mahwah, NJ: Erlbaum.

Davies, A. (1991). *The native speaker in applied linguistics.* Edinburgh, Scotland: Edinburgh University Press.

Davies, A. (2003). *The native speaker: Myth and reality.* Clevedon, England: Multilingual Matters.

Kaplan, R. B. (1999, March). The ELT: Ho(NEST) or not ho(NEST)? *NNEST Newsletter, 1*(1), 1, 5–6.

Kramsch, C. (1998). *Language and culture.* Oxford: Oxford University Press.

Medgyes, L. (1994). *The non-native teacher.* London: Macmillan.

Phillipson, R. (1992). *Linguistic imperialism.* Oxford: Oxford University Press.

Section 1

Theoretical Underpinnings

Section 1 provides a general introduction and background information to the issues discussed in this book. The readings in this section therefore serve to contextualize the chapters in the other three sections of this book. In the opening chapter, "The Nonnative English-Speaking Professionals' Movement and Its Research Foundations," George Braine, a leading figure in the NNES professionals' movement, describes the history of this movement, placing emphasis on the birth of the Nonnative English Speakers Caucus in the TESOL organization. In his chapter, Braine also provides an overview of the research focusing on NNES professionals and pays special attention to emerging research on the topic.

The remaining two chapters of this section present two personal narratives designed to promote a better understanding of the professional development process of two different types of NNES professionals: visible and invisible minorities—that is, minorities who come from white or non-white ethnic groups (Hansen, this volume). In the chapter titled "Confessions of a Nonnative English-Speaking Professional," Jun Liu, a visible minority, describes the three stages of his own professional development in the U.S., with each stage dealing with a specific dilemma. Liu's first stage, "Puzzlement," deals with the challenges to his self-confidence that he experienced as a newly arrived graduate student in the U.S. Liu's second stage, "Endeavor," focuses on what he calls the "adaptive cultural transformation" process, involving the development of strategies that allowed him to function successfully in the target culture and in his first culture by integrating values, habits, and social norms from both. Liu's final stage, "Empowerment," describes what he does now as a teacher to empower his students to learn. He concludes the chapter by stating that success as a TESOL professional is dependent on a teacher's professionalism, rather than on a teacher's background.

In the last chapter in Section 1, "Invisible Minorities and the Nonnative English-Speaking Professional," Jette G. Hansen, like Jun Liu, focuses on the notion of teachers' professionalism. She argues that teachers should be hired on the basis of what they can do and not how they look. To address this point, her chapter focuses on a topic that has received very limited attention in the literature: *invisible NNES professionals*. In the chapter, she describes the challenges faced by visible and invisible NNES professionals and argues that visible and invisible characteristics affect people's perceptions about and reactions toward NNES professionals. She also reflects on her own experiences as an invisible NNES professional in order to give this group of professionals "a voice and visibility" in the TESOL field.

The Nonnative English-Speaking Professionals' Movement and Its Research Foundations

George Braine
The Chinese University of Hong Kong

A few months ago, I received volume 4, number 1, of the newsletter published by the NNEST Caucus. The newsletter listed an impressive list of thirteen caucus events scheduled at the 2002 TESOL convention, ranging from individual presentations to colloquia and workshops and covering a variety of topics from the preparation of nonnative speaker English to strategies for academic publishing. The presenters were from Taiwan, Kazakhstan, Brazil, Panama, Lithuania, Hong Kong, Singapore, the United Arab Emirates, and, of course, the United States.

The TESOL organization has six caucuses, and one for nonnative speakers may not seem unusual to readers. Although a large number of English teachers in the United States are nonnative speakers of English and many of them are members of TESOL, they did not speak with one voice, and there was no organization that represented them until recently. Therefore, the formation of the NNEST Caucus is a narrative worth repeating. In this chapter, my aim is twofold: to narrate the recent history of the nonnative English-speaking educators' movement and to briefly describe the research that has begun to appear on the subject of nonnative teachers of English.

The Identity of a Nonnative Speaker

In an anthology titled *Teaching English to the World* (Braine, forthcoming), more than a dozen English teachers, all nonnative speakers of English, reflect upon how they became English teachers, discussing their first language backgrounds, ambitions, successes, doubts, and insecurities. This reflection and the resultant self-discovery are important because, as Brady (2002) has pointed out, teaching is very much about empathy, and unless teachers see themselves honestly and as others see them, empathy is likely to be limited.

Some nonnative speakers of English are often made acutely aware of the fact that the variety of English they speak is regarded as outside the norm, that it may be at best second-rate. For instance, a typical Hong Kong student who may have studied English for 15 years is shocked into embarrassment when an immigration officer in the United States is unable to comprehend the answers provided by the student to the officer's routine questions. Or a nonnative speaker teaching assistant, facing a classroom of North American undergraduates, draws criticism if not insults for having an unusual accent. However, other nonnative speakers, especially those who rarely come into contact with native speakers or those living in environments where the local variety of English has prestige, may not be as acutely aware of their status as nonnative speakers. I will relate my own experience here because it is a fitting prelude to my role in the NNEST Caucus.

I grew up in Ceylon (now Sri Lanka) in the 1950s and '60s, when English was commonly used in many households and in the media. I read both local newspapers and foreign magazines like the *Readers' Digest* and *Time*, as well as those distributed free by the United States Information Agency, such as a now-extinct magazine named *Free World*. The foreign magazines were glossy, attractively laid out, and had colorful pictures and eye-catching advertisements. But, when it came to text and content, the local newspapers were as well written as those published in foreign markets. English was very much a world language, and the variety used in Ceylon was on par with the best in the world.

The secondary school I attended had both local and expatriate British teachers. The local teachers were impeccable users of English, whose love of the language shone through in their enthusiasm for teaching it. Although skin color and accent were obvious markers, I could not discern a difference in the fluency and teaching styles of the local and expatriate teachers; to me, they were all English teachers. This pattern was repeated at the teachers college I attended later. In fact, all the local lecturers there had more teaching experience, and some, with graduate degrees from prestigious British and U.S.

universities, were more qualified than the single expatriate lecturer from Great Britain.

The pattern changed in the 1980s when I began to teach in the Middle East. The employment sector there showed a clear segregation. Well-paying positions in the military, education, construction, and mercantile sectors were taken mainly by Europeans and North Americans. Jobs that involved manual labor were filled mainly with South Asians and North Africans. In the case of English teachers, those from Great Britain were paid higher salaries and enjoyed better perks than better-qualified teachers from the Indian subcontinent. I remember a teacher from Great Britain, whose only qualification was a teaching certificate from the British Council, being paid a salary twice that of mine and provided with luxurious housing and other perks. Was my honors degree in English, two years of training as an English teacher, and more than 10 years of teaching experience worth only half of his six-month teaching certificate? Obviously, there was more to it than that. During my three years in the Middle East, I gradually learned that it was his identity as a native speaker of English that earned him and his compatriots the recognition that was denied to me and others from the subcontinent.

But the native/nonnative distinction hit me with full force only when I arrived in the United States in 1984 to enroll in a master of arts (MA) in TESOL program. About half of my classmates were from countries such as Bangladesh, Indonesia, Colombia, Malaysia, and Zimbabwe. All were experienced English teachers. The university itself was a microcosm of the United Nations, with students from more than 150 countries enrolled in its programs. To me, it was a tremendous experience to walk into a campus cafeteria and be able to hear numerous varieties of English being spoken, all wondrously intelligible to me. With more than a decade and a half of experience of English teaching under my belt, I applied for a tutor position at the university's language center, but I was turned down almost instantly. Instead, native speaker classmates who had no teaching experience were hired. For the rest of my stay at the university, I shelved books in the library for minimum wage while my inexperienced native speaker classmates tutored at the language center. Later, at an intensive English program in Philadelphia where I taught briefly, I came to realize that prejudice towards nonnative teachers also came from English as a second language (ESL) students. Two students who were enrolled in one of my classes complained about my accent and requested transfers to classes taught by native speakers.

During my doctoral studies at another university in the late 1980s, where the applied linguistics program enrolled a large number of students, I took the initiative to start an academic journal in applied

linguistics. I gathered a group of classmates, formed a journal committee, and wrote a successful grant proposal to fund the journal. I
expected enthusiastic support from the professors and other administrators, but, to my surprise and acute disappointment, I only met
opposition from some of these worthies, who attempted to kill the
journal even before it was off the ground. In subtle ways, I was made
to understand that foreign students were not expected to make waves
or take on initiatives. Instead, they were expected to remain low-key,
not annoy their professors, and then graduate with the least fuss and
disappear for good. It was my stubborn persistence that eventually
saw the journal becoming a reality.

The Birth of a Caucus for Nonnative Speakers in TESOL

I survived graduate school and managed to overcome the open prejudice that existed in the 1980s against the hiring of nonnative speakers
as English professors. As I began to play a more active role in TESOL,
I was bothered by the fact that topics and issues that could have been
better dealt with by nonnative speakers were often handled by others. Take, for instance, the initiation of nonnative speaker graduate
students into academic discourse. This is clearly a topic that I and
other nonnative speaker professionals had firsthand experience of,
one that we could enrich with our first-person narratives. Yet it was
handled almost exclusively by researchers who at best could only
report secondhand on the experiences of others, nonnative speaker
professionals such as myself. In essence, although nonnative speakers were present within the TESOL organization, its publications, and
conferences, they did not have visibility, recognition, or the voice they
deserved. English is a world language, but TESOL was dominated by
those who spoke American English.

To bring more visibility to nonnative speaker issues, I organized a
colloquium titled "In Their Own Voices: Non-native Speaker Professionals in TESOL" at the 30th annual TESOL convention, held in Chicago
in 1996. I invited well-known nonnative speaker scholars in applied
linguistics as well as novices to our profession to participate, and I
encouraged them to address issues that were of concern to them.
They exceeded my expectations, presenting highly charged, mainly
personal narratives that generated much interest and enthusiasm
among nonnative speakers in the audience. I especially remember
the first presentation by Jacinta Thomas. The pin-drop silence that
prevailed as she spoke, and the emotions that she evoked within me,
told me that we had struck a chord. Other speakers, such as Ulla Connor, Suresh Canagarajah, and Kamal Sridhar, also brought a strong
personal touch to their more academic presentations. Some nonna-

tive speakers in the audience claimed that they finally had a voice within TESOL. The idea for a TESOL Caucus for nonnative speakers was first proposed at this colloquium. A few weeks later, Jun Liu of the University of Arizona and Lía D. Kamhi-Stein of California State University, Los Angeles, and I began to collect signatures of TESOL members in support of the caucus. The statement we wrote in order to launch the signature drive has since been published in Bailey, Curtis, and Nunan (2001).

Around this time, Alexander Jenin, a nonnative speaker of Polish origin, wrote to *TESOL Matters* detailing the prejudices he faced in finding employment as an English teacher. I was invited to write a companion piece to Jenin's letter, and it was published under the big, bold headline "NNS and Invisible Barriers in ELT" (Braine, 1998). In the article, I pointed out that for many nonnative English-speaking teachers, qualifications, ability, and experience were of little help in the job market, where the invisible rule appeared to be "No NNS need apply." I pointed out that despite the TESOL organization's explicit opposition to hiring practices that discriminate against nonnative English speakers, most English language teaching (ELT) administrators (with some notable exceptions) did not hire nonnative English speakers. I described two frequent excuses trotted out for not hiring nonnative speakers—that ESL students prefer being taught by native speakers and that recruiting foreigners involves a complex legal process—but argued that the main reason was the subtle opposition to the increasing presence of foreigners in Western academia as teachers, researchers, and scholars. Although a similar presence of foreigners/nonnative speakers in ELT was only to be expected—there are at least four nonnative speakers to every native speaker of English—it met with opposition when scarce jobs were threatened. I argued that this was especially ironic in ELT, considering the profession's strident championing of multiculturalism, diversity, and other sociopolitical causes on behalf of ESL students and immigrants. I pointed out that while ESL students were praised and admired for the multiculturalism and diversity they bring into language classes, nonnative speaker English teachers, who could also contribute their rich multicultural, multilingual experiences, were often barred from the same classes.

I also pointed out another ironic situation. When nonnative speaker English teachers return to their countries after obtaining higher degrees and teacher qualifications in the West, they are not always able to find work. Some language program administrators—notably in Japan, Korea, and Hong Kong—sometimes prefer to hire unqualified native speakers of English instead of qualified locals. I stated that Jenin and other nonnative speakers like him were in the bewildering and frustrating position of being denied what they had been trained to do. I advised nonnative English-speaking teachers that the playing field would not be level for them, that they would have to struggle twice as hard to achieve what often comes as a birthright to their native speaker counterparts: recognition of their teaching ability and respect for their scholarship. Teaching ability alone would not be enough for obtaining employment or for career advancement. They would have to grow as professionals, taking active roles and assuming leadership in teacher organizations, initiating research, sharing their ideas through publications, and learning to network with nonnative speaker colleagues. (The full text of this article can also be found at the Nonnative English Speakers in TESOL Caucus website at *http://nnest.moussu.net/.*)

The article evoked an immediate response. I received letters and e-mail messages from nonnative English-speaking teachers from around the world, thanking me for the strident championing of nonnative speakers and saying that they finally appeared to have a voice within TESOL. Many cited personal experiences and anecdotes to support my position. I also received messages of support from native speaker colleagues, which were even more gratifying. The publicity evoked by the *TESOL Matters* article was an unexpected boost to the proposed caucus.

In 1998, we established the caucus with myself as the chair, Jun Liu as the chair-elect, Lía D. Kamhi-Stein as the newsletter editor, and Aya Matsuda, then at Purdue University, as the webmaster. The first formal meeting of the caucus was held at the TESOL convention in 1999, which coincided with the publication of my book *Non-Native Educators in English Language Teaching.* The overall aim of the caucus is to strengthen effective teaching and learning of English around the world while respecting individuals' language rights. Specifically, the major goals are to create a nondiscriminatory professional environment for all TESOL members regardless of native language and place of birth, encourage the formal and informal gatherings of nonnative speakers at TESOL and affiliate conferences, encourage research and publications on the role of nonnative speaker teachers in ESL and English as a foreign language (EFL) contexts, and promote the role of nonnative speaker members in TESOL and affiliate leadership positions. The caucus uses a biannual newsletter, an active listserv, and the website to publicize its activities and disseminate information among the membership. The website also lists a bibliography of publications that have appeared under the topic. At the time of this writing, the list included more than 82 items. Another notable achievement has been the election of Jun Liu as a board member of TESOL and of Lía Kamhi-Stein as the president of California TESOL (CATESOL).

Research on Nonnative Speaker Issues

A movement in an educational context could be relevant and popular, but it cannot grow without the backing of sound research and pedagogy. This section will summarize the research carried out in the area of nonnative speaker English teachers. But first, I will digress briefly to explore the terms *native speaker* and *nonnative speaker* and their implications to ELT.

A nonnative speaker of a language is invariably defined against a native speaker of that language. Naturally, nonnative speakers are thereby assigned to a second-class, inferior position vis-à-vis native speakers. Nevertheless, the notion of the native speaker and all the linguistic, social, and economic connotations that accompany it are open to controversy. Although Chomsky's (1965) use of the term *native speaker* has no doubt bolstered the linguistic authority of native speakers, he defined a native speaker of a language as an "ideal speaker-listener, in a completely homogeneous speech community, who knows its language perfectly" (p. 3). At best, such a speaker is an abstraction with no resemblance to a living human being.

In terms of English language pedagogy, the well-known applied linguist Henry Widdowson (1994) has pointed out that native speakers become "custodians and arbiters not only of proper English but of proper pedagogy as well" (p. 387) due to the use of authentic, naturally occurring English for instructional purposes. When the emphasis is moved from the contexts of use to contexts of learning, the advantage of the native speaker teacher disappears. Accordingly, Widdowson argued that native speakers have "no say . . . no right to intervene or pass judgement" (p. 385) on how English develops internationally. Another well-known applied linguist, Claire Kramsch (1997), attributed the idealization of the native speaker to the emphasis on spoken communication in foreign language pedagogy since the 1960s. She argued that native speakers do not speak the idealized, standardized version of their language; instead, their speech in influenced by geography, occupation, age, and social status. She questioned why foreign language students who have a multilingual perspective on the target language, its literature, and its culture should emulate the idealized but nonexistent native speaker.

According to Phillipson, the author of *Linguistic Imperialism* (1992), the origins of a number of fallacies regarding the place of native speakers in language pedagogy could be attributed to the Commonwealth Conference on the Teaching of English as a Second Language held in 1961. Phillipson has pointed out that one of the key tenets of the conference was that "the ideal teacher of English is a native speaker" (p. 185) because native speakers of a language have a better command of fluent, idiomatically correct language forms; are more knowledgeable about the cultural connotations of a language; and are the final arbiters of the acceptability of the language. According to Phillipson, these abilities could be instilled through teacher training. In addition, insights into the language learning process, the mastery of correct forms and appropriate use of the language, and the ability to analyze and explain the language are within the reach of nonnative speaker teachers, too. Further, nonnative speakers of a language have undergone the process of learning a language, which makes them better qualified to teach the language than those who acquired it as a birthright. Phillipson attributed what he termed the "native speaker fallacy" to the period when language teaching was synonymous with the teaching of culture.

Let us now turn to research on the subject of nonnative teachers of English. Although nonnative speakers may have been English teachers for centuries, this appears to be an area hardly touched by research. In fact, even descriptive accounts of nonnative English-speaking teachers appear to be scarce. This may have been due to the fact that the topic was an unusually sensitive one, long silently acknowledged but too risky to be discussed openly. In English-speaking countries, the authority of the native speaker teacher was supreme. In most non-English-speaking countries, there appeared to be power struggles between the imported native speakers and the local nonnative speaker teachers. For the most part, having been openly relegated to a second-class position in 1961, nonnative English-speaking teachers may have opted for a reluctant acceptance of their status. Peter Medgyes, himself a nonnative speaker, appears to be the first to have brought the issues concerning nonnative speaker English teachers to the open, with two articles in the *ELT Journal* titled "The Schizophrenic Teacher" (1983) and "Native or Non-native: Who's Worth More?" (1992). He soon followed with a groundbreaking book, *The Non-native Teacher* (first published by Macmillan in 1994 and reissued by Hueber in 1999), in which he boldly discussed previously untouched topics under chapter titles such as "Natives and Non-natives in Opposite Trenches" (1999, p. 25), "The Dark Side of Being a Non-native" (p. 33), and "Who's Worth More: The Native or the Non-native" (p. 71).

In his book, Medgyes advanced four hypotheses based on his assumption that native and nonnative English-speaking teachers are "two different species" (p. 25). The hypotheses were (1) that the native and nonnative speaker teachers differ in terms of language proficiency and in terms of teaching practice (behavior), (2) that most of the differences in teaching practice can be attributed to the discrepancy in language proficiency, and (3) that both types of teachers can be equally good teachers on their own terms. The best known example of Medgyes' research (Reves & Medgyes, 1994) was the result of an international survey of 216 native and nonnative English-speaking teachers from 10 countries (Brazil, Czechoslovakia, Hungary, Israel, Mexico, Nigeria, Russia, Sweden, Yugoslavia, and Zimbabwe). The objective was to examine the following hypothesis: native and nonnative English-speaking teachers differ in terms of their teaching practice (behaviors); these differences in teaching practice are mainly due to their differing levels of language proficiency, and their knowledge of these differences affects the nonnative speaker teachers' "self-perception and teaching attitudes" (p. 354). The questionnaire consisted of 23 items, of which 18 were addressed to both native and nonnative speakers and 5 to nonnative speakers only. Most of the questions were closed-ended and meant to elicit personal information of the subjects and their teaching contexts. The open-ended questions were meant to elicit the subjects' self-perceptions and their opinions relating to the three hypotheses. The overwhelming majority of the subjects, by their own admission, were nonnative speakers of English. In their responses, 68% of the subjects perceived differences in the teaching practices of native speaker and nonnative speaker teachers. Eighty-four percent of the nonnative speaker subjects admitted to having various language difficulties, vocabulary and fluency being the most common areas, followed by speaking, pronunciation, and listening comprehension. Only 25% of the subjects stated that their language difficulties had no adverse effect on their teaching. In view of these findings, Reves and Medgyes (1994) suggest that "frequent exposure to authentic native language environments and proficiency-oriented in-service training activities" (p. 364) might improve the language skills of nonnative speaker teachers. Further, in order to enhance the self-perception of these teachers, they should be made aware of their advantages as language teachers.

Applying Medgyes' approach, Samimy and Brutt-Griffler (1999) surveyed and interviewed 17 nonnative speaker graduate students who were pursuing either an MA or a Ph.D. in TESOL at a university in the United States. Their students, referred to by the researchers as a "rather sophisticated group of nonnative speakers of English" (p. 134), were from Korea, Japan, Turkey, Surinam, China, Togo, Burkina Faso, and Russia. (Russia is the only country where this study overlapped with that of Reves and Medgyes.) Although they used Medgyes' questionnaire to collect quantitative data, Samimy and Brutt-Griffler also gathered qualitative data through classroom discussions, in-depth interviews, and analysis of autobiographical writings of the student subjects. The aims of the study were to determine how these graduate students perceived themselves as professionals in the ELT field, if they thought there were differences in the teaching behaviors of native speakers and nonnative speakers, what these differences were, and if they felt handicapped as nonnative English-speaking teachers. Responding to the questionnaire, more than two-thirds of the subjects admitted that their difficulties with the language affected their teaching from "a little" to "very much." Nearly 90% of the subjects perceived a difference between native speaker and nonnative speaker teachers of English. They identified the former group as being informal, fluent, and accurate; using different techniques, methods, and approaches; being flexible; using conversational English; knowing subtleties of the language; using authentic English; providing positive feedback to students; and having communication (not exam preparation) as the goals of their teaching. Nonnative English-speaking teachers were perceived as relying on textbooks, applying differences between the first and second languages, using the first language as a medium of instruction, being aware of negative transfer and psychological aspects of learning, being sensitive to the needs of students, being more efficient, knowing the students' background, and having exam preparation as the goal of their teaching. However, they did not consider the native speaker teachers superior to their nonnative speaker counterparts.

One of the first doctoral-level studies on native and nonnative teachers' issues was conducted by Ofra Inbar at Tel Aviv University in Israel. In *Native and Non-native English Teachers: Investigation of the Construct and Perceptions*, Inbar (2001) set out to investigate the effects of the native/nonnative distinction on the pedagogical perceptions of English teachers in Israel. The study was conducted in two phases. In the first phase, data were gathered through self-reports of 102 English teachers on the factors that accounted for the teachers' self-identification as native or nonnative speakers of English. In its second phase, self-reports of 264 English teachers formed the basis for the determination of how their self-identity as native or nonnative speakers of English affected their pedagogical perceptions. Results from the first phase indicated that the teachers' native speaker identity could be explained by nine variables, two of which could best predict this identity: (1) having spoken English from the age of zero to six and (2) others' perception of them as native speakers of English. Findings from the second phase showed that the teachers' native or nonnative speaker background did not account for differences in most pedagogical perceptions. Self-identified native speakers tended to consider native speaker teachers superior and expressed more confidence in using the English language and teaching about culture. Nonnative speaker teachers, on the other hand, reported having better relations with students and feeling more confident in using the L1 to facilitate teaching. Interviews with nine teachers confirmed the results from the self-reports.

The research so far had focused on nonnative English-speaking teachers. The students, who were ultimately the most affected by the native and nonnative dichotomy, had not been investigated. This gap was partly filled by Lucie Moussu, whose MA thesis at Brigham Young University, Utah, was titled *English as a Second Language Students' Reactions to Nonnative English-Speaking Teachers* (2002). Moussu's research questions were threefold: (1) What feelings and expectations do the students have at first when taught by a nonnative speaker English teacher, and why? (2) What other variables (gender, age, first language, etc.) influence the students' perceptions of their nonnative speaker teachers at the beginning of the semester? (3) How do the variables of time and exposure to nonnative speaker teachers influence the students' perceptions of their teachers?

Moussu's subjects were four nonnative English-speaking teachers from Japan, Argentina, Ecuador, and Switzerland and 84 ESL students above the age of 17, both males and females, from 21 different countries and studying at an intensive English program attached to a U.S. university. All students responded to two questionnaires, one given the first day of class and the second given 14 weeks later on the last day of class. Over the 14-week semester, three separate sets of interviews were also conducted with six students. Analysis of the data shows that from the beginning of the semester, the students had positive attitudes towards their nonnative speaker teachers. For instance, 68% of the students said that they could learn English just as well from a nonnative speaker as from a native speaker, 79% expressed admiration and respect for their nonnative speaker teachers, and as many as 84% of the students expected their class with such a teacher to be a positive experience. The Korean and Chinese students expressed negative feelings toward their nonnative speaker teachers more frequently than other students. Time and exposure to the teachers only made their opinions more positive by the end of the semester. For instance, to the question "Would you encourage a friend to take a class with this nonnative English-speaking teacher?" only 56% of the students had answered "yes" at the beginning of the semester. By the end of the semester, 76% had answered "yes" to the same question.

Kristy Yan Liang's master's research (2002) at California State University, Los Angeles, also investigated students' attitudes toward nonnative English-speaking teachers. Specifically, the study was designed to investigate 20 ESL students' attitudes towards six ESL teachers' accents and the features of these teachers' speech that contributed to the students' preference for teachers. Five of the teachers were nonnative speakers from different language backgrounds, and the other was a native speaker.

The students listened to brief audio recordings delivered by the six nonnative English-speaking teachers and rated and ranked the teachers' accents according to a scale of preference. Data were collected through questionnaires that included information on the students' background, their beliefs about teaching, and their ranking of the teachers in the study. The results showed that, although the students rated pronunciation/accent in the ESL teachers' speech as very important, pronunciation/accent did not affect the students' attitudes toward their last nonnative English-speaking teachers in their countries. In fact, the students held generally positive attitudes toward the teachers in their home countries, and pronunciation/accent was not as relevant as it appeared in the first place (see Lippi-Green, 1997, for information on attitudes toward teacher ethnicity). Further, personal and professional features as derived from the teachers' speech—such as "being interesting," "being prepared," "being qualified," and "being professional"—played a role in the students' preference for teachers. In conclusion, Liang (2002) suggests that, instead of focusing on ESL teachers' ethnic and language background, the discussion on nonnative English-speaking teachers should focus on their level of professionalism.

So far, what has been missing is an investigation of both teachers and students, and Yin Ling Cheung (2002) fulfilled this need with her research on the attitudes of the university students in Hong Kong towards native and nonnative teachers of English. Cheung's objectives were to determine the attitudes of the university students in Hong Kong towards native and nonnative teachers of English, the strengths and weaknesses of these native and nonnative teachers from the perspective of students, and the capability of native and nonnative English teachers in motivating the students to learn English. She also attempted to determine if there was any discrimination against nonnative English-speaking teachers in Hong Kong.

Cheung triangulated her data collection with the use of questionnaires, interviews, classroom observations, and post-classroom interviews. The questionnaire was distributed to 420 randomly selected undergraduates from a variety of majors at seven universities in Hong Kong. Most of the students (98%) were Cantonese or Putonghua speakers, and 99% of them had learned English in either Hong Kong or China. Twenty-two university English teachers (ranging from department head to instructor) at six universities and 10 students from three universities were also interviewed. The majority of the teachers were expatriates, with about 60% being native speakers of English. Nearly 90% had been resident in Hong Kong for more than six years. The results showed that both students and teachers saw native and nonnative teachers having their respective strengths. A high proficiency in English, ability to use English functionally, and the awareness of the cultures of English-speaking countries were the strengths observed in native English-speaking teachers. In the case of nonnative teachers, the ability to empathize with students as fellow second language learners, a shared cultural background, and the emphasis they placed on grammar were seen as their strengths. As for teacher competency, both students and teachers stated that teachers should be well-informed about the English language, able to make learning relevant and fun, good at motivating students, able to encourage independent learning and thinking, sensitive and responsive to students' needs, and able to respect students as individuals with their own aspirations. Not all students and teachers were of the opinion that there was discrimination against nonnative English-speaking teachers in Hong Kong.

Two more studies conducted in Hong Kong are noteworthy here. Both examined Hong Kong learners' reactions to native speakers' and nonnative speakers' accents (Forde, 1996; Luk, 1998). The results of these studies were similar, Luk's showing that most learners preferred Received Pronunciation (RP) and expressed a desire for English teachers speaking RP. Forde's study showed that most learners preferred Standard American English and RP English accents to Hong Kong, Australian, and Yorkshire accents. In fact, Luk went so far as to suggest that accents of English teachers could have "negative pedagogical and psychological effects on the students" (p. 104).

Conclusion

The relative merits of native and nonnative English teachers have been extensively discussed by Davies (1991), Widdowson (1994), Medgyes (1992), and Boyle (1997) in recent years. As Medgyes (2001) has noted, "NESTs [native English-speaking teachers] make better *language* models, [and] non-NESTs can provide better *learner* models" (p. 436). The nonnative teachers, having been second language learners themselves, "have deeper insights into . . . the learning process" (Medgyes, 2001, p. 437). Native speaker teachers, on the other hand, are capable of creating an "English-rich" environment in the classroom to enhance student motivation. Further, native speaker teachers have been found to teach *the* language more than the *rules* of the language, and they have not been found to adhere to the textbook. As Cook (1999) pointed out, multilingual (nonnative speaker) teachers are probably more capable and qualitatively different than the monolingual (native speaker) teachers.

Beginning with the pioneering research of Medgyes, it is heartening that native and nonnative teacher issues have now become a legitimate area of research. One characteristic of this research is that, to date, most of these studies have been conducted by nonnative speaker researchers. Another is that not until 2002 (with the research of Moussu, Liang, and Cheung, who are all novice researchers at the MA level) did the research extend to students' attitudes and preferences, probably the most crucial factor in the native and nonnative teacher issues. The sensitive nature of the factor and the need to be politically correct may have influenced more experienced researchers to steer clear of this topic. In fact, the need to be politically correct may have also affected the responses of native speaker teachers to the topic, especially in Cheung's (2002) research. Nevertheless, it's heartening to note that younger researchers are breaking ground in areas that need investigation.

One important factor that emerges from the research is the need for more education, for both nonnative speaker teachers and their students. Nonnative teachers must be made aware that English is no longer a unitary language, that there are so-called Englishes, each with its own identity and recognition in social, economic, and national contexts. As long as they are mutually intelligible, these Englishes will continue to coexist and thrive. They are the varieties that can be transmitted from teacher to student for generations. If they decline to the level of Pidgins, as they are doing in some contexts, they will no longer be acceptable beyond these narrow contexts. As far as students are concerned, they, too, must be made aware that English has no owners, that it is their language, and not a dead language to be studied from textbooks but a vigorous and thriving mode of communication at their service. The local variety, taught by local teachers, is as good as any variety taught by expatriates.

I would like to end this chapter with a quote from a nonnative teacher of English. After the publication of my book *Non-native Educators in English Language Teaching*, I received many messages of support and empathy from fellow nonnative teachers. Surprisingly, four years after the book's publication, an occasional message still arrives. One that came last month read as follows: "When I was reading the book . . . I almost burst into tears several times. I found so many similar experiences/stories/struggles from my life described in this book. It was really good to know that there are so many people working on the topic, making nonnative English-speaking teachers known, trying to find ways to make our lives better. I am not lonely!"

References

Bailey, K. M., Curtis, A., & Nunan, D. (2001). *Pursuing professional development: The self as source*. Boston: Heinle & Heinle.

Boyle, J. (1997). Imperialism and the English language in Hong Kong. *Journal of Multilingual and Multicultural Development, 18*(3), 169–181.

Brady, B. (2002, September). The "NNESTessity" of professional self-discovery. *NNEST Newsletter, 4*(2), 6–7.

Braine, G. (1998, February/March). NNS and invisible barriers in ELT. *TESOL Matters, 8*(1), 14.

Braine, G. (1999). *Non-native educators in English language teaching.* Mahwah, NJ: Erlbaum.

Braine, G. (forthcoming). *Teaching English to the world.* Alexandria, VA: TESOL.

Cheung, Y. L. (2002). *The attitude of university students in Hong Kong towards native and non-native teachers of English.* Unpublished master's thesis, Chinese University of Hong Kong, People's Republic of China.

Chomsky, N. (1965). *Aspects of the theory of syntax.* Cambridge: MIT Press.

Cook, V. (1999). Going beyond the native speaker in language teaching. *TESOL Quarterly, 33*(2), 185–209.

Davies, A. (1991). *The native speaker in applied linguistics.* Edinburgh, Scotland: Edinburgh University Press.

Forde, K. (1996). A study of learner attitudes towards accents of English. *Hong Kong Polytechnic University Working Papers in ELT and Applied Linguistics, 1*(2), 59–76.

Inbar, O. (2001). *Native and non-native English teachers: Investigation of the construct and perceptions.* Unpublished doctoral dissertation, Tel Aviv University, Israel.

Kramsch, C. J. (1997). The privilege of the nonnative speaker. PMLA: *Publications of the Modern Language Association, 112*(3), 359–369.

Liang, K. Y. (2002). *English as a second language (ESL) students' attitudes towards non-native English-speaking teachers' accentedness.* Unpublished master's thesis, California State University, Los Angeles.

Lippi-Green, R. (1997). *English with an accent: Language, ideology, and discrimination in the United States.* London: Routledge.

Luk, J. C. M. (1998). Hong Kong students' awareness of and reactions to accent differences. *Multilingua, 17*(1), 93–106.

Medgyes, P. (1983). The schizophrenic teacher. *ELT Journal, 37*(1), 2–6.

Medgyes, P. (1992). Native or non-native: Who's worth more? *ELT Journal, 46*(4), 340–349.

Medgyes, P. (1999). *The non-native teacher.* Ismaning, Germany: Hueber.

Medgyes, P. (2001). When the teacher is a non-native speaker. In M. Celce-Murcia (Ed.), *Teaching English as a second or foreign language* (3rd ed., pp. 429–442). Boston: Heinle & Heinle.

Moussu, L. (2002). *English as a second language students' reactions to nonnative English speaking teachers.* Unpublished master's thesis, Brigham Young University, Provo, Utah.

Phillipson, R. (1992). *Linguistic imperialism.* Oxford: Oxford University Press.

Reves, T., & Medgyes, P. (1994). The non-native English speaking EFL/ESL teacher's self-image: An international survey. *System, 22*(3), 353–367.

Samimy, K. K., & Brutt-Griffler, J. (1999). To be a native or nonnative speaker: Perceptions of "non-native" students in a graduate TESOL program. In G. Braine (Ed.), *Non-native educators in English language teaching* (pp. 127–144). Mahwah, NJ: Erlbaum.

Widdowson, H. G. (1994). The ownership of English. *TESOL Quarterly, 28*(2), 377–389.

Confessions of a Nonnative English-Speaking Professional

Jun Liu
University of Arizona, Tucson

At a recent meeting of the oral comprehensive examination committee for a doctoral student in the Second Language Acquisition and Teaching Interdisciplinary Program at the University of Arizona, I briefly introduced myself to the graduate representative from a different discipline. I was not prepared for the question he threw back at me: "So, are you a graduate student?" I noticed that the other committee members who knew me were startled by the question. The doctoral candidate came to my rescue, saying, "No, Dr. Liu is my committee chair." I smiled and then focused on the procedure of the oral exam. On my way home that evening, the question reentered my mind, and I could not help thinking of a number of pertinent issues regarding how I am perceived.

Recent publications in our profession reveal a growing interest in the concerns of nonnative English-speaking (NNES) professionals and the roles they play as TESOL professionals (Braine, 1996, 1997; Kamhi-Stein, 2000; Liu, 1999; Samimy & Brutt-Griffler, 1999). Generally, TESOL research has focused on the experiences of ESL/EFL learners and effective ways to help them learn English (e.g., Brown, 2000; Celce-Murcia, 2001; Hadley, 2001; Li, 1998; Liu & Richards, 2001; Manzo & Manzo, 1997; Mitchell & Vidal, 2001; Norris & Ortega, 2000; Richards & Rodgers, 2001). Recently, however, research in the field has expanded to include the impact that NNES professionals have on their students (e.g., Braine, 1996; Kresovich, 1988; Liu, 1998; McNeill, 1994; Medgyes, 1994; Palfreyman, 1993; Rampton, 1990). Although in

25

the U.S. the majority of professionals in applied linguistics and TESOL speak English as their first language (L1), NNES professionals clearly play an important role as well. Additionally, their interests, concerns, and perspectives have compelled the profession to explore the complexities of the native/nonnative speaker constructs (some leading researchers are Davies, 1991; Kramsch, 1998; Liu, 1999; Medgyes, 1992). This exploration has led many researchers to challenge the stereotype that NNES professionals who were born and educated in EFL contexts fall short of native proficiency in English (Bautista, 1997; Crystal, 1997; Kachru, 1992; Kachru & Nelson, 1996; Medgyes, 1994; Paikeday, 1985; Rampton, 1990).

Admittedly, numerous differences exist between native speakers and nonnative speakers of English. Obvious ones include the process of learning English and the context in which English is learned. In this chapter, I will reflect on my own experiences as a NNES professional, initially as an international graduate student and currently as a faculty member in a U.S. research university. My reflection comprises three parts, each focusing on a particular dilemma I faced as I progressed along the continuum of my professional development. The first part is titled "Puzzlement" and addresses the question: How did I feel when my self-confidence was challenged by school expectations in the target culture? The second part is titled "Endeavor" and addresses the question: How did I attempt to develop adaptive cultural transformation competence[1] and to create multiple identities appropriate for different communities? The third part is titled "Empowerment" and addresses the question: What did I do as a NNES teacher to empower my students to learn?

My intention is to share my experiences both with other NNES professionals and with my native English-speaking (NES) colleagues who have not experienced a similar process. Ultimately, I aim to achieve a better understanding and appreciation of those in the TESOL field who consider themselves NNES professionals.

Puzzlement

I came to the U.S. in 1991 to pursue my Ph.D. in second and foreign language education at Ohio State University (OSU). With a decade of experience teaching EFL in a college in China, upon my arrival in the U.S. I was very confident of my proficiency in English. However, from the beginning there were many occasions when I felt very awkward and thought that I had failed to achieve communicative competence. For example, when I arrived at the airport in Columbus, Ohio, I was picked up by an acquaintance who kindly took me to his house for dinner. As soon as we reached his house, his wife asked me if I wanted something to drink. Because of my Chinese sense of politeness, I said, "No, thanks." Actually I was very thirsty and expected her to ask me again. But to my surprise, she served herself a drink and started talking with me while preparing dinner. About half an hour later, the dinner was ready, and this time she asked me directly if I cared for a glass of root beer. Although I did not quite hear the modifier of the word "beer," I accepted her offer without hesitation, thinking that a glass of beer, whatever it was, would help me relax after a 17-hour stressful flight. No sooner had I taken the first sip than I realized that American beer had a very special taste. Such a different flavor soon became too unique to appreciate. To please my hosts, I kept drinking, pretending that I really enjoyed the beer, while waiting for a chance to request something else to drink. What I did not expect was that the hostess, impressed by my speed of drinking, took my glass and said, "So you like the taste, and I bet you cannot find it in China, eh?" "Yes, well, you see . . ." I tried to search for words polite enough to show my dislike of the taste. But she interpreted my hesitation as indicating approval, although my Chinese culturally conditioned "yes" response was not intended to mean "yes" in this context. Sure enough, my empty glass was soon filled again with the same beverage. This time, however, I did not finish it, afraid of having the glass refilled again. I used my Chinese strategy of implicit polite refusal by sipping it but a little at a time. Half an hour later, the glass was still full.

A couple of months into the first quarter at OSU, I began to realize the difference between the English people spoke in daily communication and the English I had learned from reading 18th- and 19th-century British and American literature books. The idiomatic expressions I knew from books and from tapes sometimes caused confusion in communication; the canned proverbs, jokes, or tongue twisters I consciously carried into conversation were not received as humorous. What was worse, some British poems I proudly inserted in conversation to reveal my solid background in literature sometimes made me sound comical. Oftentimes, I was dissatisfied with my conversational English and began to question how successful I had been at learning and teaching English in China.

Pragmatic incompetence apart, my lack of cultural experience on many occasions aggravated my frustration in communication. I felt ashamed that my knowledge of English, which was mainly obtained from books, did not help me feel comfortable in daily communication. One day I had a conversation with a rental agent about the distinction between furnished and unfurnished rooms because I did not understand the variety of rental packages. Fifteen minutes into the conversation, the landlord, who was obviously impatient with my endless questions and the puzzled expression on my face, quit talking with me and showed me the apartment instead. When visiting McDonald's, I literally questioned the meaning of "to go" when I first ordered a combo, because I did not know where else I could go other than to the fast-food restaurant in order to eat the hamburger. I was somewhat confused and offended one day when a taxi driver asked me to sit in the back seat while the passenger seat in front was available. I felt extremely uncomfortable when in one of the courses I took during my first quarter, I noticed that the professor sat on the edge of the front desk while teaching. I was equally surprised to notice that some of my classmates brought soft drinks and potato chips into class. In Chinese culture, this behavior is not acceptable because it is perceived as disrespectful to teachers. Here in the U.S., nobody in class seemed to care. It took me almost a year before I realized that while shopping for clothes, I could actually try on every piece before I bought it, and I could return anything I decided I didn't like. Behavior patterns that were known by others in the U.S. represented new concepts for me. The problem, in my case, was not the language, since I could tell the difference between the language I used and the language spoken by others. The problem was that the U.S. culture overshadowed my linguistic abilities. The beliefs, values, and norms that governed my social behavior no longer seemed to function well in this new environment. What I needed then, and what I later benefited from, was the desire and courage to embark on a journey of what I will call adaptive cultural transformation.

Endeavor

Achieving adaptive cultural transformation in the U.S. was not easy. The biggest challenge that I encountered in this process was finding a balance between my Asian cultural background and the U.S. cultural environment I was in and between my dual identities—in the Chinese and in the U.S. communities. I was highly motivated both instrumentally and integratively[2] to adapt to the U.S. culture, to gain new experiences in order to understand and appreciate the target culture. But my Chinese self, characterized by Asian beliefs, values, customs, and habits as illustrated by my earlier experiences in the U.S., often presented conflicts in the process of my adaptive cultural transformation. That transformation required determination and a willingness to recognize my own native culture and to understand and respect the target culture.

In North America, I am regarded as a visible minority due to my Asian appearance. In order to achieve my second language (L2) social identity, to be accepted as a member of the target culture, which was a very important factor for success in my professional career, I focused my attention on improving my communication skills and mannerisms and even my appearance. As a result of my cultural adaptation, I am now often mistaken for a Chinese-American. While being identified as a Chinese-American can be a symbol of successful acculturation, it is not necessarily interpreted that way in the Chinese community. I found it difficult to be Westernized when I was with my Chinese friends. For instance, in a Chinese-only group, speaking English would be regarded as odd or showing off; likewise, dressing like the U.S. population would be considered a sign of being alienated from the Chinese inner group.

Sometimes I preferred to reveal my Chinese ethnic identity when talking about something I was very proud of, such as Chinese ethnic foods, which I cook without using recipes, and China's long history with numerous dynasties. Sometimes I preferred to conceal my Chinese ethnic identity when the topic under discussion was something for which China is often criticized, such as the treatment of intellectuals or the nature of the government bureaucracy.

As I believe that social identity is dependent on the social context, I know that my social identity has multiple dimensions. Each has its function in the right context. I present myself as a different person in different social groups and communities. In China, I was very quiet in class as a sign of respect for teachers, but I became very outspoken in class at OSU as a sign of cooperation with teachers. I was not very talkative in Chinese communities in the U.S. because I did not want to show off. But I was very enthusiastic when talking about China and Chinese people among U.S. friends, as I considered myself a cultural informant. I seldom wrote Chinese letters to my relatives and friends in China, yet I was not afraid of losing my Chinese. But I wrote almost every day in English because I still saw weakness in my writing in English. Therefore, I came to realize that I have to maintain different identities in different contexts and to vary my communication styles depending on when and where I speak about what and to whom.

I also found that a social identity sometimes requires mutual acceptance. Even if I want to be affiliated with an ethnic group, I might be rejected. In order to know the U.S. culture well, for several consecutive years I spent Christmas Eve at the homes of my U.S. friends, even though I was invited again and again by my Chinese friends to go to their Chinese Christmas parties. One Christmas, when I wanted to be with my Chinese friends for a change, I was unfortunately not invited. I was told later by my Chinese friends that they thought I would decline their invitation if they asked me again. I felt bad about this experience. But perhaps my friends were right; affiliation with a certain ethnic group is reciprocal. How you want to be identified is incomplete without considering what others might think of you.

In my journey of adaptive cultural transformation, I gradually perceived my Chinese cultural boundaries as permeable and flexible. Instead of letting my Chinese culture and my well-established L1 social identity become a shield that blocked me from constructing my L2 identity in the U.S. culture, I became open-minded and was willing to participate in various social activities to give myself opportunities to experience and understand the target culture. I was considered a fluent English speaker by many native English speakers in the U.S. But in my first quarter at OSU, I was afraid to speak up in the courses I took. I was overwhelmed by the various teaching styles used by professors, by the amount of information presented in my classes, by the amount of reading to be completed before each class meeting, by the weekly testing format, and by the outspokenness of my classmates. As a result, I kept quiet and tried to figure out how to carve a niche for myself in the new classroom culture. I conducted numerous "experiments" on myself in adapting to this special social setting—the academic content classroom. I tried to speak up when I was very certain of something, but initially I failed because I was nervous about making grammatical mistakes. I tried several times to focus on basic concepts in the readings and give my interpretations of the concepts when they were discussed in class. This purposeful preparation somewhat helped my participation. However, I still felt nervous about speaking up in class, as I noticed slightly unnatural tones in my voice. Nevertheless, I kept trying and reflecting on my own experiences in participation and interaction with classmates. A couple of quarters later I realized that my participation in classes had become instantaneous, improvised, and effortless.

Learning some of the "normal" behavior rules in classroom communication in the target culture and unlearning some of the "normal" classroom behavior rules in my own culture gradually brought about an internal transformation. In time, I deviated from the accepted classroom patterns of my original culture and acquired the new patterns of the target classroom culture. This process, referred to as the stress-adaptation-growth process (Kim, 1988) in a classroom setting, led to my increased functional fitness and to a greater congruence and compatibility between my internal state and the conditions of the U.S. classroom environment. As a result, my increased oral participation in content courses gradually made me aware of my successful existence in class. I could hear my voice in discussions, and I had a sense of belonging. This increased self-confidence also gradually enabled me to attain a level of communicative success beyond the classroom setting that allowed me to meet my social needs, including making friends with people from different cultural backgrounds and seeking graduate research and teaching assistantships across campus.

More self-confidence also improved my psychological state in that I achieved lower levels of stress and anxiety, higher self-esteem, and the ability to be more creative in work and study and to have a sense of personal fulfillment.

My increased classroom participation enhanced my ability to function in my L2 and thus improved the effectiveness of my communication in the target culture outside the classrooms. It also affected my psychological state and self-identification, which changed from being monocultural to being increasingly intercultural. Instead of feeling bound exclusively to the Chinese culture, I had a more fluid intercultural identity (Gudykunst & Kim, 1984) that I expressed by observing and practicing different sets of social values, beliefs, and norms in different cultural communities. Such an intercultural identity with cognitive, affective, and behavioral flexibility allowed me to adapt to situations and to creatively manage or avoid the conflicts that occur frequently in intercultural communication settings. It is through this dynamic and continuous process of cultural adaptive transformation that I have gradually moved toward becoming increasingly intercultural.

Like many nonnative English speakers in the U.S., I underwent an adjustment period in my process of adaptive cultural transformation. Now I am a professor who teaches both graduate and undergraduate courses in applied linguistics and L2 pedagogy in the Department of English at the University of Arizona. Whenever I teach a class that includes many NNES students, they always remind me of myself when I first came to the U.S. Although I understand that these students are new to the culture, I still expect them to take risks and to make efforts to adapt themselves effectively to the U.S. culture. An encounter with another culture can only lead to openness if the students can suspend the assumption of difference, perceiving the new culture not as strange or alien but, instead, as a culture to learn about, adjust to, and transform into.

Empowerment

When I began teaching English composition to NNES graduate and undergraduate students at OSU, I often encountered suspicion from my students. This suspicion usually came from those who walked into my classes presuming that their English teacher would be a native English speaker, an understandable assumption. Eventually, my smiles and understanding, my correct pronunciation of their names with 10 or more syllables, my anecdotes about my English learning experiences, my encouragement, and my detailed and constructive comments and suggestions on their first assignment all helped me to win their trust and admiration. It is true that I am not a native speaker of English and never will be. But the quality of language teaching is not merely determined by native or nonnative speaker status, and I believe my students came to recognize this.

The language I speak and the way I teach make a difference in the students' perception of me, a Chinese person teaching English in the U.S. I remind myself constantly that since I am teaching English in an English environment, the only way I can make up for my lack of nativeness is by being aware of it. This keeps me constantly striving for a higher goal, since I recognize that a journey of self-cultivation and refinement usually ends when one no longer feels the need for improvement.

I also believe that the success of NNES professionals in TESOL lies in our modesty. My students appreciate me because I tell them that I need to consult my native speaker colleagues about a word, a phrase, or a sentence. My students appreciate me because I provide them with examples of my struggles completing difficult writing tasks. They appreciate me because they feel free to comment on different drafts of a summary or paper and to criticize papers, including mine. As a NNES professional, I empower my students through empathy, sailing with them to the shore instead of summoning them from the shore.

The following two examples illustrate how I as a NNES instructor empowered my NNES students when I taught ESL composition at OSU.

Example 1: Being a Participant in the Peer Review Process

Context. International graduate students at OSU represent 129 countries, and their ability to function in English varies greatly. Almost 85% participate in course work offered through the ESL composition program, the largest post-admission ESL writing program in the U.S. The ultimate goal of this program is to bring students' expository writing skills to a level at which they can perform successfully as writers in university courses. Upon enrollment, all international graduate students are required to take a one-hour writing placement exam. Based upon this exam, holistically evaluated by ESL composition staff, students are then placed in one of three English courses (106G, 107G, and 108.02). Only a small number of highly qualified students are exempted from the courses.

The three courses have different purposes. English 106G is designed to help graduate students develop the fluency and basic skills needed for academic writing. The emphasis of English 107G is to help students develop advanced skills in academic writing. English 108.02, the last course in the sequence, helps students develop the skills necessary to write about research findings. In the fall of 1995, I conducted an action research project[3] in the intermediate ESL writing class (107G). Because developing advanced writing skills was the objective of this course, students were expected to write polished essays incorporating organization patterns most frequently found in academic prose. There were three major tasks in this course—writing a definition paper, writing a problem-solution paper, and performing data analysis. Each task was to be completed with three drafts. Between the first and second drafts, peer review activities, in which a group of three or four students collaborated and commented on each paper, usually with the help of a structured peer review sheet, were incorporated. Between the second and the final drafts, one-on-one teacher-student conferences were held. In these conferences, each student came to the teacher's office at a pre-assigned time and the teacher went through the paper with the student, pointing out rhetorical as well as grammatical errors and making various suggestions for revision.

Problems. Although the two activities, peer review and one-on-one tutorials (also known as writing conferences), were generally welcomed by the students, problems occurred with each of the activities. In the peer review session, students often felt uncertain, not sure they should trust the comments of peers who were at the same linguistic level. Their insecurity often led to a lack of enthusiasm toward this activity. Meanwhile, without the presence of the instructor, some students came to peer review sessions underprepared because of their heavy course loads, communicating disrespect to others and seriously hindering the mutual exchange among peers. This problem of students not trusting their peers and arriving without adequate preparation called into question the real value of peer review.

Another problem was related to the one-on-one teacher-student conferencing. Besides totally exhausting the teacher, who repetitively talked with each individual student about similar rhetorical or grammatical mistakes, the tutorials were of questionable benefit, as the students often followed the instructor's advice without fully understanding the comments. They were able to revise their drafts based on the teacher's comments, but it became evident that the students frequently did not remember the reasons for their revisions and thus made the same mistakes again in later assignments.

Action. To resolve these problems, I incorporated peer review activities into the conferencing. As the instructor as well as a NNES teacher who had gone through a similar learning process, I participated in the peer review activities by assuming the role of a peer. Instead of dominating the discussion, I had the group select a leader to facilitate the discussion. I sometimes participated in the discussion by confirming peers' comments and sometimes questioned the writer's and peers' comments in order to stimulate further discussion. I gave my written comments on peer review sheets at the end of the discussion of each student's paper, as did the other peers. As a participant, my role was not only to offer comments but also to provide support and encouragement so that the student whose paper was being reviewed would feel comfortable and confident in assessing the different options and suggestions from peers (myself as peer included). The peers, on the other hand, would have to be well prepared to actively participate in commenting, arguing, and debating issues of concern when their teacher was present as a peer.

Findings. Data were collected via surveys, open-ended questionnaires, and interviews with the ESL students in an effort to address three research questions:

1. How do students in ESL composition courses perceive peer review, tutorials, and peer review with and without the instructor?
2. Why do they like or dislike peer review with the instructor as opposed to either peer review without the instructor or one-on-one tutorials?
3. What salient factors are involved or need to be addressed regarding the effectiveness of peer review with the instructor?

Both survey and open-ended questionnaires revealed that the majority of students liked peer review with the instructor because they could easily check with the instructor when receiving feedback from different perspectives. This made students feel more secure. The majority of the students thought that peer review with the instructor facilitated their decision making about which feedback to accept or reject. Also, the interview data revealed the students' belief that peer review with the instructor helped prepare them to be careful, critical, and sensitive reviewers of others, as well as of their own papers. By contributing and listening to the critiques of their peers' papers, they were more aware of their own writing problems and were better able to revise their own writing.

Implications. Combining peer review with student-teacher conferencing was an attempt to empower NNES students in their academic writing classes. The success of this attempt was enhanced by a number of factors. The primary factor, I believe, was my NNES status. As I had gone through a similar process of learning how to write in English for academic purposes, my role as a peer was easily accepted and naturally maintained. Any uneasiness students felt about being judged or evaluated was soon overtaken by the excitement and enthusiasm created by their active participation. The preceding example thus shows how a NNES professional can serve as a role model by sharing learning experiences, anticipating difficulties in writing in English, and providing needed help and timely advice in the composing processes.

Example 2: Sharing My Own Academic Writing Experiences

Context. ESL students who are learning to write academic papers often request samples that the teacher considers high quality. Because of their L1 writing training, international students in general, and Asian students in particular, tend to value the content and rhetoric of these samples. They make a realistic assessment of how they can work effectively and efficiently to produce similar high-quality papers. To address this need, the writing teacher feels compelled to find writing models.

The problem. It is very difficult to match the students' current writing skills with a sample paper that will serve as a model; that is, professional writing samples (e.g., published journal articles) are either rhetorically too sophisticated for the students to appreciate at their current English proficiency levels or too long for them to imitate. As a result, many ESL students do not benefit from reading models, despite their expressed desire to have them. Using previous students' writing (anonymous and with consent) as samples for class discussion is welcomed by students. Such student sample papers provide a realistic product for students to emulate. However, a problem with student sample papers is that the teacher cannot explain why certain ideas were included in the text or what revisions were made during the process of writing. Therefore, the process of writing and revising, a very important aspect to include in the teaching of writing, not only is unrevealed but cannot be revealed.

Action. In order to show the writer's mindset in composing and revising, I used my own writing samples. I would usually give my students an early draft on the same topic as the one they had been given, without disclosing that I was the author. I invited students to critique the paper in small groups in class. In the next class, I would show them a second draft based on their comments and suggestions and invite them to make further comments. A few days later, I would show them the final draft and ask them to compare it with the previous drafts and justify why certain changes had been made or not. At this time I would claim authorship and share with my students the processes of writing and revision, as well as the dilemmas I faced in the writing process.

Findings. In looking at the results of the action research project, I mainly focused on one question: What effect does the use of my writing samples have on students' attitudes toward writing and on the improvement of their own writing? My observations, my informal interviews with undergraduate and graduate students, and the end-of-term evaluations over several quarters produced consistently positive findings. The majority of students not only welcomed the use of my samples but also felt that they benefited from understanding my thought processes in shaping a paper through several drafts. They also realized the importance of feedback from both teacher and peers in the process of writing and revising. Such awareness contributed to their enthusiasm and attention in undertaking peer review activities and accepting teacher comments.

Implications. By using my own writing and by undertaking revision based on my students' input, the writing process became lively and engaging. By sharing my experiences as a NNES writer, I demonstrated to my ESL students that no one can write a good paper without revisions and no one can effectively revise a paper without receiving comments and critiques. This sharing greatly empowered my students to understand the processes of writing, peer critiquing, and revising and led them to understand the importance of reflecting on their own writing experiences.

In teaching ESL composition courses, I also shared with students my struggles in transitioning from writing in my L1 to writing in my L2. I told my students that although in China I had succeeded in publishing many papers and books written in Chinese, during my first few quarters at OSU I had difficulty writing papers in English because of the influence of my L1. It was not the content but the discourse that made the difference. My Chinese way of thinking had a great impact on how I composed in English. I soon realized that in order to maintain my L2 literacy and L2 social identity, I had to understand the fundamental thinking processes that the target culture accepted and the way that my L1 culture could be accepted. I learned U.S. discourse and rhetoric, and I made an effort to adapt my writing style to fit the general preference of a U.S. audience. The result? I have had a few papers published. However, the process of adaptation does not mean that I lost my Chinese writing style. I still see the legitimacy and beauty of Chinese writing, even though I do not practice it in U.S. academia.

Despite the success of my action research, dilemmas have surfaced and have raised many questions. Will my prescription of strategies restrict my students' freedom of thought and expression? Will my requirement that students adopt U.S. academic standards do a great disservice by inhibiting them from reflecting their own cultures and ideologies? Will my dense reading and writing assignments burden students to the extent that they become passive learners? Will the use of my early writing as samples limit my students' opportunities to see model articles? Will my emphasis on discourse in writing discourage students from concentrating on eliminating grammatical errors? As I continue to think about these questions, I am reminded of other issues important to teaching ESL composition, such as learner autonomy, self-directed learning, and self-empowerment.

Afterthoughts

As a nonnative English speaker, I am proud to be a member of the TESOL profession. I am also proud to be aware of the ramifications of being a NNES professional. The success of TESOL professionals does not depend on whether they are native speakers or nonnative speakers of English; however, nonnative speakers might depend on different instructional approaches than those used by native speakers. Therefore, we need to consider several questions. How can we as nonnative speakers of English take advantage of our experience learning the language we are teaching and collaborate with our NES colleagues to make teaching more effective and rewarding? How can we incorporate nonnative speakers' viewpoints regarding factors such as authenticity in language, social identity in communities, and cultural diversity in language classrooms? How can we best provide opportunities for our NNES students to empower themselves? And finally, what can we, as NNES professionals, do to empower ourselves? I believe we need to constantly ask ourselves these questions because in the process of forming questions, we can begin to find answers.

Notes

1. Adaptive cultural transformation competence is the knowledge that enables an individual to communicate appropriately and effectively in the target culture by expanding his or her social identity to one that blends the new set of values, habits, and social norms endorsed in the target culture with those in the home culture. Such a higher-level competence is needed in appropriate and effective cultural adaptation, accommodation, and acculturation in order to develop successful second language proficiency in multiple contexts.
2. Instrumental motivation commonly refers to the desire of a learner to achieve proficiency for reasons connected to another goal (e.g., to attain career, financial, or educational goals). Integrative motivation, on the other hand, refers to the learner's desire to achieve proficiency due to a positive attitude toward the target language and culture and a desire to become like members of that target culture (Gardner & Lambert, 1972).
3. Action research involves participant intervention in a real-life classroom setting. Most frequently, the researcher participant poses a research question and then seeks to answer this question by collecting data and closely examining actual practices in the chosen context. This research typically culminates in suggestions that would improve the teaching practice (Nunan, 1989).

References

Bautista, M. L. S. (1997). *English is an Asian language: The Philippine context.* Sydney, Australia: Macquarie Library.

Braine, G. (1996, March). *In their own voices: Non-native speaker professionals in TESOL.* Colloquium presented at the 30th annual meeting of Teachers of English to Speakers of Other Languages, Chicago, IL.

Braine, G. (1997, March). *Non-native-speaking TESOL educators.* Colloquium presented at the 31st annual meeting of Teachers of English to Speakers of Other Languages, Orlando, FL.

Brown, H. D. (2000). *Teaching by principles: An interactive approach to language pedagogy* (2nd ed.). Englewood Cliffs, NJ: Prentice-Hall.

Celce-Murcia, M. (Ed.). (2001). *Teaching English as a second or foreign language* (3rd ed.). Boston: Heinle & Heinle.

Crystal, D. (1997). *English as a global language.* New York: Cambridge University Press.

Davies, A. (1991). *The native speaker in applied linguistics.* Edinburgh, Scotland: Edinburgh University Press.

Gardner, R. C., & Lambert, W. E. (1972). *Attitudes and motivation in second language learning.* Rowley, MA: Newbury House.

Gudykunst, W. B., & Kim, Y. Y. (1984). *Communicating with strangers: An approach to intercultural communication.* New York: Random House.

Hadley, A. O. (2001). *Teaching language in context* (3rd ed.). Boston: Heinle & Heinle.

Kachru, B. B. (Ed.). (1992). *The other tongue: English across cultures* (2nd ed.). Chicago: University of Illinois Press.

Kachru, B. B., & Nelson, C. L. (1996). World Englishes. In S. L. McKay & N. H. Hornberger (Eds.), *Sociolinguistics and language teaching* (pp. 71–102). New York: Cambridge University Press.

Kamhi-Stein, L. D. (2000). Adapting U.S.-based TESOL education to meet the needs of non-native English speakers. *TESOL Journal, 9*(3), 10–14.

Kim, Y. Y. (1988). *Communication and cross-cultural adaptation: An integrative theory.* Philadelphia: Multilingual Matters.

Kramsch, C. (1998). The privilege of the intercultural speaker. In M. Byram & M. Fleming (Eds.), *Language learning in intercultural perspective: Approaches through drama and ethnography* (pp. 16–31). New York: Cambridge University Press.

Kresovich, B. M. (1988). *Error gravity: Perceptions of native-speaking and non-native speaking faculty in EFL.* (ERIC Document Reproduction Service No. ED311732)

Li, D. (1998). "It's always more difficult than you plan and imagine": Teachers' perceived difficulties in introducing the communicative approach in South Korea. *TESOL Quarterly, 32,* 677–702.

Liu, J. (1998, March). *The impact of NNS professionals on their ESL students.* Colloquium presented at the 32nd annual meeting of Teachers of English to Speakers of Other Languages, Seattle, WA.

Liu, J. (1999). Nonnative-English-speaking professionals. *TESOL Quarterly, 33,* 85–102.

Liu, J., & Richards, J. C. (2001, March). *An international survey of language teaching methods.* Paper presented at the 35th annual meeting of Teachers of English to Speakers of Other Languages, St. Louis, MO.

Manzo, A., & Manzo, U. (1997). New eclecticism: A pedagogical perspective for literacy and learning. *Reading Research and Instruction, 36*(3), 191–198.

McNeill, A. (1994). *Some characteristics of native and non-native speaker teachers of English.* (ERIC Document Reproduction Service No. ED386067)

Medgyes, P. (1992). Native or non-native: Who's worth more? *ELT Journal, 46*(4), 340–349.

Medgyes, P. (1994). *The non-native teacher.* London: Macmillan.

Mitchell, C. B., & Vidal, K. E. (2001). Weighing the ways of the flow: Twentieth century language instruction. *Modern Language Journal, 85*(1), 26–38.

Norris, J. M., & Ortega, L. (2000). Effectiveness of L2 instruction: A research synthesis and quantitative meta-analysis. *Language Learning, 50*(3), 417–528.

Nunan, D. (1989). *Understanding language classrooms: A guide for teacher-initiated action.* Englewood Cliffs, NJ: Prentice-Hall.

Paikeday, T. M. (1985). *The native speaker is dead! An informal discussion of a linguistic myth with Noam Chomsky and other linguists, philosophers, psychologists, and lexicographers.* Toronto: Paikeday Publications.

Palfreyman, D. (1993). "How I got it in my head": Conceptual models of language and learning in native and non-native trained EFL teachers. *Language Awareness, 2*(4), 209–223.

Rampton, M. B. H. (1990). Displacing the "native speaker": Expertise, affiliation, and inheritance. *ELT Journal, 44*(2), 97–101.

Richards, J. C., & Rodgers, T. (2001). *Approaches and methods in language teaching* (2nd ed.). New York: Cambridge University Press.

Samimy, K. K., & Brutt-Griffler, J. (1999). To be a native or non-native speaker: Perceptions of "non-native" students in a graduate TESOL program. In G. Braine (Ed.), *Non-native educators in English language teaching* (pp. 127–144). Mahwah, NJ: Erlbaum.

Invisible Minorities and the Nonnative English-Speaking Professional

Jette G. Hansen
University of Arizona, Tucson

You are not a nonnative speaker of English.

These words were spoken to me as I was staffing the Nonnative English Speakers in TESOL (NNEST) Caucus booth at the TESOL convention in New York City in March of 1999. While these words may have been spoken in jest, there was a serious undercurrent to them—I did not "look" like a nonnative speaker of English, nor did I sound like one with my American–accented English, and therefore I did not fit into the stereotype of a nonnative speaker of English. In short, because I did not look or sound like a nonnative speaker, I could not possibly be one.

I had never had my nonnativeness challenged so directly before. My native language is Danish and I did not begin learning English until I was 10 years old. However, because I have a native-like command of English and I am an invisible[1] minority due to my physical appearance, I am often mistaken for a native speaker of English. This comment may appear to be a compliment and a testimony to my achievements in acquiring English; however, there may also be negative consequences of this misidentification. First of all, since I am perceived to be a native speaker of English, there is sometimes the assumption that I have fully acquired the English language and the cultural customs of the English as a second language (ESL) context, in my case the

United States; second, being identified as a native speaker of English typically implies monolingualism and monoculturalism, which may suggest that I cannot be a native speaker of another language or have another cultural identity, e.g., being viewed as an "American" and a native speaker of English effectively obscures my Danish identity and linguistic and cultural background. Finally, and more seriously, being identified as a native speaker can minimize or even erase my ESL learning experiences. Yet these experiences are the reason I became a TESOL professional, and my self-identification as a nonnative speaker of English is the identity that drives my research and teaching.

In this chapter, I am going to describe my own experiences in learning and teaching ESL in relation to being an invisible immigrant minority, a nonnative speaker of English, and, more important, an invisible nonnative speaker of English. Invisible nonnative English-speaking teachers may be perceived as native speakers by individuals both outside and inside the TESOL profession, including by their students, and this fact may render them invisible within the NNEST discourse community. Because of the invisibility of this group of nonnative speakers' voices, there has been very little focus on the experiences of this group of English language teachers within the growing discourse on NNEST—to my knowledge, only Liu (1999a, 1999b) and this text deal explicitly with this population of teachers. Therefore, my goal in this chapter is to explore some of my experiences as an invisible nonnative speaker of English in terms of being an ESL learner, an ESL and an English as a foreign language (EFL) teacher, and a TESOL educator, in order to give this population of teachers a voice and visibility within the NNEST discourse.

My Experiences as an ESL Learner: How I Learned English and "Lost" My Danish Identity

Developing First Language Literacy Skills in Denmark

I was born in Denmark. Both of my parents were teachers in the Danish public school system and placed a high value on literacy. As children, my older sister and I were always encouraged to read: One of my mom's goals is to never let a birthday or Christmas go by without including at least one book as a gift. Our house has always been filled with books, to the extent that our living room resembles a library. My parents' open encouragement of reading has sparked a life passion—every member of my family is an avid reader.

While writing may not have been encouraged as openly, it was certainly not ignored. One of my earliest memories of writing is of my mom helping my sister and me "write" our own newspapers, by clipping letters and words from old newspapers and pasting them into a notebook to create our own version of the news. I was both reading and writing before I entered school, thanks to an older sister who, proud of her own new ability to read and write, was eager to teach her younger sibling and to be a teacher like mom and dad. From the time I could put letters together to form words, I wrote songs, usually as a gift in honor of my mom or dad's birthday. These songs and my later attempts at poetry had my mother convinced that I would someday be a writer.

There are two things I remember from this time. First, I am left-handed, and when I entered first grade, my teacher began to teach me to write with the right hand. My mom soon noticed this, and since then the only time I have tried to write with the right hand has been in the vain attempt to call myself ambidextrous. Second, I remember trying to teach a younger friend how to read and write and my amazement at her outright refusal to be taught. I later found out that her teacher was teaching reading and writing through a special system and did not want any other teaching to interfere. At eight years of age, I had survived my sister's rather haphazard teaching and was doing just fine in second grade, and so I thought both my friend's teacher odd and my friend dumb not to want to read sooner. Needless to say, my early views of pedagogy were a bit skeptical.

Acquiring English as a Second Language in the United States

Whereas my first language (L1) experience was marked with success and sweetly comical memories, my second language (L2) experience could best be described as a struggle. After the death of my father and due to various health and financial reasons, my mother decided to leave Denmark for the United States when I was 10 years old. We settled in a very small town in northern Wisconsin. To say the school district was unprepared for my sister and me is an understatement: This was 1977, and ESL instruction was just starting to be a component in many urban school districts. It was certainly not an issue in Elcho, Wisconsin, where no foreigners had entered the school system before. Unfortunately for me, English education began in the fifth grade in Denmark at that time, and so when we moved to the United States, I had had no prior exposure to this strange new language. My sister had studied English in school for two years and so knew a bit of English, and my mom knew some English as well. However, by the time I entered the Elcho Public School System in September of 1977, my English was limited to three words: *yes, no,* and *love.*

In retrospect, I realize that there were positive aspects to attending school in a small district; at the time, however, all I could see were the negatives. While the school really was at a loss about how to deal with my sister and me, what they lacked in skills and materials, they made up for in personal attention. We were moved along slowly in the mainstream classes but were not expected to keep up with our peers in the beginning. Not surprisingly, the only subject I initially understood was math; I was even lost in gym class, since we played softball and not soccer or handball, the sports I was accustomed to playing in Denmark. To our horror, my sister and I were also pulled out of class once a day to spend an hour with a special needs tutor. This added a significant stigma to our already "different" identities in school and, more significantly, affected our own view of ourselves: We had been viewed as high achievers by our teachers in Denmark and now were told we could not keep up with our peers. My sister rebelled against this stigma and refused to go to the tutor—not knowing quite what to do with her, the tutor eventually left her alone. I wanted to rebel, but at 10 years of age, I was afraid to and also did not quite have the language to do so successfully; therefore, I kept going to the tutor for several months. This stopped one day when the teacher in charge of the center admitted to my mother that they were at a loss about what to do with me, since I was outperforming all the other students. In retrospect, I believe the tutoring helped me quite a bit, especially with vocabulary and spelling, though at the time, I viewed it as a nuisance and one more symbol of my differentness.

In a way, I was part of a community language learning situation comprised of my tutor, my fifth-grade teacher, my classmates, and my mom and sister—where I was often the only student. My fifth-grade teacher, Mrs. Bucholtz, was patient and kind and encouraged the other students to help me, although she strictly forbade them to teach me any swear words. The other students had mixed reactions to me: Most of the boys saw me as odd and probably stupid as well and were not afraid to tease me when the teacher or some of the more sensitive classmates were not around. Many of the girls were my peer language tutors; they unwittingly used Total Physical Response (TPR) to teach me words like *run* and *jump,* and they gave it their best effort to teach me abstract vocabulary as well. A vivid memory of this time is of me playing on the monkey bars during recess and, after I had struggled with the word *fun* for quite a while, the lightbulb in my head suddenly went off when I realized what the word meant. My girlfriends were excited and proud that their teaching had worked, and this episode was recounted often through the years as we reminisced about my early years in the United States. It was a highly contextualized learning experience—perhaps this is why I remember it so well.

At home, my mom worked hard with us every night to make sure we could understand and complete our homework. My mom remembers this as a time when I was falling asleep over my books at night since I stubbornly refused to stop until I had completed all the work—I did not want to be that different from everyone else in class the next day. Frustration at not being able to understand the homework, as well as a lack of patience with my own perceptions of the slowness of my English acquisition, also reduced me to tears in the beginning. Writing in English was especially difficult, and I was angry and upset that I was not able to write in English, since writing in Danish had not been difficult to learn.

It was a hard time, but I did learn. One of my earliest recognitions of achievement was based on reading: My fifth-grade class was divided into three reading-group levels based on students' abilities to pass reading tests corresponding to three different proficiency levels. I was placed into the lowest level when I first arrived, and I stayed in that level for several months. It was difficult for me to be called a poor reader, and worse yet, to actually not be able to read the material well. Even though the letters were familiar to me, I couldn't quite grasp the sound or the meaning of the new words formed from the familiar letters. Some of the letters also looked a bit different—I had to "relearn" writing in script, as the Danish letters *j* and *t* are written a bit differently from the English letters. For example, while cursive English *t* is written with a slash across the top, the Danish cursive *t* may have a loop at the bottom and no slash, especially in lowercase form (in uppercase, it resembles the English *T*). In uppercase cursive form, the Danish *J* may be written with a loop as well, whereas in lowercase it may be dotted like the English *j*.[2]

In order to move to a different reading level, students had to do well on two tests in a row—the tests were composed of multiple-choice questions focusing on the vocabulary in and comprehension of a particular reading passage, a different one for each reading group and thus proficiency level. Students took these tests every few weeks, after they had finished reading and studying the vocabulary of a particular passage. If students did well on the test for their particular level twice in a row, they were considered able to advance to the higher reading level (and vice versa). There was not a lot of upward (or downward) movement, so when I climbed to the intermediate level, the other students were surprised. The surprise probably also had something to do with my slowly changing persona: I was no longer the "slow" learner I had been viewed as before, and I was developing a U.S. identity on the surface because of the U.S. clothes and shoes I had begged my mother to buy. There was a particularly obnoxious boy in the highest reading group, and when I moved into the intermediate group, he loudly announced that I would never be able to move up to his reading group. A few months later I did.

The upward movement in reading levels stands out as the clearest indicator of my increasing English literacy: Within a year of arriving in the United States, I had surpassed many of my peers in reading ability. I became fluent in English very rapidly—too rapidly in retrospect, for somewhere between the seventh and eighth grade, my accent disappeared and, except for my name, any visible markers of a Danish identity disappeared. Unlike many immigrant children, I was able to acquire both Basic Interpersonal Communicative Skills (BICS) and Cognitive Academic Language Proficiency (CALP) (Cummins, 1981) in a few years. Research (e.g., Collier, 1989; Cummins, 1991; Thomas & Collier, 1997) suggests that immigrant children may acquire the oral language skills necessary to communicate fluently in social contexts, also referred to as BICS, after several years in the L2 context. In contrast, it may take them between five and seven years to acquire the cognitive academic language skills to keep up with their peers academically if they are literate in the L1 and between seven to nine years if they are not literate in the L1, as the literacy in the L2 and attainment of cognitive strategies and academic skills resulting from previous literacy and schooling experiences are thought to be transferable to acquisition of L2 literacy and academic skills. My own rapid acquisition of basic oral communication skills and cognitive academic language proficiency skills can be credited to my strong L1 literacy skills, as well as to attention from both teachers and peers at school and to parental attention and help at home. Another factor that influenced my learning was that for me, reading, writing, listening, and speaking were all integrated. In effect, I was receiving content-based instruction wherein all four skills areas—listening, speaking, writing, and reading—were integrated within contextualized and meaningful tasks and activities. I was learning to spell words as I was learning the meanings of words and how to pronounce them. While my peers were learning the sound-symbol correspondences of words they already knew how to pronounce (the phonic method), I learned both the sound and spelling simultaneously, and perhaps I had an easier time connecting the two as I had no preconceived notions of how the words should be spelled and therefore no phonetic interference. In fact, spelling was one of my strong points, and in the seventh grade, I won the grade-level spelling bee and competed in the schoolwide spelling bee. English became my favorite and easiest subject in school and my major as an undergraduate and graduate student.

In 1982, after having lived in northern Wisconsin for five years, my family moved to Milwaukee, Wisconsin, where I began 10th grade in a suburban high school. No one asked me, "Where are you from?" Instead, I was asked, "How did you get such an unusual name?" In this new environment where I had no history, I was seen as no different from anyone else except for having a name that was difficult to spell and pronounce; in effect, I had become an invisible nonnative speaker of English.

Balancing Two Languages and Identities

Though permanent residents of the United States, my family members and I have all retained our Danish citizenships. My family was fairly sheltered from contact with other Danes both in the remote northern Wisconsin town of Elcho and in urban Milwaukee. The Danes that did live in Milwaukee or the surrounding area were mostly second or third generation, and many of them did not speak Danish. Our submersion within the L2 culture and language and our unintended physical distance from our L1 culture and language had a reverse effect on our language and identity—it nurtured them and made the bonds to Denmark stronger rather than eroding the ties and supplanting the language. Although my family fostered my emerging English literacy, we have always maintained Danish as our home language, and having brought many Danish books with us to the United States, we read in Danish if we chose to. To this day, we speak only Danish with one another, and if English speakers are around, we still prefer to speak Danish to one another and then translate what we speak about if others are listening. We have strong familial and friendship ties to Denmark, and these ties have grown stronger over the years as my sister and I have begun developing our own relationships and traveling on our own to Denmark. At my sister's wedding, family and friends flew in from Denmark for the celebration; my nephew is a Danish citizen and is being raised bilingually in Danish and in English although his father is American and the family lives in the United States.

My mother has always nurtured our Danish identities by fostering Danish language use within the family. Had we not maintained our Danish, I would probably not identify myself as strongly as a Dane, since I would have a difficult time assimilating into the Danish culture when I go home to Denmark if I did not speak Danish. These trips home are filled with a lot of joy, but they are also filled with sadness, since I often wonder who I would be and what I would have become had I stayed in Denmark. It is a time when I search for the Danish identity I hold on to so hard in the United States. When I am in the United States, I perceive myself as very Danish, and I mourn the loss of the accent that would signify my identity to the rest of the world. Paradoxically, the linguistic markers I mourn the loss of in the United States are present in my Danish. A number of years ago, when it had been quite a few years between visits to Denmark, a store assistant in Copenhagen asked me how I had learned such good Danish. Good as it was, it wasn't *quite* right. During that same trip, a Danish professor of English told me that I spoke Danish with "an American mouth"—syntactically and phonologically. In an ironic twist of fate, I have become a visible minority—linguistically due to my Danish attrition and physically due to my U.S. clothes—in my native culture.

While it is not surprising that I have suffered L1 attrition, this attrition is not permanent—rather, the more frequently I return to Denmark, the more I am able to "re-learn" the Danish I have lost. Also, quite like being told that I was not good enough to move into the highest reading group in fifth grade spurred me to work harder to acquire English, comments like those by the store assistant and the professor have spurred me to work on my Danish so that I am not "different" from other Danes. In recent years, I have had more opportunities to travel to Denmark, and with each trip my Danish becomes more and more indistinguishable from that of Danish speakers in Denmark. I often read novels in Danish, and I have begun writing e-mails in Danish to friends and relatives—both these activities reestablish my Danish literacy and help it to flourish.

While I struggle to become invisible once again in my native culture—to reclaim my Danish identity, culture, and language—I struggle to become visible in my adopted culture and language. Because I look and sound American, most people assume that I am a native speaker of English and a U.S. citizen. This is not surprising—however, what is surprising is that even after I reveal that I am not a native speaker of English and that I am a Danish citizen, many people still have a difficult time accepting me as anything other than American. In terms of visible surface markers of my Danish identity, all I have is my name—and this is often interpreted as a colorful selection by hippie parents during the 1960s rather than a symbol of ethnic identity. With the loss of a perceptible Danish accent came linguistic prejudice—because I don't sound Danish, I can't possibly be Danish. Over the years, I've been asked countless times why I have not become a U.S. citizen (and this is sometimes combined with an explicit criticism of my choice to remain a Danish citizen). Even when I try to explain how I feel inside, I find that people perceive that I am hanging on to my Danishness as though I had no right to it—that with the acquisition of an American accent I should forfeit my right to membership in another ethnic group. My—and my family's—resistance to complete assimilation is not well understood. I wonder, if I had a more noticeable Danish accent, would it be more acceptable?

More difficult is the erasure of my L2 learning experiences and the minimization of the difficulty of learning English as a child when these experiences are acknowledged (e.g., when people acknowledge that I am a nonnative speaker rather than assuming, and/or insisting, that

I am a native speaker). It is commonly assumed that it is easy for children to acquire an L2—that they just "absorb" it naturally and effortlessly. Therefore, my revelation that I began learning English when I was 10, rather than as an adult, is often greeted with responses about how easily children pick up an L2. However, as my own case illustrates and as an abundance of research documents (cf. Collier, 1989; Cummins, 1991; Thomas & Collier, 1997), learning an L2 as a child can be extremely difficult and time-consuming, especially for school-age children, who must acquire subject matter knowledge along with linguistic knowledge. Immigrant children are also often socially and academically marginalized both in and out of school (Kramsch & Lam, 1999). As illustrated by my own experience, immigrant children not only may have a difficult time keeping up with their peers academically—even if they are literate in the L1—but may be further stigmatized by being pulled out of class for special instruction or by being placed in special instructional programs. These children may be further marginalized by their differences in clothing, food, behaviors, and so on. Being perceived as different from other children because of physical and behavioral characteristics along with being marginalized academically may also lead to social isolation. These children may be teased by their less sensitive classmates and avoided by others (I vividly remember a fourth-grade girl not wanting to sit next to me on the school bus). It is a huge task for immigrant children to try to become socialized within U.S. norms—in order to not be perceived as different and therefore to avoid being teased, left alone, and having no friends—while also being expected to acquire academic content matter and language skills.

Additionally, while many immigrant children may be successful at appearing to be "fluent" in English due to their acquisition of BICS, they can be misinterpreted as having acquired the academic skills necessary to keep up with the subject matter content of their age-level peers, and this can lead to mainstreaming (cf. Carger, 1996). These children may be in academic jeopardy if they in fact have not yet acquired the skills necessary to keep up with academic demands. Furthermore, moving to a new environment can be traumatic, with the loss of familiar surroundings, friends, belongings, family members, and so on. It is also important to note that most child immigrants, such as myself, do not themselves choose to immigrate to another country—these decisions are most often made by their parents, for various reasons. While some families and/or children may wish or be forced to assimilate completely (i.e., to replace their native language and customs with those of the L2 culture in order to become absorbed into the L2 culture), others—like my own family—may acculturate (i.e., adapt some of the customs and language of the L2 culture while retaining their own language and customs as well). This group of immigrants may have a second identity that is often invisible to others. It is not surprising that in his study of seven nonnative speakers of English, all of whom were ESL teachers, Liu (1999b) found that "among the seven participants, the three . . . who had learned English in the U.S. at an early age seemed to have the most problems, though different ones, in categorizing themselves as NSs or NNSs" (p. 95). Perhaps growing up in a society wherein monolingualism, rather than multilingualism is promoted, and where acculturation without assimilation is not completely understood, straddling two cultures and two languages can be conflicting because one may be expected to make a choice between being an American or not and being a native speaker of English or not. Children such as myself who have grown up bilingually and biculturally are often unable to make that choice.

From an ESL Learner to an English ESL/EFL Teacher and TESOL Educator

Balancing My Native and Nonnative Identities

It has now been 25 years since my family immigrated to the United States. While I will probably always wonder what my life would have been like had my family remained in Denmark and who and what I would have become, my experiences as an immigrant child and L2 learner have enriched my life and opened up a career that I might not otherwise have entered. I became an ESL/EFL teacher because I am an ESL learner, and I became a TESOL educator because of my experiences in both teaching and learning English. After obtaining both a bachelor's and a master's degree in English literature, taking courses in TESOL, and teaching ESL while working on my master's degree, I taught EFL in Japan for one and a half years. After returning to the United States, I taught ESL in various community colleges, intensive English programs, composition programs, and spoken English programs, and I earned a doctorate in foreign and second language education from Ohio State University.

As an ESL/EFL teacher and now as a TESOL educator, I bring my nonnativeness into the classroom. Because I am Caucasian and have an American English accent, my students assume that I am a native speaker of English. Just like I had to find a balance between my Danishness and Americanness in terms of my own identity, I have also had to find a balance between my own perceived status as a nonnative speaker of English and the other-identification my students have of me as a native speaker. When I first began teaching ESL, I was not sure to what extent my nonnative status would affect my students' perceptions of my abilities as an ESL teacher. It wasn't until I had gained enough confidence in my own abilities to teach effectively that I began revealing that I was a nonnative speaker of English. Additionally, I initially hesitated to reveal I was a nonnative speaker because I did not want my students to feel intimated by my L2 proficiency. Over time, I have become more comfortable with revealing my background as I have realized that it can be a benefit in the classroom. When I reveal my nonnative status to students, it has been to show empathy and to also discuss what problems I encountered when I learned English. Being a nonnative speaker of English helps me understand their language learning experience in a more personal manner, which then helps me develop more effective pedagogical practices. Usually, my students greet my revelation with initial surprise and then admiration of my L2 proficiency. I try to use this as an opportunity to discuss factors influencing L2 acquisition, and I emphasize that I have been learning and using English in the L2 context for a number of years. Rather than intimidating my students, I find that talking about my own L2 learning experiences helps us to develop rapport, since the students know that once I, too, was like them. It also helps us discuss crosslinguistic similarities and differences as we compare English with their native language and with my own.

As a TESOL educator, I also find that being a nonnative speaker offers unique benefits in the classroom. I feel very fortunate to be an ESL learner and to have had 10 years experience teaching the English language both internationally and in the United States—and in a variety of settings (higher education, community college, language schools, etc.)—before becoming a university educator. All these experiences make me a better teacher, since I can approach a course and a topic from multiple perspectives. For example, in teaching a course in applied phonology for master of arts and Ph.D. students, I was able to discuss the topic matter from the perspective of a phonology researcher, a pronunciation teacher, and an L2 learner who still has difficulty with some English consonants. I am not afraid to share my own language use mishaps and problems with my students, and in my teaching, to help illustrate specific points, I often contrast the Danish and English language and culture (and others with which I am familiar). I find this helps students understand the experiences of learners, where their frustrations might be, and what makes learning and, very important, *using* English or any other language difficult, even for native speakers. I see it as a way of getting students "inside" the language and the language learning experience. I believe the multiple perspectives with which I approach a course and topic allow me to help my students gain insight into the topic matter and also provide an important meeting ground among students themselves and between myself and my students, since all of us have some experience in learning and using a language.

However, I look and sound like a native speaker, so even after I reveal that I am not, it is still difficult for people to accept me as a nonnative speaker. The reality is that my English phonology has traces of my L1 and that there are some words I still cannot pronounce accurately. One of my strategies as a young learner of English when I was asked to read aloud and encountered an unknown or unpronounceable word was to skip it entirely or replace it with a synonym—all the while hoping these text modifications were not too noticeable. I had particular difficulty with the word *physician*—it looked painful to pronounce, and I could not master the pronunciation of the *ph,* even though I could easily pronounce an *f* (this sound-symbol correspondence does not exist in Danish). Realizing that it was hopeless, I soon became adept at replacing the word with *doctor* without skipping a beat. Remarkably, no one ever corrected me or commented on this behavior. While I learned to pronounce *physician* in time—though I continue to prefer the term *doctor*—I still stumble across *diary* and *dairy* and *phase* and *phrase,* and I will forever pronounce *zoo* just like *Sue.* I know my weaknesses and, like many language learners, have an arsenal of strategies to deal with them—avoidance being my preferred strategy still.

While I may be able to hide some of my linguistic difficulties, I have more difficulty hiding the gaps in my U.S. cultural knowledge. All the U.S. children's songs, stories, and TV shows I know I've learned as an adult. One of my jobs in Japan was teaching English to young children between ages three and five for one hour per week. The classes consisted mostly of singing songs (e.g., "The ABC Song," "Head, Shoulders, Knees, and Toes") and doing various TPR activities. I dreaded this weekly class not only for the pressure the parents put on the children to actually speak English (many of them were still struggling with speaking Japanese!) but also because I had to learn every song and story before the class, as they were not part of my own childhood.

The United States is multicultural, and there is no *one* U.S. culture. However, because ESL/EFL textbooks and materials market certain U.S. (or British, etc.) traditions as the epitome of the culture, students do have assumptions about what people in the United States look like, what they sound like, and how they live their lives. Because we retained our Danish customs and traditions in my family, it has taken us a long time to adopt and celebrate—if we do at all—U.S. holidays. While we have been celebrating Thanksgiving for many years now, it wasn't until two years ago that my mom made cranberry relish, and we still have not adopted pumpkin pie. While cranberry relish, pumpkin pie, and children's stories may not appear to be profound differences between my childhood and that of my U.S. peers, they are symbolic of deeper differences—while we live in the U.S., my family retained our L1 culture, and identity. Retaining our L1 culture does not mean that we have not adopted or celebrated U.S. holidays, but it does mean that when we do adopt customs and ideologies, we do it on our terms—that is, within the larger framework of our Danish identities and ideologies. In essence, if there are two similar celebrations in the United States and Denmark, we prefer to celebrate with Danish traditions (e.g., we have a Danish Christmas). For celebrations that do not exist in Denmark or are not as commonly celebrated in Denmark, we may adopt aspects of those celebrations that do not conflict with our Danish identities and culture (e.g., while we may grill out on the Fourth of July and watch fireworks, we may not display a U.S. flag). It has taken me years to feel comfortable singing the U.S. national anthem, because I felt it was unpatriotic toward Denmark to do so. I was in middle school at a time when schoolchildren still recited the Pledge of Allegiance every morning, and I always sat silently at my desk during this activity. Even as a child, I was acutely aware of my own identity and felt that engaging in these activities was wrong or improper. Perhaps this is why I (and my mother and sister) have retained Danish citizenship. At the same time, our framework has become infused with the new customs, culture, and ideology of the United States. We have acculturated to this society and therefore are not truly *only* Danish anymore. Perhaps this is why we all still choose to live in the United States.

Being an Invisible Nonnative Speaker of English on the Job Market

As far as I know, I have never been denied an ESL/EFL teaching job because I was a nonnative speaker—though this is impossible to know for certain. I am not sure what employers assume about my English proficiency or native speaker status when they look at my curriculum vitae, although the ones that have contacted me for a position have assumed that I was a native speaker because of my U.S. educational background. It is impossible to know whether questions about my native speaker status were a factor when I was not contacted for a position I applied for. The only time native speaker status was explicitly a criterion of employment was when I worked in Japan. When I applied for the job I would eventually take at a private language school, I did not reveal my nonnative status—nor did I state I was a native speaker—even though the advertisement for the position explicitly stated only native speakers need apply. The interview for the position was held over the phone, and it was only after I had been offered the job and the discussion turned to visa processing that I revealed I was a Danish citizen. I was surprised to learn that this news was actually greeted positively, since this meant that processing of the visa would go more smoothly and quickly.

Even though the ad for the position was for native speakers only, this did not prepare me for the ideology of the EFL market in Japan. Of 12 full-time teachers, I was the only one who had any ESL/EFL teaching experience or had any course work in TESOL and L2 acquisition. All of us were Caucasian and from Great Britain, the United States, Canada, Australia, or New Zealand, except for one U.S. citizen, who was biracial Japanese-American but looked Caucasian. While the school employed part-time teachers of English who were Japanese, they were typically only allowed to teach the beginning-level classes—all intermediate or advanced classes were taught by "native" speakers. I witnessed the difficulty of a Jamaican native speaker of English to get hired at language schools in the midsize city I lived in. Despite being highly qualified, she could not find work in our city—eventually she found a teaching position in Tokyo. The teachers at my language school were also often sought out for different classes based on our accents—some students only wanted speakers of British English, while others wanted speakers of American English or Australian English. After a colleague from Great Britain left Japan, I inherited one of her private students, an older upper-class Japanese housewife who only wanted to learn British English. Despite her preference for British English, she accepted me as her teacher, though I struggled with the British text and the expectation that I would be teaching her British English. While I loved my time in Japan, these experiences tarnished my idealistic notions about language teaching. However, rather than drive me from the field, they fed into my already very personal investment in English language teaching—and propelled me to enter a Ph.D. program in TESOL.

The Past as a Bridge to the Present

I taught ESL/EFL for over 10 years before becoming a TESOL educator, and I am currently an assistant professor of English language/linguistics and second language acquisition and teaching at the University of Arizona. My research and teaching interests are grounded in my most poignant memories from long ago. The struggles of my mother in acquiring the sound system of English, our achievements in reading English due to our love of reading in Danish, the peer tutoring that was promoted by my fifth-grade teacher, learning the meaning of the word *fun* as my friends and I swung on the monkey bars during recess—while these events took place over 25 years ago, they still drive me to continually challenge myself as a researcher and as a teacher. Not surprisingly, my main research agenda is on the effect of social and linguistic forces on L2 acquisition, especially with regard to phonology. Because of my memories of being "tutored" (quite successfully) by my fifth-grade classmates, I became interested in utilizing peer response activities in my L2 writing classroom. I have recently co-authored a book on peer response, *Peer Response in Second Language Writing Classrooms* (Liu & Hansen, 2002). The difficulties of my mother as an immigrant woman—she lost her professional identity as a head schoolteacher in Denmark and had to start all over again—are reflected in my interest in gender and L2 development opportunities. In short, being a nonnative speaker of English is an integral part of *who* I am, *what* I do, and *why* I do it.

Nonnative English-Speaking Teachers and the TESOL Profession

My goal in this chapter has been to explore some of my own experiences as an invisible immigrant minority, a nonnative speaker of English, and an invisible nonnative speaker of English, in order to bring visibility to the issues nonnative speakers like myself may have. As my own experiences as an ESL learner, ESL/EFL teacher, and TESOL educator reveal, there are benefits as well as drawbacks to being labeled as either a native or a nonnative speaker. While being perceived as a native speaker has no doubt had a positive influence on my students' views of my abilities as a teacher in terms of my being considered knowledgeable about the language and the culture—as well as having a positive effect on my being hired for certain teaching positions—it conflicts with my self-identification as a nonnative speaker and my actual cultural and linguistic knowledge. While I have learned to balance these two identities both inside and outside the classroom, the balancing act is still a struggle that I am not sure will ever really cease.

Another goal of this chapter has been to explore the assumptions we make about individuals based on characteristics such as race, ethnicity, and speech—and the way these visible traits often obscure and minimize the unique experiences and abilities nonnative speakers—visible and invisible—bring to the TESOL profession. For visible minority nonnative speakers, this may mean that their L2 learning experiences are visible on the surface while their proficiency in the L2 and ability to teach it are erroneously obscured. For invisible minority nonnative speakers, the opposite may be true: While their L2 proficiency may not be questioned (as they may be perceived to be native speakers), their L2 learning experiences—the very experiences that may have brought them into the TESOL profession—may be concealed. In that sense, the issues that visible and invisible nonnative speakers face are similar: For both groups, visible characteristics often obscure or belie strengths as nonnative-speaking teachers of English. Therefore, both visible and invisible nonnative speakers, as well as native speakers, need to join forces in TESOL to ensure that the real way teachers are hired and evaluated in our profession is by virtue of what they can *do*—by their professionalism and teaching ability—and not by how they look.

Notes

1. Per Reitz (1980), invisible minorities are from white ethnic groups while visible minorities are from non-white ethnic groups.
2. While these conventions vary to some extent, these are still common cursive forms, and they were the forms I was taught in school in Denmark.

References

Carger, C. L. (1996). *Of borders and dreams: A Mexican-American experience of urban education.* New York: Teachers College Press.

Collier, V. P. (1989). How long? A synthesis of research on academic achievement in a second language. *TESOL Quarterly, 23*(3), 509–531.

Cummins, J. (1981). The role of primary language development in promoting educational success for language minority students. In Office of Bilingual Bicultural Education, California State Department of Education (Ed.), *Schooling and language minority students: A theoretical framework* (pp. 3–49). Los Angeles: Evaluation, Dissemination, and Assessment Center, California State University, Los Angeles.

Cummins, J. (1991). Interdependence of first- and second-language proficiency in bilingual children. In E. Bialystok (Ed.), *Language processing in bilingual children* (pp. 70–89). Cambridge: Cambridge University Press.

Kramsch, C., & Lam, W. S. E. (1999). Textual identities: The importance of being nonnative. In G. Braine (Ed.), *Non-native educators in English language teaching* (pp. 57–72). Mahwah, NJ: Erlbaum.

Liu, J. (1999a). From their own perspectives: The impact of non-native ESL professionals on their students. In G. Braine (Ed.), *Non-native educators in English language teaching* (pp. 159–176). Mahwah, NJ: Erlbaum.

Liu, J. (1999b). Nonnative-English-speaking professionals in TESOL. *TESOL Quarterly, 33*(1), 85–102.

Liu, J., & Hansen, J. G. (2002). *Peer response in second language writing classrooms.* Ann Arbor: University of Michigan Press.

Reitz, J. G. (1980). *The survival of ethnic groups.* Toronto: McGraw-Hill Ryerson.

Thomas, W. P., & Collier, V. P. (1997). Two languages are better than one. *Educational Leadership, 55*(4), 23–26.

Questions for Reflection

1. In his chapter, Braine describes the history of the NNEST Caucus. As explained by Braine, the establishment of the caucus has contributed to the understanding of the strengths NNES professionals bring to the language classroom, has increased the visibility of NNES professionals, and has contributed to the legitimization of research on NNES professionals and the issues that are of concern to them. What are some of the actions that the caucus could take in order to prevent NNES professionals from experiencing prejudice like that experienced by Braine?

2. Liu describes his process of professional development in the U.S. Reflect on the process of professional development experienced by other NNES teachers that you know. In what ways have the processes they have experienced been similar to the one described by Liu? In what ways have the processes been different from the one described by Liu? What factors have contributed to making the processes similar or different?

3. Hansen argues that visible and invisible NNES professionals face similar challenges since visible and invisible characteristics affect people's perceptions about and reactions toward NNES professionals. Do you agree with Hansen? What are the consequences of such challenges? How would you respond to these challenges?

4. The chapters by Braine, Liu, and Hansen deal with the multiple identities of NNES professionals. In what ways can such identities contribute to strengthening the instructional practices of NNES professionals?

Section 2

Focus on Research

Braine (this volume), in discussing the dynamics of the NNES professionals' movement, argues that "a movement in an educational context could be relevant and popular, but it cannot grow without the backing of sound research." Section 2 presents four research studies that advance the field by exploring issues related to NNEST professionals from different perspectives. In the opening chapter, "Nativism, the Native Speaker Construct, and Minority Immigrant Women Teachers of English as a Second Language," Nuzhat Amin focuses on immigrant women teaching in adult ESL programs in Canada. In her chapter, she argues that the race of immigrant women is perceived as a marker of being nonnative speakers of English. She further argues that native speakers of English are perceived as having a White accent, usually associated with countries where English is a dominant language (e.g., the United States, Canada, or Great Britain). In her chapter, she reports on the challenges experienced by eight minority immigrant women who teach ESL to adults in Toronto, Canada. The results of Amin's study indicate that the challenges that these women experience are the result of being viewed as nonnative speakers of "Canadian English" and of being women of a racial minority. Her findings also show that while the women in her study are aware that they are perceived as outsiders to Canada, they also view themselves as being effective teachers. More importantly, the participants attribute their effectiveness to their implementation of instructional practices that draw on their status as nonnative speakers of English. Based on these findings, Amin questions the validity of the native speaker model that is used in ESL programs and recommends "dismantling the native/nonnative speaker dichotomy and reconceptualizing the native speaker norm."

The next chapter, "Teaching in Kindergarten through Grade 12 Programs: Perceptions of Native and Nonnative English-Speaking Practitioners," by Lía D. Kamhi-Stein, Annette Aagard, Angelica Ching, Myoung-Soon Ashley Paik, and Linda Sasser, switches the focus of the discussion from minority women teaching adult ESL to native and nonnative English-speaking professionals (male and female) teaching kindergarten through grade 12 (K–12). Their study compares the perceptions of NES and NNES professionals in relation to their professional preparation, their level of job satisfaction, and their degree of comfort teaching various skill areas. Kamhi-Stein et al. conclude that the K–12 NES and NNES professionals who participated in their investigation are best characterized by a complex set of similarities and differences. Drawing on the findings of the study, Kamhi-Stein et al. suggest that Medgyes' (2001) notion that NES and NNES professionals are "different species" (p. 434) does not necessarily capture the complexity involved in being a NNES professional (a point articulated by Pasternak & Bailey, this volume).

The following chapter, "Children of a Lesser English: Status of Nonnative English Speakers as College-Level English as a Second Language Teachers in the United States," by Ahmar Mahboob, Karl Uhrig, Karen L. Newman, and Beverly S. Hartford, focuses on a topic that has not been investigated before. The chapter presents the results of an empirical study designed to provide information on the hiring criteria favored by administrators of college-level intensive English programs (IEPs) in the U.S. The results of the study show that more program administrators than not consider "native English speaker" to be an important hiring criterion, so much so that it was found to be a statistically significant criterion in explaining the presence or absence of nonnative English-speaking teachers in an IEP. Two other such criteria also found to be significant in this respect were "recommendation" and "teaching experience." The results of the study also show that there is a lower proportion of nonnative English-speaking teachers to native English-speaking teachers in actual practice in U.S.-based IEPs. According to Mahboob et al., these results suggest that within the profession of English language teaching in the U.S., nonnative speakers of English are treated as "children of a lesser English."

In the last chapter of this section, "Native or Nonnative: What Do Students Enrolled in an Intensive English Program Think?" Ahmar Mahboob investigates ESL students' attitudes toward native and nonnative English speakers teaching in an IEP in the U.S. The results of this investigation suggest that ESL students in the U.S. do not have a clear preference for either native or nonnative English speakers; rather, they feel that both types of teachers have unique attributes that contribute to their education. The findings of this study also demonstrate that the importance given to the "native English speaker" hiring criterion by program administrators is not shared by students.

Nativism, the Native Speaker Construct, and Minority Immigrant Women Teachers of English as a Second Language

Nuzhat Amin
University of Toronto, Canada

There was a sharp knock on the door of my university office. A graduate student whom I often see at departmental seminars and parties popped his head inside the door and said, "Do you know any native speakers [of English]?" He had a sheet of paper with approximately 20 sentences and phrases, and he wanted a native speaker to go over them. I offered to look at them. He reluctantly handed me the sheet, and I did not find it difficult to give him the "correct" answers. Indeed, the problems and questions were so simple that most teachers of English as a second language (ESL)—particularly at the higher levels, where there is emphasis on colloquialisms and where you are supposed to have a "feel" for the language—could easily have answered them. I pointed out a few phrases that I would not use and others that I considered to be acceptable. He thanked me and, as he was leaving, said, "Would a native speaker agree with you on these suggestions?"

I do not know what this Ph.D. candidate did with my input, but I suspect that he did not use it. This seemingly innocuous incident was one of many that left me, first, puzzled about my "nonnative speaker" status and, second, wondering what the significance of the native speaker is. The first question that comes to mind when I think of such incidents is: What linguistic knowledge does a native speaker of English have that someone who has studied English for many years does not or cannot have? In other words, what is the definitive distinction that this student was trying to voice? And why did the student assume that I am not a native speaker of English? Is it because of my race—because I am a visible minority woman? Is it also because I have a Pakistani accent?[1]

The "native speaker of English" is such a powerful construct, one so embedded in myth, that it is daunting to attempt to disentangle fact from fable. As Nayar (1994) puts it: "Generations of applied linguistic mythmaking in the indubitable superiority and the impregnable infallibility of the 'native speaker' has created stereotypes that die hard" (p. 4). This mythmaking, I suggest, is not only about language competence but is deeply embedded in discourses of racism and colonialism that inform both individual and institutional understandings and evaluations of speakers of nonnative Englishes. The more recent critical literature says as much. For instance, Kachru (1997) considers the native speaker to be a linguistic colonial construct. Pennycook (1998) reaches a similar conclusion, claiming that the native speaker is yet another legacy of colonialism. And Paikeday (1985), commenting on who is seen as a native speaker, says that when people recruit "native speakers" of English, the term appears to be a codeword for White Anglo-Saxon protestants.

I take the position in this chapter that the native speaker construct is embedded in the larger discourses of nativism[2] that position visible minority immigrant women as nonnative to the predominantly English-speaking nations of the First World (e.g., to Canada or the U.S.) and that nativist discourses are being mobilized through the native speaker concept. I further argue that immigrant women from the Third World,[3] or from what Kachru (1992) terms Outer Circle and Expanding Circle countries—i.e., countries where English has a history of institutionalized functions and where it has foreign language standing, respectively—are considered nonnative to the predominantly English-speaking countries of the First World, or Inner Circle. By virtue of their race and birth status, these immigrant women are therefore considered nonnative speakers of English and outsiders to Inner Circle societies. To borrow Brah's (1996) words in the context of England, racial minority immigrants are seen as living "in" Canada or the U.S. but are not seen as being "of" these countries.

This chapter is based on a study that investigates the experiences of visible minority immigrant women teachers of ESL in Canada (Amin, 2000). Highlighting data from six of the eight participants in the study, in this chapter I explore their encounters with the discourses of the native speaker and of nativism. I first describe my study, after which

I detail its theoretical underpinnings. I then describe the challenges faced by the minority ESL teachers interviewed and how they negotiate these challenges in the classroom. Finally, I look at the implications of my research for English language teaching (ELT).

The Study

From 1998 to 1999 I conducted interviews with eight minority immigrant women who had taught or were teaching ESL to adult immigrants in Toronto, Canada, in government-financed language programs known commonly as "Settlement ESL." The purpose of my research was to investigate how nativism, in particular the concept of the native speaker, is manifested in the context of ESL and how minority immigrant women teachers of ESL negotiate this linguistic manifestation of cultural nativism (see Amin, 2000, for details of the study).

A few facts about the racial makeup of Canada are helpful here in order to situate the study. In the decade after World War II, one-half of all Canada's immigrants came from the United Kingdom. During the late 1960s, a series of reforms in immigration policy was introduced that resulted in more immigrants coming from countries other than the U.K. Hence, in 1994, only two percent of Canada's immigrants came from the U.K. ("All the King's Horses," 1999). Toronto attracts a large number of the immigrants who come to Canada—approximately 48% of Toronto's population are immigrants, and by year 2001 foreign-born residents will comprise the majority of the Toronto population (City of Toronto, 1998). The overwhelming majority (86%) of teachers in the province's Settlement ESL courses are women, and 35% of them are nonnative speakers (Power Analysis, 1998). The definition of native speaker and nonnative speaker of English used in the Power Analysis study was based on "the first language" (L1) that the instructor learned (B. Power, personal communication, August 25, 1999). Such statistics and judgments about native and nonnative speakers are problematic. The statistics do establish, however, (a) that the local teaching force is multiracial and multicultural and (b) that many ESL teachers are likely to be confronted with nativist discourses.

My participants were visible minority women who grew up in the Third World, immigrated to Canada as adults, and had taught or were teaching Settlement ESL to adult immigrants. These women had backgrounds similar to mine in that English was a major language in their lives in their countries of origin and continued to be a major language in their lives in Canada. I began my interviews with two minority teachers whom I identified with the help of the Toronto and Ontario branches of the professional organization Teachers of English as a Second Language (TESL). The rest were chosen through the "snowball sampling technique" (Bogdan & Biklen, 1992, p. 70); that is, I asked the first two teachers interviewed to recommend others. The participants were randomly selected, and data collection consisted of open-ended semi-structured interviews. The participants were Arun from India, Dina from Surinam, Fayza from Egypt, Iffat from India and Pakistan, Jane from China, Patsy from Kenya, Tasneem from Pakistan, and Violet from Jamaica.[4]

My research questions were the following:

1. How is nativism, in particular the concept of the native speaker, manifested in the context of ESL?
2. How do visible minority immigrant women teachers of ESL negotiate nativism and the native speaker construct?

Theoretical Background

My study draws on three notions. The first notion is that a racial minority woman's English is heard as the English of a nonnative speaker, of a foreigner. Fiction writer Bharati Mukherjee, who is originally from India and now lives in the U.S., supports this notion by describing her experience as a linguistic and racial Other in her (1985) short story "Hindus." In this story, Leela, the protagonist, expresses well the idea that mouthing English perfectly does not automatically put the speaker in the native speaker category.

Second, this study relies on the notion that the native speaker concept is embedded in nativist discourses that position only Inner Circle speakers of English as having legitimate claims to belonging to their country and of having English as their native language. According to Davies (1991), the first recorded use of *native speaker* is the following definition by Bloomfield (1933): "The first language a human being learns to speak is his native language, he is a native speaker of this language" (p. 43). Such a definition and other definitions in modern sources (see Amin, 2000, for a discussion on this topic) emphasize conditions and qualities such as (a) birth, parentage, childhood, and (b) intuition. These qualities appear to be embedded in the original meaning of native as "natural." The emphasis in these widely accepted definitions is on the intuition of native speakers who, it is suggested, cannot help knowing what they do about English. This intuition is seen as being tied to the fact that their "mother tongue," or first language, is English.

Third, this study draws on the concept that an immigrant woman's race is a marker of being an immigrant woman and of being nonnative to Inner Circle societies. I argue that this experience of Otherness is reproduced in the ESL classroom through the imagining of the native speaker as White. This concept influences the teaching, classroom materials, and relations between the teacher and learners. The race of the idealized native speaker is spelled out by Leung, Harris, and Rampton (1997), who, building on Rampton's earlier (1990) research, argue that there is an "abstracted notion of an idealised native speaker of English from which ethnic and linguistic minorities are automatically excluded" (p. 546). Leung, Harris, and Rampton appear to be saying that even visible minorities who are born and have grown up in the First World are not seen as native speakers. Another marker of being nonnative is having an accent that is different from the norm of the ESL classroom. I argue that accents, like race, are socially organized, are a linguistic manifestation of nativism, and constitute a new and effective form of racism. Brutt-Griffler and Samimy (1999) argue that "national origin and accent" (p. 416) are crucial characteristics that are socially held to represent those of the native speaker. Drawing on my earlier work (Amin, 1994), I would go one step further and say that a native speaker is imagined as having a White accent, one that is associated with Inner Circle countries such as Great Britain, the U.S, and Canada.

Findings

The challenges faced by nonnative women teachers have been well documented in the recent literature (for a discussion on the topic, see Amin, 1999; Kamhi-Stein, 1999; Thomas, 1999), and hence I will take only a brief look at the main difficulties reported by my participants. In a Canadian setting, I see all these challenges as stemming from the construction of minority immigrant women as being non-Canadian and the privileging of the native speaker of "Canadian English" by Settlement ESL programs in Canada.

Challenges Faced by Minority Women Teachers

My participants indicated that some of their students initially reacted so negatively to having a non-White teacher that they decided not to return. Fayza, who, as a new immigrant, was formerly a student in an ESL class, recognized the investments immigrants have in learning English from a teacher whom they consider to be a Canadian. As I have argued elsewhere (see Amin, 1997), there appears to be a strong connection between the attitudes of the students—many of them new immigrants—to nonnative teachers and their investments in learning English. What are some of these investments? As Rockhill and Tomic (1995) point out, new immigrants who are learning English are defined as other, as culturally and linguistically inferior; the discourse of ESL is such that it promises liberation once one has acquired English, and hence new Canadians are invested in what they term "Canadian English." To appreciate what "Canadian English" symbolizes to new Canadians, I turn to Peirce's (1993) study in which she examines the complex interrelationships between power, identity, and language learning of immigrant women. Peirce reveals how much immigrant women want to "speak like them [the dominant group]" (p. 1) to negotiate their social identity. Peirce argues that English should be seen not primarily for its instrumental value, as Ng (1990) sees it, but as constitutive of and constituted by social identity. It is clear that ESL learners have a great investment in learning Canadian English (see Amin, 1997), while minority immigrant women are positioned as being non-Canadian and hence unable to teach Canadian English.

Nativist discourses that position minority teachers as outside the nation and as nonnative to Canadian English are best exemplified by Iffat's narrative. Iffat's many degrees in English could not compensate her students for what they saw: a visible minority woman and the only non-White teacher in the school. Iffat named one ethnic group after another who "were very hard on me." One such group was from a neighboring country to Pakistan.

Nuzhat: Like what did they say?

Iffat: "Oh, you're Pakistani." And they, they'd sort of imply that, "Look here, we are in Canada and I'm being taught English by a Pakistani."

But in the multiracial class that she habitually taught, it was not only students of color who were "hard" on her.

Iffat: East Europeans would say, "Ohhh. So you're from Pakistan." They'd just sit there and make me feel sort of bad that, you know . . .

Nuzhat: So your, your problem with students, over the next 20 or 30 years, did the situation with the students remain the same?

Iffat: Yes, it did remain the same. Because there were all these new immigrants coming in. And every time there would be a revolution somewhere, we would have a whole bunch of new students.

The students at this school were new immigrants, and as Iffat taught the beginners, her students were often those who were very recent arrivals. She says that as the program was only three months long, she could not tell if the students' idea of an ideal ESL teacher changed with time—whether, in fact, this thinking was reinforced or lessened.

Another manifestation of nativism is that minority teachers are perceived as *learners* of English. The interconnected discourses of native speaker, L1, and mother tongue emphasize birth, heredity, and innateness of linguistic ability (see Christophersen, 1988), and hence nonnative teachers can be disadvantaged by being seen as having acquired English rather than having English as part of their inheritance from a mother or father. The recurrent theme in Arun's narrative is that she is considered to be a language learner.

> *Arun:*   Students ask me a lot of questions: "Where did you learn English?" "You've learned English well." "How many years did it take you to learn English?" "How long have you been in Canada?" These are the first reactions, because right away when they find out that I'm not from Canada, [they think] I might be lacking in some way. It might be accent or proper Canadian English.

> *Nuzhat:*   But what if the teacher was a visible minority woman who was born in Canada or came here as a child?

> *Arun:*   It would still be the same. The initial response would be, "Oh, she who herself has learned, how can she teach us?"

Arun is making three points. First, ESL students in Canada want a Canadian teacher. Second, students think of Arun as a person who has learned the language and therefore cannot teach it, thus reflecting one of the strongest tenets of ELT, that the ideal teacher is one who has been immersed in English from birth. The third point follows from the second—that if you are not born in an English-only environment, you cannot ever learn English well enough to teach it and definitely will never speak it as well as a native speaker. There is a growing body of literature that shows that a person who has been a language learner can be a better teacher in certain situations than a native speaker or someone who has not formally learned English (see Tang, 1997; Widdowson, 1994). However, it appears that the Inner Circle has been successful in promoting the mystique of the elusive native speaker among new immigrants in ESL programs in Canada. In this context it is worth citing Davies (1991), who points out that there is *no* definition of the native speaker; the only definition seems to be negative, that is, the "native speaker would be someone who is *not* a learner" (p. x). To me, the significance of this negative definition is that "ESL learner" is construed as a static, unchanging identity, so there is no possibility of moving from the identity of ESL learner to that of native speaker. Hence Arun's students think that she cannot be a *teacher* of English.

Nonnative Identities as a Source of Empowerment

The women's experiences in ESL indicate that discourses of colonialism continue to adhere to English in Canada and interlock with racism, sexism, imperialism, and the women's Third World status to discredit their claim of being valid ESL teachers. The narratives suggest that the teachers are aware of the nativist discourses that position them as Other but also strongly point to the following findings: (a) The participants feel that they are effective teachers despite initial nonacceptance by their students and colleagues and despite being constantly judged against the native speaker norm; and (b) they build effective pedagogies on their ascribed nonnative status, and, in fact, they are more effective in the classroom when they build their pedagogies on their nonnative identities, rather than when they try to follow the native speaker norm. I now look at some of the successful classroom strategies in which the teachers foreground their differences.

Build community. One such pedagogical strategy common to the teachers is that they build community with their students on the basis of their commonalities and thus provide the social conditions identified by Peirce (1993) as conducive to language learning. Jane says this of her bilingual Mandarin-English class:

> *Jane:* Bilingual, they are from my culture, so they perceive me as a bridge between the two worlds. You feel you are highly appreciated. You bring the two worlds together.

Jane feels successful in the bilingual class primarily because her students and she share a common language, culture, and ethnicity.

Tang's (1997) study of Cantonese-speaking teachers teaching English in Hong Kong offers insight into the strengths of bilingual teachers who share the L1 of their students, and hence it is relevant to bilingual ESL programs in any country. The teachers in Tang's study reported that having a common mother tongue is a useful instructional tool in teacher-student interaction. Some respondents reported also that their experiences as ESL learners gave them a privileged understanding of the problems and weaknesses of their students. Tang adds that nonnative teachers can empathize with their learners and thus attend to their errors, especially those that are due to transfer from their L1. Tang's findings concur with Widdowson's (1994) view that nonnative teachers can be more effective than native teachers in certain situations.

In the context of Canada, a study of Settlement ESL programs for adult immigrants in Ontario shows that 14% of ESL teachers are fluent in Chinese and that 23% of ESL students in Ontario first learned to speak Chinese (Power Analysis, 1998). Assuming that many of these adults were at some time in bilingual ESL programs, it could be argued that Jane's feelings of success are probably common among teachers of bilingual ESL programs for ethnic Chinese students.

Like Jane, Dina works hard at fostering community with her students. As she is multilingual and familiar with a number of cultures, she uses these qualities to establish an environment conducive to language learning.

> *Dina:*   They loved [being in my class] because they could converse with me in their own language, so if there was a problem, they would come to me, and I could understand their culture. It was as if I was an ally to them, rather than an enemy.

She describes a particular class where her students were Iranians, ethnic Chinese people from Hong Kong, and Koreans and where she felt particularly successful:

> *Dina:*   And since I knew their culture and religion and customs, it was, "Oh, yes, you understand what I'm talking about. How important Ramadan is, how important Eid and Nauruz are."

One of Dina's successful pedagogical strategies for creating community with her students is to show her familiarity and acceptance of their institutions—many of which are not validated by White Canada. Jane says that she is successful in the bilingual class because she shares a common language, culture, and ethnicity with her students. While Dina does not share the languages of all her students, she and her students have many commonalities.

Like Jane and Dina, Fayza forges community with her students, but she builds on the shared experience of being nonnative and immigrant. She articulates the pressures felt by some new immigrants to assimilate:

> *Fayza:*   The students, they come here, they are in a hurry, they want to be recognized and integrated, and part of this society, and that's why they want to destroy their identity completely, their values, and they want to identify with this native completely. Some of them even imitate their way of talking, the way they dress, even if it doesn't suit them. But they *want* to be Canadian.

It appears, then, that as Fayza makes connections between language and culture, she recognizes also the self-hatred that her students suffer from, a self-hatred she recognizes because she experienced it as a new immigrant. She tells her students that as a new immigrant and as an ESL student, she, too, wanted to erase her roots, and she draws on her experience to caution them that "people respect you more when you respect yourself."

> *Fayza:* But they [students] have to know also that they have to keep their identity. When you come to Canada, it doesn't mean that you have to be Canadian, that you have to have everything like a born Canadian. Like you have to want his values, his traditions, his language, everything. You have to keep your identity. Identity is very important. You have also to realize that your roots and traditions and values are important.

Disrupt native speaker myths of birth, intuition. The teachers build their pedagogies on an experience that is associated with being nonnative speakers—the experience of having been ESL learners—and this experience provides them with a privileged understanding of the problems and weaknesses their students face in learning English (see Tang, 1997). Tasneem's experience of Otherness in a number of sites has made her mindful of the negative messages that her students are receiving about their social identities as ESL learners. She describes how she is an agent in her students' empowerment:

> *Tasneem:* Some of my Chinese students say that English is very difficult, and I tell them: You can learn it. I learned it. I wasn't born speaking English. My mother doesn't speak English. We learned English in school.

Tasneem is stressing two related points: first, English is not her mother tongue; second, English can be learned. She thus challenges the discourse that you have to be born in an English-speaking family and that English has to be your mother's or father's L1 in order for you to know English well. She is telling her students: "Don't give up. I did it, and so can you"—much needed words of encouragement for adult students who often feel that learning English well is an impossible goal. Clearly, Tasneem has embraced a nonnative position as one from which she can effectively negotiate her teaching.

Use anti-racist materials. Another way these teachers demythologize the native speaker is with the materials that they bring into the classroom. Since immigrants have to face the stereotype of what is a valid and acceptable accent and since the Settlement ESL classroom uses native speaker accents as the norm, Dina focuses on disrupting the stereotype of what accent a teacher or a person of authority should have. In place of commercial audiotapes that use what I've termed "White accents," she often makes her own tapes that include a variety of voices, including her own. In this way, she disrupts her students' thinking that their minority teacher's accent is different from the accents they hear on the commercial tapes and thus perceive as authoritative.

Jane describes her students' understanding of a Canadian accent: "The English they hear on TV, the English they hear around them, they recognize as Canadian." Like Dina, Jane self-consciously uses tapes with a variety of accents, thus encouraging her students to rethink their understanding of a Canadian accent to include those voices and those accents that they do not hear on mainstream television and radio.

The experience of being a linguistic and racial Other, both inside and outside ESL, has also sensitized Arun to interracial and interethnic tensions among her students, and she addresses these tensions in a nonthreatening way. Among the materials that she has found effective in addressing and diffusing these tensions is a video called *The Eye of the Beholder* (Reynolds, 1953), in which all four witnesses to a death describe the incident differently. Arun uses this video to discuss how human beings turn our prejudiced perceptions into "facts." To explain this process, she gives the hypothetical example of a woman having four or five negative experiences with a few Vietnamese people, leading her to attribute these negative qualities to all Vietnamese people.

Nuzhat: Are you doing this only to address students' racism against other students or is this also your way of dealing with what's happening to you [that is, not being accepted as a good English teacher]?

Arun: Exactly. It serves my purpose, too. . . . [Prejudices] have roots. . . . There are historical reasons for dislikes [of a particular ethnic group]. After these exercises, my students learn how to respect everybody. That's what I want them to do before learning English—to have respect for everyone in the class.

In sum, Dina, Jane, and Arun draw on materials that challenge the belief that the White native speaker is the only valid ESL teacher.

Prepare effective lessons. It was not a surprise when all the participants said that they believe teachers should have extensive training, more than a two- to three-month TESL course. It therefore did not surprise me that they had all spent a great amount of time upgrading their skills in teacher training institutes. All eight teachers talked about how hard they work to produce good, effective lessons. This message came through most poignantly and clearly in Fayza's interview, for she explained *why* she had to work so hard:

Fayza: I was so conscientious. When you become a teacher, and it's not your native language, after all, it's your second language so you become so conscientious, and you want to do your best to compensate or to make up for that or to make them feel that they have achieved their goal somehow. You don't want to disappoint your students, right? Then you get a good feedback sometime.

Nuzhat: You seem like a very hardworking and conscientious person. Would you have done the same [gone to such pains] if you were teaching, say, Arabic? Or was it because you were teaching English and you felt that somehow you had to?

Fayza: Yes, I would have done probably the same if I were teaching Arabic. But in a more relaxed [way]. No doubt about it, it's a challenge, teaching English, because you have to know more about the culture. No matter how long you have learned the language, no matter how long you have been using the language, still you have to be aware of all aspects of the language. But with your own native language, sometimes you take it for granted.

I asked Fayza if her students ever asked the supervisor for a native speaker teacher.

Fayza: Yes. True. But eventually not so many of them do that. These are adult students, and they are looking for a good teacher to help them with their language difficulties. They soon realize that it's not just the color of the skin [that they should go by]. Is she a good teacher? That is the bottom line. Your reputation gets around. If you are a dedicated teacher and you are doing a good job, then the word gets around and then there will be no problem.

The many hours of hard work that Fayza put in to overcome her perceived deficiency helped to make her a popular and successful teacher. Although the belief that teachers have to compensate for not being native speakers might be problematic, it is common among nonnative teachers (see, e.g., Kamhi-Stein, 1999) because of the un-realistic—written or unwritten—goal of many ESL and EFL programs worldwide that students should learn to speak like native speakers (see Kachru, 1990a; Sridhar, 1994).

A Pedagogy of Empowerment

The participants in my study have opened up possibilities for their students, for nonnative teachers, and for all those involved in ESL, by showing that although native speakers are privileged by our profession, nonnative speakers can also lay valid claim to full competency in English. They also show that good pedagogy is not the province of the native speaker but is dependent on learning the craft or skill of teaching ESL. These are big steps toward the empowerment of nonnative speakers, both students and teachers, for, as Widdowson (1994) has pointed out, the association of the native speaker with ownership of English and good pedagogy is a dominant discourse of ELT.

What do the participants' pedagogical strategies imply for decolonizing the ESL classroom? Here I turn to Simon (1992), who distinguishes between "pedagogy" and "teaching" (p. 56). According to Simon, "When we teach, we are always implicated in the construction of a horizon of possibility for ourselves, our students, and our communities. . . . To propose a pedagogy is to propose a political vision" (pp. 56–57). Simon emphasizes that we teachers need to concern ourselves with the enhancement of human possibility whereby we encourage our students to "envisage versions of a world that is 'not yet'—in order to be able to alter the grounds upon which life is lived" (p. 57). By disrupting dominant stereotypes of who can claim full competency in English and by showing that nonnative speakers are effective teachers, my participants are engaging in a transformative critique of their own lives and of the lives of their adult learners. These teachers' nonnative pedagogies also have implications for ELT.

Implications for English Language Teaching

As noted earlier, the data indicate that, to varying degrees, the teachers do not use the native speaker as their model; rather, they build effective pedagogies based on their difference and on their ascribed nonnative speaker status. But while the teachers try to decolonize the classroom, the extent to which they can transform ESL is limited by the confines of their profession. Although the native speaker norm is being questioned by linguists (e.g., Braine, 1999; Nayar, 1994), many ESL and EFL programs worldwide continue to have as a goal that students learn to speak like native speakers (Kachru, 1990a; Sridhar, 1994). In this section I will look at the ramifications of my study for our profession. I will first address the responsibilities of professional organizations in ELT and then suggest a reassessment of teacher training programs that would result in a revision of Settlement ESL programs.

Responsibilities of the Professional Organizations

One term that is "overdue for compulsory retirement" in linguistics, according to Christophersen (1988, p. 15) is *native* as used in phrases like *native language* and *native speaker.* Christophersen suggests also redefining the terms *first language* and *mother tongue* on the basis that they are misleading and confusing. A person's mother tongue may or may not be their mother's tongue, nor is a person's L1 always that which they learned first, because first can mean either the language the person learned first or the language that is first in importance. Cheshire (1991) and Ferguson (1992) have made similar arguments.

The narratives of the participants in my study indicate that such a reconceptualization of these concepts is indeed long overdue because the native speaker model is not a pedagogically sound principle in all contexts. For example, in many ESL programs worldwide, the native speaker norm is frequently used when teaching higher-level classes, the rationale being that students want to learn idiomatically appropriate language and to appreciate the cultural connotations of the language (see Phillipson, 1992). But according to Phillipson (1992), teachers who are nonnative speakers can acquire this competence through teacher training.

My position in this chapter has been that the native/nonnative speaker division is not solely based on proficiency and that many nonnative speakers are fully proficient in English. In addition, the native speaker model divides the profession according to a caste system and should therefore be eliminated (Kachru, 1990b; Pennycook, 1992; Phillipson, 1992). Organizations like the American Association for Applied Linguistics (AAAL), TESOL, and TESOL affiliates should therefore actively dismantle the native/nonnative speaker dichotomy.

Such an initiative, as Widdowson (1994) has recommended, should involve an inquiry into the craft of teaching ESL and EFL, since, as the participants have shown, teaching English well is not a racial or biological quality but a craft, a skill that has to be learned. Phillipson (1992) makes a similar point when he asserts that teachers are made rather than born and that "the untrained or unqualified native speaker is potentially a menace" (p. 195). This inquiry should address the interlinked issue of world Englishes. English has evolved away from its original base of Inner Circle societies and has become indigenized in a number of postcolonial countries. Historically, native speakers have decided whether a variety of English is valid. However, as Kachru (1992) and Sridhar and Sridhar (1992), among others, have argued, the rules used to decide on the validity of a particular variety of nonnative English are culturally and linguistically biased. Kachru (1992) adds that native speakers of mother English define any deviation from mother English in the indigenized varieties of English as not a difference but an error, for the norm that they use is that of English as used in native contexts.

What then can TESOL or other professional organizations do to validate the different varieties of English that exist outside Inner Circle countries? Quirk (1990) has dismissed any attempts at acceptance of these new varieties of English as "liberation linguistics." His stand continues to be that Standard British English should be the norm internationally. Kachru (1991) considers Quirk's insistence to be unrealistic and misguided, as it ignores the reality of world Englishes. Therefore, Kachru suggests a dialogue on the issue of international standardization. Such a dialogue is much needed now so that ESL and EFL programs worldwide can have a clearer direction in terms of which variety of English is the best model for a particular context.

Implications for Teacher Preparation

Kamhi-Stein (1999) notes that the messages of what a nonnative teacher cannot do stand in the way of nonnative speakers realizing their full potential, causing them to limit their career choices. Some of her teacher trainees tell her that since they speak what they call "a deficient variety of English," they are "qualified only to play the role of assistants of native English-speaking teachers" (p. 149). One of the consequences of this international hegemony of the native speaker is that nonnative speakers may see themselves as speakers of indigenized varieties of English and hence self-impose limits on their aspirations. As the discourses of the native speaker appear to be particularly disempowering for new teachers, I suggest that a curriculum that would attempt to overcome these potentially disempowering discourses in teacher education programs is a meaningful first step toward dismantling the native/nonnative speaker dichotomy.

I now make suggestions for training new teachers, both native speakers and nonnative speakers, that will encourage them to explore new models and new pedagogies. I need to point out that the participants in my study are not new to this profession; that, as teacher trainees and as new teachers, they might have used the native speaker model because it is the model actively promoted by TESL programs; and that they have had to create and develop their own nonnative pedagogies in order to be effective teachers. Although I have termed their pedagogies "nonnative," I wish to emphasize that both native and nonnative teachers can learn from these pedagogies as they aim to eliminate the native/nonnative speaker dichotomy.

Sanaoui's (1997) *Directory of ESL Teacher Preparation Programs in Ontario* outlines the curriculum of programs in Ontario, and it is clear that by and large they focus narrowly on second language acquisition, teaching methods, and linguistics, without placing these fields in their sociopolitical context. More recently, some of the TESL programs in the U.S. have begun to address sociopolitical issues (Tollefson, 1995). However, there appears to be little acknowledgment of the existence, much less validity, of the international varieties of English, nor is there questioning of concepts such as first language, mother tongue, and native speaker. Thus, in many ways, TESL programs in both Canada and the U.S. are helping to maintain the status quo. My proposal encourages trainees not to privilege the native speaker, given (a) that the native speaker construct does not have a sound linguistic basis (and hence a pedagogy based on this norm is not always effective) and (b) that the native speaker model is a way of "Othering" those seen as nonnative to English and nonnative to the nation. Rather than representing effective practices, pedagogies that make the native speaker the norm are promoting an unequal division between White First World teachers and teachers who come from the rest of the world. This nonlinguistic underpinning of the native speaker construct has to be made transparent in TESL programs so that both native and nonnative teachers can make informed choices about what and how to teach.

I further suggest that the discourse of "empowerment"—through the acquisition of a Canadian, British, or American accent—is problematic. Lippi-Green (1997) argues that it is not possible for adults to eliminate their accent and that even if adult immigrants could change their accents, the intersection of race, gender, class, and Third World status would be factors in their continuing disempowerment. Goldstein (1999) therefore questions the value of emphasizing a certain accent and pronunciation in ESL. In addition, such accent-reduction discourses of empowerment for students are disempowering for their nonnative teachers who may have one of the stigmatized accents that students are being encouraged to unlearn in order to succeed. Hence, both good pedagogy and social justice demand that TESL programs in Canada, the U.S., and elsewhere rethink this emphasis on native speaker accents.

I have so far addressed the need for all teacher trainees to question the native speaker model and explore new pedagogies. Now I will look at how TESL programs can equip the nonnative trainees for the special challenges that they will face in this profession. Kamhi-Stein (1999) makes a strong case for integrating instruction on issues related to nonnative speakers in TESL preparation programs. She further argues that such programs should allow future teachers to develop an understanding of their assets, beliefs, and values and should also promote improvement of the teacher trainees' competencies. In such an approach, the teacher preparation curriculum provides teacher trainees with many opportunities to examine their nonnative speaker status in relation to theories of language acquisition, methodology, and curriculum design. It also allows them to examine the cultural and social factors affecting second language development. Such a curriculum would be a meaningful attempt to counter discourses in ELT that promote the notion that the native speaker is the best model.

Conclusion

In this chapter I have argued that the native speaker is a linguistic manifestation of nativist discourses that position visible minority immigrant women as being nonnative to Canada or the U.S. and, thus, as being nonnative speakers of English. I have also argued that native speakers are imagined as having Inner Circle accents and that accents, like race, are socially organized, are a linguistic manifestation of nativism, and constitute a new and effective form of racism. I have indicated that minority teachers are aware of their positioning as nonnative, as the Other of ESL, and that they often draw on their experience of otherness to build successful pedagogies and to disrupt native speaker mythologies. I have then looked at some of the implications of my study for the teaching of English as a second or foreign language worldwide; more specifically I have recommended that professional organizations should actively work toward dismantling the native/nonnative speaker dichotomy and reconceptualizing the native speaker norm. I have also recommended that teacher education programs make transparent the nonlinguistic underpinnings of the native speaker construct so that both native and nonnative teachers can make informed pedagogical choices.

I conclude on an optimistic note. While the pedagogies employed by the participants in the study were developed in the context of Settlement ESL programs in Toronto, the teachers' narratives of resisting native speaker and nativist discourses and of setting up a counterdiscursive paradigm in their ESL classrooms foreground strategies that can be employed by nonnative teachers in any classroom situation. These narratives tell a larger tale than ESL: by challenging the notion that the native speaker of English is the only valid teacher of English, not only are the teachers decolonizing ESL and decolonizing English, but they are also decolonizing our collective imagination.

Notes

1. There is no one Pakistani accent. Accents in Pakistan, as in Canada, are on a continuum. I am referring to how my accent indicates that I did not grow up in Canada and to the implications of this fact.

2. "Nativism" refers to the belief that the national culture is embodied in certain groups of people who were born in that country. It further refers to the belief that these native-born individuals are native speakers and that one born outside that country to parents speaking another language cannot attain native speaker status.
3. I do not use the term *Third World* unproblematically. Said (1994) has pointed out that the binary divisions of Third World and First World signify dominated and dominant. My use of these binaries in this article is an attempt to make transparent the continuing power inequalities between the two spheres that make it possible for the First World to produce and maintain such dichotomies as native/nonnative speaker. In addition, I am thus indicating that discourses of nativism continue to construct non-White immigrant women living in Canada as Third World inhabitants, signaled by the status of nonnative speaker that is ascribed to them.
4. Participants granted me permission to use data from their interviews in this study. I changed their names to protect their identities.

References

All the king's horses (1999, August 21). *Toronto Star,* pp. J1–J3.

Amin, N. (1994). *Minority women teachers on ownership of English.* Unpublished master's thesis, Ontario Institute for Studies in Education, University of Toronto, Canada.

Amin, N. (1997). Race and the identity of the nonnative ESL teacher. *TESOL Quarterly, 31,* 580–583.

Amin, N. (1999). Minority women teachers of ESL: Negotiating White English. In G. Braine (Ed.), *Non-native educators in English language teaching* (pp. 93–104). Mahwah, NJ: Erlbaum.

Amin, N. (2000). *Negotiating nativism: Minority immigrant women ESL teachers and the native speaker construct.* Unpublished doctoral dissertation, Ontario Institute for Studies in Education, University of Toronto, Canada.

Bloomfield, L. (1933). *Language.* New York: Holt, Rinehart, & Winston.

Bogdan, R. C., & Biklen, S. K. (1992). *Qualitative research for education: An introduction to theory and methods* (2nd ed.). Boston: Allyn & Bacon.

Brah, A. (1996). *Cartographies of diaspora: Contesting identities.* New York: Routledge.

Braine, G. (1999). From the periphery to the center: One teacher's journey. In G. Braine (Ed.), *Non-native educators in English language teaching* (pp. 15–27). Mahwah, NJ: Erlbaum.

Brutt-Griffler, J., & Samimy, K. K. (1999). Revisiting the colonial in the postcolonial: Critical praxis for nonnative-English-speaking teachers in a TESOL program. *TESOL Quarterly, 33,* 413–431.

Cheshire, J. (1991). Introduction: Sociolinguistics and English around the world. In J. Cheshire (Ed.), *English around the world: Sociolinguistic perspectives* (pp. 1–12). New York: Cambridge University Press.

Christophersen, P. (1988). "Native speakers" and world English. *English Today,* *4*(3), 15–18.

City of Toronto (1998). *Together we are one: A summary paper on diversity in Toronto.* Toronto: Author.

Davies, A. (1991). *The native speaker in applied linguistics.* Edinburgh, Scotland: Edinburgh University Press.

Ferguson, C. (1992). Foreword to the first edition. In B. B. Kachru (Ed.), *The other tongue: English across cultures* (2nd ed., pp. xiii–xvii). Chicago: University of Illinois Press.

Goldstein, T. (1999). Accents, ebonics, and crossing: Thinking about language, race relations, and discrimination [Review of the book *English with an accent: Language, ideology, and discrimination in the United States*]. *TESOL Quarterly, 33,* 597–604.

Kachru, B. B. (1990a). *The alchemy of English: The spread, functions, and models of non-native Englishes* (2nd ed.). Oxford: Pergamon.

Kachru, B. B. (1990b). World Englishes and applied linguistics. *World Englishes, 9*(1), 3–20.

Kachru, B. B. (1991). Liberation linguistics and the Quirk concern. *English Today, 7*(1), 3–13.

Kachru., B. B. (Ed.). (1992). *The other tongue: English across cultures* (2nd ed.). Chicago: University of Illinois Press.

Kachru., B. B. (1997). English as an Asian language. In M. L. S. Bautista (Ed.), *English is an Asian language: The Philippine context* (pp. 1–23). Sydney, Australia: Macquarie Library.

Kamhi-Stein, L. D. (1999). Preparing non-native professionals in TESOL: Implications for teacher education programs: In G. Braine (Ed.), *Non-native educators in English language teaching* (pp. 145–158). Mahwah, NJ: Erlbaum.

Leung, C., Harris, R., & Rampton, B. (1997). The idealised native speaker, reified ethnicities, and classroom realities. *TESOL Quarterly, 31,* 543–560.

Lippi-Green, R. (1997). *English with an accent: Language, ideology, and discrimination in the United States.* London: Routledge.

Mukherjee, B. (1985). *Darkness.* Markham, Ontario: Penguin.

Nayar, P. B. (1994). Whose English is it? *TESL-EJ, 1*(1). Retrieved April 7, 2001, from *http://www-writing.berkeley.edu/TESL-EJ/ej01/f.1.html*

Ng, R. (1990). Racism, sexism, and visible minority immigrant women in Canada. In *Zeitschrift der Gesellschaft für Kanada-Studien, 10*(2), 21–34. Neumünster, Germany: Karl Wachholtz.

Paikeday, T. M. (1985). *The native speaker is dead! An informal discussion of a linguistic myth with Noam Chomsky and other linguists, philosophers, psychologists, and lexicographers.* Toronto: Paikeday Publications.

Peirce, B. N. (1993). *Language learning, social identity, and immigrant women.* Unpublished doctoral dissertation, Ontario Institute for Studies in Education, University of Toronto, Canada.

Pennycook, A. (1992). *The cultural politics of teaching English in the world*. Unpublished doctoral dissertation, Ontario Institute for Studies in Education, University of Toronto, Canada.

Pennycook, A. (1998). *English and the discourses of colonialism*. London: Routledge.

Phillipson, R. (1992). *Linguistic imperialism*. Oxford: Oxford University Press.

Power Analysis. (1998). *Study of ESL/EFL services in Ontario*. Toronto: Author.

Quirk, R. (1990). Language varieties and standard language. *English Today, 6*(1), 3–10.

Rampton, B. (1990). Displacing the "native speaker": Expertise, affiliation, and inheritance. *ELT Journal, 44,* 97–101.

Reynolds, S. (Producer). (1953). *The eye of the beholder.* [Motion picture].

Rockhill, K., & Tomic, P. (1995). Situating ESL between speech and silence. In J. Gaskell & J. Willinsky (Eds.), *Gender in/forms curriculum: From enrichment to transformation* (pp. 209–229). New York: Teachers College Press.

Said, E. (1994). *Culture and imperialism*. New York: Alfred A. Knopf.

Sanaoui, R. (1997). *Directory of ESL teacher preparation programs in Ontario*. Toronto: TESL Ontario.

Simon, R. (1992). *Teaching against the grain: Texts for a pedagogy of possibility*. Toronto: Ontario Institute for Studies in Education.

Sridhar, K., & Sridhar, S. N. (1992). Bridging the paradigm gap: Second language acquisition theory and indigenized varieties of English. In B. B. Kachru (Ed.), *The other tongue: English across cultures* (2nd ed., pp. 91–107). Urbana: University of Illinois Press.

Sridhar, S. N. (1994). A reality check for SLA theories. *TESOL Quarterly, 28,* 800–805.

Tang, C. (1997). On the power and status of nonnative ESL teachers. *TESOL Quarterly, 31,* 577–580.

Thomas, J. (1999). Voices from the periphery: Non-native teachers and issues of credibility. In G. Braine (Ed.), *Non-native educators in English language teaching* (pp. 5–14). Mahwah, NJ: Erlbaum.

Tollefson, J. W. (1995). Introduction. In J. Tollefson (Ed.), *Power and inequality in language education* (pp. 1–8). New York: Cambridge University Press.

Widdowson, H. G. (1994). The ownership of English. *TESOL Quarterly, 28,* 377–388.

Teaching in Kindergarten through Grade 12 Programs: Perceptions of Native and Nonnative English-Speaking Practitioners

Lía D. Kamhi-Stein
California State University, Los Angeles

Annette Aagard
Palomar College

Angelica Ching
California State University, Los Angeles

Myoung-Soon Ashley Paik
La Puente Hacienda Unified School District

Linda Sasser
Alhambra School District

Over the past few years, interest has grown in issues related to language and ethnic minority practitioners in the field of teaching English to speakers of other languages (TESOL). Recent publications have looked at the perceived advantages and disadvantages of nonnative English-speaking teachers (NNESTs) in English as a foreign language (EFL) and English as a second language (ESL) classrooms (e.g., Braine, this volume; Medgyes, 1992, 1994; Samimy & Brutt-Griffler, 1999), perceived attitudes toward NNESTs (e.g., Amin, 1997, this volume; Tang,

1997), and the struggles and triumphs of NNESTs (e.g., Braine, 1999, this volume; Connor, 1999; Liu, this volume; Thomas, 1999).

Much of the research just cited has focused on NNESTs in EFL contexts (Medgyes, 1992; 1994; Tang, 1997), adult ESL classes (Amin, 1997), or college-level courses (Braine, 1999; Thomas, 1999). The present study was designed to focus on practitioners in kindergarten through 12 (K–12) contexts, specifically K–12 practitioners from a language minority background. The focus on this group was motivated by two factors. First, there is limited, if any, research focusing on NNESTs teaching at the K–12 level. Second, prior research (Kamhi-Stein, Lee, & Lee, 1999) and informal interviews of Master of Arts (MA) TESOL students suggest that U.S.-based NNESTs seem to favor teaching at the K–12 level over other levels. However, at this time there is no information regarding the perceptions of U.S.-based K–12 NNESTs. Given this gap in the literature, we designed the current study to compare the differences in perceptions regarding professional preparation and job satisfaction between K–12 native English-speaking teachers (NESTs) and NNESTs. The study was also designed to look at the perceptions of K–12 NESTs and NNESTs regarding their English language skills and teaching preferences.

Background

This investigation included four broad areas of research: (a) teacher confidence, (b) self-perceived language needs, (c) self-perceived prejudice, and (d) mentoring concerns. Following is a summary of research in each of the four areas.

Teacher Confidence

A few studies have focused on factors affecting the confidence of teachers from ethnic and language minority backgrounds. For example, Freeman, Brookhart, and Loadman (1999) investigated beginning teachers in high-diversity schools and concluded that these teachers "tend to encounter a complex and challenging teaching environment, struggle to form meaningful relations with their students, and be less satisfied with their jobs" (p. 107). In another study of five novice Cantonese-dominant secondary English teachers in Hong Kong, Pennington and Richards (1997) reported that the teachers discarded a communicative methodology in favor of a product-oriented approach to instruction. Possible factors explaining this finding include the following: a heavy teaching load, large class sizes, students' low proficiency in English and lack of discipline, closeness in age between the students and beginning teachers, personal experience of the new teachers while in school, low job satisfaction, low perceived effectiveness in their first year of teaching, and the school culture. Another factor affecting the confidence of NNESTs is challenges to their credibility (Samimy & Brutt-Griffler, 1999; Thomas, 1999). According to Thomas, NNESTs are challenged by professionals in the TESOL field, by professional organizations, and by students.

Self-Perceived Language Needs

The self-perceived language needs of NNESTs is another area of research that has received some attention within the literature. Specifically, several studies have identified pronunciation (Barkhuizen, 1997; Tang, 1997), writing, vocabulary (including idioms and slang), and cultural knowledge as areas of perceived difficulty (Kamhi-Stein et al., 1999; Liu, 1999; Samimy & Brutt-Griffler, 1999; Tang, 1997). While two studies (Kamhi-Stein et al., 1999; Samimy & Brutt-Griffler, 1999) have shown that lack of English proficiency does not have a negative effect on the instructional practices of NNESTs, another study (Li, 1998) has concluded that, in some cases, NNESTs view their variety of English as deficient and argue that lack of English proficiency constrains them when implementing communicative methodologies.

Self-Perceived Prejudice

Research has also shown that another area of concern for NNESTs is self-perceived prejudice based on ethnicity or nonnative status or both (Amin, 1997; Canagarajah, 1999; Kamhi-Stein et al., 1999; Thomas, 1999). Montemayor (1991) also identified a few critical issues that minority teachers face as they begin teaching, some generic to all teachers and some specific to their situation:

1. They may face isolation and separation from their ethnic group culture.
2. They may experience teacher bashing and the media's distrust of public education.
3. They may be expected to advocate for their ethnic group and solve emerging problems. Also, they may be relied on to communicate with parents, especially when language is a factor.
4. They may "burn out" trying to meet the needs of bilingual programs while working under the stigma of teaching in a "bilingual," rather than a "regular," program.
5. They may feel they were hired to fill a quota and provide a minority presence, thus making them feel conspicuous and out of place.

Mentoring Concerns

According to Stallworth (1994), it is critical that the teaching profession attract qualified minorities, including those who come from fields outside the teaching profession, since these professionals "bring with them a larger repertoire of life experiences and skills learned in the field and not just from academic preparation" (p. 27). While the mentoring of NNESTs has received no attention in the TESOL field, research suggests that the lack of availability and low quality of mentoring are barriers frequently faced by minority teachers. For example, Stallworth (1994) found that novice teachers from a minority background feel "isolated and incompetent" in their new environment; however, they tend to feel less intimidated when they secure at least one colleague as a mentor to assist them in answering questions "in a nonjudgmental manner" (p. 29). Novice teacher support—in the form of conferencing with mentors, being observed by mentors, and receiving tuition-free graduate courses—has been reported to be helpful and to promote teacher retention (Smith, 1989–1990).

Blankenship et al. (1992) outline a set of principles for effectively inducting all beginning teachers while focusing particularly on minority teachers' needs, including the following: (a) the need to meet with other teachers to reflectively discuss classroom experiences, (b) the need to observe experienced teachers, (c) the need to incorporate new and innovative instructional methodologies and resources, (d) the need to learn how to manage time and paperwork wisely, and (e) the need to develop classroom management ideas with diverse student populations.

In summary, the studies reviewed in the preceding sections suggest that ethnic and language minority teachers are often faced with challenges to their professional credibility and with prejudice based on ethnicity or nonnative status. Additionally, while so far very little, if any, research has focused on NNESTs and mentoring issues, some research suggests that lack of quality mentoring is a barrier faced by minority teachers in general. Still missing from the literature is research designed to compare the perceptions of K–12 NESTs and NNESTs in relationship to their professional preparation, their level of job satisfaction, and their teaching preferences.

Research Questions

This study was guided by three research questions.

1. To what extent, if any, are there differences in the perceptions of K–12 NESTs and NNESTs regarding their professional preparation?

2. To what extent, if any, are there differences in the perceptions of K–12 NESTs and NNESTs regarding their job satisfaction?
3. To what extent, if any, are there differences in the perceptions of K–12 NESTs and NNESTs regarding their English language skills and teaching preferences?

Method

Participants

Participants in this study were selected according to two criteria: (a) language status (NESTs and NNESTs) and (b) the type of institution in which they taught (K–12). The participants in this study were 55 NESTs and 32 NNESTs teaching in K–12 programs in southern California. All of the 55 NESTs reported being born in the U.S. Additionally, nearly 65% of the NESTs reported being Caucasian; 13% reported being Asian; 7% reported being African-American, Latino, or other; and the remaining 16% did not provide information on race or ethnicity.

Of the 32 NNESTs, 59% reported they were born outside the U.S. Specifically, 31% of NNESTs were born in Mexico, 13% in Taiwan, 9% in Korea, and 6% in El Salvador and Vietnam. The other 41% were born in the U.S. Among the 32 NNESTs, 44% reported being Latinos, 38% reported being Asian, 9% reported being Caucasian, 3% reported being African-American, and 7% did not report race or ethnicity. Additionally, at the time of the study, 88% of the 32 NNESTs reported having lived in the U.S. for 10 or more years and the remaining 12% reported having lived in the U.S. from 6 to 9 years. While 41% of the NNESTs reported speaking Spanish as a first language, only 19% reported speaking Spanish at home at the time of the study.

Instrument

A survey was designed to provide information on the preceding three research questions.[1] Survey items were developed based upon a national survey of graduates of teacher education courses (Loadman, Freeman, Brookhart, Rahman, & McCague, 1999). A pilot copy of the survey was administered and revised. The revised version of the survey instrument had three main sections requiring participants to respond to questions on a Likert scale as well as to open-ended questions. The first section, "Demographic Information," contained 14 questions designed to provide information on the participants' age, ethnic background, and degrees completed and in progress. The second section, "Professional Information," contained 66 questions designed to provide information on the participants' schools and their current teaching assignments, the participants' reported job sat-isfaction and future plans, and the participants' perceptions regarding the quality of formal mentoring they received and the quality of their interactions with school faculty and staff. The third section, "Language Background," contained 21 questions designed to provide information on the participants' perceptions regarding their English language skills as well as perceptions about the NNESTs' strengths and weaknesses.

Data Collection and Analysis

The survey was distributed and collected in two ways. First, copies of the survey were administered during the summer quarter of 2000 within the Charter College of Education at California State University, Los Angeles (CSULA). Second, copies of the survey were mailed to selected K–12 programs with a stamped, self-addressed return enve-lope. Mailed responses were collected over a six-week period.

Survey responses were analyzed using quantitative and qualitative techniques. Specifically, survey responses were analyzed for descriptive statistics (means, standard deviations, overall frequencies, and percent-ages) using the Statistical Package for the Social Sciences, version 9.0 (1998). Open-ended responses were analyzed qualitatively by engaging in a process of recursive reading of the survey instruments, identifying recurring responses, and assigning them to tentative themes (Strauss & Corbin, 1990). The process was completed by naming the themes.

Findings

This section presents findings for the quantitative and qualitative analyses.

Quantitative Findings

General profile of the participants. Table 1 shows that NESTS and NNESTs had a variety of teaching assignments. However, as can be seen in Table 1, a larger percentage of NNESTs reported teaching early elementary grades (NNESTs = 41%, NESTs = 18%). Additionally, while the same percentage of NESTs and NNESTs reported teaching senior high school (16%), a larger percentage of NESTs reported teaching middle school or junior high school (NESTs = 26%, NNESTs = 22%).

Table 2 presents information on the participants' length of service in their current positions. According to the results presented in the table, NESTs were somewhat more experienced than NNESTs. Spe-cifically, 25% of the NESTS and 13% of the NNESTs had been in their current positions for four years or more.

TABLE 1.   Teaching Assignment by Language Status

Teaching Assignment	NESTs		NNESTs	
	N	%	N	%
Preschool	2	4	0	0
Early elementary	10	18	13	41
Upper elementary	5	9	3	9
Middle school/junior high	14	26	7	22
Senior high school	9	16	5	16
Early and upper elementary	2	4	1	3
Senior high school and adult ESL	0	0	1	3
Early elementary and adult ESL	0	0	1	3
Senior high school and IEP	0	0	1	3
Other combinations	13	23	0	0
Total	55	100	32	100

TABLE 2.   Current Teaching Experience by Language Status

Length of Service in the Current Teaching Position	NESTs		NNESTs	
	N	%	N	%
Less than one year	12	22	3	9
One to two years	19	35	17	53
Two to four years	10	18	8	25
More than four years	14	25	4	13
Total	55	100	32	100

Perceptions regarding professional preparation. Table 3 presents descriptive statistics for the participants' perceptions regarding professional preparation. As can be seen in the table, both NESTs and NNESTs viewed their credential program preparation as being between "average" and "above average." In contrast, while NESTs rated their MA program preparation as being between "average" and "above average," NNESTs rated their MA program preparation as being "above average." These results show that the NNESTs' perceptions about their MA program preparation were slightly more positive than those of the NESTs.

Perceptions regarding job satisfaction. Tables 4 and 5 present information on the participants' perceptions regarding job satisfaction. As indicated in Table 4, NESTs and NNESTs were similar in their overall job satisfaction. Specifically, the mean for overall job satisfaction for NESTs and NNESTs was closer to "positive" than to "somewhat positive," although NESTs (M = 3.94, SD = 1.02) were slightly more positive than NNESTs (M = 3.83, SD = .83). As shown in Table 5, the job feature that NESTs and NNESTs rated highest (between "positive" and "very positive") was "interactions with students." While "salary/fringe benefits" received the lowest mean rating for NESTs (between "negative" and "somewhat positive"), "general work conditions," including

TABLE 3.   Perceptions about Professional Preparation

	NESTs		NNESTs	
Type of Program	M	SD	M	SD
Credential	3.55	.59	3.71	.69
MA	3.60	.50	4.00	.95

Note: Scale: 1 = unacceptable, 2 = below average, 3 = average, 4 = above average, 5 = exceptional.

TABLE 4.   Perceptions regarding Overall Job Satisfaction

	NESTs		NNESTs	
Quality Rating	M	SD	M	SD
Overall satisfaction	3.94	1.02	3.83	.83

Note: Scale: 1 = very negative, 2 = negative, 3 = somewhat positive, 4 = positive, 5 = very positive.

TABLE 5.   Perceptions regarding Various Job Features

	NESTs		NNESTs	
Job Features	M	SD	M	SD
Interactions with students	4.44	.79	4.50	.72
Interactions with colleagues	3.98	.95	3.84	1.10
Professional autonomy	3.96	.88	3.73	.74
Interactions with parents	3.81	.96	3.87	.99
Interactions with administrators	3.87	1.07	3.61	1.02
Opportunities for professional advancement	3.34	1.04	3.53	.98
General work conditions	3.30	1.22	3.00	1.11
Salary/fringe benefits	2.78	1.11	3.30	.93

Note: Scale: 1 = very negative, 2 = negative, 3 = somewhat positive, 4 = positive, 5 = very positive.

class size and workload, received the lowest mean rating for NNESTs ("somewhat positive").

Table 6 summarizes the participants' perceptions regarding the quality of faculty-staff interactions. As shown in the table, "respect for minorities" was the variable that received the highest mean rating. Specifically, both groups viewed faculty and staff interactions to be "respectful of minorities" ($M = 4.11$, $SD = .98$ for NESTs; $M = 4.11$, $SD = 1.01$ for NNESTs). In contrast, the two groups ranked different variables lowest. NESTs gave "networking" a mean rating of 3.67, indicating that the participants' views about faculty-staff "networking" was between "somewhat positive" and "positive." The lowest ranked feature for NNESTs was "clarity of school requirements" ($M = 3.34$, $SD = 1.11$), indicating that the NNESTs' mean rating of "clarity of school requirements" was closer to "somewhat positive" than to "positive."

TABLE 6. Perceptions regarding Faculty and Staff Interactions

Features of Faculty and Staff Interactions	NESTs		NNESTs	
	M	*SD*	*M*	*SD*
Respect for minorities	4.11	.98	4.11	1.01
Sharing of resources	3.97	.91	3.65	.97
Respect for novice teachers	3.90	1.04	3.67	1.14
Openness to new ideas	3.77	1.19	3.62	.97
Clarity of school requirements	3.77	1.09	3.34	1.11
Networking	3.67	.96	3.42	.91

Note: Scale: 1 = very negative, 2 = negative, 3 = somewhat positive, 4 = positive, 5 = very positive.

NESTs and NNESTs did not differ in their perceptions regarding their schools' support. As indicated in Table 7, the mean for "quality of formal mentoring" for both groups was between "average" and "strong." Additionally, both groups of practitioners reported meeting with their mentor teachers at least "once a month." However, the slightly higher mean for NESTs (M = 3.61, SD = .92 vs. M = 3.29, SD = .91 for NNESTs) suggests that NESTs meet somewhat more frequently with their mentor teachers than NNESTs.

Table 8 presents a ranking of the participants' perceptions regarding the different kinds of support received. According to the table, "support from family and friends" was at the top of the ranking for both NESTs and NNESTs. Following in the ranking in descending order for both groups were "support from school colleagues," "support from school administrators," and "support from pre-service courses."

Participants' perceptions regarding their English language skills. Table 9 summarizes the participants' perceptions regarding their English language skills. As can be seen in the table, while NESTs viewed their overall language skills as being between "very good" and "excellent," NNESTs perceived their overall English language skills as being "very good" or close to "very good." Additionally, NESTs and NNESTs differed in the individual language skill areas that they rated highest and lowest. Specifically, the highest self-rated skill area was "reading" for NESTs and "listening" for NNESTs. In contrast, the lowest self-rated skill area was "grammar" for NESTs and "pronunciation" for NNESTs.

Table 10 summarizes information on the participants' self-reported degree of comfort teaching the different skill areas. As shown in the table, while the means for NESTs were within the close to "comfortable" and "comfortable" categories, the means for NNESTs were within the "comfortable" category. Table 10 shows that NESTs reported feeling comfortable teaching pronunciation, speaking, listening, writing,

TABLE 7. Perceptions regarding School Support

Mentoring Ratings	NESTs		NNESTs	
	M	SD	M	SD
Quality of formal mentoring	2.32	.82	2.50	.52
Frequency of formal mentoring	3.61	.92	3.29	.91

Note: Scale, quality of mentoring: 1 = weak, 2 = average, 3 = strong; scale, frequency of mentoring: 1 = never, 2 = once a semester, 3 = once a month, 4 = once a week.

TABLE 8. Ranking by Type of Support Currently Received

Type of Support Received	NESTs		NNESTs	
	M	SD	M	SD
Support from family and friends	4.20	.78	3.79	.79
Support from school colleagues	3.76	.97	3.70	.88
Support from school administrators	3.62	1.07	3.34	1.11
Support from pre-service courses	3.37	.96	3.13	.90

Note: Scale: 1 = unacceptable, 2 = below average, 3 = average, 4 = above average, 5 = exceptional.

TABLE 9. Perceived English Language Skills by Language Status

Skills	NESTs		NNESTs	
	M	SD	M	SD
Overall	4.35	.76	3.97	.78
Reading	4.45	.79	4.13	.75
Listening	4.42	.74	4.22	.83
Speaking	4.27	.87	3.88	.66
Pronunciation	4.29	.94	3.75	.88
Writing	4.22	.92	3.81	.83
Grammar	4.09	.89	3.97	.93

Note: Scale: 1 = poor, 2 = fair, 3 = good, 4 = very good, 5 = excellent.

TABLE 10. Teaching Comfort in English by Language Status

Skills	NESTs		NNESTs	
	M	SD	M	SD
Pronunciation	3.26	.76	3.25	.67
Speaking	3.24	.70	3.28	.63
Listening	3.24	.78	3.38	.61
Writing	3.11	.86	3.25	.62
Reading	3.11	.90	3.41	.61
Grammar	2.98	.81	3.25	.72

Note: Scale: 1 = not comfortable at all, 2 = somewhat comfortable, 3 = comfortable, 4 = very comfortable.

TABLE 11. Self-Perceptions about Instructional Abilities

| | Self-Perceptions about Instructional Abilities | |
Language Status	M	SD
NESTs	3.82	.69
NNESTs	4.04	.64

Note: Scale: 1 = inferior, 2 = below average, 3 = average, 4 = better than average, 5 = exceptional.

and reading, in decreasing order, but close to comfortable teaching grammar. In contrast, NNESTs reported feeling comfortable teaching all six skill areas on the table, including reading, listening, speaking, writing, pronunciation, and grammar, in decreasing order.

Table 11 summarizes information regarding the participants' perceptions about their instructional abilities. As can be seen in the table, the mean rating for NESTs was slightly lower than that for NNESTs. While NNESTs perceived themselves to be "better than average" teachers, NESTs perceived themselves to be between "average" and "better than average," although their mean rating was closer to "better than average" than "average."

Qualitative Findings

The open-ended survey questions, answered by NESTs and NNESTs, were analyzed qualitatively in order to identify the perceived difficulties faced by NNESTs as well as their sources of strength. The analysis allowed the identification of two areas of perceived difficulty: "communication skills" and "vocabulary skills." According to the survey respondents, effective communication was sometimes hindered by the "nonnative" status of students and teachers alike. One teacher noted: "Nonnativeness both from students and teachers may hinder effective communication" (#74). However, another participant made the following comment:

> Sometimes they [NNESTs] are afraid that they're going to make a mistake when speaking; they need to realize that everyone makes mistakes when speaking and writing. (#35)

The respondents noted that "vocabulary skills" were the second area of difficulty for NNESTs. Specifically, survey respondents agreed that lack of adequate vocabulary might interfere with NNESTs' ability to teach. One commented, "Lack of prior knowledge of vocabulary is a hindrance when teaching."

The qualitative analysis of the open-ended survey questions allowed the identification of three sources of strengths for the NNESTs:

"cultural awareness," "empathy," and "linguistic advantage provided by the nonnative status." First, the survey respondents agreed that NNESTs can strengthen the school curriculum by bringing to the classroom their "cultural awareness," involving, but not limited to, an understanding of two or more cultures, multicultural experiences, and a broad worldview. A participant summarized this idea as follows:

> Diverse cultural background contributes to a multicultural learning environment, which can help students broaden their perception of the world. (#46)

Second, many of the survey respondents explained that another feature that characterized NNESTs was their empathy. They explained that second language (L2) students usually see their NNESTs as role models with whom they can identify and relate. Specifically, NNESTs were seen as being able to understand the difficulty of learning a new language since they had gone through the L2 learning process and were, therefore, especially sensitive to the language needs of their ESL students. The following observations reflect these points:

> NNES teachers tend to be more successful in reaching students who can relate culturally or linguistically to them. (#16)

> Because of their nonnative status, they had to "rise" above and usually, in my experience, they were better teachers, more sensitive too . . . (#127)

> [NNESTs have] the ability to understand the difficulty of learning a new language, different methods of acquiring the English language . . . and can share personal experiences. (#76)

Finally, survey respondents agreed that NNESTs are characterized by what might be called a "linguistic advantage provided by the nonnative status." Many survey respondents teaching elementary grades agreed that the NNESTs' ability to communicate with their students' parents promoted positive parent-teacher rapport. At the same time, survey respondents explained that NNESTs become interpreters of the U.S. school culture for students. They also help immigrant parents understand how U.S. schools operate and how they can assist their children in becoming successful learners. The following two comments reflect what was said about this issue:

> They provide a communication link to some students; similar to an interpreter . . . (#37)

[They have] good communication skills with parents who speak their language and ability to translate school newsletters, etc. . . . (#113)

Discussion and Conclusions

This study provided information on K–12 NNESTs, a group of practitioners that, so far, have received little attention within the literature on nonnative English-speaking professionals. The results of this study showed that K–12 NESTs and NNESTs were similar and different in a number of ways. First, NESTs and NNESTs shared positive views of their pre-service and in-service training. Specifically, both NESTs and NNESTs were positive about their preparation in credential and MA programs, although NNESTs were slightly more positive than NESTs.

Second, both NESTs and NNESTs rated the formal mentoring they received in their schools as being between "average" and "strong" (although the mean rating for NESTs was closer to average). Both groups reported meeting with their mentors at least "once a month," although NESTs reported meeting with their mentor teachers more often than NNESTs did. In any case, this fact did not affect the NNESTs' perceptions about the quality of the mentoring received, as shown by the small difference in mean ratings between NNESTs and NESTs.

Third, NESTs and NNESTs reported that they received support not only from formal networks, that is, mentoring programs organized by the teachers' schools, but also from informal networks such as school colleagues and family and friends. However, both NESTs and NNESTs had slightly more positive perceptions about informal support networks than formal support networks. It could well be the case that the informal support provided by colleagues, friends, and family contributes to the creation of a positive school climate (Stallworth, 1994) and to the prevention of teacher "burnout," a factor that can ultimately threaten teacher retention.

A further similarity between NESTs and NNESTs was their self-reported job satisfaction. Specifically, the mean rating for overall job satisfaction for both groups was closer to "positive" than to "somewhat positive," although the mean rating for NESTs was slightly more positive than that for NNESTs. Several job features that received high mean ratings (i.e., "interaction with students," "interactions with colleagues," "professional autonomy," "interactions with parents," and "respect for minorities") may have positively affected the level of job satisfaction for both NESTs and NNESTs. Common to these job features is the fact that they emphasize human relationships that teachers need to build if they are to function successfully in the school environment.

On the other hand, other job features (e.g., "salary/fringe benefits," "general work conditions") may have negatively affected both NESTs and NNESTs' level of job satisfaction. These job features focus on the administrative structure of schools, and teachers, regardless of language status, may have felt that they had little control over such factors, thereby negatively contributing to the teachers' overall job satisfaction mean ratings. Future research needs to look at larger samples and rely on inferential analysis techniques to determine the extent to which various job features contribute to a high or low level of job satisfaction.

NESTs and NNESTs were also similar in that both groups' perceptions of their English language skills were positive. However, when compared to NNESTs, NESTs were found to have slightly more positive views of their English language skills. Specifically, while the mean ratings for the NESTs' self-reported English language skills ranged from "very good" (for grammar) to close to "excellent" (for reading), the means for NNESTs were close to "very good" (for pronunciation) or within the "very good" category (for listening). The fact that both NESTs and NNESTs exhibited positive perceptions about their English language skills did not support findings in prior studies (e.g., Medgyes, 1992, 1994, 2001). This difference could be attributed to the fact that the NNESTs in this study were different from NNESTs in other studies. Most of the NNESTs in the current study had resided in the U.S. for 10 or more years, and, in turn, length of U.S. residence may have positively affected the NNESTs' perceptions about their language skills.

Regarding the participants' English language skills, two observations are in order. First, neither pronunciation nor speaking was considered to be an area of concern for NNESTs (although pronunciation turned out to be the skill area with the lowest mean rating for NNESTs and speaking was ranked as the fourth-best skill area for NESTs and NNESTs). This finding did not support findings in prior studies that showed that both pronunciation and speaking were areas of concern for NNESTs (Medgyes, 1994). The findings in the current study could be explained by the fact that the NNESTs differed from the teachers in Medgyes' investigation in their length of U.S. residence as well as in their opportunities to be exposed to and to use the English language. Second, in this investigation, grammar was ranked as the third-best skill area for NNESTs, and it was ranked as the weakest skill area for NESTs. The study's findings related to grammar confirm a prior study (Kamhi-Stein et al., 1999) showing that long-term U.S. residence was negatively related to NNESTs' views about their English grammar skills. Additionally, while the NNESTs in this study reported feeling comfortable teaching grammar, their mean rating for degree of comfort teaching grammar was lower than that for teaching reading, listening, speaking, writing, and pronunciation. It would seem that, in the area of grammar, the NNESTs in this study were different from EFL teachers in other studies (e.g., Medgyes, 1994; Tang, 1997) who felt that grammar was one of their strongest skill areas. Again, these results could be attributed to the fact that most of the NNESTs in the study had lived in the U.S. for 10 years or more and that length of U.S. residence may have affected the participants' perceptions regarding their grammar skills in English.

NESTs and NNESTs differed in more than one way. First, while 41% of the NNESTs in this study reported teaching elementary grades, only 18% of the NESTs in this study reported teaching at that level. This finding suggests that NNESTs may find teaching elementary grades to be an appealing career choice (Kamhi-Stein et al., 1999). This result may be explained by the qualitative findings in this investigation, supporting the notion that when teaching elementary grades, NNESTs have a linguistic advantage both inside and outside the classroom because of their first language (L1) skills. NNESTs may strengthen the school curriculum by bringing a unique worldview to the classroom. Outside the classroom, NNESTs who share their students' L1 can easily communicate with parents and can serve as cultural brokers. However, great caution should be taken when making generalizations about these findings since the sample in this study was small and not randomly selected. It is unclear whether the same results would be obtained with a larger, randomly selected sample.

Second, NNESTs were slightly less positive than NESTs in their evaluation of school administrators ("support from school administrators" and "interactions with administrators"), although there was wide variation in the participants' responses. One possible explanation for the NNESTs' slightly less positive attitude could be that a higher percentage of NNESTs had been in their current teaching position for four years or less. Most probably, these novice teachers need their school administrators to play a proactive role in assisting them to adapt to and cope with the demands of their new positions (Kamhi-Stein, 2000).

NNESTs were also slightly more positive about their instructional abilities than were the NESTs. The NNESTs' slightly more positive perception was reflected in the group's slightly higher mean ratings for degree of teaching comfort for various skill areas such as speaking, listening, writing, reading, and grammar. The differences in perceptions could be attributed to the NNESTs' slightly more positive views about their professional preparation. It could also be argued that three other factors—the NNESTs' strong sense of cultural awareness, their empathy, and their ability to communicate with their students' parents—also contributed to the NNESTs' positive perceptions about their instructional abilities.

Taken together, the results of this study do not support Medgyes' (2001) idea that NNESTs and NESTs are "two different species" (p. 434), that is, membership in one group excludes membership in the other group. Rather than showing that NESTs and NNESTs belong in "different camps," the results of this study showed that the long-term U.S. residents from a nonnative English-speaking background and the U.S.-born native English speakers who participated in this study were characterized by a complex set of similarities and differences. Among the similarities are the teachers' views about their professional preparation, their perspectives on formal and informal mentoring networks, their level of overall job satisfaction, and their perceptions about their English language skills. NESTs and NNESTs in this study differed in the grades they tended to teach (with a higher percentage of NNESTs teaching early elementary grades), in their evaluation of school administrators (with NNESTs being slightly less positive), and in their perceptions about their instructional abilities (with NNESTs having more positive perceptions). In this study, the similarities and differences between the two groups of participants could be explained, at least in part, in terms of the NNESTs' length of U.S. residence, which may have contributed to making the NNESTs and NESTs in this study more similar than different.

Given the findings of this study, four recommendations are in order. First, further research needs to be conducted to provide in-depth information about the career choices of NNESTs in ESL and EFL settings. This line of research would seek to answer questions such as the following: To what extent, if any, do NNESTs favor teaching a particular age-group? To what extent, if any, do NNESTs favor teaching in a particular setting (e.g., adult ESL programs vs. community college ESL credit programs)? Finally, what are the reasons for these preferences?

Second, future case studies need to be conducted to develop profiles of exemplary K–12 school administrators who have successfully supported newly hired teachers in general and NNESTs in particular. This line of research would help identify the conditions that must be in place for NNESTs to become an integral part of the school culture and, ultimately, achieve professional success. Some of the questions these case studies should seek to answer about these exemplary administrators include:

1. What kinds of resources do they commit to assist NNESTs in the successful transition from graduate student to novice teacher?
2. What role, if any, do they play in helping NNESTs develop as professionals?

3. What kind of teaching situation (specifically the teaching load, class size, and class structure) do they assign to NNESTs during their first year on the job?
4. What role do they play in helping NNESTs understand the purposes and consequences of the various types of evaluations implemented?

Third, the findings in this investigation support the notion that nonnative status contributes to the development of positive self-perceptions regarding professional practices. Teachers in the current study viewed their nonnative status as a professional asset. Future research needs to develop profiles of NNESTs in different instructional settings in order to help develop an in-depth understanding of the relationship among pedagogical practices, self-perceptions about professional preparation, and self-perceptions about English language proficiency.

Fourth, this study has shown that it is not possible to assert that native and nonnative English speakers are "two different species" (Medgyes, 2001, p. 434), since a variety of factors may contribute to making NESTs and NNESTs more similar than different. Therefore, future investigations need to continue exploring the impact that different variables (e.g., length of residence in different types of settings, professional preparation, work experience, and so on) may have on the self-perceptions, instructional beliefs, and instructional practices of NNESTs.

Completed research in the arenas just outlined would contribute to the understanding of the complex set of factors that affect nonnative English-speaking professionals, ultimately benefiting both nonnative English-speaking professionals and their students.

Note

1. A complete copy of the survey instrument is available from Lía D. Kamhi-Stein, Charter College of Education, California State University, Los Angeles, 5151 State University Drive, Los Angeles, CA 90032.

References

Amin, N. (1997). Race and the identity of the nonnative ESL teacher. *TESOL Quarterly, 31,* 580–583.
Barkhuizen, G. (1997). Predicted problems of elementary school ESL teachers: Implications for teacher education. *TESL Reporter, 30,* 17–26.
Blankenship, C. S., Burton, J. M., Faltis, C., Lodge, N., Rice, R., & Santos, S. L. (1992). *Embracing cultural diversity in colleges of education: Minority recruitment and retention project.* (ERIC Document Reproduction Service No. ED362469)

Braine, G. (1999). From the periphery to the center: One teacher's journey. In G. Braine (Ed.), *Non-native educators in English language teaching* (pp. 15–28). Mahwah, NJ: Erlbaum.

Canagarajah, A. S. (1999). Interrogating the "native speaker fallacy": Non-linguistic roots, non-pedagogical results. In G. Braine (Ed.), *Non-native educators in English language teaching* (pp. 77–92). Mahwah, NJ: Erlbaum.

Connor, U. N. (1999). Learning to write academic prose in a second language: A literacy biography. In G. Braine (Ed.), *Non-native educators in English language teaching* (pp. 16–29). Mahwah, NJ: Erlbaum.

Freeman, D. J., Brookhart, S. M., & Loadman, W. E. (1999). Realities of teaching in racially/ethnically diverse schools: Feedback from entry-level teachers. *Urban Education, 34,* 89–114.

Kamhi-Stein, L. D. (2000). Adapting U.S.-based TESOL teacher education to meet the needs of nonnative English speakers. *TESOL Journal, 9*(3), 10–14.

Kamhi-Stein, L. D., Lee, E., & Lee, C. (1999, March). *NNS teachers in TESOL programs.* Paper presented at the 33rd annual meeting of Teachers of English to Speakers of Other Languages, New York.

Li, D. (1998). It's always more difficult than you plan and imagine: Teachers' perceived difficulties in introducing the communicative approach in South Korea. *TESOL Quarterly, 32,* 677–703.

Liu, D. (1999). Training non-native TESOL students: Challenges for TESOL teacher education in the West. In G. Braine (Ed.), *Non-native educators in English language teaching* (pp. 199–212). Mahwah, NJ: Erlbaum.

Loadman, W. E., Freeman, D. J., Brookhart, S. M., Rahman, M. A., & McCague, G. J. (1999). Development of a national survey of teacher education program graduates. *Journal of Educational Research, 93*(2), 76–89.

Medgyes, P. (1992). Native or non-native: Who's worth more? *ELT Journal, 46,* 340–349.

Medgyes, P. (1994). *The non-native teacher.* London: Macmillan.

Medgyes, P. (2001). When the teacher is a non-native speaker. In M. Celce-Murcia (Ed.), *Teaching English as a second or foreign language* (pp. 429–442). Boston: Heinle & Heinle.

Montemayor, A. (1991). Retaining an ethnically diverse teaching force. In E. G. Cuellar & L. Huling-Austin, (Eds.), *Achieving an ethnically diverse teaching force* (pp. 29–34). Austin: Texas Education Agency. (ERIC Document Reproduction Service No. ED340687)

Pennington, M. C., & Richards, J. C. (1997). Reorienting the teaching universe: The experience of five first-year English teachers in Hong Kong. *Language Teaching Research, 1,* 149–178.

Samimy, K. K., & Brutt-Griffler, J. (1999). Perceptions of NNS students in a graduate TESOL program. In G. Braine (Ed.), *Non-native educators in English language teaching* (pp. 129–146). Mahwah, NJ: Erlbaum.

Smith, A. L. (1989–1990). Collaborative induction model to support first-year minority teachers. *Action in Teacher Education, 11*(4), 42–47.

Stallworth, B. J. (1994). *New minority teachers' perceptions of teaching.* (ERIC Document Reproduction Service No. ED383660)

Statistical package for the social sciences (Version 9.0). (1998). Chicago: SPSS.

Strauss, A., & Corbin, J. (1990). *Basics of qualitative research: Grounded theory procedures and techniques.* Newbury Park, CA: Sage.

Tang, C. (1997). On the power and status of nonnative ESL teachers. *TESOL Quarterly, 31,* 577–580.

Thomas, J. (1999). Voices from the periphery: Non-native teachers and issues of credibility. In G. Braine (Ed.), *Non-native educators in English language teaching* (pp. 5–14). Mahwah, NJ: Erlbaum.

Children of a Lesser English: Status of Nonnative English Speakers as College-Level English as a Second Language Teachers in the United States

Ahmar Mahboob
East Carolina University

Karl Uhrig
Indiana University, Bloomington

Karen L. Newman
Indiana University, Bloomington

Beverly S. Hartford
Indiana University, Bloomington

Today, it is an uncontested fact that English is the fastest growing language in the world. It is also accepted that there are more non-native speakers of English than there are native speakers (Alatis & Straehle, 1997). According to a British Council (1986) report, there are as many as two billion people learning English globally and who have "some awareness of English" (p. 4). More recently, Kachru (1996) writes, "there are now at least four non-native speakers of English for every native speaker" (p. 241). Keeping these facts in mind, it could be concluded that the large majority of English language teachers around the world are nonnative speakers. In fact, Reves and Medgyes (1994), based on a survey of 216 English as a second language (ESL) and English as a foreign language (EFL) teachers in 10 countries, report that "in two-thirds of the schools there were no NESTs [native English-speaking teachers], while only one third of the schools employed both NESTs and non-NESTs" (p. 356). Canagarajah (1999) also states that up to 80% of the English language teachers globally are nonnative speakers of English.

As a consequence of the high demand for learning English and the corresponding cadre of English language teachers and specialists, a large number of teachers (both pre- and in- service) come to countries where English is a native language to be trained as teachers of English. According to one study that looked at 173 graduate programs in North America (including the United States and Canada), 40% of the students preparing to be English teachers in Teaching English to Speakers of Other Languages (TESOL) and applied linguistics programs were nonnative speakers (Liu, 1999). Kamhi-Stein (1999) reports that the number of nonnative English speakers from either an international or a U.S. background, in at least one U.S.-based institution, was as high as 70%. These figures provide evidence that programs that prepare ESL/EFL teachers in North America (specifically the United States) attract a high number of nonnative speakers of English.

While literature on nonnative English-speaking teachers (NNESTs) (Braine, 1999; Cook, 2000; Medgyes, 1992; Tang, 1997) suggests—and in fact presupposes—that the number of NNESTs working in English language programs (ELPs) in native English-speaking countries is disproportionate to the number of NESTs (and to the number of nonnative English-speaking graduate students in TESOL, applied linguistics, and/or language education programs), there are no empirical studies that report the proportion of NNESTs to NESTs working in ELPs. The present study is designed to fill this gap in the literature by presenting the results of a survey of college-level ELPs in the United States.[1]

In addition to investigating the numerical status of NNESTs in relation to NESTs, the survey results also evaluate the weight that program administrators give to various hiring criteria, including the native/nonnative English speaker status of potential teachers. Medgyes (1992), focusing on the United Kingdom, states that program administrators prefer native speakers because they are "aware that international students studying in Britain preferred to be taught by native-speaking English teachers. This demand would have to be satisfied by the school principal . . ." (p. 344). However, Medgyes' report is based on an informal "straw poll" (p. 343). The current study provides empirical evidence to evaluate such claims on the issues of hiring/nonhiring of NNESTs in college-level ELPs in the United States.

The Study

Participants

The participants in this study were 503 college-level ELPs listed in a publication entitled *English Language and Orientation Programs in the United States,* published by the Institute of International Education in 1997. The ELPs listed in this publication were spread throughout the 52 states of the United States. All the programs in this study were college-level intensive English programs (IEPs); thus, all discussion in this study is limited to college-level IEPs and should not be extended or generalized to K–12 or other types of programs.

One hundred and twenty-two surveys were completed, and 24 surveys were returned unopened because of "unknown addressee" status. Thus, the response rate, based on a total of 479 IEPs that received the survey, was 25.5%. The geographical distribution of the programs that responded was not tracked.

The surveys were addressed to program administrators. Teachers, regardless of language status, were not asked to complete any surveys for this study. Thus, the results of this study are based on feedback from program administrators only.

Survey

The survey developed for the purposes of this study consisted of three sections (see Appendix A for a copy of the survey). The first section contained questions that pertained to the criteria that administrators use to hire and evaluate English language teachers in their programs. There were 10 criteria that the program administrators rated on a 6-point Likert scale (ranging from 0 to 5, where 0 implied "least important" and 5 implied "most important"). The 10 criteria listed were: "accent," "U.S. citizenship," "U.S. nationality," "dialect," "educational experience," "enrollment in associated academic program," "ethnicity," "native English speaker," "recommendation," and "teaching experience." In addition to the question on hiring criteria, a number of other questions related to the programs were also included in this section. These questions were used as distractors and will not be analyzed in this chapter.

The second section contained questions about teacher demographics, including whether they were native or nonnative English speakers, male or female, and graduate or undergraduate students in an affiliated teacher preparation program. The information collected in this section also looked at the total number of international students in their affiliated graduate programs. It should be kept in mind that the results from the question on international students do not include nonnative English-speaking graduate students who are U.S. citizens.

The third section contained questions about student demographics in the IEPs, such as how many students there were in each program, which countries they represented, and what proportion of them went on to study at a university or college in the U.S. This last section is not relevant to the current study and therefore will not be discussed in this chapter.

Data Analysis

Once the completed surveys were received by the researchers, the data were entered using the Statistical Package for the Social Sciences, version 10.0.7 (2000). Subsequent analysis was performed with the aid of this statistical software. Teacher demographics were studied using descriptive statistics, including totals, percentages, and means. The hiring criteria were analyzed using a variety of statistical methods. In order to study the importance of each individual criterion, the mean, mode, and standard deviation for the various criteria were calculated. The relationships among the various criteria were explored using a hierarchical cluster analysis, designed to allow the identification of relatively homogeneous groups of variables. The hierarchical cluster analysis used Pearson correlations to measure the relationship between the various criteria (for a complete description of hierarchical cluster analysis, see Mahboob, 2003). In order to understand which criteria best explain the ratio of NNESTs employed in a program, a multivariate linear regression analysis using the stepwise method was conducted. In this case, the dependent variable was the ratio of NNESTs employed in a program, and the independent variables included the 10 hiring criteria rated by program administrators.

Results and Discussion

The two sections of the survey relevant to the present chapter were the instructor section and the administrative section. Within these sections, there were a number of questions that were utilized to keep the survey broad-based and to divert the attention of the respondents from the sensitive issue of NESTs and NNESTs. Before discussing the results of specific sections of the survey, the demographic information of the teachers will be presented.

The results of the survey analysis show that out of the 122 respondents, 115 program administrators provided information about the gender of the teachers employed in their programs. There was a total of 1,394 teachers in these 115 programs. Of these teachers, 1,016 were female and 378 were male. Thus, 72.8% of the teachers in the 115 IEPs were female and 27.2% were male. This figure implies that the majority of ESL teachers, approximately three-fourths, are female.

Table 1 provides a list of all the countries represented in the study and the number of teachers from each of these countries. The distribution of the countries in Table 1 suggests that there is no preference in hiring NNESTs based on their country of origin. By extension, it further suggests that Kachru's (1992) distinction between countries of the "Expanding Circle" (where English has a long history because of a colonial past and where it is used as an official language—e.g., Pakistan, India, Singapore) and countries of the "Outer Circle" (where English has recently gained popularity and where it is not used as an official language—e.g., Japan, China, Brazil) does not impact the distribution of NNESTs working in the IEPs.

The results presented in Table 1 also show that none of the program administrators listed the U.S. as a country of origin for any of their NNESTs. However, teachers who are born in the U.S. but who are not native speakers of English do exist. Therefore, it is possible that the

TABLE 1. Distribution of NNESTs Based on Their Country of Origin

Country of Origin	N	Country of Origin	N
Taiwan	8	Austria	1
China	6	Bulgaria	1
Brazil	5	Cambodia	1
Germany	5	Croatia	1
Russia	5	Ghana	1
Turkey	5	Greece	1
Japan	4	Guyana	1
Korea	4	Holland	1
Mexico	4	Italy	1
Morocco	4	Kenya	1
Poland	4	Kuwait	1
Czech	3	Latvia	1
Finland	3	Middle Eastern	1
Iran	3	Nepal	1
Lebanon	3	Nicaragua	1
Chile	2	Norway	1
Colombia	2	Pakistan	1
Egypt	2	Palestine	1
India	2	The Philippines	1
Israel	2	Romania	1
South Africa	2	Spain	1
Vietnam	2	Switzerland	1
Angola	1	Thailand	1
Argentina	1	Ukraine	1
Asian	1		
Total = 107			

program administrators failed to report the NNESTs who were born in the United Sates, or they might have reported information by country of heritage rather than origin. However, the current data do not provide any evidence to support either hypothesis. This issue needs to be further explored in a follow-up study.

Administrators were also asked to provide information on the teachers' language status. The results of the survey analysis show that 118 program administrators (out of the 122 respondents) provided answers to the relevant questions and reported having 1,313 NESTs and 112 NNESTs on their staff. These numbers mean that out of a total of 1,425 teachers, 7.86% were NNESTs and 92.14% were NESTs. The 112 NNESTs were hired by 50 of the 118 IEPs. Therefore, at the time of the survey, 68 IEPs (57.6%) employed only NESTs and 42.40% employed both NESTs and NNESTs. These results show that college-level IEPs in the United States do not have an equal representation of NNESTs and NESTs.

Program administrators were also asked to provide detailed information about the total number of teachers employed by their program and the distribution of these teachers based on their status as "native" or "nonnative" speakers of English and—in their capacity as instructors—as "full-time," "part-time," "graduate students," and/or "others." The results of the analysis are given in Table 2.

Table 2 shows that there were a higher number of NESTs in each category. There were 634 full-time NESTs compared to 25 full-time NNESTs. This implies that only 3.80% of the full-time staff was comprised of NNESTs. The percentage of full-time NNESTs was the lowest among the four categories of teachers listed. In addition to the full-time teachers, there were 550 part-time NESTs compared to 54 NNESTs. This implies that 9% of the part-time instructors were NNESTs. There were 110 native English-speaking graduate students teaching in the IEPs as compared to 29 nonnative English-speaking graduate students. Thus, 21% of the graduate student teacher population was comprised of NNESTs. This was the highest percentage of NNESTs in any category. The last category of teachers was listed as "others." There were 19

TABLE 2.   Distribution of NESTs and NNESTs by Position

Type of Position	NESTs		NNESTs	
	N	%	N	%
Full-time (with benefits)	634	96.20	25	3.80
Part-time (not graduate students)	550	91.00	54	9.00
Graduate students	110	79.00	29	21.00
Others (please specify)	19	83.00	4	17.00
Total	1,313	92.14	112	7.86

NESTs in this category and 4 NNESTs, meaning that 17.00% of teachers in the "others" category were NNESTs.

The total number of teachers in each of the IEPs surveyed ranged from 1 to 74, with the total number of NESTs in each of the various programs ranging from 1 to 68 and with the total number of NNESTs ranging from 0 to 14. Thus, the highest number of NNESTs in any of the programs was 14 (out of a total of 37 teachers). In order to understand the relationship between the number of NESTs and NNESTs in a program, ratios were calculated. However, before presenting the results of the ratio analysis, it is important to understand the function and the properties of the ratio. Ratios are used to display information about frequencies in relation to each other. Thus, theoretically, the ratio of NNESTs will be 0 if there are no NNESTs in a program, and it will be 1 if all the teachers in a program are NNESTs.

The actual distribution of the ratio in the 118 programs that provided information regarding the number of teachers in their program ranged between 0 and .4. As already noted, the majority of the programs ($N = 68$) did not have any NNESTs at the time of the survey. Therefore, they had a ratio of 0. In addition, among the 50 IEPs that did hire NNESTs, a high number of IEPs had a low ratio, implying that the proportion of NNESTs in these programs was low. The program with the highest ratio had a ratio of .4, implying that 40% of the teachers in this program were NNESTs. This program had a total of five teachers, of which three were NESTs and the other two NNESTs. The program with 14 NNESTs had a ratio of .378 (the second highest ratio). There were 16 IEPs with a ratio of .2 (meaning that at least 20% of the teachers in these programs were NNESTs). The majority of the programs (24 of them) had a ratio of less than .2 (meaning that less than 20% of the teachers in these program were NNESTs). This last finding shows that, in general, college-level IEPs in the United States that have hired NNESTs have similar proportions of NNESTs and NESTs in their programs (assuming, of course, that there are similar proportions of NNESTs seeking such jobs).

The survey also asked the program administrators to provide information about any undergraduate or graduate programs with which they were affiliated. One hundred and twenty program administrators responded to this question; out of these, 26 indicated that their program was affiliated with a department of applied linguistics, TESOL, or language education, and only 21 program administrators provided detailed information on the distribution of their undergraduate/graduate student population. Thus, the results given in Table 3 are based on 21 programs only.

As Table 3 shows, the number of undergraduate students enrolled in the programs with which the 21 IEPs are affiliated was 297. The

TABLE 3. Distribution of Student Population in the Program with Which the IEPs Are Affiliated

Type of Students Enrolled in the Program Affiliated with the English Language Program	Total Number of Students	Average Number of Students per Program ($N = 21$)
Undergraduate students	297	14.14
Graduate students	356	16.95
International graduate students	173	8.23

number of graduate students was 356, and out of these, 173 were international students. These results mean that of 356 graduate students in 21 programs, 48.59% are international students. This figure is comparable to that found elsewhere in relevant literature (see Kamhi-Stein, 1999; Liu, 1999).

In this study, the respondents were not asked to provide the number of nonnative English-speaking graduate students who are U.S. citizens. According to Kamhi-Stein (personal communication), there may be a substantial number of graduate students who are U.S. citizens and consider themselves nonnative speakers of English. Thus, the 48.59% in this study only represents the percentage of international graduate students in the 21 programs that provided information on their visa status and may not reflect the total percentage of nonnative English-speaking graduate students in the programs. It is possible that the actual number of nonnative graduate students is higher than the 48.59% presented earlier.

The number of international graduate students in a program was correlated with the ratio of NNESTs employed in the affiliated intensive English program (IEP). The results of this analysis show that no significant correlation was found between the ratio of NNESTs in an IEP and the number of international graduate students in its affiliated teacher preparation program. This lack of a correlation implies that the number of international (nonnative) students in a graduate program is not related to the number of NNESTs employed in an affiliated IEP. This result supports the idea that the IEP administrators do not place much emphasis on "enrollment in associated academic program" as a criterion for hiring prospective instructors.

The ratio of NNESTs who were also graduate students in an affiliated program was correlated with the number of international graduate students (if any) in those programs. This was done to verify the aforementioned lack of a significant correlation between the number of international graduate students and the ratio of NNESTs in a program. There were 10 IEPs that employed graduate students enrolled in the programs with which they were affiliated. The result of the analysis for the 10 IEPs that hired graduate students showed that there was not a significant correlation between the number of international graduate students enrolled in a program and the ratio of graduate students from a nonnative English-speaking background teaching in an affiliated program (p = .57). This lack of a significant correlation supports the earlier finding that there is not a relationship between the ratio of NNESTs employed in an IEP and the presence or absence of international students in an affiliated program.

Administrative Questions

This part of the study asked the respondents to rank 10 criteria in making hiring decisions: "accent," "citizenship," "nationality," "dialect," "educational experience," "enrollment in affiliated educational program," "native English speaker," "recommendation," "ethnicity," and "teaching experience." The results for this question, presented in Table 4, are based on 122 responses (100% of the surveys that were received). Table 4 provides a ranking of the mean ratings, as well as the mode and standard deviation for each criterion.

As shown in Table 4, "teaching experience" received the highest mean rating among the 10 hiring criteria (M = 4.28). In addition, the standard deviation for this criterion was relatively low (at 1.35) when compared to standard deviations for other criteria, indicating that the respondents were in general agreement with one another about the importance of this criterion in their hiring decisions. "Educational experience" was the second highest ranked criterion. Its mean was 4.15 with a standard deviation of 1.35. Moreover, the mode was 5, suggesting that a high number of respondents believe that educational experience is a key criterion in making hiring decisions.

TABLE 4.   Ranking of Mean Ratings, Standard Deviation, and Mode for the Various Hiring Criteria

	Mean Ratings		
Hiring Criteria	M	SD	Mode
Teaching experience	4.28	1.35	5
Educational experience	4.15	1.35	5
Recommendation	3.55	1.37	4
Native English speaker	2.86	1.83	5
Accent	2.86	1.66	4
Dialect	1.93	1.69	0
Citizenship	1.24	1.61	0
Nationality	1.13	1.47	0
Enrollment in affiliated academic program	1.08	1.54	0
Ethnicity	0.74	1.08	0

Note: Scale 0 = not important at all, 1 = not very important, 2 = slightly important, 3 = somewhat important, 4 = moderately important, 5 = very important.

Table 4 also shows that program administrators find the "recommendation" criteria to be important in making hiring decisions. It received a moderately high mean rating of 3.55 and a standard deviation of 1.37. The mean for the "native English speaker" criterion was 2.86. However, when viewing this mean in light of a mode of 5 and a standard deviation of 1.83 (the highest for any of the criteria listed), it can be seen that program administrators were, in fact, split in their rating of this criterion. Table 5 shows this split in the IEP administrators' rating of this criterion. As can be seen in the table, 45.9% of the respondents indicated that this criterion was moderately to highly important in making hiring decisions, while 29.5% of the respondents felt that this criterion was not very important or not important at all.

Figure 1 illustrates the results presented in Table 4. As can be noted in the figure, the bars form a U curve. This U curve, also known as an

TABLE 5. Importance in Hiring: Relative Weight Given to the "Native English Speaker" Criterion

Relative Weight Given to the "Native English Speaker" Criterion	N	%
Not important at all	20	16.4
Not very important	16	13.1
Slightly important	13	10.7
Somewhat important	17	13.9
Moderately important	24	19.7
Highly important	32	26.2
Total	122	100.00

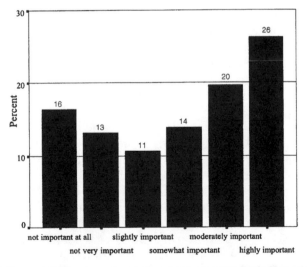

FIG. 1. Relative weight, in percentage, given to the "native English speaker" criterion

inverted bell curve, is indicative of bimodalism, implying that most respondents preferred to rank the "native speaker" criterion at either the lower end (0–1) or the higher end (4–5). This also accounts for the high standard deviation of this criterion.

As Table 5 and Figure 1 suggest, the native/nonnative status of a potential teacher is an issue in the field: administrators consider it either very important or not important at all. The high mode of 5 (see Table 4) suggests that being a native speaker is an important criterion for a majority of the administrators (59.8% of the respondents considered it at least somewhat important). The importance given to the criterion suggests one reason why NNESTs seem to be underrepresented in IEPs in the United States.

The results presented in Table 4 also show that the mean rating received by the hiring criterion entitled "accent" was 2.86 with a standard deviation of 1.66 and a mode of 4. This relatively high mean rating considered in the light of the high mode suggests that "accent" forms an important criterion for making hiring decisions for quite a number of programs. A question that would be of interest here, although not asked in the current survey, would be about administrators' preference of specific accents and how they define accent in general.

Table 4 also shows that "dialect" received a mean rating of 1.93 and a mode of 0 but had one of the highest standard deviations among the criteria (SD = 1.69). Clearly, this result shows that there was notable variation among the respondents regarding the importance of dialect in making hiring decisions, but since the mean rank remains low, overall, this criterion was not very important for most program administrators.

U.S. citizenship was ranked low, with a mean of 1.24. Since the mode for this criterion was 0, the implication is that most administrators think that it is not of much importance in making hiring decisions. Like citizenship, U.S. nationality was rated low by the respondents. The mean for this criterion was 1.13 with a relatively low standard deviation of 1.47. The mode for this criterion was also 0, implying that many respondents did not find it useful in making hiring decisions.

The results of the study also show that the criterion titled "enrollment in associated academic program" was not considered very important by most of the program administrators (see Table 4). The majority of the respondents found this criterion to be of little value in making hiring decisions. The mean rating for this criterion was 1.08 with a standard deviation of 1.54. The mode for this criterion was 0. The lack of importance given to this criterion is an important finding. As documented in relevant literature cited earlier (Kamhi-Stein, 1999; Liu, 1999), there is a high number of international students in academic programs in TESOL and applied linguistics. A lack of importance given to potential teachers' affiliations to associated degree/professional programs suggests that nonnative graduate and undergraduate students enrolled in such programs do not necessarily receive any special consideration just because of their links to affiliated programs. Thus, it seems, there may not be a notable relationship between an IEP being affiliated to a graduate degree program and the number of NNESTs that the IEP hires.

As shown in Table 4, "ethnicity" received the lowest mean rating among all the criteria ($M = .74$). The standard deviation, also the lowest, was 1.08. The mode for this criterion was 0. Taking all these figures into account, these results suggest that ethnicity was of very little value to most of the respondents when they made hiring decisions. A lack of emphasis on ethnicity is interesting. According to Amin (1999), an unmarked ESL teacher is an Anglo-white male native speaker of English. Amin's comment suggests that ethnicity, as well as gender, may play an important role in making hiring decisions. However, the present data are not sufficient to evaluate the role of these two criteria as suggested by Amin.

Relationship and Hierarchy between Various Criteria

In order to understand the relationship between various criteria, a hierarchical cluster analysis was conducted. This analysis allowed the identification of relatively homogeneous groups of variables. The hierarchical cluster analysis performed in this study used Pearson correlations to measure the relationship between various criteria.

The results of the hierarchical cluster analysis show that the 10 criteria fall into three major clusters. These three clusters have been labeled "professional background," "linguistic background," and "personal background." This classification is important because it groups together the different criteria. The order in which these three clusters are described here represents the average importance given to the criteria in each cluster.

Three criteria, "educational experience," "teaching experience," and "recommendation," fall into the "professional background" cluster. All of these criteria deal with professional qualifications of teachers. There is a very close relationship between "educational experience" and "teaching experience" ($r = .771, p < .001$), and these two criteria are also related to "recommendation." Another three criteria, "accent," "dialect," and "native English speaker," fall into the "linguistic background" cluster. Within this cluster, "accent" and "dialect" are more closely (but not highly) related to each other ($r = .509, p < .001$) than to "native English speaker." The last cluster, "personal background," is formed by four criteria, "U.S. citizenship," "U.S. nationality," "ethnic-

ity," and "enrollment in associated academic program." These criteria
deal with various aspects of teachers' personal background. Within
this cluster, "U.S. citizenship" and "U.S. nationality," perhaps unsur-
prisingly (because of the similarity in their meaning), form the closest
relationship (r = .806, p < .001). These two criteria are also related to
"ethnicity" and to "enrollment in associated academic program."

Relationship between Total Number of NNESTs and Criteria for Hiring

In this section, the relationship between various criteria and the ratio
of NNESTs in a program is reported. This relationship is first presented
through a correlation between the 10 criteria and the ratio of NNESTs
working in a program. The results based on this correlation analysis
help identify significant relationships between any of the criteria and
the ratio. Table 6 presents the results of the analysis.

Table 6 shows that the "native English speaker" criterion had the
highest (negative) correlation with the ratio of NNESTs in a program.
In addition, this was the only significant correlation found between
any of the 10 criteria and the ratio of NNESTs in an IEP (r = −.375, p
< .001). The negative value of the correlation is important. It implies
that the less importance the administrators gave to the "native English speaker" criterion, the higher the number of NNESTs in an IEP
was. Conversely, the more importance the administrators gave to the
"native English speaker" criterion, the lower the number of NNESTs
in that IEP was.

It is important to point out that while "educational experience,"
"teaching experience" and "recommendation" had a higher mean
rating than "native English speaker," they did not correlate with the
actual ratio of NNESTs in a program. This observation suggests that,

TABLE 6.   Correlation of the Ratio of NNESTs and NESTs in a Program
and the 10 Hiring Criteria

Hiring Criteria	Pearson Correlation	Sig. (2-tailed)
Accent	−.014	.899
U.S. citizenship	−.141	.204
U.S. nationality	−.071	.526
Dialect	−.036	.750
Educational experience	−.103	.356
Enrollment in associated academic program	.016	.884
Ethnicity	−.138	.215
Native English speaker	−.375*	.001
Recommendation	.090	.419
Teaching experience	−.022	.842

*Correlation is significant at the .01 level (2-tailed).

in making hiring decisions, the importance given to being a "native English speaker" is more significant than the professional background of teachers.

A correlation analysis only studies two variables at a time. Therefore, in addition to the correlation analysis, a multivariate linear regression using the stepwise method was conducted in order to explain the ratio of NNESTs in a program. A linear, stepwise regression was used to find the independent variables that best explained the dependent variable. In this case, the dependent variable was the ratio of NNESTs employed in a program, and the independent variables included the 10 hiring criteria rated by program administrators. Table 7 presents the results of the regression analysis.

The results presented in Table 7 show that the dependent variable, the ratio of NNESTs in a program, may be explained by focusing on three independent variables, that is, three criteria. The three independent variables that significantly explain the dependent variable are "recommendation," "native English speaker," and "teaching experience." Among these, the most significant independent variable was "native English speaker" with the highest t-value of -4.498 ($p < .001$). The second statistically significant independent variable was "recommendation" with a t-value of 2.659 ($p < .01$), and the third statistically significant independent variable was "teaching experience" with a t-value of 2.383 ($p < .05$).

The negative t-value of "native English speaker" implies that the ratio of NNESTs in a program will be higher if the program administrator of that program ranks "native English speaker" as an unimportant criterion. Thus, there may be a greater number of NNESTs in a program if the administrator of that program places a low emphasis on the "native English speaker" criterion. This finding is also supported by the negative correlation discussed earlier and shows that there is a relationship between the importance given to the "native English speaker" factor and the actual ratio of NNESTs in a program.

In addition to the "native English speaker" criterion, "recommendation" was found to be a significant independent variable that explains the ratio of NNESTs in an IEP. This result means that administrators

TABLE 7. Results of the Regression Analysis

| Hiring Criteria | Unstandardized Coefficients | | Standardized Coefficients | | Level of Significance |
	B	Std. Error	Beta	t	
Recommendation	1.83E-02	.007	.579	2.659	.009
Native English speaker	−2.20E-02	.005	−.617	−4.498	.001
Teaching experience	1.42E-02	.006	.525	2.383	.019

who place emphasis on recommendation letters are more likely to hire NNESTs in their program, given that all other variables are equal. This finding suggests that for NNESTs to be hired, they must provide strong references.

The last important result of the regression analysis shows that "teaching experience" also explains the ratio of NNESTs in a program. This finding implies that administrators who may hire NNESTs look for high educational qualifications in their teachers (all other variables being equal). Thus, NNESTs who are hired must have high educational qualifications in a related field.

In summary, the results of the regression analysis suggest that if the administrator considers "native English speaker" to be an important criterion for hiring, and if not much weight is given to recommendations and teaching experience, that program will have a low ratio of NNESTs. In other words, these results may be interpreted to suggest that for NNESTs to obtain a job in a particular college-level IEP in the United States, they must have strong recommendation letters and high educational qualifications in TESOL or applied linguistics or a related field, and, most important, they must apply to a program whose administrators do not believe that being a native speaker is an important characteristic of an ESL teacher.

It should be noted that the three significant variables belonged to either the "professional background" cluster or the "linguistic background" cluster. The variables in the "personal background" cluster were not found to be significant. This lack of importance given to personal background by program administrators when making hiring decisions was also observed earlier in the discussion of the mean ratings of the 10 criteria. This confirmation of results based on different analytical procedures adds reliability to the findings.

The finding that administrators favor the hiring criterion titled "native English speaker," taken together with the low number of NNESTs in the 118 IEPs surveyed (7.9%), provides empirical evidence to support Cook's (2000) and Medgyes' (1992) observations that administrators prefer to hire native speakers over nonnative speakers.

Summary of Findings and Conclusion

The results of the college-level IEPs' survey, based on data collected from 118 IEP administrators throughout the United States, showed that out of a total of 1,425 ESL teachers in these programs, only 112 were NNESTs. Thus, it can be concluded that the number of NESTs working in IEPs is substantially higher than the number of NNESTs.

The correlation analysis shows that the number of international students in a graduate program is not related to the number of

NNESTs working in an affiliated IEP. The lack of a significant correlation suggests that the presence or absence of international graduate students in a graduate degree program is not related to the number of NNESTs who teach in the affiliated IEP. The results of the analysis of the survey also show that more program administrators consider "native English speaker" an important criterion than do not (59.8% of the respondents considered it at least "somewhat important"). A correlation analysis between the various hiring criteria and the ratio of NNESTs working in a program further suggests that there is a link between a low number of NNESTs in IEPs and administrators' emphasis on "native English speaker" status. A negative correlation was found between the relative importance given to "native English speaker" in the hiring process and the ratio of NNESTs in a program. This negative correlation suggests that the more importance a program administrator gives to a teacher's status as a native speaker, the smaller the ratio of NNESTs in that program will be. In addition to the correlation, a regression analysis with the ratio of NNESTs being the dependent variable and the 10 criteria being the independent variables was conducted. The results of this regression analysis showed that the criterion "native English speaker" most significantly explains the ratio of NNESTs in a program. Two other significant independent variables that significantly explained the ratio of NNESTs in a program were "recommendation" and "teaching experience."

In summary, an analysis of the surveys collected from 122 college-level IEPs revealed the following:

1. Most program administrators give a rating of "somewhat important" to teachers' "native English speaker" status.
2. There is a significant negative correlation between the relative importance given to the "native English speaker" hiring criterion and the ratio of NNESTs in that program (this was the only criterion that significantly correlated with the ratio); that is, the more importance program administrators give to the "native English speaker" criterion, the smaller the number of NNESTs employed in their programs will be.
3. There is a lower proportion of NNESTs to NESTs in actual practice in U.S.-based IEPs.
4. There is a lack of a significant correlation between the number of NNESTs employed in an IEP and the number of international graduate students in an affiliated program.
5. The criteria "native English speaker," "recommendation," and "teaching experience" were found to be the only three significant independent variables (out of a total of 10 independent variables) that significantly explain the ratio of NNESTs in a program.

While the response rate in this study was respectable, future studies relying on mailed surveys should consider including a second mailing or sending the survey to a randomly selected subset of the total number of IEPs to increase their response rate. Also, future studies should give respondents an opportunity to list additional criteria that they might use in making hiring decisions. This might reveal factors that administrators consider important in hiring that were not included in the survey. Finally, in addition to collecting data from college-level IEPs, future studies should collect data from IEPs associated with various community colleges across the United States as well as K–12 educational institutions.

At this time, based on the results of this investigation, it can be concluded that "native English speaker" status is an important factor in the hiring of teachers at college-level IEPs. Regardless of other qualifications that NNESTs might have, they are not equally represented in U.S.-based IEPs, even though NNESTs comprise a majority of the world's English teachers and a substantial number of graduate students in TESOL graduate classes in the U.S. Taking into consideration the results of this study, it can be said that nonnative speakers of English are treated as "children of a lesser English" in the profession of English language teaching in the United States. Should U.S.-based IEPs seek to offer their international students exemplary role models of nonnative English-speaking teachers, and should they seek to reflect a realistic and inclusive picture of the diversity represented by world Englishes, then IEPs would do well to examine their hiring practices and include increasing numbers of NNESTs among their staff.

Appendix A

ENGLISH LANGUAGE PROGRAMS SURVEY

I. Administrative Questions

1. On a scale of 0 to 5 (0 being the least important and 5 being the most important), please rank *each* of the following criteria for hiring ESL instructors in your English Language Program.

_____ Accent	_____ Enrollment in associated academic program
_____ American citizenship	_____ Ethnicity
_____ American nationality	_____ Native English speaker
_____ Dialect	_____ Recommendation
_____ Educational experience	_____ Teaching experience

2. What professional development opportunities (seminars, workshops, classes, etc.) are available on a pre-service or an ongoing basis to your instructors?

3. Which of the following criteria do you use to evaluate instructors in your English Language Program? (You may mark one or more of the following.)

_____ Student evaluations	_____ Classroom observations
_____ Other (please specify)	

4. Do you use an integrated/holistic approach to language teaching, or do you teach skills (listening, speaking, reading, writing, and grammar) in separate classes?

5. How many ability levels (e.g., Three: 1 = beginning, 2 = intermediate, 3 = advanced) are there in your English Language Program?

6. Which of the following criteria do you use when placing students into various levels in your English Language Program? *You may mark one or more of the following.*

_____ TOEFL score	_____ Michigan Test
_____ In-house placement exam	_____ Others (please specify)
_____ Class grades	

II. Instructor Questions

7. Do you have an undergraduate or a graduate program affiliated with your English Language Program? (e.g., applied linguistics, TESOL, language education, etc.)

   Yes   No

   If "yes," please answer the following questions:

   a.   How many undergraduate students do you have in the program?
   b.   How many graduate students do you have in the program?
   c.   How many of those graduate students are international students?

8. How many instructors are there in your English Language Program?

   a.   How many are females?
   b.   How many are males?

9. How many of your English Language Program instructors are:

   Full-time (with benefits):   Native speakers[2] _____
                                         Non-native speakers_____

   Part-time (not graduate students):   Native speakers _____
                                         Non-native speakers _____

   Graduate students: Native speakers _____
                                         Non-native speakers_____

   Others (please specify):   Native speakers _____
                                         Non-native speakers_____

10. Do all your instructors have specific training in English as a Second Language (ESL), linguistics, Foreign Language Teaching (FLT), etc.?

    Yes   No

    If you answered "no," what are the minimum required educational qualifications for instructors in your English Language Program?

11. Do your graduate students teach as paid instructors, or do they teach as part of a practicum experience?

12. If you have any instructors who are non-native speakers, which countries are they from?

III. Student Questions

13. How many students are currently enrolled in your English language program?

14. Which countries are represented among your students? Which countries have the highest representation?

15. Approximately what proportion of your students go on to study at a university or college in the United States?

_____ 5–10%   _____ 50–75%
_____ 10–25%   _____ 75–100%
_____ 25–50%   _____ Unknown

Notes

An earlier version of this study was presented at the 36th annual meeting of Teachers of English to Speakers of Other Languages, Salt Lake City, UT, April 2002.
1. All four authors contributed to the design of the survey instrument used for this study. However, the first author was responsible for the analysis presented in this chapter (see Mahboob, 2003, for a complete version of the study).
2. The term *native* here includes American, Australian, and British English, and so on.

References

Alatis, J., & Straehle, C. (1997). The universe of English: Imperialism, chauvinism, and paranoia. In L. A. Smith & M. Forman (Eds.), *World Englishes 2000* (pp. 1–20). Honolulu: University of Hawaii.

Amin, N. (1999). Minority women teachers of ESL: Negotiating white English. In G. Braine (Ed.), *Non-native educators in English language teaching* (pp. 93–104). Mahwah, NJ: Erlbaum.

Braine, G. (1999). *Non-native educators in English language teaching*. Mahwah, NJ: Erlbaum.

British Council. (1986). *English language and literature* (Activity Report No 4). London: Author.

Canagarajah, A. S. (1999). Interrogating the "native speaker fallacy": Non-linguistic roots, non-pedagogical results. In G. Braine (Ed.), *Non-native educators in English language teaching* (pp. 77–92). Mahwah, NJ: Erlbaum.

Cook, V. (2000). The author responds . . . *TESOL Quarterly, 34,* 329–332.

Institute of International Education. (1997). *English language and orientation programs in the United States.* Annapolis, MD: Author.

Kachru, B. B. (1992). Teaching world Englishes. In B. B. Kachru (Ed.), *The other tongue: English across cultures* (2nd ed., pp. 355–365). Chicago: University of Illinois Press.

Kachru, B. B. (1996). The paradigms of marginality. *World Englishes, 15*(3), 241–255.

Kamhi-Stein, L. D. (1999). Preparing non-native professionals in TESOL: Implications for teacher education programs. In G. Braine (Ed.), *Non-native educators in English language teaching* (pp. 145–158). Mahwah, NJ: Erlbaum.

Liu, D. (1999). Training non-native TESOL students: Challenges for TESOL teacher education in the West. In G. Braine (Ed.), *Non-native educators in English language teaching* (pp. 197–210). Mahwah, NJ: Erlbaum.

Mahboob, A. (2003). *Status of nonnative English speakers as ESL teachers in the United States.* Unpublished doctoral dissertation, Indiana University, Bloomington.

Medgyes, P. (1992). Native or non-native: Who's worth more? *ELT Journal, 46*(4), 340–349.

Reves, T., & Medgyes, P. (1994). The non-native English speaking EFL/ESL teacher's self-image: An international survey. *System, 22*(3), 353–367.

Statistical package for the social sciences (Version 10.0.7). (2000). Chicago: SPSS.

Tang, C. (1997). On the power and status of nonnative ESL teachers. *TESOL Quarterly, 31*(3), 577–580.

Native or Nonnative: What Do Students Enrolled in an Intensive English Program Think?

Ahmar Mahboob
East Carolina University

The work on nonnative English-speaking teachers' (NNESTs) issues, for the most part, has examined the self-perceptions and personal histories of NNESTs themselves. Recently there has been some work on administrative issues as well (Flynn & Gulikers, 2001; Mahboob, Uhrig, Newman, & Hartford, this volume). In addition to this work, some researchers (Cook, 2000; Liu, 1999; Medgyes, 1992) have discussed the underrepresented status of NNESTs within English as a second language (ESL) and English as a foreign language (EFL) programs. These researchers have pointed out that program administrators generally prefer hiring native English-speaking teachers (NESTs) to NNESTs because administrators perceive that ESL students do not want NNESTs as their teachers. However, perceptions of ESL students are not well represented in the literature on NNESTs, especially the perceptions of ESL students in the United States.

Mahboob et al. (this volume) present the results of a study focusing on the hiring criteria of English language program (ELP) administrators in the United States. The results of their study show that the majority of program administrators agree that the "native English speaker" criterion is important in making hiring decisions. The results of the study showed that the more importance program administrators gave to the "native English speaker" criterion, the lower the ratio of NNESTs employed in their programs was. These results support

121

the idea that program administrators perceive "nativeness" to be
important and give it significant weight when hiring teachers. These
findings, thus, provide empirical support to claims that there is a
bias in favor of NESTs in the profession (Braine, 1999; Cook, 1999;
Medgyes, 1992).

As mentioned earlier, the literature on NNESTs suggests that the
reason why program administrators stress "nativeness" is that they
perceive that students in their programs prefer NESTs over NNESTs.
However, administrators' perceptions have not been systematically
studied. And there currently are only a few studies of students' perceptions of and preferences for "nativeness" in a teacher (Cook, 2000;
Liang, 2002). In one, Cook (2000) summarizes his findings and states,
"nowhere is there an overwhelming preference for NS [native speaker]
teachers. Being an NS is only one among many factors that influence
students' views of teaching" (p. 331). Cook further states that while
program administrators believe that students prefer native speaker
teachers, students in various countries themselves do not have an
"overwhelming preference" (p. 331) for NESTs. He believes that "nativeness" is not a major factor in influencing students' views. However,
Cook does not discuss the reasons for these perceptions.

The purpose of this study is to explore ESL students' perceptions
of both NESTs and NNESTs and to investigate what students think
about the "native" status. The study also investigates factors that
influence students' perceptions of their teachers. Students' perceptions presented in this chapter are, when possible, compared and
contrasted with teachers' perceptions of themselves and with other
references to related research on NNESTs.

The Study

The purpose of this study is to evaluate ESL students' attitudes toward
NESTs and NNESTs. In order to do this, the study relies on qualitative
data (Hyrkstedt & Kalaja, 1998). The use of qualitative data to explore
students' attitudes is a break away from traditional methods used in
attitude studies and has several advantages.

Most studies of language attitudes and perceptions tend to use one
of three methods. Ryan, Giles, and Sebastian (1982) present a detailed
overview of these methods. According to them, the technique of "content analysis of societal treatment" (p. 7) relies on the use of existing
documents that may be available as well as ethnographic observations that do not explicitly solicit information from respondents. In
contrast to this technique, the "direct measurement" (p. 7) technique
solicits respondents' beliefs and attitudes by using individual or group
interviews/questionnaires. A third method used in language attitude

studies, the "indirect measurement" (p. 7), became widely used in the 1960s (with the studies of language attitudes toward English and French in Montreal). This indirect method, popularly known as the "matched-guise approach," uses pre-recorded oral stimulus in different varieties as spoken by a single speaker. Listeners' attitudes toward the various guises (i.e., different varieties that are actually spoken by the same person) are recorded and then analyzed.

Although these three methods have been extensively used in research on language attitudes, their validity and reliability have been questioned. The criticism against the matched-guise technique is particularly severe. In summarizing the problems associated with this technique, Hyrkstedt and Kalaja (1998) state,

> To begin with, the technique has been criticized for its low reliability and validity, as it is difficult to generalize findings from experiments and apply them to real-life situations; second, for its uncritical choice of speech samples and insensitive treatment of subjects. In addition, the technique separates the attitude object from its evaluation. More importantly, the technique forces subjects to respond along dimensions that have been worked out by researchers, instead of along dimensions of their own choice. (p. 346)

In order to avoid these problems, especially the last one listed, Hyrkstedt and Kalaja used a "discourse-analytic" technique to explore the attitudes toward English in Finland. Hyrkstedt and Kalaja gave a "letter-to-the-editor" to their respondents (80 college students), asking them to write a response to the letter. The response essays were collected by the researchers and coded. In coding the essays, the researchers created categories of responses and counted the distribution of comments in each category. However, instead of categorizing the responses based on predefined categories, the researchers let the categories evolve out of the data. In this sense, they based their analysis in grounded theory (Babchuk, 1997), which also stresses the importance of allowing categories to emerge from data rather than using a priori categories. The findings of the study were then discussed based on the categories that evolved out of the responses and the distribution of the responses (as either positive or negative) among the categories.

Hyrkstedt and Kalaja's technique of studying language attitudes avoids the criticism discussed earlier that was leveled against other techniques used in studies on language attitudes. In addition, the development of categories based on the data (in contrast to an analysis that uses predefined categories) allows for an exploratory analysis of the data. The current study has adopted the discourse analytic technique in studying and analyzing ESL students' perceptions of NESTs and NNESTs.

Participants

In order to elicit students' perceptions of NNESTs, all students enrolled in an intensive English program (IEP) at a large midwestern university were invited to write an essay on a given topic. Students in this program are provided with classroom instruction for four to five hours daily. This IEP has both native and nonnative English speakers as language instructors. Thus, the participants in this study were familiar with having NNESTs as teachers in the United States. However, whether or not the particular student writers in this study had studied with a NNEST in this IEP was not explored.

A total of 37 students volunteered to participate in the essay writing. All were adults and came from diverse linguistic backgrounds. The language proficiency of these students varied; however, based on a holistic evaluation of their essays, the students were at either an intermediate or an advanced level. Because of the small size of the program (the total number of students in the program was approximately 200) and in order to maintain complete confidentiality and anonymity, biographical information about the students was not collected.

Instrument

Following the technique used by Hyrkstedt and Kalaja (1998), participants in this study were given a stimulus topic and asked to write their reactions to the stimulus. The cue given to them stated:

> Some students think that only native speakers can be good language teachers. Others think that nonnatives can also be efficient teachers. What is your opinion about this issue? Please feel free to provide details and examples.

As can be noted in the preceding stimulus, impartiality was maintained in the statement. Students were therefore free to explore and write their own perceptions regarding this issue. In order to not influence students' essay content, the essay writing was supervised by one of the teachers (a native speaker of Anglo-American English) in the program. Neither the researcher, a nonnative English speaker, nor any other NNESTs were present during the time the students wrote these essays. The students were informed of the strict confidentiality and anonymity of their essays and were told that their essays would not be used to evaluate them in any way. Students were given 35 minutes to write their essays.

Data Analysis

Out of the 37 essays collected, 4 were discarded because the essays were written entirely on the students' English language learning experience in their own countries, which (although interesting) was not a focus of the current study. One additional essay was disqualified because the student wrote off topic. Thus, the results of the study are based on 32 ESL student essays.

Students' responses to the stimulus were analyzed using a discourse analytic technique, following Hyrkstedt and Kalaja (1998). The 32 essays were coded by four readers (the use of multiple coders has been advocated by Babchuk, 1997). No a priori categories were used in the analysis of the essays; rather, the categories emerged as a result of the analysis. Emphasis on not having a priori categories stemmed from the fear that predetermined categories may perpetuate ideas that did not reflect the students' actual perceptions as well as distract the researcher from observing other uncategorized dynamics in the data.

In the first stage of the analysis, the four readers coded the essays individually. Each individual read and coded the essays using different-colored highlighters for the various types of comments that they found important. Then, the four readers got together and generated a list of categories of students' comments about both NESTs and NNESTs. These categories were then labeled. Any differences in opinion or categorization were resolved after a brief discussion. The total number of comments in each category was counted. This count was distributed within a category based on whether a comment was positive (+) or negative (–) in its evaluation. The final stage in the analysis involved sorting the individual categories into major groups and labeling the groups.

Findings

Three broad groups of categories encompassing 10 individual categories emerged from the data analysis. The first group, "linguistic factors," included "oral skills," "literacy skills," "grammar," "vocabulary," and "culture." The second group, "teaching styles," included "ability to answer questions" and "teaching methodology." The third group, "personal factors," included "experience as a second language (L2) learner," "hard work," and "affect." Following are the results of the analysis.

Linguistic Factors

As noted earlier, there were five linguistic factors that students referred to in their discussion of NESTs and NNESTs. The distribution of comments across these factors is given in Table 1.

TABLE 1. Distribution of Comments for the Linguistic Factors

	NESTs		NNESTs	
	Positive Comments	Negative Comments	Positive Comments	Negative Comments
Linguistic Factors	(N)	(N)	(N)	(N)
Oral skills	15	0	5	5
Literacy skills	0	0	3	0
Grammar	0	4	12	0
Vocabulary	8	0	4	0
Culture	6	0	4	1
Total	29	4	28	6

Table 1 shows that there were 67 comments distributed over the five linguistic categories. There were 29 positive and 4 negative comments about NESTs and 28 positive and 6 negative statements about NNESTs. These results are presented next.

Oral skills. The category of "oral skills" included comments that discussed the teaching of listening and speaking/pronunciation. The teaching of oral skills was considered the forte of the NESTs. There were 25 statements in this category, the highest for any one category. Fifteen of these comments discussed the role of NESTs, while the other 10 discussed the role of NNESTs in teaching this skill.

All 15 students' comments related to NESTs were positive. In general, these comments stated that native speakers can provide an ideal model for pronunciation. The following two examples from the essays express students' perceptions of NESTs' ability to teach oral skills:

> The best part of having native speakers as teachers is you can learn natural pronunciation from them. And it is very effective to your listening and speaking. (Student #8)

> . . . when native speakers teach, students can learn right rhythm and pronounciation (Student #34)

These two statements show that NESTs were preferred as teachers of oral skills because "you can learn natural pronunciation from them." This is interesting because research in L2 acquisition indicates that pronunciation is one of the linguistic skills that is the hardest to acquire at a native speaker level for adult ESL students (Dalton-Puffer, Kaltenboeck, & Smit, 1997). However, the results just presented support findings by Arva and Medgyes (2000). In their study of teacher perceptions, they found that the communicative ability of NESTs is perceived to be their strongest attribute by both NESTs and NNESTs. Thus, students' perceptions about NNESTs' oral skills are corroborated by studies focusing on the self-perceptions of EFL teachers (see Lippi-Green, 1997, for information on the relationship between teacher accentedness and ethnicity).

As compared to NESTs, NNESTs received mixed reviews as teachers of oral skills. Out of the 10 comments that referred to NNESTs, 5 were positive and the other 5 were negative. The positive comments elaborated on the NNESTs ability to identify the exact problems with their learners' pronunciation and to teach them how to correct it. The following example illustrates this:

> . . . non-native speakers try to teach our mistakes. . . . I think that English pronunciation are difficult for Asian. . . . he [NNEST] always found my mistakes of English (Student #1)

On the other hand, the negative comments regarding NNESTs' ability to teach oral skills mostly focused on NNESTs' perceived nonstandard pronunciation. Students felt that NNESTs were not the best teachers for oral skills because they were themselves nonnnative-like. The following statement is an example of such comments:

> Although they sometime have problem in pronunciation . . . students can get many other from non-natives. (Student #6)

This student states that NNESTs are not good teachers of oral skills because of their "problematic" pronunciation; however, the student feels that ESL students can learn other skills from NNESTs.

Interestingly, some students felt that while NNESTs can be good teachers of listening, they may not be good teachers of speaking. One student discussed this issue at some length and wrote,

> Non-native speakers speak worse than native speakers. But pronuncian is just one part of language. Although non-native speakers cannot speak very well and they have a limit, on the contrary they can teach very well other parts of language; grammar, reading, writing and even listening. (Student #26)

This student, like many others, considered the speech of native speakers as standard and all other variations as being "worse" or less than standard.

Another student expressed concern about the prejudice experienced by nonnative English speakers who have an accent that differs from what is expected to be the mainstream accent:

> Some people have a prejudice about pronunciation, which mean non-native speaker's pronunciations is a little different, so their teaching is not good. I

think that is bad idea. Important thing is teacher's knowledge not pronunciation. If we can understand teacher's pronunciation, it's not a problem. In
IEP, some teachers are non-native speaker but I think they have more zeal
and wider knowledge. (Student #33)

This student raises a number of important issues. The student points
out that there is a "prejudice" within the student body against NNESTs'
pronunciation. However, this student also suggests that not all students feel this way. For this student, teachers' knowledge, not their
accent or pronunciation, is important. The student also points out
that in the program in which he or she studies, there are a number
of NNESTs who have "more zeal and wider knowledge" than NESTs.
This reference to NNESTs in his or her own program suggests that this
student has been taught by at least one nonnative English speaker.
This student's comment suggests the possibility that students' perceptions of NNESTs may be different (and may change) based on whether
they have or have not studied with a nonnative English speaker in
the United States. The comment may be interpreted to suggest that
students who have not studied with NNESTs may find pronunciation
to be an important factor, while those who have studied with them
find teachers' knowledge to be a more important factor.

Though not focusing on students themselves, the results of a study
by Reves and Medgyes (1994) in an EFL setting supports the notion
that EFL teachers from a nonnative English-speaking background may
feel "deficient" in their language skills. Similarly, in another study, Arva
and Medgyes (2000) refer to statements from NNESTs indicating that
their oral skills were not very good. Arva and Medgyes quote one nonnative English-speaking teacher who felt that "because this is a learnt
language, it doesn't come spontaneously" (p. 361). However, in contrast to the current study, Arva and Medgyes' study was conducted in
a secondary school EFL setting (Hungary). Furthermore, the NNESTs in
their study had lived in an English-speaking country for a very limited
time—between two weeks and one and a half years. Thus, it is unclear
whether NNESTs in the United States, especially those who have been
here for a long time, share the same self-perceptions regarding their
oral skills as the NNESTs in Arva and Medgyes' study.

Samimy and Brutt-Griffler (1999) investigated the self-perceptions
of nonnative teacher trainees enrolled in a master of arts program in
teaching English to speakers of other languages (TESOL) in the United
States. Samimy and Brutt-Griffler specifically refer to work by Reves
and Medgyes and state,

The present study led us to a different conclusion from that of Reves and
Medgyes (1994). Namely, unlike the causal relationship that they established

between NNS professionals' command of English and impoverished self-image, the results of this study seem to suggest otherwise. In other words . . . they did not express a sense of inferiority vis-à-vis native speaker professionals. (p. 141)

In yet another study of NNESTs' self-perception in the United States, Mahboob et al. (2002) also report that they did not find any negative self-evaluation based on NNESTs' language skills. Rather, they found that the NNESTs were very confident in their language skills and their ability to teach ESL. One nonnative English-speaking teacher in their study said:

I feel fully integrated; I don't have any doubts about my abilities [to teach English]. . . . Perhaps I am even more competent than they [my colleagues] are!

The contrast between the preceding findings for NESTs and NNESTs and the studies by Reves and Medgyes (1994) and Arva and Medgyes (2000) may be a result of the setting. While Reves and Medgyes and Arva and Medgyes report on data collected in EFL settings, Mahboob et al. (2002) and Samimy and Brutt-Griffler (1999) base their analysis on data collected in the United States. Therefore, the relationship between the instructional settings (EFL vs. ESL) and NNESTs' self-perceptions needs to be further investigated.

Literacy skills. Literacy skills, in this study, included reading and writing. The number of comments for literacy skills was lower as compared to those for oral skills. There were only three comments in this category. These comments discussed the positive role of NNESTs in teaching these skills.

One student wrote:

One of the reason I thought non-native speakers can teach English well is the person who came from non-native English country can teach grammar, reading, and listening also. (Student #6)

This statement shows that the student felt that NNESTs can be good teachers of reading, grammar, and listening. (This statement was also included in the "oral skills" and "grammar" categories because of its reference to those skills.)

Another student wrote:

[NNESTs] could . . . be better in writing than native speaker . . . (Student #16)

This comment is interesting because not only does it state that NNESTs are good teachers of writing, but it further implies that they are "better" than NESTs.

The positive evaluation of NNESTs as teachers of literacy skills and an absence of any positive comments about NESTs suggests that students find NNESTs to be good at teaching literacy skills (both reading and writing). One reason for this, as given by one of the students, is that to be good writers, both native and nonnative speakers need to learn how to write. The following statement shows that some students realize that literacy skills and oral skills are different in nature and that both native and nonnative speakers need to develop their reading and writing skills:

> Also, in writing subject . . . it is not a matter about pronunciation of language any more. Native speakers also need to know these writing skills when they are writing. So native speakers also are required to take a writing class. (Student #25)

It is interesting to note that the student argument just presented mirrors arguments in the literature on NNESTs. Kramsch and Lam (1999) state,

> The controversy surrounding the respective privileges of native speakers (see, for example, Kramsch, 1997) becomes moot when we deal with written language. For no one could argue that people are "born" into reading and writing. . . . both have to be schooled into literacy and into certain types of academic literacy in order to use language in its written form. (p. 57)

The similarity between Kramsch and Lam's statement and that of the student shows that ESL students are aware of the complexities of literacy acquisition and are sensitive to the equality between NESTs and NNESTs in their literacy achievements.

Grammar. Within the "linguistic factors" group, grammar was the category in which NNESTs received the strongest positive comments. There were 16 comments in this category. Twelve were positive comments that discussed the strength of NNESTs in teaching grammar, and 4 were negative comments that described NESTs' weakness in teaching this aspect of the language.

The following is an example of a student's comment elaborating on NNESTs' strength as grammar teachers:

> So . . . they [NNESTs] can be good grammar teachers like a TOEFL and TOEIC. (Student #22)

This example shows that students find NNESTs' grammar teaching important for their ability to do well on standardized tests of English, such as the Test of English as a Foreign Language (TOEFL) and the

Test of English for International Communication (TOEIC). A pertinent observation here is that NNESTs, especially those who were international teacher trainees in the United States, need to take the TOEFL and/or the Graduate Record Examination (GRE) in order to be admitted to many academic programs across the country. Thus, NNESTs' experience of taking these tests may aid them in their ability to help their students prepare for the tests.

In their study of NNESTs' self-perceptions in the United States, Mahboob et al. (2002) found that NNESTs were aware of their strength in teaching grammar. In addition to showing self-confidence, the NNESTs in the Mahboob et al. study also stated that their native English-speaking colleagues valued their expertise in grammar. Arva and Medgyes (2000) also found that NESTs acknowledged NNESTs' better understanding of grammar. They give the following example from an interview with a native English-speaking teacher:

> The non-native teacher has learnt grammar and is able to convey that to people very clearly with no wastage, whereas I would have to more often look up to find out what it was I was being asked about. (p. 362)

Arva and Medgyes also cite two other NESTs who acknowledged their limitations as grammar teachers:

> This is wrong and this is the correct way you should say it, I know, but I can't explain why it's wrong or right. (p. 361)

> Most native teachers I know never really came across grammar until they started teaching it. So you have to learn it as you go along. (p. 361)

In the preceding examples, NESTs express their feeling that although they know how to use the language, they are not aware of its rules explicitly. This lack of a grammatical understanding appears to be noticeable to the students. It is probably based on observing this inability of NESTs to satisfactorily explain grammatical concepts that ESL students in the present study labeled NESTs as not being good teachers of grammar. While discussing this perceived weakness, one student stated:

> Sometimes native speakers are not structure teachers, because even though they speak the language perfectly, and understand the structure very well, they do not know what is the pain, because they did not have the pain. (Student #8)

It is interesting to note that the student's comment supports the perceptions of the native English-speaking teacher in the study by Arva and Medgyes (2000). The student just quoted states that while native speakers can "speak the language perfectly," they are not good at teaching its grammatical structure. This statement also attributes the NESTs' inability to teach structure to their lack of experience of explicitly learning it.

Vocabulary. Students stated that both NESTs and NNESTs can be good teachers of vocabulary. There were 12 statements in this category, and all of them were positive. There were more statements that supported the idea that NESTs are better teachers of vocabulary than NNESTs. An example statement that showed that NESTs are good vocabulary teachers follows:

> Many slang words and new vocabulary. Native speakers can explain it easily. (Student #19)

The following is an example of a statement that supports the idea that NNESTs are good vocabulary teachers:

> Next, non-native English teacher can give the definitions of the words that we cannot understand. (Student #12)

There were no negative comments in this category. Thus, both NESTs and NNESTs were considered to be effective teachers of vocabulary, though NESTs received more positive comments than NESTs.

Culture. A number of students discussed the teaching of culture in relation to NESTs and NNESTs. There were six comments supporting the idea that NESTs have the ability to teach culture. An example of such a comment follows:

> By the conversation with Americans, I can learn some pronunciation, slang and American culture. (Student #5)

The preceding example shows that some students perceive that they can acquire an understanding of U.S. culture from NESTs.

Four comments also supported the notion that NNESTs can be a source of cultural knowledge. This view was expressed by one student in the following statement:

> Sometimes, we [students] cannot understand some specific words because we do not have cultural background. For these situation, they [NNEST] can explain the word's definitions more easily than explaining of native speaker. (Student #12)

In contrast to the four comments supporting the idea that NNESTs were a good source of cultural knowledge, one comment disagreed with the notion. Following is the comment reflecting this idea:

You can learn a foreign language perfectly, but you will always keep your
conception of the world . . . (Student #35)

This quotation shows how, for some students, no matter how well
one learns a new language, one will always maintain their cultural
heritage, and this will influence their teaching ability.

Teaching Styles

As already noted, the second group of categories was labeled "teaching styles." There were two categories of comments that were placed
in this group: "ability to answer questions" and "teaching methodology." Table 2 presents the distribution of comments across categories.

As the table shows, there were a total of 13 comments in this category. Four of them, all negative, described NESTs; while the other 9,
all positive, described NNESTs. The results of the analysis follows.

Ability to answer questions. This category included statements that described students' satisfaction or dissatisfaction with
the explanations or answers that teachers provided. There were
seven comments in this category. Interestingly, all comments about
NESTs were negative while all comments about NNESTs were positive. The following statement from one of the students exemplifies
the case:

In my opinion, I can get sufficient answer from non-native rather than natives
in some questions . . . (Student #22)

This statement suggests that while NESTs cannot provide "sufficient
answer" to students' questions, NNESTs' responses satisfy them. The
following comment supports the same idea:

Sometimes I have questions . . . non-native speakers are better teachers than
native speakers. (Student #5)

TABLE 2.   Distribution of Comments for Teaching Styles

	NESTs		NNESTs	
Teaching Styles	Positive Comments (*N*)	Negative Comments (*N*)	Positive Comments (*N*)	Negative Comments (*N*)
Ability to answer questions	0	3	4	0
Teaching methodology	0	1	5	0
Total	0	4	9	0

Teaching methodology. As in the previous category, titled "ability to answer questions," students found that NNESTs employed teaching methodologies that promoted enhanced learning. Two students stated:

> And they [NNESTs] can teach the most efficient way to study the language for foreigners. (Student #33)

> . . . The non-native teacher who also might have same experience and situations as me. So they knew how I could feel. . . . And they also know the way they taught effectively. (Student #28)

In contrast to the positive evaluation of NNESTs' teaching skills, one of these same students felt that NESTs did not use appropriate teaching methodologies:

> [NESTs] don't have patience about hearing the other countries' speaker's stories. (Student #28)

One possible explanation for students' positive evaluation of NNESTs' methodology is that their teaching styles may match their students' learning styles. In a study on learning styles, Peacock (2001) found that students expressed discomfort when their EFL teachers' teaching styles did not match their learning styles. Peacock found that Hong Kong EFL students preferred "kinesthetic" and "auditory" learning styles and disfavored "individual" and "group" styles. In comparison, he observed that local NNESTs favored "kinesthetic," "group," and "auditory" styles, while Western NESTs only favored "kinesthetic" and "group" styles. Peacock concluded that EFL teachers should implement a balanced approach to instruction as a means to accommodate a variety of learning styles. A study of NNESTs' self-perceptions also reveals that they are very confident of their teaching abilities (Kamhi-Stein, Aagard, Ching, Paik, & Sasser, this volume). In their study of NESTs and NNESTs in K–12 programs in California, Kamhi-Stein et al. suggest that the NNESTs' strong sense of cultural awareness and empathy may contribute to the teachers' positive self-perceptions about their instructional practices. It is interesting to note that these two characteristics, cultural awareness and empathy, were also found to be categories that emerged in the analysis of students' perceptions. However, it should be noted that Kamhi-Stein et al. conducted their study in a K–12 setting. Teachers' perceptions regarding their teaching methodology in adult ESL programs may differ.

Personal Factors

Three categories of comments were grouped together as "personal factors." There were a total of 30 comments in this group. The distribution of these comments is provided in Table 3.

Table 3 shows that, much like in the case of the "teaching styles" group, NESTs only received negative comments, if any, while NNESTs received positive comments.

Experience as a L2 learner. This category received the second largest number of comments (N = 19). Fifteen of these comments support the idea that NNESTs are better teachers because they have had the experience of learning English themselves, while the other four stated that NESTs are not good teachers because they have not had the experience of learning English.

A number of issues discussed in the essays—for example, NESTs' perceived weakness and NNESTs' perceived strength in teaching grammar and answering students' questions—were attributed to teachers' experience, or a lack of experience, as ESL learners. The following statement by one of the students exemplifies this:

> Because they [NNESTs] learned the language which they teach now, they know what problems do students have in learning language. For example, native speakers have never learned grammar, so most of them don't know how to teach grammar. (Student #9)

Almost half of the ESL students (15 out of 32) in this study felt that NNESTs' experience of learning English as a L2 makes them aware of the problems that ESL learners may face. The students therefore feel that NNESTs are better equipped to help them. They also feel that NNESTs have more empathy for them because of this experience. Discussing this point, one student stated:

> Non-native teachers also have studied the language as foreigner, so, the teachers have many experiences about the language. During the teachers'

TABLE 3. Distribution of Comments for Personal Factors

	NESTs		NNESTs	
	Positive Comments	Negative Comments	Positive Comments	Negative Comments
Personal Factors	(N)	(N)	(N)	(N)
Experience as a L2 learner	0	4	15	0
Hard work	0	0	5	0
Affect	0	0	6	0
Total	0	4	26	0

study they realized many problems that can't be found by native teachers. (Student #3)

It is interesting to note that in studies of NNESTs' self-perceptions, NNESTs seem to be aware of this advantage. Lee and Lew (2001) report that teacher trainees enrolled in a master of arts program in TESOL "unanimously agreed that the most valuable asset is their experience as learners of English" (p. 146). They present the following quotation from one of their participants who shared her advantage of having had the experience of learning English:

> I can understand and feel what the professor is saying about the theories, and I can put myself into the learners' shoes when I am preparing a lesson plan. (p. 146)

This quotation shows that the participant in Lee and Lew's study was able to extract the appropriate message from her graduate TESOL classes and applied this understanding to her own teaching.

In another study of NNESTs' self-perceptions, Liu (1999) quotes one of his participants, Ms. I:

> I also briefly mention my experience learning English so that they realize that I went through the same process that they are going through now. I want them to feel that I have also experienced learning English as a second language. . . . [Ms I. then explains the reason for doing this and adds:] it is important not only having had experience teaching languages but more importantly having been a student of a second/foreign language. This creates and establishes trust and rapport with the students at their level of experience. (p. 171)

This quotation further confirms that not only are NNESTs aware of their advantage of having been L2 learners, but they also utilize this benefit to their advantage in their teaching.

An interesting observation in relation to this category is that many TESOL programs in the United States have a foreign language requirement for their teacher trainees. This suggests that many ESL teachers have had at least some experience of learning a second/foreign language. However, the ESL students in this study did not show awareness of this fact.

Hard work. There were five comments in this category, and all of them supported the idea that NNESTs were hard workers. Some students felt that to be a nonnative English speaker and a teacher of English in the United States, NNESTs have to work very hard. One student wrote:

I felt that the people who study very hard for another language can be speaker without any problem. . . . Non-native speaker can do . . . teaching easily. (Student #32)

Another student forwarded the same idea when he or she stated:

I think non-natives can be a good teacher they try to study and practice hardly. (Student #4)

In contrast to the comments describing NNESTs as hard workers, there were no comments that described NESTs as hard workers. An absence of comments about NESTs in this category should not necessarily be taken as a sign that students do not consider them hard workers. Rather, the absence of comments may be interpreted as a factor of the category itself: native English speakers do not need to work hard to be good speakers of English.

Hard work also comes out as a marker in several studies that look at NNESTs' self-perceptions (Kamhi-Stein, 1999; Lee & Lew, 2001). Kamhi-Stein (1999) refers to a former student who "found herself working twice as hard as any of her [NEST] colleagues in order to gain acceptance of her ESL students" (p. 150). This reference shows that NNESTs feel that they need to work harder to prove themselves. Regardless of the reason for this hard work, a study of student perceptions shows that ESL students recognize this hard work and appreciate their NNESTs for it.

Affect. Six statements were placed in this category. All of these were positive statements about NNESTs. This category was related to NNESTs "experience as a L2 learner." Some students felt that NNESTs could empathize with them and provide them emotional support because they had gone through the process themselves and knew how it felt. One student stated:

The non-native teacher who also might have same experience and situations as me. So they knew how I could feel . . . (Student #28)

Another student specifically stated that NNESTs are more empathetic:

I think non-native speakers can be better language teachers because of their empathy and diverse culture. (Student #21)

Arva and Medgyes (2000) explain that NESTs themselves realize their shortcoming in being unable to appreciate the process that their students go through. They cite the following statement from a native English-speaking teacher:

Being a native speaker, it is difficult for you to appreciate what the students
are going through when they are learning English. (p. 362)

The reference to Arva and Medgyes' study provides support and
validity to this study of ESL students' perceptions. It also shows that
ESL students have a keen observation and are sensitive to their teachers' (both NESTs or NNESTs) relative strengths and weaknesses.

One student focused on the relationship between language proficiency and affect at some length by sharing a story about two friends
who were piano teachers. This student wrote:

When I lived in Japan. I had a friend who is a piano teacher. She learned
playing the piano at University. But her playing quarity is not good. On the
other hand, I had another friend who is also piano teacher. She graduated
a very famous music university. So, she is a really good piano player. Both
of them teached piano to children. They were completely different because
teacher who is a good player could teach a high level tequnick but the
another teacher couldn't teach a high level teq. But the result was strange.
Students who were taught by a good player teacher couldn't improve their
play, but another students could improve. I considered well about this result.
The teacher who can teach high level teq. to children couldn't teach how
playing piano is interesting, but the teacher who can't teach high level teq.
could teach how playing piano is interesting, also she couldn't show high
level playing but could teach how to learn.

In this case, the teacher who is not high level can be a good teacher. I think
it is same as English teacher. If an English teacher is not a native speakers,
he can teach how to enjoy English and learn English. And also he can teach
a correct answer to his students. (Student #33)

For this student, the skills that a person has do not necessarily
translate into teaching ability. The student felt that NNESTs could
teach language learners how to "enjoy" English as well as be able to
provide appropriate answers to their questions. While this student
believes that NESTs have a higher level of language proficiency, the
student suggests that NNESTs can be effective, too, since they can
teach learners how to "enjoy" the language learning process.

Summary of Findings and Discussion

Data for this study were collected using a discourse analytic technique. The advantage of using this technique was that the analysis
and findings were grounded in qualitative data rather than based
on a priori categories. The findings of this study are collated in
Table 4.

TABLE 4. Distribution of Positive and Negative Comments for NESTs and NNESTs

	NESTs		NNESTs	
Categories	Positive Comments (*N*)	Negative Comments (*N*)	Positive Comments (*N*)	Negative Comments (*N*)
Linguistic factors				
Oral skills	15	0	5	5
Literacy skills	0	0	3	0
Grammar	0	4	12	0
Vocabulary	8	0	4	0
Culture	6	0	4	1
Teaching styles				
Ability to answer questions	0	3	4	0
Teaching methodology	0	1	5	0
Personal factors				
Experience as a L2 learner	0	4	15	0
Hard work	0	0	5	0
Affect	0	0	6	0
Total	29	12	63	6

Table 4 shows that the distribution of perceived strengths for the two groups of teachers is complementary. Thus, while NESTs are seen as good at teaching oral skills, NNESTs are seen as good at teaching literacy skills and grammar. Table 4 also shows how NNESTs' experience of having studied the language themselves is perceived as their strongest characteristic.

The results of this study support several of Medgyes' (2001) assumptions regarding the "bright side of being a non-NEST" (p. 436). Although the focus of his work is on EFL settings, a comparison of his assumptions with the results of this study is informative. The data collected in this study support Medgyes' assumption that "non-NESTs can teach learning strategies more effectively" (p. 436). This assumption is supported by the students' belief that their NNESTs' understanding of L2 teaching comes from their own L2 learning experience. Learners felt that as a result of this experience, NNESTs were able to anticipate and explain concepts better than NESTs. They felt that explanations given by NNESTs were more satisfactory than those provided by NESTs.

The students' preference of NNESTs' teaching methodology is especially interesting when considered in light of the research conducted in the 1980s. In the 1980s there was a perception that to become good teachers, NNESTs should not only improve their linguistic skills to match those of native speakers, but they should also adopt the teaching practices and methods of NESTs. The following extract from Sheorey (1986), himself a nonnative English speaker, illustrates this point:

> the study gives an indication of which errors are most irritating to native ESL teachers, a finding which we can use to bring our own error-evaluation practices in line with those of native teachers. I am assuming here that acquiring a native-like sensitivity to errors is a proper goal (however elusive it might be) for non-native ESL teachers, and that we should seek to adjust our error-evaluation practices accordingly. (p. 310)

This reference supports the idea that the goal of NNESTs should be to acquire native-like teaching sensitivity. The results from the present study of student perceptions not only negates the need for NNESTs to become native-like in their pedagogical practices but indeed suggests that they have unique characteristics that students find lacking in NESTs, especially in the teaching of grammar and the ability to answer questions. Thus, statements from earlier studies, such as Sheorey (1986), need to be reanalyzed in light of the findings discussed here that suggest that "acquiring a native-like sensitivity" is not "a proper goal" for NNESTs. Rather, the unique teaching abilities of both NESTs and NNESTs complement each other and together provide a better learning environment for L2 students.

The students in this investigation also perceived NNESTs to be more understanding and empathetic toward them. They felt that NNESTs, again based on their L2 learning experience, could provide affective support that NESTs were not equipped to do. As a result of NNESTs' experience of being L2 learners, it is possible that their teaching methodology fits their students' expectations. McCargar (1993) reports that students come to a class with a number of expectations and that they feel disappointed if these expectations are not met. In this study, students' reference to NNESTs' ability to answer questions satisfactorily and to provide empathy suggests that NNESTs have a firsthand understanding of how to meet their students' expectations.

The perception that NESTs are more skilled in their language competence was shared by a majority of the students in their essays. The students perceived NNESTs to be good at teaching all skills except speaking and pronunciation. This perception of NNESTs' "less-than-native-like" pronunciation is one possible reason why the students in this study do not share Medgyes' idea that NNESTs provide their students an imitable model. In fact, none of the students' essays in this study discusses the role of NNESTs as providing good learner models. Students only refer to NNESTs' experience as L2 learners in relation to their ability to better answer students' questions, provide empathy, and use appropriate teaching methodologies. They do not feel, or at least explicitly state, that NNESTs provide them with good learner models.

Students feel that the NNESTs' English is not perfect and therefore they are not the ideal "language models" (Medgyes, 2001, p. 436) for them. This negative perception of the NNESTs' oral skills is also supported by a number of attitudinal studies that evaluate perceptions of individuals from various countries and language backgrounds toward different varieties of English. For example, Forde (1996) studied the attitudes of Chinese elementary school children toward different varieties of English and reported that the respondents preferred native varieties of English (both American and British) over local models. Forde also found that the respondents linked teachers' variety of English to their ability to teach. In other studies of language attitudes, Chiba, Matsuura, and Yamamoto (1995); Dalton-Puffer et al. (1997); and Jarvella, Bang, Jakobsen, and Mees (2001) found attitudes toward Japanese, Austrian, and Dutch varieties of English, respectively, to be less favorable as compared to a native variety of English. The results of the current study, focusing on an ESL setting, support the findings in EFL settings. The students in the current study believe that NESTs are their "language models" (Medgyes, 2001, p. 436). As one of the students put it, "I want the *truth* [emphasis added] pronunciation which non-natives teachers can't speak or use voice like native speakers." This student's use of "truth pronunciation" reflects the views of students who may feel that there is an "ideal," "true," and/or "correct" pronunciation of English. Bhatt (2002), in his discussion of the historical influences on the TESOL field, points out that the Chomskian notion of an "ideal native speaker" has permeated the field and is responsible for such perceptions. This perceived importance of an "ideal native speaker" model is especially interesting in ESL because there is ample linguistic evidence that adult ESL learners cannot achieve native-like pronunciation. Dalton-Puffer et al. (1997) raised a similar point and argued that "the prominence of native speaker in language teaching has obscured the distinctive nature of the successful L2 user and created an unattainable goal for L2 learners" (p. 185). However, regardless of an understanding of the weaknesses of a native speaker model by academics, it is perceived to be the eventual goal by ESL learners in this study.

This emphasis on pronunciation by the students may be one factor that influences administrators' perception that students do not want nonnative teachers, and it may be one cause of program administrators' ranking of the criterion "accent" as important in making hiring decisions (Mahboob et al., this volume). This understanding of students' preference for "native" accent might also be a reason that Flynn and Gulikers (2001) list "accent" to be an important criterion employed by administrators in hiring NNESTs.

Medgyes' (2001) assumption regarding the benefit students might have from NNESTs sharing their mother tongue was not supported by the results of this study. However, this may be because the essays focused on students' experience of learning English in the United States and not their home countries. The nature of ESL classes in the United States is such that students from multiple mother tongues take the same class. Thus, even if NNESTs share the mother tongue with one group of students in their classes, they may not be able to use it for instructional purposes in a multilingual class. It is also possible that the students in this investigation had not had the experience of having a nonnative English-speaking teacher who shared their mother tongue during their stay in the United States. A future study of NNESTs in an EFL setting or in an ESL setting where students share their teachers' mother tongue will be better able to evaluate the validity of this assumption.

Conclusions

The strongest finding of this study is that NESTs are perceived to be best for teaching oral skills. In addition to oral skills, NESTs are also perceived as being stronger in their ability to teach vocabulary and culture. However, some students perceive them as being weak in their ability to teach grammar. Furthermore, some students also perceive that NESTs are not always able to answer their questions well.

A number of characteristics that favored NNESTs were mentioned in the essays. These included "linguistic factors," such as the NNESTs' ability to teach literacy skills and grammar, and "teaching styles," including their ability to use appropriate teaching methodologies and to satisfy students' questions. NNESTs were also perceived to have strengths related to "personal factors," including their experience of being L2 learners, being hardworking, and providing affective and emotional support. In contrast to their strengths, NNESTs were criticized by some students as being unable to teach oral communication skills. This weakness appeared to be rooted in the students' belief that in order for them to acquire a "true" and "correct" pronunciation, they must have native speaker models.

In summary, the results of this study show that ESL students in the United States do not have a clear preference for either NESTs or NNESTs; rather, they feel that both types of teachers have unique attributes. Students find that there are strengths in the way NNESTs teach them when compared to NESTs. This is an important finding and shows that students are not naive and do not necessarily buy into the "native speaker fallacy" (Phillipson, 1992) that only native speakers can be good language teachers. The findings of this study clearly demonstrate that the importance given to the "native English speaker" hiring criterion by program administrators (Mahboob et al., this volume) is not shared by students. Both NESTs and NNESTs working collaboratively can provide a better learning environment to ESL students. This is best exemplified in the following quotation from one student:

> In my opinion, learning language have various ways and skills. You can't learn a language well just use one skill. Therefore, the different experiences from native and non-native speakers also can be your teacher when you learn a foreign language. You can get wonderful linguistical learning skills from different people and ways. (Student #5)

However, it should be noted that the present study was based on only 32 essays. A future study with a larger number of essays may reveal additional dimensions of students' perceptions of NESTs and NNESTs. A future study should also incorporate a secondary data collection task. In this way, it will be possible to add to the reliability of the results. Furthermore, biographical data should be collected from the participants in order to explore whether personal backgrounds make a difference in students' perceptions. Finally, a future study should include students in programs other than college-level IEPs. Other types of programs, such as community colleges and K–12, should be the focus of future research. It is possible that students' attitudes in these institutions may be different.

Implications for Classroom Teaching

The results of the study of students' perceptions have implications for classroom teaching for both NNESTs and NESTs. One of the primary implications is that NNESTs should feel confident about their teaching methodology. The results of this study show that students appreciate their teaching methods and the emotional support that they provide to their students. NNESTs should also actively reflect on and use their own language learning experiences to develop techniques and methods that they believe will help their students. An important implication of this study is that NNESTs should realize that even though they may not sound like native speakers, students do not necessarily hold that against them. Students will appreciate teachers who work hard on their lesson plans and use their experience to teach their classes. Another implication of this study is that students, in general, do not share the assumption that many administrators have: that ESL students prefer NESTs. Students are perceptive of the positive qualities that NNESTs possess and the contributions that they make.

The results of the study also have instructional implications for NESTs. Students find that NESTs can help them understand the culture of the host environment. NESTs should use this positive evaluation and build on it. However, at the same time, the negative evaluations of their ability to teach grammar and answer students' questions should lead them to reflect on how they can improve these aspects of their teaching. They might want to consider using varied teaching methods and styles and rethink the way they respond to students' questions. They may also consider team teaching, collaborating, or exchanging ideas and experiences with NNESTs. Such collaboration will be mutually beneficial to both NNESTs and NESTs.

Implications for ESL Teacher Education Programs

The findings of this investigation give support to a collaborative model of teacher education (Matsuda, 1999). Recent work in teacher preparation (e.g., de Oliveira & Richardson, this volume; Matsuda, 1999; Matsuda & Matsuda, this volume) suggests that, with the current demographics of the graduate student population in TESOL programs, the model of teacher education that is most beneficial to all students is a collaborative one. In this collaborative model, native and nonnative teacher trainees exchange notes and have a continuous dialogue that allows them to develop the skills that the other group excels in. Such a model of teacher education seems to be supported by the findings discussed in this chapter. With the complementary distribution of skills and attributes of NESTs and NNESTs, as perceived by the ESL students in this investigation, collaboration between the two will promote a better teaching-learning setting for ESL students.

NNESTs in the United States may discuss issues about the teaching of oral skills and culture with NESTs. Similarly, NESTs can benefit from discussing how NNESTs present and teach various grammatical points and what methods they use to explain problematic issues to their students. NESTs can also benefit from talking to NNESTs about their experiences as English language learners. This might include a discussion of linguistic and other areas that NNESTs have found problematic in their own learning of the language and ways in which they overcame these problems. A discussion of these issues will provide an opportunity to NNESTs to reflect on their learning experiences and use them more actively in their own teaching.

Collaboration between native and nonnative teacher trainees can be achieved using various techniques. For example, TESOL program faculty may choose to use journal exchanges as part of their course requirements (Matsuda & Matsuda, this volume). Faculty may also assign groups or pairs to write reports or complete assignments focusing on topics that require collaboration between native and non-native speakers. Faculty teaching practicum courses may consider pairing native and nonnative speakers as team teachers. They may also consider having both NESTs and NNESTs observe each others' classes (Brady & Gulikers, this volume).

Finally, TESOL programs may consider developing a "buddy-teacher program," in which native and nonnative teacher trainees are paired as "buddies." In addition to having an educational purpose, such a program may also provide emotional and other types of support to nonnative students who may be international students and new to the United States (Brady & Gulikers, this volume).

Implications for Program Administrators

The results of this study have a number of implications for administrators of IEPs in the United States. In particular, the results of this study have implications for program administrators who do not hire NNESTs because of their perception that ESL students only want NESTs. The results of this study show that ESL students do not prefer NESTs. Rather, this study revealed that students value both NESTs and NNESTs. This study showed that students feel that both NESTs and NNESTs contribute uniquely to their ESL learning experience in the United States and that together they can provide the best learning environment.

Based on these results, program administrators should consider making hiring decisions based on language and teaching expertise and not on the teachers' native or nonnative status. It should be noted that being a native speaker does not guarantee linguistic expertise (Pasternak & Bailey, this volume; Rampton, 1990). By focusing on teachers' teaching abilities and teachers' professional qualifications rather than their native or nonnative status, program administrators will create a context of learning for their students that will be more supportive of their needs not only as language learners but also as individual human beings.

References

Arva, V., & Medgyes, P. (2000). Native and non-native teachers in the classroom. *System, 28,* 355–372.

Babchuk, W. A. (1997, October). *Glaser or Strauss? Grounded theory and adult education.* Paper presented at the Midwest Research-to-Practice Conference in Adult, Continuing, and Community Education, Michigan State University, East Lansing.

Bhatt, R. M. (2002). Experts, dialects, and discourse. *International Journal of Applied Linguistics, 12*(1), 74–109.

Braine, G. (1999). From the periphery to the center: One teacher's journey. In G. Braine (Ed.), *Non-native educators in English language teaching* (pp. 15–28). Mahwah, NJ: Erlbaum.

Chiba, R., Matsuura, H., & Yamamoto, A. (1995). Japanese attitudes toward English accents. *World Englishes, 14,* 77–86.

Cook, V. (1999). Going beyond the native speaker in language teaching. *TESOL Quarterly, 33*(2), 185–209.

Cook, V. (2000). The author responds . . . *TESOL Quarterly, 34,* 329–332.

Dalton-Puffer, C., Kaltenboeck, G., & Smit, U. (1997). Learner attitudes and L2 pronunciation in Austria. *World Englishes, 16*(1), 115–128.

Flynn, K., & Gulikers, G. (2001). Issues in hiring nonnative English-speaking professionals to teach English as a second language. *CATESOL Journal, 13*(1), 151–160.

Forde, K. (1996). A study of learner attitudes towards accents of English. *Hong Kong Polytechnic University Working Papers in ELT and Applied Linguistics, 1*(2), 59–76.

Hyrkstedt, I., & Kalaja, P. (1998). Attitudes toward English and its functions in Finland: A discourse-analytic study. *World Englishes, 17*(3), 345–357.

Jarvella, R. J., Bang, E., Jakobsen, A. L., & Mees, I. (2001). Of mouths and men: Non-native listeners' identification and evaluation of varieties of English. *International Journal of Applied Linguistics, 11*(1), 37–56.

Kamhi-Stein, L. D. (1999). Preparing non-native professionals in TESOL: Implications for teacher education programs. In G. Braine (Ed.), *Non-native educators in English language teaching* (pp. 145–158). Mahwah, NJ: Erlbaum.

Kramsch, C., & Lam, W. S. E. (1999). Textual identities: The importance of being non-native. In G. Braine (Ed.), *Non-native educators in English language teaching* (pp. 57–72). Mahwah, NJ: Erlbaum.

Lee, E., & Lew, L. (2001). Diary studies: The voices of nonnative English speakers in a master of arts program in teaching English to speakers of other languages. *CATESOL Journal, 13*(1), 135–149.

Liang, K. Y. (2002). *English as a second language (ESL) students' attitudes towards non-native English-speaking teachers' accentedness.* Unpublished master's thesis, California State University, Los Angeles.

Lippi-Green, R. (1997). *English with an accent: Language, ideology, and discrimination in the United States.* London: Routledge.

Liu, J. (1999). Nonnative-English-speaking professionals in TESOL. *TESOL Quarterly, 33*(1), 85–102.

Mahboob, A., Uhrig, K., Newman, K. L., & Hartford, B. S. (2002, April). *Perceptions of non-native speaking teachers.* Paper presented at the 36th annual meeting of Teachers of English to Speakers of Other Languages, Salt Lake City, UT.

Matsuda, P. K. (1999, October/November). Teacher development through native speaker–nonnative speaker collaboration. *TESOL Matters, 9*(5), 1, 10.

McCargar, D. F. (1993). Teacher and student role expectations: Cross-cultural differences and implications. *The Modern Language Journal, 77*(2), 192–207.

Medgyes, P. (1992). Native or non-native: Who's worth more? *ELT Journal, 46,* 340–349.

Medgyes, P. (2001). When the teacher is a non-native speaker. In M. Celce-Murcia (Ed.), *Teaching English as a second or foreign language* (pp. 429–442). Boston: Heinle & Heinle.

Peacock, M. (2001). Match or mismatch? Learning styles and teaching styles in EFL. *International Journal of Applied Linguistics, 11*(1), 1–20.

Phillipson, R. (1992). *Linguistic imperialism.* Oxford: Oxford University Press.

Rampton, M. B. H. (1990). Displacing the "native speaker": Expertise, affiliation, and inheritance. *ELT Journal, 44*(2), 97–101.

Reves, T., & Medgyes, P. (1994). The non-native English speaking EFL/ESL teacher's self-image: An international survey. *System, 22*(3), 353–367.

Ryan, E., Giles, H., & Sebastian, R. (1982). An integrative perspective for the study of attitudes toward language variation. In E. Ryan & H. Giles (Eds.), *Attitudes towards language variations: Social and applied contexts* (pp. 1–19). London: Arnold.

Samimy, K. K., & Brutt-Griffler, J. (1999). To be a native or non-native speaker: Perceptions of "non-native" students in a graduate TESOL program. In G. Braine (Ed.), *Non-native educators in English language teaching* (pp. 127–144). Mahwah, NJ: Erlbaum.

Sheorey, R. (1986). Error perceptions of native-speaking and non-native-speaking teachers of ESL. *ELT Journal, 40*(4), 306–312.

Questions for Reflection

1. In her chapter, Amin describes a variety of effective classroom strategies implemented by the nonnative English speakers she investigated. According to Amin, the strategies challenge the validity of the native English speaker model. Observe a classroom taught by a NNES professional of your choice. What other strategies stemming from the teacher's nonnative English speaker status can you identify in the classroom? How effective are the strategies?

2. In their study of K–12 teachers, Kamhi-Stein et al. found that, when compared with NES professionals, NNES professionals had more positive perceptions about their instructional abilities. To what factors, other than those described by Kamhi-Stein et al., could you attribute the differences in perceptions?

3. According to Kamhi-Stein et al., their findings do not necessarily support Medgyes' (2001) idea that NES and NNES professionals are "two different species" (p. 434). Where do you stand on this issue? What factors contribute to your position?

4. In their chapter, Mahboob et al. conclude that "'native English speaker' status is an important factor in the hiring of teachers at college-level IEPs." However, Mahboob, in his chapter, concludes that ESL students enrolled in an IEP do not buy into the "native speaker fallacy." What are the implications of these two studies for professional groups like the Nonnative English Speakers in TESOL Caucus? In what ways could the findings presented in the two studies be used to enhance the preparation of native and nonnative English-speaking professionals?

5. The study by Mahboob et al. focuses on NNES professionals in the U.S. How could you build upon their study in an investigation of hiring criteria in EFL settings?

6. Review the studies described by Braine in Section 1 and the studies in Section 2. Identify gaps in the literature on NNES professionals and decide what direction future research should take.

Section 3

Focus on Teacher Preparation

It can be fairly stated that one of the areas in which the NNES professionals' movement has had the greatest impact is teacher education. Section 3, which focuses on teacher education, presents five chapters discussing theory, research, and practices that examine issues related to nonnative English speakers enrolled in teacher preparation programs. Common to the chapters in the section is the idea that language teacher preparation programs should create conditions in which all teachers, regardless of their language background, succeed.

Section 3 opens with Mindy Pasternak and Kathleen M. Bailey's "Preparing Nonnative and Native English-Speaking Teachers: Issues of Professionalism and Proficiency." The authors argue that the debate about native and nonnative teachers has been overly simplistic, that language proficiency is not the same as nativeness, and that language proficiency and professional development should be viewed "as continua rather than as categorical absolutes." Another argument put forward in this chapter is that effective teachers, regardless of language status, must have both declarative knowledge—"knowledge *about* something"—and procedural knowledge—"ability to do things." As explained by Pasternak and Bailey, in the case of "EFL and ESL teachers and teacher trainers, declarative and procedural knowledge entail at least three key areas: (1) knowing about and how to use the target language, (2) knowing about and how to teach in culturally appropriate ways, and (3) knowing about and how to behave appropriately in the target culture." Pasternak and Bailey illustrate these ideas by presenting fictionalized accounts of teachers they have known. The chapter concludes with a discussion of the implications of their ideas for pre-service and in-service language teacher preparation.

In the next chapter, "Autonomy and Collaboration in Teacher Education: Journal Sharing among Native and Nonnative English-Speaking Teachers," Aya Matsuda and Paul Kei Matsuda argue that teacher education programs should implement a "collaborative model" of teacher preparation. Such a model "strives for integration (NESTs and NNESTs), cooperation (mutual sharing), and addition (NEST

151

strengths plus NNEST strengths), all of which can lead to the type of collaboration that increases the effectiveness of teacher education programs." In their chapter, Matsuda and Matsuda describe an online journal sharing project as an example of such a collaborative model. They also discuss how such a project can strengthen the preparation of novice teachers and encourage them to engage in collaborative learning.

In the subsequent chapter, "Nonnative English-Speaking Student Teachers: Insights from Dialogue Journals," Donna M. Brinton examines the dialogue journal entries of NNES student teachers enrolled in a practicum course. Brinton's objective in analyzing the journal entries is to document the challenges faced by NNES student teachers. According to Brinton, some of the factors affecting NNES student teachers reflect concerns typical of *all* novice teachers, regardless of their language status. Other factors affecting NNES student teachers seem to be anchored in their nonnative status. In her chapter, Brinton concludes that "it is the teacher educators' responsibility to foster in the TESOL practicum an atmosphere that is pedagogically meaningful and supportive for both NES and NNES student teachers."

The following chapter, "Enhancing the MA in TESOL Practicum Course for Nonnative English-Speaking Student Teachers," by Brock Brady and Goedele Gulikers, builds upon Brinton's idea that teacher educators are responsible for creating contexts that are "pedagogically meaningful and supportive." In their chapter, Brady and Gulikers explain that the practicum course offered in many master of arts in TESOL programs in North American/British/Australian (NABA) settings, relies most often on the assumption that student teachers share the educational values and beliefs of those in NABA settings. As explained by Brady and Gulikers, there is a need for the practicum experience to be made more meaningful and transparent to NNES student teachers from non-NABA settings. With this idea in mind, Brady and Gulikers discuss how the practicum course at the American University was redesigned to address the cross-cultural needs of NNES student teachers from non-NABA settings. Brady and Gulikers conclude their chapter by stating that in responding to the needs of the NNES student teachers, they have created conditions in which all student teachers enrolled in a practicum course, native and nonnative English speakers alike, benefit.

In the last chapter of Section 3, "Preparing Nonnative English Speakers for EFL Teaching in Hong Kong," Icy Lee switches the attention from the practicum course to a teacher preparation program and from teacher preparation programs in NABA settings to teacher preparation programs in EFL settings. In her chapter, Icy Lee, a NNES teacher educator herself, uses the case of Hong Kong to describe the power imbalance between NES and NNES professionals. She also argues that NNES teacher educators, with firsthand knowledge of their pre-service teachers' native language, have the unique advantage of being able to identify their trainees' areas of strength and weakness. Drawing on these ideas, Icy Lee describes the strategies she uses to aid in the process of empowering nonnative English speakers for EFL teaching in Hong Kong. She concludes the chapter by stating that making non-native English speakers aware of how to capitalize on their strengths will improve their self-perceptions and strengthen their instructional practices.

Preparing Nonnative and Native English-Speaking Teachers: Issues of Professionalism and Proficiency

Mindy Pasternak
Monterey Institute of International Studies

Kathleen M. Bailey
Monterey Institute of International Studies

This chapter addresses the issues of language teacher professionalism and proficiency from the teacher educator's perspective. We begin by discussing the concepts of procedural knowledge and declarative knowledge, raising issues about the relative strengths of (and challenges faced by) native and nonnative English-speaking teachers. We use the profiles of five different teachers to show that the debate about native versus nonnative teachers in our field is overly simplistic and unhelpful. Then we address the interplay of proficiency and professional development, viewing these constructs as continua rather than as categorical absolutes. Next we review some of the literature comparing the perceived strengths of native and nonnative speaking teachers, before examining the speaking skill in some detail. We conclude with a brief discussion of some implications of the foregoing for pre-service and in-service teacher training.

The way many laypersons, students, and employers view nonnative speaking teachers has often been a huge source of justified frustration for well-prepared, highly proficient nonnative English-speaking teachers (NNESTs) over the years (Bailey, Curtis, & Nunan, 2001). In many countries, the blond, blue-eyed backpacker who runs out of money and looks for work may have better luck getting a position teaching English than a local teacher with a master's degree or an advanced diploma in TESOL. There is no justification for this practice other than the folk belief that native English-speaking teachers (NESTs) are somehow inherently superior—an unquestioned assumption that has been called the "native speaker fallacy" (Braine, 1999; Canagarajah, 1999; Phillipson, 1992).

The debate over the qualifications of NESTs versus NNESTs is highly controversial. To begin, accepted definitions of *native* and *nonnative* do not hold up under scrutiny, and researchers, linguists, and teachers generally agree that the term *native speaker* is not particularly precise. Medgyes (2001) summarizes the widely held notion that "a native speaker of English is traditionally defined as someone who speaks English as his or her native language, also called mother tongue, first language, or L1" (p. 430). A nonnative speaker of English, presumably, is everyone else who speaks English but does not fit this definition. However, as Kaplan (1999) points out, there is "no satisfactory definition of the term *native speaker*, and in the absence of such a definition, the negative term is quite impossible to define" (p. 5).

In spite of the problems in agreeing upon a precise definition of these terms, English as a second language (ESL) and English as a foreign language (EFL) teachers who are *perceived* as speaking a language other than English as their mother tongue—regardless of their actual proficiency with English—are typically labeled as "nonnative" English speakers. This label can sometimes contribute to the perception that they are not as proficient at English language teaching as their "native" English-speaking counterparts (Kamhi-Stein, 1999). As a result, NNESTs in both ESL and EFL settings often find it difficult to compete with NESTs for teaching positions (Braine, 1999; Medgyes, 2001).

Additionally, the demand for English language classes in both ESL and EFL settings far outweighs the supply of so-called native teachers. Actual numbers of individuals who use English as a second or foreign language are hard to determine, though Crystal (1997) suggests a conservative estimate of around 450 million nonnative users of English. Crystal points out, however, that more radical estimates—those that include speakers with a lower level of English language fluency and awareness—are closer to one billion. Compared to his estimate of 400 million native speakers of English, the number of nonnative speakers of English is enormous. It is simply not logical to assume that there are enough NESTs (qualified or otherwise) to meet the global demand for English teachers; nor is it logical to assume that hiring a native over a nonnative teacher is always the best administrative decision. As we will see, research suggests that NNESTs have many strengths that are sometimes not recognized by potential employers.

Furthermore, in many areas of the world, the vast majority of English language teachers are nonnative speakers of English. Due to cultural, historical, economic, and geographical factors, these NNESTs themselves may never have had instruction from NESTs. They also may not have had much exposure to target language speech, for either input or interaction. As a result of these and other factors, some NNESTs' fluency (e.g., in listening and speaking) may be far less developed than their accuracy (e.g., in grammar and writing), and often NNESTs doubt their own abilities as qualified language teachers. Yet many people (ourselves included) believe that NNESTs have a great deal to offer their students and may be as effective as or even more effective than some NESTs (see, e.g., Liu, 1999; Medgyes, 1999). In order to view the relative strengths of native and nonnative English-speaking teachers, we will propose some simple frameworks that will allow us to examine individual teachers' attributes. As a starting point, we will contrast procedural knowledge and declarative knowledge.

Procedural and Declarative Knowledge

There is a useful distinction between declarative knowledge and procedural knowledge, which can shape our discussion of the relative strengths and weaknesses of native and nonnative English teachers. *Declarative knowledge* "includes all of the things we know and can articulate" (Nunan, 1999, p. 3). In other words, declarative knowledge is our knowledge *about* something. When we have declarative knowledge on a topic, we can discuss that topic confidently. In our profession, important kinds of declarative knowledge minimally include knowledge (1) about the target language (e.g., its rules and their exceptions), (2) about the target culture (e.g., its norms and taboos), and (3) about teaching (e.g., knowing about content and formal schemata in teaching reading and listening). In a field as broad as English language teaching, declarative knowledge covers all the topics we have studied and learned that we can discuss—with students, parents, colleagues, administrators, legislators, and so on.

To be effective language teachers, however, we must have superior procedural knowledge as well. *Procedural knowledge* is the ability to do things, our skills (Nunan, 1999; see also Anderson, 1980, 1983). The difference between procedural knowledge and declarative knowledge can be summarized as knowing *how* versus knowing *about*. So, for EFL and ESL teachers, in terms of the target language, procedural knowledge would include being able to carry on conversations in English. Other important kinds of procedural knowledge relate to teaching—for instance, knowing how to plan lessons, how to treat students' oral errors, or how to conduct pair work.

For EFL and ESL teachers and teacher trainers, declarative and procedural knowledge entail at least three key areas: (1) knowing about and how to use the target language, (2) knowing about and how to teach in culturally appropriate ways, and (3) knowing about and how to behave appropriately in the target culture. These issues are depicted in Figure 1, where a few illustrations have been provided.[1]

Both NESTs and NNESTs will face challenges with regard to their declarative and procedural knowledge, though these challenges will probably differ. Of course, native-speaking teachers of any language may have a natural advantage in terms of their procedural knowledge about how to use their own variety of the target language and how to behave in their segment of the target culture. However, without the proper professional preparation and the experience of learning new languages themselves, NESTs may lack both procedural and declarative knowledge about how to teach and declarative knowledge about the language itself. Unfortunately, it is not unusual to hear untrained NESTs respond to students' grammar questions by saying, "I don't know why. That's just the way we say it."

Compared to their native-speaking counterparts, nonnative-speaking teachers may have much stronger declarative knowledge about the target language, given their years of study and formal instruction. For high-level learners of English with good academic backgrounds, this formal study can lead to both declarative and procedural knowledge, particularly with regard to the organizational features of English (i.e., their grammatical and textual competence; Bachman, 1990). Their

	Examples of Declarative Knowledge	Examples of Procedural Knowledge
About the Target Language	The ability to explain grammar rules and their exceptions	The ability to use grammar rules appropriately in speaking or writing
About Teaching	The ability to explain the rationale for using jigsaw activities in communicative language teaching	Skill in setting up communicative jigsaw activities in pair work or group work
About The Target Culture	The ability to explain norms of kinesics and proxemics used by members of the culture during interaction	Being able to behave appropriately in terms of nonverbal behavior and physical spacing when interacting with members of the culture

FIG. 1. Key areas of declarative and procedural knowledge in English language teaching

pragmatic competence (i.e., their illocutionary and sociolinguistic competence) may be weaker, especially if they have had little interaction with native and other English speakers in context over time. If they have had appropriate professional preparation opportunities, NNESTs may also have excellent declarative and procedural knowledge about language teaching. What NNESTs may lack is the experience base for using the target language confidently and behaving appropriately in the target culture, two examples of procedural knowledge.

To illustrate some possible combinations, let us consider the profiles of five teachers. These accounts are fictionalized, but they are all based on teachers we have known.

Kim is a young but somewhat experienced teacher. He taught English in secondary school in his home country for two years but wanted to improve both his English and his skills and confidence as a teacher. Kim enrolled in an intensive English program in the U.S. and then entered a master's degree program in TESOL. Although he experienced some difficulty with the graduate course work and projects due to his English proficiency, Kim successfully completed the program. His English fluency, vocabulary, and grammatical accuracy improved during this time, as did his use of communication strategies. Although his English is still heavily accented and is sometimes halting when he talks with new people or discusses unfamiliar topics, his confidence and skills as an EFL teacher have increased markedly.

Lua is a novice EFL teacher. She wanted to be an engineer, but her English scores on the national secondary school exit exams were too low, so she could not study engineering at the university. Instead, she was slotted into a three-year teacher training curriculum. Her preparation for teaching EFL included courses on Shakespeare, Chaucer, and modern British poetry. She has never had the opportunity to travel outside her own country. She teaches in a secondary school near her home, where she conducts her English classes in the students' first language, following the prescribed curriculum and preparing her students for their exams.

Tom is an inexperienced teacher of EFL. He grew up in Australia and traveled in Asia as part of a study-abroad program in college. There he developed a fascination for martial arts and Asian culture. After finishing his degree, Tom returned to Asia and found a job teaching English while he studied martial arts. Tom holds conversation classes for beginners and lower-intermediate students at a commercial language school that advertises that its teachers are all native speakers of English. There is no pre-service or in-service training for the teachers. All Tom's lessons are based on the school's textbooks. At each class, the students read passages from the book aloud and then answer the comprehension questions in the text. He corrects the students' grammar and pronunciation errors by having them repeat the oral models he provides.

Elena is an experienced EFL teacher who completed an advanced diploma in the U.K. some years ago. She has taught English for Academic Purposes (EAP) for many years at a university in her home country. She is spending a semester as a visiting scholar at a university in an English-speaking country in order to update her skills and conduct original research. While her English fluency, vocabulary, grammar, and pronunciation are quite advanced, she has a great deal of difficulty writing academic papers. Furthermore, she regularly offends her professors and classmates with her very aggressive, even rude, verbal behavior. Elena is consistently surprised by her interlocutors' reactions to her attempts to communicate her ideas and needs in English.

Monika is an experienced ESL teacher who was raised in western Canada. She has an advanced degree in language teaching and has decided to try teaching EFL to broaden her experience. However, now that she is working in a new country, she finds the students to be uncooperative. They often speak in their first language, which she doesn't know, so she wonders what they are saying about her. Also, they are hesitant to speak English in class and regularly whisper and share answers during tests. Monika feels the students are unmotivated to learn and disrespectful to her as a teacher. She plans to leave this school as soon as her contract is done.

Clearly these five teachers have different attributes. Some are stronger in their declarative knowledge about English, while others have greater procedural knowledge. They also vary in their knowledge of teaching and their knowledge of culture—both the target cultures of the countries where English is spoken and the learners' home culture. These five people have entered the English language teaching profession by very different pathways. Some have had appropriate teacher education experiences, and some have not.

We turn now to a discussion of proficiency and professional development. We will use our five fictional English teachers to illustrate the complexity of these issues as they relate to the debate on NESTs versus NNESTs.

Proficiency and Professional Development

The widely believed "native speaker fallacy" and the simplistic debate about the merits of native versus nonnative teachers may lead us to overlook some very important issues. Teachers may be fully proficient in the target language whether or not they are native speakers in the chronological sense of which language(s) they learned in infancy.

But a teacher's target language proficiency is only one element of professionalism. Another concern is whether the person has the appropriate education to be a language teacher. We see these two issues—proficiency and professional preparation—as continua, as shown in Figure 2 (Bailey, forthcoming).

Certainly, professional preparation is not the same thing as nativeness, and it should not be equated with language proficiency. Whether a native or a nonnative speaker, a teacher without any formal training cannot be said to be professionally prepared. But like proficiency, professional preparation is a continuum, and there are various types of professional education available depending on the position a pre-service teacher is seeking or the kind of updating an in-service teacher needs. We believe that, as teachers, we can and should continue to pursue professional development throughout our lives. We would even argue that it is possible for us as teachers to become relatively *less* prepared than we once were if we don't keep up with new developments and research and are unable to meet our students' changing needs.

Quadrant 1 in Figure 2 apparently represents the most desirable set of attributes for any language teacher to possess—being both

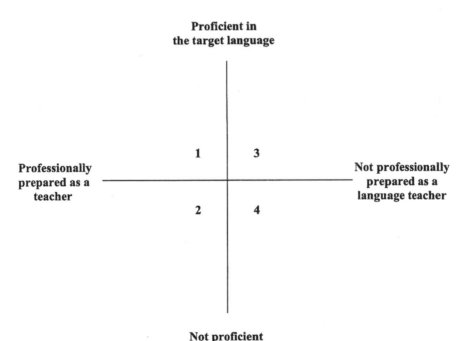

FIG. 2.   Continua of target language proficiency and professional preparation

proficient in the target language and professionally well prepared. Yet even being a professionally prepared native speaker is no guarantee of success as a teacher. As we saw, Monika, a native English-speaking teacher with an advanced degree in our field, is struggling in her new context as an EFL teacher. Likewise, Elena, who also fits in Quadrant 1, is having difficulty as a visiting scholar in an ESL context. In spite of her years of experience and training and her advanced linguistic competence, her lack of sociolinguistic competence is a serious drawback.

Quadrant 4, which represents teachers who are not proficient and who lack professional preparation, is clearly the least desirable. This is Lua's situation. She is a product of the education system in which she now teaches. Without further training and without the opportunity to interact in English with native and proficient nonnative speakers, it is difficult to see how Lua will be able to improve either her professionalism or her English proficiency.

But what about Quadrants 2 and 3? The comparison rests on many variables, including local needs and constraints. There may be instances when a professionally prepared nonnative English-speaking teacher such as Kim, who has good English ability (Quadrant 2), and a native speaker of English like Tom, who has little or no training (Quadrant 3), are the candidates for a teaching position. If the choice, then, is between an untrained native English-speaking teacher (like Tom, from Quadrant 3) and a trained nonnative English-speaking teacher (such as Kim, from Quadrant 2), we feel the nonnative English-speaking teacher should be given greater consideration for a teaching position. One could argue that Tom might pursue training as a language teacher, which could move him into Quadrant 1 eventually, but for the moment his only asset appears to be his procedural knowledge of the target language and of Australian culture. Kim, on the other hand, possesses both declarative and procedural knowledge about language teaching, has declarative knowledge and some communicative skill in the target language, and has had a lengthy immersion experience in the target culture. Although his English is not perfect, he has much to offer his students, whose needs, first language, educational context, and cultural values he understands well.

Proficiency, represented by the vertical axis in Figure 2, is defined as "knowledge, competence, or ability in the use of a language, irrespective of how, where, or under what conditions it has been acquired" (Bachman, 1990, p. 16). Experience has shown that individuals can have different proficiency levels in the four traditional skills. Someone who is an adept reader of a foreign language, for example, may have limited speaking proficiency. Likewise, many language learners (though typically not language teachers) develop spoken fluency without ever learning to read or write in the target language—particularly if its script differs from that of their first language. Spoken fluency may also mean that the learner has a facility for understanding and confidently utilizing the more colloquial features of a language, such as slang and idioms. Being fluent does not necessarily mean, however, that the learner has developed accurate use of grammatical forms, clear pronunciation, and so on.

Proficiency is not necessarily equated with nativeness, and certainly not all native speakers are equally skilled users of English. There are varying degrees of proficiency: being proficient is a continuum, rather than an either-or proposition. Apparently people can continue to develop their second language proficiency throughout the span of their lives, although some features of language (e.g., pronunciation) seem to be more difficult to change, while others (such as vocabulary) continue to develop regularly, as we read, study, and interact with others.

Whether or not a teacher is proficient depends on how we define this multifaceted construct. In terms of a narrow view of linguistic competence, Elena can be said to be proficient. If we consider sociolinguistic and pragmatic competence, there are huge gaps in her proficiency, which cause many problems in her role as a visiting scholar at an English-medium university.

Furthermore, individual learners have their own goals for studying the target language, goals that may be positively or negatively affected by the language proficiency and professional preparation of their teachers. At one time a major purpose for studying a foreign language was to be able to read the literature written in that language. Another important goal was often to pass a test in order to gain access to educational or employment opportunities, where one might or might not have to use the target language. But with 20th-century advances in global transportation and rapid, interactive communication, the development of speaking and listening skills has also become a central goal for many language learners. And often those learners use English to communicate with other nonnative speakers, rather than exclusively with native English speakers. Over 20 years ago, Smith noted,

> English is being used by non-native speakers to communicate with other non-native speakers. The countries of ASEAN (Association of South East Asian Nations) use English in their official meetings to represent themselves and their cultures. Japanese businessmen use English in K.L., Malaysia to represent their company's policy. Singaporeans use English to tell others about their "way of life." New literatures in English have appeared from India, the Philippines, the South Pacific as well as Africa—literature written

in English by non-native speakers intended for a world audience—not just
a native-speaking audience. (1981, p. 13)

As a result of these trends, speaking and listening have recently been
emphasized more, since English has come to be widely used in literature, science, technology, and commerce.

Subsequently, NNESTs have experienced pressure to increase their
own target language speaking and listening skills as well, in order
to rise to the challenges posed by their students' changing needs.
However, experts such as Liu (1999), Medgyes (1994, 1999, 2001),
and Morley (1991) feel that many TESOL preparation programs lack
the necessary language training component and that nonnative
teacher trainees and in-service NNESTs would benefit greatly from
more focused instruction in areas of speech and fluency, listening,
and pronunciation.

We have asserted that both NESTs and NNESTs have strengths as
English teachers. Likewise, we have claimed that both groups may
have gaps in their professionalism. We turn now to what some of the
available literature has to say about these claims.

Relative Strengths of Native- and Nonnative-Speaking English Teachers

Many researchers (see, e.g., Flynn, 1999; Lee, 2000; Tang, 1997) suggest
that NNESTs can be extremely effective as English language teachers.
What NNESTs may sometimes lack in terms of English language proficiency is offset by a different—but equally valuable—set of skills. For
example, Shaw (1979) points out that "a native teacher may partially
or even completely lack the kinds of insight necessary for an English
language teacher to prepare and execute his classes" (p. 12). Shaw
also observes that "non-native speaker teachers are typically better
able . . . to control the complexity of their speech in an elementary
class" (ibid.).

Murphy-O'Dwyer (1996) claims that, as teachers, "native speakers
have just as much to learn (and in many cases much more) than nonnative speakers" (p. 21). For example, she suggests that NNESTs who
have studied the target language formally often have better insights
into the structure and use of the language than do untrained native
speakers who may have little or no explicit declarative knowledge of
their first language. Furthermore, Murphy-O'Dwyer notes that NNESTs
have a distinct advantage over monolingual native speakers in that
"they already have a successful language learning experience behind
them, which they can draw on to inform their teaching" (ibid.).

In Medgyes' (1999) opinion, when compared to the strengths and
weaknesses of NESTs, NNESTs have the advantage in that they can

- provide a good learner model for imitation,
- teach language learning strategies more effectively,
- supply learners with more information about the English language,
- anticipate and prevent language difficulties better,
- be more empathetic to the needs and problems of learners, and
- make use of the learner's mother tongue. (p. 178)

It is important to point out, however, that this pendulum swing—from the native speaker fallacy to the viewpoints just expressed—seems to disregard the fact that not all NNESTs are guaranteed to possess all of these strengths, nor does it acknowledge that not all NESTs will lack them. A nonnative teacher for whom a high level of English proficiency comes rather easily, for example, might not always be sympathetic toward the problems of learners for whom learning English is a challenge. Further, unlike Monika in the previous scenario, many NESTs—particularly in EFL settings—do speak their students' mother tongue and are able to use that knowledge in the classroom. Therefore, the wise program administrator or teacher educator would take a step back from an "all-or-nothing" stance with regard to the relative strengths or weaknesses of native- versus nonnative-speaking teachers and would consider instead the strengths and weaknesses of each individual teacher or teacher candidate.

It is also important to consider the language goals of the students with whom each teacher trainee is working or will work. A teacher whose students' need for English is primarily to read scientific texts, for example, must have highly developed procedural and declarative knowledge with regard to reading as well as the discourse and lexicon of science and technology. If the students are preparing to be English-speaking tour guides or to work with visitors in the hospitality industry, the teacher will need a high level of English speaking and listening skills, in addition to declarative and procedural knowledge of English pragmatics and politeness routines. As we will see, however, research has indicated that many NNESTs lack confidence in their ability to speak English well. We turn now to a discussion of speaking (and to some extent listening) as these skills relate to the declarative and procedural knowledge of NNESTs.

Speaking and Listening Skills

Speaking a second or foreign language well can be challenging for anyone, but nonnative teachers face an additional challenge: the expectation that language teachers will have excellent speaking skills. This expectation is not unreasonable. After all, we want language learners to have both good linguistic models and good role models. However, unrealistically high expectations—perhaps especially those held by NNESTs themselves—can be overwhelming.

Apparently, many NNESTs feel inferior when compared to their native English-speaking teacher counterparts, especially in areas of language fluency and communication. For example, Tang (1997) reports on a survey of 47 NNESTs, examining their perceptions of the "proficiency and competency" of NESTs and NNESTs. Her subjects felt that NESTs were superior to NNESTs in areas of fluency such as speaking (100%), pronunciation (92%), and listening (87%). She found that NNESTs "were felt to be associated with accuracy rather than fluency" (p. 578). In a survey conducted by Medgyes (1994; see also Reves & Medgyes, 1994), 325 teachers from 11 countries, 86% of whom were NNESTs, completed self-report questionnaires about their perceived behavior as English language teachers.[2] Results showed that the NNESTs "viewed themselves as poorer listeners, speakers, readers, and writers" (p. 33) than their native English-speaking teacher counterparts. These NNESTs identified speaking and fluency, pronunciation, and listening as most problematic after vocabulary and idiomatic and appropriate use of English. Areas of accuracy, such as grammar and writing skills, were mentioned far less frequently, and "reading skills and cultural knowledge were not even mentioned" (Medgyes, 2001, p. 434) by the NNESTs surveyed.

Speaking and listening are often not formally taught in undergraduate and graduate TESOL programs, as these programs tend to assume that their teacher trainees already know how to speak English. In other words, such programs apparently assume that the majority of these teacher trainees fall into Quadrant 3 of Figure 2: they are highly proficient in the target language but are not yet professionally prepared as teachers (the reason that the teacher trainees would be applying for such programs). However, Medgyes (1999) says that language training is ignored in many TESOL programs. (He specifically points to his own Centre for English Teacher Training at the Eötvös Loránd University in Budapest.) Medgyes also suggests that because language improvement is not considered to be a key issue, "trainees will not bend over backward to make linguistic progress" (p. 191). Therefore, teacher trainees are not likely to become near-native speakers of English, something he says is necessary in order for NNESTs to be "effective, self-confident, and satisfied professionals" (p. 179). In order to help NNESTs achieve this goal, he emphasizes the importance of including language training in pre-service education.

Medgyes is not the only one to stress the need for focused language training. According to Liu (1999), an excellent command of English is "extremely important for quality ESOL teaching," where *excellent com-*

mand is defined as "fluent and idiomatic use of the English language" (p. 204). However, Liu also says that nonnative TESOL students' needs have been overlooked in terms of helping them improve their English proficiency as it relates to their future success as teachers (but see Johnson, 1990). The teacher trainees feel the lack, too. In a survey of 59 nonnative TESOL students, Liu (1999) found that only 14% felt they had the English language proficiency needed to be a "truly qualified teacher" (p. 205). Almost half (49%) weren't sure, and 37% replied with a definite "no." Therefore, he says, nonnative TESOL students "need help or training to improve their English" (p. 205).

Listening comprehension and pronunciation accuracy rate highly among NNESTs as areas in which they feel their English proficiency is lacking. Medgyes and Liu suggest that focused training in these areas will be beneficial for nonnative TESOL students and current NNESTs (both in terms of improving their English proficiency and in improving their own self-confidence as qualified English language teachers). Morley (1991) agrees, saying that nonnative teacher trainees who plan to teach ESL or EFL "need special attention paid to communicative skills in general and to pronunciation intelligibility in particular" (p. 492). Celce-Murcia, Brinton, and Goodwin (1996) say that NNESTs "who expect to serve as the major model and source of input in English for their students" require "special assistance with pronunciation," though they point out that the goal is not to expect NNESTs to sound like native speakers but merely to help them "to surpass the threshold level so that their pronunciation will not detract from their ability to communicate" (p. 8). These authors do not define "threshold level." Presumably the point at which an individual's pronunciation affects his or her ability to communicate will vary depending on the interlocutors and the situation in which communication occurs.

The link between pronunciation ability and listening comprehension is also widely discussed. Gilbert (1993) claims that "how you hear English is closely connected with how you speak English" (p. 3). Morley (1991) suggests that in terms of programming principles for teacher education, there should be "a focus on the link between listening and pronouncing/speaking and a need to expand the nature and range of pronunciation-oriented activities" (p. 494).

There is some evidence that pronunciation instruction does lead to improved listening and speaking. For example, a study by Cenoz and Lecumberri (1999) found that Basque and Spanish students who received specific English phonetics training, including aural discrimination exercises, improved in the discrimination of English simple vowels and diphthongs.

In Canada, Derwing, Munro, and Wiebe (1998) studied the effects of three types of instruction on ESL learners' speech. Three groups of subjects were given (1) training on segmental accuracy, (2) instruction with a global focus (e.g., suprasegmental emphasis), or (3) no specific pronunciation instruction. These authors found that "three aspects of oral production—comprehensibility, accent, and fluency—showed improvement as a result of instruction" (p. 405). The segmental accuracy group, whose instruction included identification and discrimination tasks, showed a greater improvement in accentedness over the other two groups, while the global focus group showed clear improvement in comprehensibility and fluency.

While researchers have studied the effects of pronunciation instruction on nonnative speaker comprehensibility, accuracy, and fluency, there appears to be relatively little research measuring the effect of focused training for NNESTs by NESTs on the pronunciation intelligibility and listening comprehension of pronunciation contrasts of NNESTs. Pasternak (2002) investigated the effect of instruction by NESTs on the pronunciation intelligibility and the receptive aural discrimination of American English sounds by NNESTs in China. She tested 33 Chinese middle school teachers of English before and after a four-week intensive English language workshop that focused on conversation, listening, and pronunciation skills. The analyses revealed statistically significant improvement between the Chinese teachers' pre- and post-test scores for the aural discrimination assessment. Their pronunciation intelligibility results were somewhat less clear, though one of the two raters did perceive statistically significant improvement following the instruction. The results suggest that language learners' aural discrimination of phonemic contrasts does indeed improve with focused instruction and that such instruction may also contribute to the learners' own pronunciation intelligibility. Given that all of the participants had been trained as English teachers but had limited proficiency (i.e., they were in Quadrant 2 of Figure 2), it seems that even a short, intensive training program that exposes NNESTs to native speech may be beneficial to their listening and speaking skills.

The oral fluency of 15 in-service EFL teachers in Hong Kong was investigated by Lam (1995). These teachers were randomly sampled from those enrolled in a 20-week course intended "to extend the fluency and enhance the confidence of participants in spoken English" (p. 133). Lam adds, however, that how the teachers' fluency is expected to change—if at all—is not spelled out. Lam found no statistically significant differences in the teachers' pre-course and post-course fluency, either with subjective ratings or with three objective measures (speech rate, number of filled pauses per T-unit,[3] and percent of T-units followed by a pause; see Lam 1995). She discusses the possibility that the teachers may have made gains in fluency that were not captured in these measurements or that a "ceiling effect" may have come into play; that is, these EFL teachers "were adults who had already mastered quite an advanced level of spoken English," and they "might have reached a 'ceiling' as regards their development of speech rate" (p. 138). A third possibility, which Lam does not suggest, is that these teachers' English fluency did not discernibly improve during the course.

Another study in Hong Kong did not directly measure speaking skills, but its findings are useful here. Crew (1995) investigated changes in the English proficiency of 198 full-time teacher trainees. Some were enrolled in a three-year Chinese-medium curriculum (N = 69), while the rest (N = 129) were enrolled in a two-year English-medium curriculum. Both groups were tested three times with three parallel forms of the Oxford Placement Test (OPT) (Allan, 1984). The OPT consists of two 100-point subtests. The first covers reading and listening, while the second assesses the test takers' knowledge of grammar (both function and structure). The OPT was given to the two groups at the beginning, midpoint, and end of their respective curricula.

Crew (1995) documented a curious trend in both the Chinese- and English-medium trainees' OPT results. First, "there was a general pattern of slight gain [between OPT1 and OPT2], followed by a marked decline and overall loss of English proficiency [between OPT2 and OPT3]" (p. 123). Second, the Chinese-medium trainees made much greater gains between OPT1 and OPT2 than did their English-medium counterparts. The three forms of the OPT used the multiple-choice format to assess the test takers' receptive skills and English grammar knowledge. There was no direct speaking assessment included in this battery.

The in-service EFL teachers in Lam's (1995) research and the 198 trainees in Crew's research were all studying in Hong Kong, although 17 of the English-medium trainees in Crew's study went to the U.K. for a six-week program. That immersion group showed nearly the same average gains as the Chinese-medium trainees (+4.2 and +4.7, respectively, at the second OPT administration). Their third set of OPT scores also showed a marked decline, however.

One further study must be noted. Kelch and Santana-Williamson (2002) found that ESL students' attitudes toward teachers' accents were *not* related to the teachers' nativeness. Rather, the students' attitudes correlated with their *perceptions* of the teachers' nativeness. Kelch and Santana-Williamson conclude that "non-native speakers not only can and do possess the same professional attributes and qualifications as native speakers, but they can further contribute to a healthy learning environment by displaying great sensitivity to the needs of L2 learners and serve as more realistic role models than native speakers" (p. 58; see also Samimy & Brutt-Griffler, 1999).

This brief review of some literature on NNESTs' speaking and listening skills shows that in some circumstances, nonnative teachers make significant improvement in their English language skills, given appropriate programs of instruction. This review also suggests that how NNESTs' speaking and listening skills are measured is an important factor to consider.

Implications for Pre-service Teacher Training: Closing Comments

We began this chapter by arguing that the debate of the past several decades over the native English-speaking teacher versus the nonnative English-speaking teacher is overly simplistic. Instead, the key issues to be considered in language teachers' pre-service and in-service education and in employment decisions are the individual teachers' proficiency and professional preparation. We described five different ESL/EFL teachers as examples and considered some of the different challenges faced by native- and nonnative-speaking teachers in terms of their declarative and procedural knowledge. Finally, we have reviewed some of the research literature on NNESTs, specifically with regard to speaking and listening skills, including their own attitudes about their strengths and weaknesses. We will close by returning briefly to the proficiency and preparation of our five teachers.

We believe that pre-service and in-service teacher education programs can help teachers improve their English proficiency as well as their professionalism. Furthermore, the distinction between declarative and procedural knowledge provides us with a framework for assessing those areas where improvement is needed. Regardless of whether a teacher is a native or a nonnative speaker of the language, we can assume that the greater the procedural and declarative knowledge in any given area of English language teaching is, the more confident the teacher will be. In that regard, the framework discussed here for considering target language proficiency and professional preparation can also be used by teacher educators and trainees in assessing and tracking the trainees' development with regard to their proficiency in English. In Figure 3 we use the continua from Figure 2 and the constructs from Figure 1 to provide a means by which trainees or teacher educators can estimate the trainees' level of proficiency and/or confidence at various points in time. We have labeled the continua as *declarative knowledge* and *procedural knowledge,* with their endpoints representing either a *developed* or an *undeveloped* state.

The chart in Figure 3 can be used as a simple diagnostic tool for evaluating English teachers' proficiency or professional preparation or both. For example, prior to taking courses on English syntactic and discourse structures or on English phonology, both NESTs and

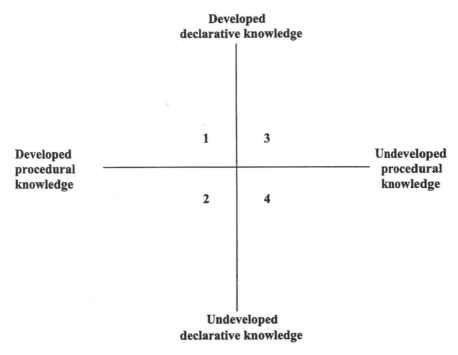

FIG. 3.   Framework for estimating developing proficiency and increasing confidence

NNESTs might evaluate their declarative knowledge as undeveloped. (We argue, however, that due to their own educational experiences as learners of English, many NNESTs will initially have stronger declarative knowledge about the target language than will their native English-speaking teacher trainee counterparts.) Similarly, before and after a practicum course, both NNESTs and NESTs may be able to rate themselves on the continuum of developing procedural knowledge about teaching. The question remains as to what teacher training programs can do to help NNESTs develop their procedural knowledge (i.e., their skilled use) of the target language.

Language teacher preparation programs can do a great deal to ensure that their students have the opportunities they need in order to feel more confident and prepared when they graduate. For example, a comprehensive and ongoing needs assessment (e.g., student surveys, interviews, focus groups) can help faculty ensure that the curriculum supports the current students' needs. Program orientations can include a learner-training component for both NESTs and NNESTs, incorporating elements such as class participation, academic training, and relationship building. Such training may help avoid the communication problems that naturally occur when students from different cultures mix in a single academic setting. Furthermore, a thorough academic advising system, wherein every student has an advisor, will enable students to complete program requirements successfully. Where possible, NNESTs can be encouraged to enroll in EAP courses that are designed to help nonnative students develop their academic English, including their speaking skills.

What has become of our five ESL/EFL teachers?

Kim's work as an EFL teacher in his home country has improved and his confidence has greatly increased as a result of his sojourn in an English-speaking country and his efforts to complete his master's degree. We hope he will continue to improve his English and sustain his professional development by getting involved in professional teaching associations, attending English cultural events, using the Internet, and so on.

Tom is still teaching conversation courses. If he continues teaching English, we hope his affinity for Asia will lead him to obtain the appropriate training as a language teacher. He may be a "natural" teacher, but even talented, natural teachers can improve their declarative and procedural knowledge about the target language, the target culture, and language teaching.

Elena soon realized that the gaps in her sociolinguistic competence were causing problems, and she set out to study this topic and improve her own productive skills. While she still seems somewhat aggressive to her native-speaking colleagues, she has learned to slow her speech, to smooth the intonation contours a bit, and to use mitigating strategies in making requests in English. In short, she has developed her sociolinguistic skills.

Monika, our professionally prepared native speaker, may learn more about the culture and language of her host country and decide to stay. If she tries to learn the students' first language, she may be more sympathetic to their needs and better prepared to cope with their behavior. Otherwise, she may simply leave the country and try to find work that is within her comfort zone.

We are hopeful that Lua will someday have opportunities to upgrade her professional skills and her English proficiency. The systemic constraints of her current context make it difficult to see how she could improve her English without significantly increased opportunities for interaction and/or instruction. Nevertheless, it is possible that she will make an important contribution to her own students' education.

We want to close with the words of Pavlenko and Lantolf (2000), who note that in order to deconstruct the concept of native speaker, we must "separate two important issues: being born in a certain geographic place versus having a participant status in a discursive community" (p. 169). Many nonnative speaking teachers "may forever claim allegiance to the place of their birth [but] they also undeniably belong in their second self-chosen world, not as observers but as full-fledged participants" (ibid.). In the context of this chapter, that second self-chosen world is the discursive community of professional language teaching. A teacher's level of participation in this community does not and should not depend on issues of "nativeness" but rather on each individual's unique blend of professional preparation and proficiency. There is room in this community—and a great need—for well-qualified teachers, regardless of their place of birth.

Notes

1. Of course, other important professional areas, such as assessment and curriculum design, could also be added to the figure.
2. Medgyes (2001) does suggest that the results be interpreted cautiously, as the questionnaire format elicited the teachers' "stated" behaviors rather than their "actual" behaviors (p. 434).
3. A T-unit is a "terminable unit" or independent clause plus any and all dependent clauses attached to it. See Gaies, 1980; Larsen-Freeman, 1978.

References

Allan, D. (1984). *Oxford placement tests.* Oxford: Oxford University Press.

Anderson, J. R. (1980). *Cognitive psychology and its implications.* San Francisco: W. H. Freeman.

Anderson, J. R. (1983). *The architecture of cognition.* Cambridge: Harvard University Press.

Bachman, L. F. (1990). *Fundamental considerations in language testing.* Oxford: Oxford University Press.

Bailey, K. M. (forthcoming). *Language teacher supervision: A casebook approach.* Boston: Heinle & Heinle.

Bailey, K. M., Curtis, A., & Nunan, D. (2001). *Pursuing professional development: The self as source.* Boston: Heinle & Heinle.

Braine, G. (1999). Introduction. In G. Braine (Ed.), *Non-native educators in English language teaching* (pp. xiii–xxi). Mahwah, NJ: Erlbaum.

Canagarajah, A. S. (1999). Interrogating the "native speaker fallacy": Non-linguistic roots, non-pedagogical results. In G. Braine (Ed.), *Non-native educators in English language teaching* (pp. 77–92). Mahwah, NJ: Erlbaum.

Celce-Murcia, M., Brinton, D. M., & Goodwin, J. M. (1996). *Teaching pronunciation.* Cambridge: Cambridge University Press.

Cenoz, J., & Lecumberri, L. G. (1999). The effect of training on the discrimination of English vowels. *International Review of Applied Linguistics in Language Teaching, (37)*4, 261–275.

Crew, V. (1995). When does a carrot become a stick? Changing attitudes and English language proficiency of Hong Kong student teachers. In D. Nunan, R. Berry, & V. Berry (Eds.), *Language awareness in language education: Proceedings of the International Language in Education Conference, 1994* (pp. 117–131). University of Hong Kong, People's Republic of China.

Crystal, D. (1997). *The Cambridge encyclopedia of language* (2nd ed.). Cambridge: Cambridge University Press.

Derwing, T. M., Munro, M. J., & Wiebe, G. (1998). Evidence in favor of a broad framework for pronunciation instruction. *Language Learning, 48*(3), 393–410.

Flynn, K. (1999, March). Hiring nonnative English speakers to teach ESL: An administrator's perspective. *NNEST Newsletter, 1*(1), 7.

Gaies, S., J. (1980). T-unit analysis in second language research: Applications, problems, and limitations. *TESOL Quarterly, 14*(1), 53–60.

Gilbert, J. B. (1993). *Clear speech: Pronunciation and listening comprehension in North American English* (2nd ed.). Cambridge: Cambridge University Press.

Johnson, R. K. (1990). Developing teachers' language resources. In J. C. Richards & D. Nunan (Eds.), *Second language teacher education* (pp. 269–281). Cambridge: Cambridge University Press.

Kamhi-Stein, L. D. (1999). Preparing non-native professionals in TESOL: Implications for teacher education programs. In G. Braine (Ed.), *Non-native educators in English language teaching* (pp. 145–158). Mahwah, NJ: Erlbaum.

Kaplan, R. B. (1999, March). The ELT: Ho(NEST) or not ho(NEST)? *NNEST Newsletter, 1*(1), 1, 5–6.

Kelch, K., & Santana-Williamson, E. (2002). ESL students' attitudes toward native- and nonnative-speaking instructors' accents. *CATESOL Journal, 14*(1), 57–72.

Lam, W. Y. K. (1995). Investigating the oral fluency of 15 EFL teachers: A quantitative approach revisited. In D. Nunan, R. Berry, & V. Berry (Eds.), *Language awareness in language education: Proceedings of the International Language in Education Conference, 1994* (pp.133–147). University of Hong Kong, People's Republic of China.

Larsen-Freeman, D. (1978). An ESL index of development. *TESOL Quarterly, 12*(4), 439–448.

Lee, K. (2000, March). A hundred miles. *NNEST Newsletter, 2*(1), 11.

Liu, D. (1999). Training non-native TESOL students: Challenges for TESOL teacher education in the West. In G. Braine (Ed.), *Non-native educators in English language teaching* (pp. 197–210). Mahwah, NJ: Erlbaum.

Medgyes, P. (1994). *The non-native teacher.* London: Macmillan.

Medgyes, P. (1999). Language training in teacher education. In G. Braine (Ed.), *Non-native educators in English language teaching* (pp. 177–195). Mahwah, NJ: Erlbaum.

Medgyes, P. (2001). When the teacher is a non-native speaker. In M. Celce-Murcia (Ed.), *Teaching English as a second or foreign language* (3rd ed., pp. 429–442). Boston: Heinle & Heinle.

Morley, J. (1991). The pronunciation component in teaching English to speakers of other languages. *TESOL Quarterly, 25*(3), 481–520.

Murphy-O'Dwyer, L. M. (1996, April/May). Putting the T in TESOL. *TESOL Matters, 6*(2), 21.

Nunan, D. (1999, August/September). So you think that language teaching is a profession, part 1. *TESOL Matters, 9*(4), 3.

Pasternak, M. (2002). *Hug or hog? Does NEST instruction help Chinese NNESTs improve their pronunciation intelligibility and listening comprehension?* Unpublished manuscript, Monterey Institute of International Studies at Monterey, CA.

Pavlenko, A., & Lantolf, J. P. (2000). Second language learning as participation and the (re)construction of selves. In J. P. Lantolf (Ed.), *Sociocultural theory and second language learning* (pp. 155–177). Oxford: Oxford University Press.

Phillipson, R. (1992). *Linguistic imperialism*. Oxford: Oxford University Press.

Reves, T., & Medgyes, P. (1994). The non-native English speaking EFL/ESL teacher's self-image: An international survey. *System, 22*(3), 353–367.

Samimy, K. K., & Brutt-Griffler, J. (1999). To be a native or a non-native speaker: Perceptions of "non-native" students in a graduate TESOL program. In G. Braine (Ed.), *Non-native educators in English language teaching* (pp. 127–144). Mahwah, NJ: Erlbaum.

Shaw, P. A. (1979). Handling a language component in a teacher-training course. *Modern English Teacher, 3,* 12–15.

Smith, L. E. (1981). TESOL and training non-native English speakers: Are M.A. teacher education programs getting the job done? Part II. In J. C. Fisher, M. A. Clarke, & J. Schachter (Eds.), *On TESOL '80—Building bridges: Research and practice in teaching English as a second language* (pp. 12–14). Washington, DC: TESOL.

Tang, C. (1997). On the power and status of nonnative ESL teachers. *TESOL Quarterly, 31*(3), 577–580.

Autonomy and Collaboration in Teacher Education: Journal Sharing among Native and Nonnative English-Speaking Teachers

Aya Matsuda
University of New Hampshire

Paul Kei Matsuda
University of New Hampshire

The issue of nonnative English-speaking teachers (NNESTs) has attracted much scholarly and professional attention in the last few years. In 1998, a caucus was established in the Teachers of English to Speakers of Other Languages (TESOL) organization in order to address through research and networking various issues related to NNESTs. The California/Nevada affiliate CATESOL followed in December 1999 by creating an interest group devoted to the issues of nonnative language educators. Several articles and books that specifically address these issues have been published (e.g., Braine, 1999; Kamhi-Stein, Lee, & Lee, 1999; Liu, 1999; A. Matsuda, 1997; P. K. Matsuda, 1999–2000). This book adds to the growing body of literature. While it is a recent phenomenon, the growth of interest in this topic is not surprising, because the majority of English teachers in the world are nonnative speakers of the language.

Many, if not most, teacher education programs in English-dominant countries enroll both native and nonnative speakers who are pre-service or in-service teachers. In these contexts, collaboration between

NNESTs and native English-speaking teachers (NESTs) is not only desirable but may even be necessary. From the perspective of teacher educators, collaboration is desirable because it can contribute to the creation of a community in which teachers learn from their differences. In such a learning community, the professional, cultural, and linguistic diversity that teachers bring with them becomes an asset rather than a liability. From the perspective of pre-service and in-service teachers, collaborative teacher development not only makes their learning experience more positive and productive but also helps them develop the ability to work collaboratively, which may be a necessity in their future careers. After graduation, NNESTs may stay in an English-dominant country or move to countries other than their own and begin careers as English teachers. Similarly, many opportunities are available for NESTs who are interested in teaching English in countries where English is not the dominant language. In any of these teaching options, all of which are common in the TESOL profession, one is likely to be working with colleagues who have linguistic, cultural, and academic backgrounds that differ from one's own. Consequently, the ability to establish good rapport and to collaborate well with a diverse group of teachers and administrators is essential for building a successful career and for providing effective instruction for one's students.

In order to create such a learning environment, we argue for a collaborative model of native and nonnative English-speaking teacher development (P. K. Matsuda, 1999–2000). Traditionally, the evaluation of teacher development has tended to be based on the "deficit model," in which teachers are individually evaluated only in terms of qualifications they have (competence) and those that they do not have (deficits). For instance, some nonnative speakers (NNSs) may be viewed as lacking experiences in certain English genres, while some native speakers (NSs) may be viewed as lacking the metalinguistic awareness of the English language. Based on *either-or logic,* NESTs and NNESTs in this model are viewed as discrete (NESTs or NNESTs) or competitive (NESTs vs. NNESTs).

In contrast, in the collaborative model of teacher development, which is driven by *both-and logic,* "teachers see themselves as members of a collaborative community in which they share their special strengths to help each other out" (P. K. Matsuda, 1999–2000, p. 10). Because this model focuses on the learning community created by teachers and on the development of the teachers as a group, learning takes place through sharing stories and adopting, adapting, and learning from others' "approaches and strategies that are informed by differing linguistic, cultural, and educational backgrounds" (ibid.). In other words, this model strives for integration (NESTs and NNESTs), cooperation (mutual sharing), and addition (NEST strengths plus

NNEST strengths), all of which can lead to the type of collaboration that increases the effectiveness of teacher education programs.

In this chapter, we describe an example of such collaboration between NESTs and NNESTs. Specifically, we show how the use of online journal sharing maximized each teacher's strengths and encouraged teachers to learn from the diversity in the group—including, but not limited to, linguistic diversity.

Journals in Teacher Education

In recent years, the use of journals has gained popularity in teacher education programs. It has been adopted by many teacher educators as a way to monitor new teachers' progress and to provide formative responses (Bailey, 1990; Brinton, Holten, & Goodwin, 1993; Cole, Raffier, Rogan, & Schleicher, 1998; Dong, 1997; Porter, Goldstein, Leatherman, & Conrad, 1990; Thornbury, 1991). Some researchers have also used journal entries as a source of data to gain insights into the process of teacher development and to evaluate teacher education programs. Murphy-O'Dwyer (1985), in an analysis of the reflective journals of pre-service teachers in a two-week teacher education course, identified issues that concerned the teachers, including group dynamics, administrative constraints, personal variables, and presentation and content of a lesson. Similarly, Numrich (1996), in her analysis of the journals of novice English as a second language teachers, was able to identify such concerns as preoccupation with teaching behavior, transfer and rejection of the teachers' own second language (L2) learning experience, and unexpected discoveries about effective teaching and teaching frustrations (see also Brinton & Holten, 1989). Furthermore, as Dong (1997) suggests, the reflective journal can help teacher educators re-evaluate and redefine the needs of teacher education programs:

> One of the focuses in my methods course . . . is on content-area instruction. However, students' responses from their field work reveal that content-oriented ESL instruction was not often practiced in real teaching because of the departmentalization of content teachers at high schools and the isolation of ESL teachers. Peer responses made me realize that interdisciplinary collaboration and access to resources are critical to making this happen. (p. 31)

Although responses to the use of journals in teacher education have been mostly positive and enthusiastic, some limitations and concerns have been identified. The lack of motivation among teachers, for example, is one of the potential problems in the use of journals. Teachers may not fully understand the benefit of keeping reflective journals in their professional development, because the results of critical reflection are not always tangible. Teachers may also feel that the task of keeping a journal is not worth including in their already busy schedule. This is an important consideration, especially when the journal writing task is imposed by the teacher educator, because as Barkhuizen (1995) points out, teachers may perceive the purpose of the journal differently or even become suspicious of the intent of the teacher educator.

Another possible problem is appropriation, which occurs when the teacher's goals in writing journals are controlled by the teacher educator's goals for using the journals. Considering the teacher educator as the primary audience, teachers may choose to write what they think will please this person. Even when the teacher educator does not respond to the text, the sheer presence of the authority figure— however unthreatening—may make teachers overly self-conscious and sometimes defensive, influencing how they perceive and use the journal (Jarvis, 1992), and can undermine the whole purpose of using the journal. Furthermore, the teacher educator's use of journals as a data source for their own research may also raise ethical questions (Barkhuizen, 1995).

The use of journals may also isolate members of the class when it is limited to the "dialogue" between the teacher educator and individual teachers (however, for examples of interactive uses of journals, see Cole et al., 1998; Dong, 1997). While this type of interaction allows the teacher educator to focus on the specific needs of each teacher and thus may sometimes be useful for teachers with little or no experience, it may also cause the teachers to depend too much on the teacher educator for directions. Furthermore, too much focus on the individual may promote competition at the expense of cooperation among teachers. As a result, unique perspectives that teachers from diverse backgrounds bring to the group may remain untapped.

Although these limitations do exist, they are not "insurmountable" (Barkhuizen, 1995, p. 33). In our journal sharing described next, we attempted to overcome these limitations.

Description of the Context

Participants in the online journal project discussed in this chapter were four graduate teaching assistants, including both authors, who were teaching sections of first-year composition designated for ESL students (ENGL 101I) in the fall of 1996. Since this was our first time to teach ESL sections of this course, we were enrolled in a practicum course in teaching ESL writing, which involved a weekly one-hour group meeting with the mentor.

The four of us came from diverse backgrounds and had diverse experiences and interests. Betty, a native of Oklahoma, was a second-year master of arts student in linguistics and ESL and was engaged in an MA thesis research project on language and gender.[1] Her teaching career had begun the previous year when she started teaching English 101 and 102—mainstream sections of introductory composition courses. In the fall of 1996 she was teaching a section of 101 along with a section of 101I. Jack, originally from Nebraska, was in his second year in an MA program in rhetoric and composition. Like Betty, he had taught mainstream composition the previous school year. Aya, a native of Japan, was also a second-year MA student, specializing in linguistics and ESL. Her prior teaching experience included teaching English as a foreign language to secondary students in Japan and teaching mainstream introductory composition. Paul, also from Japan, was specializing in ESL composition as a second-year doctoral student in rhetoric and composition. He had worked as a tutor both as an undergraduate and as a master's student and had taught mainstream composition the previous year.

Our journal project was carried out in conjunction with this practicum, although it was independent of the course requirements. The original goal of our journal sharing project was to critically reflect on our own teaching practices and to relate our previous teaching experience to the knowledge of ESL and composition theory in our new instructional context—the first-year ESL composition course. We did not specify how often we needed to post our journal entries, but two to seven entries (about four on average) were written and exchanged each week.

As was the case in Cole et al. (1998), our reflective journal project was completely self-initiated. Some of us were in the process of developing proposals for a conference when we received the teaching assignment for the following semester. We decided to collaborate and met then, during the semester preceding the assignment, to plan our project. At this first meeting, we chose reflective journal sharing as a way to facilitate our collaboration. Although we received encouragement and support from our mentor, he neither required nor evaluated this project in any fashion; the four of us took the initiative to conceive and implement it. In fact, to prevent the possibility of appropriation, our mentor voluntarily refrained from reading our journals, allowing the four of us to express our views and discuss concerns without the fear of being judged.

We shared our journal entries and responded to each other, which helped to create a supportive and collaborative network among the four of us. This defining feature of our project also transformed the nature of the reflective journal itself—the reflection no longer was at the level of each person but became a collective endeavor. We used the journal not only for personal reflections but also for sharing ideas and stories. By doing so, we were able to develop a body of local knowledge, or what North (1987) has called "practitioner's lore" (p. 23)—a body of practical knowledge that arises from the network of teachers.

Another important feature of our journal sharing project was the use of e-mail, which, as Kamhi-Stein (2000) has also pointed out, can be a useful tool to facilitate the exchange of insights. We initially exchanged hard-copy versions of our journals, until some of us expressed interest in using e-mail as a vehicle for the exchange. The use of e-mail made our journals more interactive because we were able to share our thoughts and to respond to each other more frequently. Using e-mail also facilitated the preservation of "significant or important events for the purpose of later reflection" (Richards, 1990, p. 10).

In addition, this project included not only making and sharing journal entries but also analyzing them as a group. Several times during and after the semester, we printed out the journals and analyzed them collectively, which added another layer to our critical reflections. In the process, we also negotiated what to discuss in our future journals and how to respond to each other. The ongoing as well as retrospective analyses helped us reflect critically on our own teaching practices from multiple perspectives.

Our Journal Entries

Our journal entries addressed a wide range of issues in teaching ESL writing, because we intentionally left the focus of the journal open and flexible at the beginning. Most of our entries, however, reflected the following themes: sharing teaching ideas and information, discussing issues in L2 writing, reflecting on one's own development and practices as a teacher, and providing moral support.

Sharing Teaching Ideas and Information

As we described earlier, we initially shared our journals off-line, by leaving a copy in each other's mailboxes, and we did the same with handouts, in order to exchange teaching ideas. When we decided to use e-mail, the exchange of teaching ideas became more than a mere sharing of "recipes," because we soon started to include reflections on how each task or activity worked in the classroom. Furthermore, we often adapted each other's ideas, used them in our own classes, and reported back on how they went. For instance, Aya wrote:

I've been trying to figure out how to deal with the concept of "writing as thinking" which was one of the central issues in my 101 & 102 last year. I would like to introduce it to my 101I students, too. . . . However, my concern is that many of my students seem to be still at the stage of getting used to putting their ideas in English that makes sense, and making [them] think through writing "English" may be too much burden for them. I asked them to freewrite today in any language they like, but I'm not sure if I should or want to rely on their L1 (first language) all the time. (September 1, 1996)

Aya discussed this experience again in detail at the following weekly meeting and described the freewriting activity in which she encouraged students to use their L1, if they so chose, to initiate thinking. A few days later, Jack responded:

I stole Aya's idea for a first language freewrite, which seemed to go very well. Only one student (Luis, the near-native speaker) did not write for the full time. Because my class has two or more speakers of each first language, I did a first language group activity in which the groups evaluated each member's topics, and tried to advise on both topic selection and possible lines of development. The class seemed genuinely surprised that I was encouraging them to not speak English in an English class, and that I was not interested in looking at their work (even if I could read it). I must admit that I felt very peripheral to the class activity when all of the groups were working in their native languages. (September 5, 1996)

The online journal also provided us with a convenient way of asking questions and of exchanging information about teaching-related issues. Betty asked, for instance:

Hey, Paul and Aya. Here's a question for you: What are your teachers like in Japan compared to here? Several of my students comment on their native teachers being very personal. Any thoughts on that? I'm thinking of the implications for us as teachers. My [international] students love it when I [divulge] personal info and talk to them about their families. (September 17, 1996)

In response to this question, Paul and Aya wrote:

My teachers in Japan seemed much more impersonal than my teachers in the U.S. partly because of the class size (almost all high school classes had 40+ students). But that depends on how you deal with them—they were more personal with me because I always sat in the front row and went to their offices just to chat. Even then, teachers in Japan have a sense of distance that they have to maintain in order to keep their ethos as teachers. But I'm sure that's changing as well . . . (Paul, September 17, 1996)

My teachers from elementary and secondary schools were more personal than many professors and instructors in college/univ., but I think it is more of the difference between higher education and non-higher (??) education than the cultural difference . . . (Aya, September 17, 1996)

Because we were trying out many activities for the first time, knowing how they worked in different contexts helped us examine the usefulness and effectiveness of those activities. Furthermore, the fact that our journal often functioned as a vehicle for generating teaching materials provided a practical motivation to participate in the sharing of journal entries.

Discussing Issues in L2 Writing

While many of our discussions were related to day-to-day teaching practices, such as the ones discussed above, some of them developed into more general discussions of issues in L2 writing. For example, the issue of responding to students' texts often generated active discussion in our journal exchange and during the weekly meeting:

I stopped several times in the process of responding to their papers, thinking that I was focusing too much on grammar. . . . I am now wishing that I had a chance to give them feedback on the content and rhetorical features of their paper before I collected this version. I know both are important, but commenting on both grammar and rhetoric is probably too demanding for some students (and for me). Maybe I will start commenting on one or the other. For those who are strong in content and organization, I will provide minimum comment on these areas and provide extensive feedback on grammar and convention. For others who have problems in both "rhetoric" and "syntax" (to use Barbara Kroll's [1990] distinction), I will focus on rhetorical features. (Paul, September 29, 1996)

This type of discussion helped us connect theory and pedagogy— to apply insights from our reading, off-line discussions, and the mentor's advice to our teaching practices—because we not only shared anecdotes but also tried to make references to readings and research.

The issue of nonnative English-speaking professionals was also an important topic of discussion in our exchange. We shared our personal experiences, as the following comment from Aya describes:

I personally think both NS [native speakers] and NNS [nonnative speakers] have some good things to offer to our students. There are probably certain things that I can do and NS can't, or I cannot do but NS can—or what I can/

can't do and other NNS can't/can. So I do hope my students get someone other than me for 102I and learn something different from you guys. . . . To tell you the truth, being NNS does not have as much advantage as I first thought. And not as much disadvantage either. Or they are about the same so they cancel out. It may appear one way or the other (good or bad) on the first couple of days, but students learn to see beyond my dark hair and exotic name . . . (September 20, 1996)

In response to this comment, Betty provided her assessment of American students' attitudes toward international teaching assistants as well as her own view on the issue:

I think that the attitudes reflect both an acceptance and a reluctance to appear racist. I think that American undergrads are quicker to voice their opinion than nonnative undergrads. I think that native undergrads are more hostile to nonnative teachers—and not just of English. I have had several students write about it in their journals in the past year. Of course they don't realize that I am majoring in ESL. . . . I always turn to a more experienced teacher whenever I have questions about teaching. So naturally, I have turned to Paul, Aya, Mike T. and others. I know for a fact that Paul knows more stuff about teaching strategies—not to mention the English language—than I do. Why would I go to someone with less experience than me just because they were L1 speakers? (September 24, 1996)

This topic, as easily imagined, was a sensitive one. Although most of the discussion addressed the native and nonnative English speaker issue in general terms, we were, in a way, talking about ourselves. However, this explicit discussion was crucial in establishing our collaborative relationship, because it helped us realize the complexity of this issue as well as the richness of the diverse backgrounds that we brought to the group.

Reflecting on Our Own Development and Teaching Practices

In addition to sharing teaching ideas and discussion issues specific to ESL writing instruction, we often shared our reflections on our own strengths and weaknesses as teachers. For example, Aya wrote:

As you have probably noticed by now, I do expect a lot from my students; not so much in the quality of their work, because I know they are to improve it in this class, but trying their best, doing work on time, coming to class and participating, and that kind of stuff. When my students don't meet those expectations, I get frustrated with my students for not "fulfilling their responsibilities" and also with myself for not being able to communicate my expectation or why it's important to do the work on time. Am I expecting too much from my students? Am I not "threatening" enough? (September 24, 1996)

To this message, Betty responded:

> This is a specific response to Aya's concern about whether she is "threatening" enough or not. My students that are not doing their part have begun to do their part because their grades reflect their inactivity. They have all begun to sit up and participate. I sometimes have to [coerce] them into participating, but they are doing better. (September 25, 1996)

We did not respond as directly to these entries about our teaching as we did to other types of entries, but they still created a strong sense of sharing and interaction. Some of us felt that having someone to talk to about our own progress and frustrations was helpful in itself. Reading stories of other teachers' struggles and development also helped us get to know each other better and build a tighter and friendlier learning community.

Providing Moral Support

Finally, there were some "pep talk" entries that provided moral support. All exchanges contributed to our group morale by strengthening our collaborative network, but some remarks specifically expressed our trust in this group. For example, Betty wrote:

> I just want you guys to know that I think our mentor group is extremely productive and that we all work together very well. We have a group dynamic that is unsurpassed I'm sure in other groups. I am excited about sticking together next semester. (September 24, 1996)

What Happened Next

In the following semester, the four of us stuck together to some extent, as Betty had hoped. All of us taught ENGL 102I, an ESL section of the second course in the introductory composition sequence, and we continued to exchange our journals. The exchange was less frequent, however, because we were all using very different syllabi, making the exchange of teaching ideas somewhat difficult. We probably had also gained some confidence as ESL writing teachers and did not need the same level of support we had needed the previous semester. Nonetheless, we maintained the online journals as a vehicle for interaction and continued more informal exchanges such as conversation in our offices.

At the same time, our collaboration went beyond the realm of teaching into the realm of scholarship. From this project, each of us found and developed research topics such as (a) how our differing backgrounds affected our views and practices as teachers, (b) how ESL students' perceived and reacted to NESTs and NNESTs, (c) how group dynamics may influence the process of collaboration and of mentoring, and (d) how teachers may develop professionally through collaboration. We even presented papers collaboratively at two conferences, and some of us are continuing to explore the research interests we developed through this project.

Conclusion

Just like any project, our online journal sharing project was not without problems. We began participating in this project with different assumptions and expectations—and did not initially foresee the need to articulate them. For example, at our first collective analysis meeting, we found out that one of us had not read the others' entries while the rest of us had been reading and responding to each other. We realized that we had to decide how interactive these journal entries could and should be. After much discussion, we decided to read and respond to the journals as they were distributed and to write our own entries regularly so that all four of us could benefit from the exchange. Setting the ground rules at the beginning of the project could have prevented such problems, although in our case the process of identifying assumptions and negotiating solutions provided an additional opportunity for collaboration that may have contributed to a stronger sense of community.

Despite these small glitches, the online journal sharing project was collaborative, productive, and successful. Two factors that seem to have contributed to the success of this project were the autonomy of the participants and the opportunity they had to observe each other's growth. As described earlier, the teachers were autonomous in that the teacher educator refrained from participating. This gave us complete freedom and responsibility to shape the project. Thus, from the very beginning, we had to communicate with each other frequently and make group decisions regarding the journal sharing. In addition, other logistics of this teacher education program encouraged our individual autonomy. For instance, although we were asked to use the same syllabus, we were allowed to be flexible; we had much freedom in how we organized each lesson. With this flexibility came the need for a series of decisions that had to be made in a thoughtful, yet timely, manner, just as in any teaching context. For the four of us—novice teachers who were not always confident about their decisions—e-mail was a convenient way to share our plans and get quick feedback, and the journal sharing project provided such an arena for this exchange. In other words, the teacher autonomy that was allowed in the structure of the teacher education program created the need for networking and collaboration among teachers.

This flexibility also allowed us to explore ways to use our strengths and develop our own teaching styles, which leads to another characteristic of this project—it provided opportunities to see others grow as teachers. The online journal allowed us to have an informal, candid, and spontaneous exchange of our stories about struggles and success. We witnessed how others develop their teaching styles using their unique strengths and expertise, and we gained a better understanding of why they teach the way they do. In other words, both the general structure of this teacher education program and this particular online journal project contributed to greater teacher autonomy, which encouraged us to be different, to appreciate our differences, and to learn from the differences.

Since our collaboration was completely self-initiated and autonomous, it may be difficult to replicate it in other contexts—unless a group of teachers happen to be reading this chapter and decide to start their own version of a collaborative journal sharing project. However, teacher educators can facilitate autonomous and collaborative teacher development in a number of ways. For example, they can ask teachers to read articles on teacher reflection journals and collaboration (e.g., this chapter) prior to or at the beginning of the term, and they can encourage them to consider how they might collaborate. Discussing the rationale and strategies for collaboration in teacher development in class or at professional development workshops may also be effective in introducing teachers to the idea of collaborative teacher development. Teacher educators can also encourage collaboration by creating an e-mail list exclusively for teachers and by encouraging them to think about how they might use it to suit their own needs. Although it may be disheartening for some teacher educators not to be able to monitor or evaluate some aspects of the teachers' progress, we believe that the benefit of autonomy outweighs its cost.

The collaborative approach to teacher development, we feel, is especially important in TESOL because TESOL professionals, no matter where they go, will encounter colleagues—as well as students—who come from a wide variety of backgrounds. The experience of collaborative development in the context of a teacher development program can encourage teachers to develop a collaborative learning community in their own classrooms and, in the long run, to continue their professional development by collaborating with their colleagues.

Note

1. While the authors use their own names in this report, Betty and Jack are pseudonyms for the other participants.

References

Bailey, K. M. (1990). The use of diary studies in teacher education programs. In J. C. Richards & D. Nunan (Eds.), *Second language teacher education* (pp. 215–226). Cambridge: Cambridge University Press.

Barkhuizen, G. P. (1995). Dialogue journals in teacher education revisited. *College ESL, 5*(1), 22–35.

Braine, G. (Ed.). (1999). *Non-native educators in English language teaching.* Mahwah, NJ: Erlbaum.

Brinton, D., & Holten, C. A. (1989). What novice teachers focus on: The practicum in TESL. *TESOL Quarterly, 23,* 343–350.

Brinton, D. M., Holten, C. A., & Goodwin, J. M. (1993). Responding to dialogue journals in teacher preparation: What's effective? *TESOL Journal, 2*(4), 15–19.

Cole, R., Raffier, L. M., Rogan, P., & Schleicher, L. (1998). Interactive group journals: Learning as a dialogue among learners. *TESOL Quarterly, 32,* 556–568.

Dong, Y. R. (1997). Collective reflection: Using peer responses to dialogue journals in teacher education. *TESOL Journal, 7*(2), 26–31.

Jarvis, J. (1992). Using diaries for teacher reflection on in-service courses. *ELT Journal, 46,* 133–143.

Kamhi-Stein, L. D. (2000). Integrating computer-mediated communication tools into the practicum. In K. E. Johnson (Ed.), *Teacher preparation* (pp. 119–135). Alexandria, VA: TESOL.

Kamhi-Stein, L. D., Lee, E., & Lee, C. (1999, August/September). How TESOL programs can enhance the preparation of nonnative English speakers. *TESOL Matters, 9*(4), 1, 5.

Kroll, B. (1990). The rhetoric/syntax split: Designing a curriculum for ESL students. *Journal of Basic Writing, 9,* 40–55.

Liu, J. (1999). Nonnative-English-speaking-professionals. *TESOL Quarterly, 33,* 85–102.

Matsuda, A. (1997). Diversity: An asset in teacher development. *TESOLIN, 16*(3), 10–11.

Matsuda, P. K. (1999–2000, December/January). Teacher development through native speaker–nonnative speaker collaboration. *TESOL Matters, 9*(6), 1, 10.

Murphy-O'Dwyer, L. M. (1985). Diary studies as a method for evaluating teacher training. In J. C. Alderson (Ed.), *Evaluation* (pp. 97–128). Oxford: Pergamon.

Numrich, C. (1996). On becoming a language teacher: Insights from diary studies. *TESOL Quarterly, 30,* 131–151.

North, S. M. (1987). *The making of knowledge in composition: Portrait of an emerging field.* Portsmouth, NH: Heinemann.

Porter, P. A., Goldstein, L. M., Leatherman, J., & Conrad, S. (1990). An ongoing dialogue: Learning logs for teacher preparation. In J.C. Richards & D. Nunan (Eds.), *Second language teacher education* (pp. 227–240). Cambridge: Cambridge University Press.

Richards, J. C. (1990). What happened to methods? *Language Teacher, 14*(6), 9–10.

Thornbury, S. (1991). Watching the whites of their eyes: The use of teaching-practice logs. *ELT Journal, 45,* 140–146.

Nonnative English-Speaking Student Teachers: Insights from Dialogue Journals

Donna M. Brinton
University of California, Los Angeles

The practicum is the first time that I have ever stood up in front of a class and teach. It has been proven a very tough and rewarding job. As a beginner, I have numerous things to learn. How to talk to a big class with 50 students without my hands, legs and lips shaking, how to talk to low level students who have little English, how to plan a smooth lesson without gaps that hold up the learning progress, how to give instructions and explain new words . . . not to mention the difficulty that as a non-native speaker I sometimes lose my English when I am too nervous, I learn to cope with them. None of them is easy. But I am willing to work on my weaknesses. I feel I have more confidence as I do actual teaching. The students' support and growth is the most rewarding moment I can think of. The hard work is paid off as you sense their progress and hear they say, "Teacher, I like your lesson." I wish I could improve myself and teach more.

—Nonnative English-speaking TESOL student teacher

Nonnative English-speaking (NNES) students form a significant portion of the students enrolled in North American Teaching English to Speakers of Other Languages (TESOL) programs. To complete their degrees, these students are usually required to enroll in the field practicum in TESOL and serve as student teachers for a specified number of hours (Polio & Wilson-Duffy, 1998).

For several reasons, the student teaching requirement can be a formidable one for NNES students. The first of these stems from the underlying rationale and goals of the practicum itself—that is, to provide novice teachers with a local, field-based teaching experience under the close supervision and guidance of experienced mentors. In fact, the practicum in North American universities is not usually designed with the NNES population in mind (for a discussion on this topic, see Brady & Gulikers, this volume). Nor does it typically provide special accommodations to assist these master of arts in TESOL (MA TESOL) students in completing their practicum requirement (Samimy & Brutt-Griffler, 1999; see, however, Kamhi-Stein, 2000, for ways to tailor the practicum to NNES student teachers' needs).

Despite the fact that many NNES student teachers will eventually teach in the EFL setting, the setting in which they receive their initiation into teaching is the ESL setting. To the NNES student teacher, this is a foreign setting indeed. For one, the classroom culture and milieu often do not resemble the ones in which they, as former EFL students, learned English. In addition, they are frequently unfamiliar with the types of educational settings in which practicum placements typically occur—intensive English programs (IEPs), adult education programs, and community college noncredit or credit programs. In short, in addition to learning to teach in what is an unfamiliar and often intimidating setting, these NNES student teachers are most frequently deprived of guidance specifically tailored to teaching in the EFL setting. Govardhan, Nayar, and Sheorey (1999) note that, given the exponential growth in the need for English language instruction outside North America, this lack of preparation to teach in the EFL context is a shortcoming for both native English-speaking (NES) and NNES students enrolled in U.S. MA TESOL programs.

A second reason underlying the challenges posed by the MA TESOL practicum requirement has to do with the diverse nature of the NNES student teachers themselves. Many of these students hold international student visas. Members of this group typically return to their home countries to teach EFL, putting into practice what they learned in their North American–based graduate programs. An increasing number of the NNES students, however, are immigrants to North America. Members of this group typically intend to remain in North America, working either as ESL teachers or locating jobs teaching their first language (L1). Although worldwide NNES English language educators comprise the majority of the English language teaching workforce, in the ESL setting NES teachers predominate. This reality typically exacerbates the challenges faced by NNES students, who may perceive themselves as out of place or unqualified to perform the duties of a student teacher in this setting. Even more than their

NES counterparts, NNES student teachers tend to lack confidence in their ability to rise to the challenge of delivering quality lessons. Like the NNES student teacher cited at the outset of this chapter, this lack of confidence is often compounded by perceived or real weaknesses in the English language.

Research into the challenges faced by NNES student teachers is sparse. Although most TESOL educators who have supervised the field practicum would agree that this course is especially challenging for the NNES student teacher, this belief tends to be based on accumulated experience placing and supervising these students rather than on empirical evidence. Insight into the difficulties that NNES student teachers face is often gleaned through whole-group class discussions during practicum class sessions or through individual office-hour interactions. It may also be revealed through their journal entries (see, e.g., Brinton & Holten, 1988, 1989) or in class website bulletin board postings (Kamhi-Stein, 1999). Little documentation in the literature is available to enlighten TESOL educators on this topic (see, however, Lee & Lew, 2001).

The Present Study

Background and Context

In a previous study, Brinton and Holten (1989) found that the dialogue journal entries of NNES student teachers differed from those of their NES peers in that the NNES student teacher comments focused more on issues pertaining to activities and methodology as well as on lesson planning. More generally, Kamhi-Stein (2000) noted that NNES teachers-in-preparation perceived themselves as lacking self-confidence, language ability, and visibility and status in the profession. She also reported that they experienced prejudice based on their ethnicity or NNES status.

The context of the present study is a cross-listed TESOL field practicum course (AL/TESL C118/C218—Language Teaching Practicum) offered through the Department of Applied Linguistics and TESL at the University of California, Los Angeles (UCLA). In the cross-listed format, both undergraduate and graduate students receive instruction concurrently (i.e., in the same classroom and from the same instructors). The course consists of the following student populations:

1. Undergraduate students enrolled in UCLA's undergraduate minor emphasis in Teaching English as a Second or Foreign Language (consisting of eight courses in second language pedagogy)

2. Graduate students from a variety of departments (including those pursuing an MA in Applied Linguistics) who are completing the Teaching as a Second Language (TESL) certificate as a secondary aim

In both of these cases, the field practicum is designed to be the culminating experience in the degree program. Due to its intensive nature, the field practicum is co-taught by two instructors; student teachers are assigned to one instructor as their primary field supervisor for observational and guidance purposes. Based on the period 1995–2002, NNES students comprise approximately 46% percent of the practicum population; they divide roughly equally into the international and immigrant populations previously described.

With a view toward providing insights into the particular challenges faced by NNES student teachers, this study examined their firsthand dialogue journal accounts of the practicum collected over a five-year period. The value of such journal exchanges in capturing teacher reasoning in action (Johnson, 1999) has been variously documented (see, e.g., Bailey, Curtis, & Nunan, 2001; Gray, 1998; Holten & Brinton, 1995; Jarvis, 1996; Porter, Goldstein, Leatherman, & Conrad, 1990; Richards & Ho, 1998; Roderick, 1986; Thornbury, 1991; Woodfield & Lazarus, 1998). With specific reference to the practicum course in this study, these journals allow the field supervisor to communicate regularly with student teachers in the field, thus gaining insights into the day-to-day challenges they face and the solutions they discover (Brinton, Holten, & Goodwin, 1993). They also allow the field supervisor to deepen her relationship with the student teachers and to maximize the exchange of information among the practicum course participants.

Procedure

Dialogue journal exchanges are a standard component of the "Language Teaching Practicum" course. According to syllabus specifications, students are to reflect on their practicum experience through dialogue journal entries written to a peer. These journal exchanges take the form of five original journal entries written by each student teacher over the 10-week quarter and five responses to a peer dialogue journal partner who is also enrolled in the class and who shares a similar teaching setting. The journals provide a forum for student teachers to collaboratively probe the teaching act—asking and answering teaching-related questions, sharing ideas about issues, and problem solving. All exchanges occur via e-mail. As the instructor, I receive copies of both the original entries and the responses, which are evaluated as part of the student teachers' final practicum grade.

TABLE 1. Breakdown of NNES Participants

Undergraduate (N)		Graduate (N)	
8		6	
International (N)	Immigrant (N)	International (N)	Immigrant (N)
2	6	4	2

Occasionally, although not on a regular basis, I participate in the exchanges—especially in instances where student teachers direct questions at me and/or request an opinion.

The participants in this study consisted of 14 long-term immigrant students (U.S. residents or citizens) and international students (on an I-20 visa) enrolled in the "Language Teaching Practicum" course over the period 1995–2000. Four of the 14 students were male (one was an international undergraduate, two were international graduates, and one was an immigrant graduate). Eliminated from this participant pool were any students who characterized themselves as bilingual. The breakdown of NNES participants is shown in Table 1.

For the purpose of this study, I examined the completed dialogue journals of the 14 NNES participants. The total length of the journal entries examined ranged from 1,184 to 3,454 words, with an average journal length of 2,581 words. As I read the entries, I noted any comments that emerged from the participants' NNES status. Once this process had been completed, I clustered the comments into four general areas, each representing a recurring issue for the NNES participants, and coded each comment accordingly. The categories follow:

1. *Confidence Issues:* General lack of confidence in the ability to perform adequately in the field practicum
2. *Linguistic Issues:* Doubts about linguistic performance in class or in interactions with the students and mentor teacher; inadequate knowledge of English (e.g., the grammatical system, the sound system)
3. *Methodological Issues:* Difficulty adhering to the mentor teacher's methodology due to previous English language learning experience or strongly held beliefs regarding appropriate methodologies for teaching English
4. *Cultural Issues:* Difficulty dealing with students from other cultures; difficulty explicating North American culture

Findings

The findings of the study are generally reflective of the previously cited studies of NNES teachers-in-preparation and confirm my own experience of many years dealing with NNES student teachers. The value of the study therefore lies primarily in its confirmatory nature. However, a particular contribution of this study is that, unlike studies that rely on questionnaire or survey data (e.g., Govardhan et al., 1999; Samimy & Brutt-Griffler, 1999), this study captures in their own words the reactions of NNES student teachers as they reflect on their emerging teacher identity. Moreover, since the data were not originally collected with the specific purpose of obtaining information on NNES students, the comments that emerge from the journals may be a more reliable indicator of the challenges faced by NNES teachers than data obtained from studies specifically designed to elicit such responses.

On reading through the dialogue journal entries, one is struck both by how deeply these student teachers reflect on the act of teaching and by how they seek to overcome any challenges they encounter. In fact, it is this very reflective nature of the NNES student teachers that led my colleague Christine Holten and me (Brinton & Holten, 1989) to note the "more detailed attention paid . . . to the basic building blocks of good teaching" (p. 347) of the NNES student teachers over their NES peers. Below, I share some of their more poignant comments in each of the four coding categories.

Confidence Issues

Displaying confidence in front of students is an issue with which all teachers wrestle. This is true not only for novice teachers but for all teachers throughout their careers. No doubt even the most experienced teachers have had the experience of a certain group of students that challenged them and tested their own sense of confidence to the limits. Yet it is undeniable that novice teachers experience this lack of confidence even more acutely, often feeling that students do not respect them in their role as teacher. This is the case in the following nonnative English speaker's journal excerpt:

> I was very nervous in front of class and lacked a lot of blackboard management. So, our Friday class really helped. I noticed how my mentor teacher wrote out everything on the board and I personally don't like to write on the blackboard. I also think I lacked a lot of confidence b/c I blanked out couple of times and "messed" a lot. Now, I feel like a complete fool in class. I don't think students will see/respect me as a teacher at all. Although I had asked [mentor teacher] to help me out if I get stuck, I sort of felt like she was "monitoring" me or something. I'm sure she meant to help me out, but I was honestly really nervous. I hope to do better next time.

Feelings of being disrespected or of being unworthy of serving as a teacher are often exacerbated in cases where the mentor teacher is either less than supportive or perceived as being unsupportive. Alluded to in the preceding comment, this threat to the NNES student teachers' confidence emerges even more clearly in the following comment:

> My mentor teacher is an ex-kindergarten teacher. She is very energetic. With her energy flowing around the class, she upholds students' attention and interest. I know and feel that I am no match with her. On Thursday, she suddenly called on me to do the role-play with the whole class (I do this often with students individually but not yet the class as a whole). I was surprised, and so were the students. I was nervous and the role-play did not turn out very well. Later she said to me, "You can't accomplish what I can. You need to be confidence in front of the students. They easily pick on a teacher's nervousness. Even if you're nervous, don't show it." I have no words to say at that moment. Immediately I feel the pain. It hurts to my stomach. I know I am a very sensitive person and I may have been overreacting: she did not mean to hurt my feeling. On the other hand, I know there is truth in her words. . . . Showing confidence is how I need to be. . . . Then now, my biggest concern is that how I can achieve it. As an introverted person, I need to break the "timid-self." Besides repeatedly telling myself "You're capable doing it," I have no other ideas.

The issue of the nonnative English-speaker status is not directly addressed in either of the preceding comments. However, it is clear that nonnative English-speaker status can be a contributing factor in student teachers' lack of confidence. While the second student teacher quoted eventually grew in self-confidence and established good rapport in her practicum placement, the initial "timid-self" she displayed to both her mentor teacher and the ESL students caused her to lose face and suffer unduly during the early stages of the practicum.

Linguistic Issues

Closely tied to the issue of self-confidence is that of linguistic proficiency. The UCLA NNES student teachers represent a wide range of proficiency in English, from those who are near native to those who are still developing academic English skills. To minimize the difficulties those students with developing English language skills will encounter in the practicum, mentor teachers are always polled regarding their willingness to accept NNES student teachers. In placing student teachers, emphasis is also placed in identifying settings where the NNES student teachers' linguistic proficiency will be clearly higher than that of the students they are teaching and where they can serve as positive role models for the ESL students. However, even with these measures, the issue of language proficiency cannot be completely circumvented. The following comment from one of the international student teachers enrolled in the practicum course provides evidence of how her self-assessment of poor English language skills negatively impacts her practicum experience and her own sense of self as teacher:

> After six-week field practicum, I find my biggest obstacle as a good teacher comes from my language ability. Since my own English ability is lousy, thus, when I explain something to students, I think I unconciously make lots of errors or express unaptly. As tonight, I said "in this moment" instead of "at this moment," "after their marry" instead of "after their marriage." A language teacher, should set good example for students to model rather than confus them as I did. . . . I can sense that a qualifed language teacher should at least possess enought knowledge of the targeted language. . . . I really wonder about my teaching quality? Sometimes, I can't help to think maybe I am "brain-retarded" in learning language. (I don't improve much ever I have almost stayed here for one year. It's really frustrated!)

This comment addresses the student teacher's overall linguistic profile and her concerns regarding her ability to serve as a target model for students. However, other comments in this same category document student teachers' concern regarding their inability to provide accurate, skill-specific instruction, particularly when asked to do so "on the spot":

> Another thing I found it challenging is when students ask me to correct their grammar on the spot, and I can empathize with those who are as writing student teachers. It is really hard, especially for the nonnative speakers, like me.

Even when knowledge is not at issue and the source of the student error is evident to the student teacher, the challenge remains (and is attributed, rightly or wrongly, to the student teacher's nonnative English speaker status):

> Then, a totally unexpected thing happened. Some students began to ask questions on points that I'd never expected to have. One of them was about the word 'comprehensive' in "put together a comprehensive report." When a student said it means "easy to understand," I knew how he got to this interpretation (probably from the verb 'comprehend'). Then, other students began to say what I hadn't expected, so I didn't know how, first of all, to explain the answer and convince them with it. This was obvious because they just

kept saying what they thought the word means. The bad thing was I wasn't able to respond to them with patience and confidence. I'd never wished I were a native speaker more strongly this time than ever before.

Methodological Issues

Methodological issues surface in the journals for a variety of reasons. The first of these no doubt relates to the previous educational experiences of the NNES student teachers and their resulting strongly held beliefs about the teaching/learning process. In the following comment, the student teacher questions the mentor teacher's behavior toward students who have not completed assigned homework in a TOEFL preparation class:

> Because more than half of the students are planning to take TOEFL, [the mentor teacher] gives TOEFL exercise as a homework assignment. However, a lot of students don't do homework. Because my mentor teacher doesn't want to give any pressure to students, he doesn't blame students who didn't do homework. That is incomprehensible for me. They pay a lot of money to study English at [IEPs] and want to get a high score in TOEFL, however, they don't do their homework. What an inconsistency it is?

Although the art of elicitation (and its centrality in communicative language teaching) is heavily emphasized in the practicum class, it is a constant source of challenge for both NES and NNES student teachers. One particular NNES student teacher had failed repeatedly in her efforts during observed teaching to elicit information from students, instead falling back on teacher-delivered explanation, an approach she was accustomed to from her own EFL classes in her home country of Taiwan. In the following entry, she struggles to accept the value of eliciting information from students:

> I think [the mentor teacher] is good at leading the class in a very active and communicative way. Now I realize why she keeps on emphasizing the importance of illiciting the response from the students—this way the students would have more chance to participating in the class activity, since the teacher already knows the answer. By allowing the students to have the opportunity to speak out, they would be more concentrating on the lesson and would not feel like only getting input from the teacher without making their own output. Of course, it is somewhat hard for a new inexperienced teacher to perceive this. And I think it also needs some time for me to develop this kind of teaching skill in order not to cause too much silence during the ongoing of the class.

Yet another common topic of discussion to surface in the journals is that of error correction. In the following comment, the NNES student teacher criticizes her mentor teacher's lack of error correction, noting her own learning style preference for immediate correction:

> From the first day I entered the classroom, I have noticed that my mentor teacher does not emphasize error corrections. Fluency is placed highly above accuracy. My mentor teacher tries hard to involve as many students as she can. Students are encouraged to participate and praised constantly. . . . However, I think students need correction feedback and they themselves want to be corrected. From time to time, there are students ask me to correct their pronunciation and sentences, and I have never seen them ask my mentor teacher. . . . Yesterday, the problem of error correction struck me again. Students came up and wrote down the answers for the homework on the OHP [overhead projector]. One of the answers was "a red pair of shoes." My mentor went through the answers without any correction. I stared at "the red pair of shoes," thinking whether I should point it out. Would it be a part of students' language learning and turn into fossilization? . . . I have little tolerance for any kinds of errors and I myself will like to be corrected. I feel very uneasy on this issue and uncertain on how to deal with it. What do you think?

Cultural Issues

In Samimy and Brutt-Griffler's (1999) study of NNES TESOL graduate students, all 17 students surveyed reported inadequate knowledge of culture as a perceived deficit in their ability to function in the ESL classroom. Typically, when the topic of culture is discussed in teacher preparation, the focus of the discussion is on the student teachers' knowledge of the target culture and/or their ability to explicitly teach aspects of the target culture (i.e., in a planned lesson on culture). Alternatively, the focus of the discussion can be on the teachers' ability to display incidental cultural knowledge (Lazaraton, 2003) when topics arise spontaneously in class (e.g., during reading discussions or homework correction). However, cultural issues may also arise when NNES student teachers ally with students from their own host culture. The following comment, from a NNES student teacher of Korean descent, captures the complexities faced by a NNES student teacher teaching students from her own cultural/linguistic group:

> If you're fluent in your mother tongue and try to teach English as a nonnative speaker, like myself, students who speak your mother tongue can be both your best friends and your worst enemies (usually the former, luckily).

There is one Korean gentleman in my class who knows a great deal about English grammar. . . . I had a feeling that he didn't have much confidence in me as someone who could teach English. He never said hello or bye to me or asked me any questions during or after class. Last Thursday [the mentor teacher] gave back the quiz. . . . This gentleman was taken off a point because he used a comma before because [the mentor teacher] explained that commas are not used before subordinate conjunctions, but apparently he didn't find that explanation satisfactory, giving numerous counter examples that he had seen before. [The mentor teacher] . . . knew that I had the answer to his question and asked me if I wanted to add anything to her explanation. So I said that when a comma is used before the subordinate conjunction because, it is used as the coordinate conjunction for to provide an explanation for the preceding independent clause rather than to show a causal relationship between the two clauses. He liked my explanation and seemed to be a lot more responsive to me ever since then.

Faced with a situation in which the class is multicultural, novice NNES teachers may also find themselves advocating for students from their own cultural/linguistic group and using the L1 as a crutch, as in the following dialogue journal excerpt:

We also talked about the use of L1 in teaching. The Chinese students in the class are having a hard time getting the grammar. They want to attend the Chinese bilingual class, but their work would not let them. . . . The Chinese students end up in disadvantage. They like my help: an explanation in Chinese is much easier to understand than one in English. From today's talk, my mentor teacher seems very sensitive about this issue (I may have already irritated her). She has sympathy for the Chinese students. They want to learn but hardly progress. They are helpless and she could not do much. She thinks that I, a native Chinese speaker could help them out. However, she also believes that learning English through English instruction is more beneficial than in one's L1. If I talk to a student in Chinese, she would feel very irritated. Therefore, she hope that I would help the students in Chinese only if they have tried hard enough and still not getting the points. I think, at least at the beginning level with the focus on "survival skills" and fluency, students can learn a second/foreign language better through bilingual education. . . . In the current situation, I certainly should not irritate my mentor teacher.

This particular situation—in which the mentor teacher and student teacher were both nonnative English speakers but were from different cultural/linguistic groups—actually required intervention from me as practicum supervisor, since (as the NNES student teacher suspected) she had indeed irritated the mentor teacher by her excessive use of Chinese in the classroom.

Although allying with students from one's own cultural/linguistic group is a common occurrence, the opposite situation is equally possible—that is, NNES student teachers may experience dissonance with students from cultural/linguistic groups other than their own. This is most likely to occur in cases where a specific cultural group displays behavior or characteristics radically different from those to which the NNES student teacher is accustomed. In the following comment, a young, attractive female Korean was placed in an adult education setting in the Koreatown section of Los Angeles, where she had expected to find Korean-speaking students:

> Most of the students come from Spanish-speaking backgrounds. (I thought there would be more Korean-speaking students, but we didn't have any in class.) Students' ages ranged from early 20s to late 50s. They all wanted to learn English to get better jobs. I think this is one of the reasons why we had more male students in class. I felt quite a bit uncomfortable with students. I have never worked with adults before and some of the students seemed sort of weird. I don't know if "weird" is the right choice of word, but by the end of class, I really felt uncomfortable.

As became clear during subsequent class discussions, what had made this student teacher particularly uncomfortable was that several of the male students flirted openly with her both during break and while she presented lessons.

Other

The preceding four categories capture the bulk of the comments contained in the dialogue journal exchanges examined for this study. However, some of the student teachers' comments in this corpus elude categorization, while others cut across categories and do not neatly fit into one category or the other. I include the following comment since it clearly illustrates the uneasy (in this case, clearly painful) fit that some NNES student teachers experience in the ESL setting:

> So far, I've observed [peers'] lessons and both seemed to be having something that I don't think I have over the students in my assigned class. Although the students seemed to be relatively quiet (mine can get pretty loud in terms of responding), they seemed rather respectful towards their student teachers. Meaning, they seemed like "students" (ex, none of them during the entire lesson yawned and started talking to each other). Of course, I'm not saying that the students in my class are totally irrespectful (is this a word?) of me. But, some of them (especially the ones I hang out outside of the classroom) tend to be too comfortable with me during my lesson. They sometimes draw cute pictures of me before I come to the class and as soon

as I come in, they run to their seats and act as if nothing ever happened. I know they mean no harm and drawing pictures of me is rather a friendly gestures, but I still wish they didn't do that. I grew up more than half of my life (till I was 16) in Korea where teachers are respected second to none (except perhaps parents). It is almost unthinkable based on my childhood memories to be that comfortable with a teacher (even with a TA or student teachers). I often wondered if it's just me or the others in the teaching practicum class are getting the same kind of treatments from the students.

In this situation, the student teacher (an undergraduate international visa student who himself had begun his U.S. English language studies in an IEP prior to transitioning to a community college and finally to UCLA) too closely identified with the students in the IEP class to which he was assigned. Compounding his lack of self-confidence as a teacher was his confusion regarding the culturally appropriate role a teacher in a U.S. IEP should assume and his bewilderment concerning whether the negative student behavior he had experienced should be disciplined. Teacher educators have the responsibility to assist such students in gaining a sense of self as teacher, in creating an atmosphere that fosters respect, and in providing guidance in culturally appropriate norms of behavior and discipline.

Conclusion

It could be argued that some factors affecting NNES student teachers are the same as those affecting NES student teachers (e.g., anxieties associated with standing in front of a class of students for the first time, planning effective lessons, managing pair and group work, and eliciting contributions from students). However, other factors clearly seem to be unique to the student teachers' backgrounds as nonnative English speakers. These factors include, but are not limited to, language issues. As the current study reveals, NNES student teachers are very aware of their need to serve as a linguistic role model for students. Because of their status as nonnative English speakers, they frequently wrestle with issues of both fluency and accuracy in their teaching performance, especially in unplanned segments of classroom discourse where they are called upon to provide on-the-spot explanations. In connection with their previous classroom experiences, they may also wrestle with questions that pertain to the teaching/learning process, such as how much authority the teacher should have, what constitutes appropriate student behavior and responsibilities, whether teachers should require students to do work outside of class, and the like. Finally, they confront their perceived or real inabilities to explain the target culture to students or to expand upon issues that arise in the classroom and use them as a point of departure to address cultural issues.

In sum, it is the teacher educators' responsibility to foster in the TESOL practicum an atmosphere that is pedagogically meaningful and supportive for both NES and NNES student teachers. The present study provides concrete evidence of the types of issues that NNES student teachers face in the practicum. Although limited in nature, the data form part of the mounting evidence of the need for increased attention to this significant population in North American MA TESOL programs (see also Braine, 1999; Kamhi-Stein, 2000, 2001; Medgyes, 1994).

Polio and Wilson-Duffy (1998) provide a number of valuable suggestions for enhancing the educational experience of NNES student teachers. Although their recommendations are predicated on the unique setting into which their student teachers were placed (i.e., a low-cost course for university-affiliated individuals designed to provide novice teachers with experience delivering lessons to students in a low-stress atmosphere), many of their suggestions are also relevant to placements in other settings. First and foremost among these suggestions is that of teaming NES and NNES student teachers for both lesson planning and delivery purposes. Other recommendations include directly addressing language issues in the practicum course (e.g., by including language assistance and discussion of compensatory strategies) and placing NNES student teachers in large classes that resemble those they will teach if returning to their native countries. For additional valuable suggestions concerning how practicum courses can better address the needs of NNES student teachers, see Brady and Gulikers (this volume).

Recognition of the needs of NNES teachers is growing. Important first steps in this recognition included the creation of interest sections for NNES teachers in both TESOL and its affiliate organizations, like California TESOL (CATESOL). Additional momentum has been provided by the burgeoning literature on NNES teachers. Yet in terms of research on NNES teacher preparation programs, the voices of the NNES teachers themselves must be heard. The goal of this study has been to identify particularly salient issues faced by NNES student teachers and to present them through the voices of the student teachers themselves. Although small in scope, the study illuminates some of the major challenges faced by this important and substantial population enrolled in North America MA TESOL preparation programs.

Note

An earlier version of this study was presented at the 35th annual meeting of Teachers of English to Speakers of Other Languages, St. Louis, MO, March 2001.

References

Bailey, K. M., Curtis, A., & Nunan, D. (2001). *Pursuing professional development: The self as source*. Boston: Heinle & Heinle.

Braine, G. (Ed.). (1999). *Non-native educators in English language teaching*. Mahwah, NJ: Erlbaum.

Brinton, D. M., & Holten, C. A. (1988). *Dialog journals: A window on the act of teaching* (Report No. 1988-03-00). (ERIC Document Reproduction Service No. ED303030)

Brinton, D. M., & Holten, C. A. (1989). What novice teachers focus on: The practicum in TESOL. *TESOL Quarterly, 23*(2), 343–350.

Brinton, D. M., Holten, C. A., & Goodwin, J. M. (1993). Responding to dialogue journals in teacher preparation: What's effective? *TESOL Journal, 2*(4), 15–19.

Govardhan, A. K., Nayar, B., & Sheorey, R. (1999). Do U.S. MATESOL programs prepare students to teach abroad? *TESOL Quarterly, 33*(1), 114–125.

Gray, J. (1998). The language learner as teacher: The use of interactive diaries in teacher training. *ELT Journal, 52*(1), 29–37.

Holten, C. A., & Brinton, D. M. (1995). "You shoulda been there": Charting novice teacher growth using dialogue journals. *TESOL Journal, 4*(4), 23–26.

Jarvis, J. (1996). Using diaries for teacher reflection on in-service courses. In T. Hedge & N. Whitney (Eds.), *Power, pedagogy, & practice* (pp. 150–162). Oxford: Oxford University Press.

Johnson, K. E. (1999). *Understanding language teaching: Reasoning in action*. Boston: Heinle & Heinle.

Kamhi-Stein, L. D. (1999). Promoting collaboration: Using computer-mediated communication tools in the MATESOL practicum course. *CATESOL Journal, 11*(1), 61–80.

Kamhi-Stein, L. D. (2000). Adapting U.S.-based TESOL education to meet the needs of nonnative English speakers. *TESOL Journal, 9*(3), 10–14.

Kamhi-Stein, L. D. (Ed.). (2001). New voices in the classroom: Nonnative English-speaking professionals in the field of teaching English to speakers of other languages. *CATESOL Journal, 13*(1), 47–160. [Theme section on NNES issues]

Lazaraton, A. (2003). *Incidental displays of cultural knowledge in the nonnative-English-speaking teacher's classroom*. *TESOL Quarterly, 37*(2), 213–245.

Lee, E., & Lew, L. (2001). Diary studies: The voices of nonnative English speakers in a master of arts program in teaching English to speakers of other languages. *CATESOL Journal, 13*(1), 135–149.

Medgyes, P. (1994). *The non-native teacher*. London: Macmillan.

Polio, C., & Wilson-Duffy, C. (1998). Teaching ESL in an unfamiliar context: International students in a North American MA TESOL practicum. *TESOL Journal, 7*(4), 24–29.

Porter, P. A., Goldstein, L. M., Leatherman, J., & Conrad, S. (1990). An ongoing dialogue: Learning logs for teacher preparation. In J. C. Richards & D. Nunan (Eds.), *Second language teacher education* (pp. 227–240). Cambridge: Cambridge University Press.

Richards, J. C., & Ho, B. (1998). Reflective thinking through journal writing. In J. C. Richards (Ed.), *Beyond training: Perspectives on language teacher education* (pp. 153–170). Cambridge: Cambridge University Press.

Roderick, J. A. (1986). Dialogue writing: Context for reflecting on self as teacher and researcher. *Journal of Curriculum and Supervision, 1*(4), 305–315.

Samimy, K. K., & Brutt-Griffler, J. (1999). To be a native or non-native speaker: Perceptions of "non-native" students in a graduate TESOL program. In G. Braine (Ed.), *Non-native educators in English language teaching* (pp. 127–144). Mahwah, NJ: Erlbaum.

Thornbury, S. (1991). Watching the whites of their eyes: The use of teaching-practice logs. *ELT Journal, 45*(2), 140–146.

Woodfield, H., & Lazarus, E. (1998). Diaries: A reflective tool on an INSET language course. *ELT Journal, 52*(4), 315–322.

Enhancing the MA in TESOL Practicum Course for Nonnative English-Speaking Student Teachers

Brock Brady
American University

Goedele Gulikers
Prince George's Community College

A primary goal in structuring practicum courses in master of arts (MA) in Teaching English to Speakers of Other Languages (TESOL) programs in North American/British/Australian (NABA) settings (see D. Liu, 1999) is to ensure that the experience is meaningful to all participating students. The traditional purpose of these practica is to provide practical classroom experience to novice teachers and to facilitate the transition between "teacher training" (i.e., providing the knowledge and skills needed for language teaching) and "teacher development" (i.e., encouraging reflection on teaching so that teaching decisions are better informed) (Freeman, 1982, 1989). However, as is usually the case with teacher education, one size does not fit all, and a practicum experience that may be adequate to native English-speaking (NES) student teachers from NABA settings may respond poorly to the needs of nonnative English-speaking (NNES) student teachers from non-NABA settings (Govardhan, Nayar, & Sheorey, 1999; J. Liu, 1999).

Too often, the existence of a practicum, being a tradition and a convention, is taken as "self-evident"; that is, its purpose or existence is never questioned (Scollon & Scollon, 2001). It is a rite at the end of any teacher education program (like comprehensive examinations), a requirement to be completed and never questioned. Many NES MA in TESOL students, being well socialized in both the general culture and the educational culture of U.S. institutions (Gorsuch, 2000), make do, complete their assignments, and get through the practicum experience on intuition and habit. If they have not entirely understood the practicum structure or benefited greatly from the experience, they have still successfully "jumped through the hoop" of the practicum requirement and thus find themselves a step closer to graduation.

NNES MA in TESOL students who have earned their undergraduate degrees in home countries where English was not the language of instruction may not fare as well. There are a number of reasons why it may be much more difficult for these students, to "make their way" in their practicum. NNES student teachers from non-NABA settings may be unclear about the practicum's purpose, because they have no equivalent course in academic programs back home (Brady, 2001). If, regrettably, they are perceived as "foreign," or if, in addition, they have English proficiency limitations, they may have trouble being accepted and respected by both host instructors (also known as "mentor teachers" or "master teachers") and the host classroom students (see Amin, 1997; Tang, 1997). Moreover, if they rely on the assumptions of their home educational culture to interpret the practicum experience, they may misjudge the politeness system—involving systematic assumptions made about the power and distance of interpersonal relations—in which the host instructor and student teacher operate (MacNaughton & Clyde, 1990; Scollon & Scollon, 2001), and they may have an unclear notion of the nature of the roles that the host instructor and student teacher should play (Gee, 1996; Richards, 1998). Finally, conventional ways of teaching in their home country classrooms may not conform to the expectations of the host instructor, and even if NNES student teachers in practica do make the cultural transition and produce lessons that succeed according to the educational expectations of the NABA system, it is not clear that the approaches implemented will help them to succeed—or even to be accepted—if they return to their home country to teach (Burnaby & Sun, 1989; Flowerdew, 1999, Jin & Cortazzi, 1998).

Pragmatically, MA in TESOL programs must respond to the potential stumbling blocks that their NNES students from non-NABA settings may encounter during their practicum course, particularly because MA in TESOL programs often waive students from the practicum course if they have significant prior teaching experience (Richards & Crookes, 1988).[1] In practice, this means that NES MA in TESOL students tend to be waived more frequently from the practicum than their NNES counterparts, because being a native English speaker is too often considered sufficient qualification for being employed to teach English as a second language (ESL) or English as a foreign language (EFL) courses, even if one has little or no previous English teaching experience. Consequently, many NES students bring some prior English language teaching experience to the MA in TESOL program, and if necessary, they can build on it by teaching part-time to full-time while completing their academic program, thus becoming eligible for a waiver from the practicum requirement. As a result, it is not uncommon for a TESOL practicum course to have a much higher percentage of NNES student teachers than other courses in a MA in TESOL program.

Such is the case with the MA in TESOL program at the American University (AU). From spring 1998 to fall 2001, NNES student teachers from non-NABA settings made up between 80% and 90% of the students in the course. It may be helpful to note that almost all the domestic students who do not have English as their home language are full bilinguals who have matriculated in (and have been very well acculturated into) the U.S. educational system. Therefore, their instructional needs are very similar to those of NES domestic students. The NNES student teachers are "international students" in the sense that they have earned their undergraduate degree in their home country where English was not the language of instruction—or, in a few cases, they may have earned their secondary school diploma in their home country but then gone on to attend a U.S. university for their undergraduate degree. For this and other reasons, which will be discussed in the following sections, the practicum course of the AU MA in TESOL program has gone through several stages of modification, beginning in spring 1999.

Modifying the American University TESOL Program's Practicum Course

Throughout its history, the AU MA in TESOL practicum course has been a semester-long three-credit unit course consisting of (a) a weekly two-and-a-half-hour practicum seminar designed to address general issues of English language teaching, classroom management, and lesson preparation and (b) a practicum placement (i.e., the field experience component), where a student is assigned to an ESL classroom in order to observe teaching, assist the instructor, learn the curriculum and discourse of that particular classroom, and finally teach a certain number of classes.

The AU TESOL program was once housed in the university's IEP. In recent history, it has been housed in the Department of Language and Foreign Studies. Perhaps as a consequence of the earlier institutional structure, the MA in TESOL practicum course remained associated with the university's IEP. Consequently, the practicum seminar was taught by an instructor from the IEP, and the entire practicum placement component of the practicum was carried out in IEP classrooms.

In spring 1999, a new strategic plan was developed for the IEP (ELI Strategic Plan Committee, 1999). During the drafting of the plan, members of the IEP expressed major concerns about placing NNES student teachers in their classrooms. The claim was that the IEP students, paying high tuition, did not want to be taught by NNES student teachers. In addition, some IEP instructors complained that NNES student teachers were difficult to work with. Given these concerns, the MA in TESOL program consulted with its recent alumni who had participated in the practicum course. The most salient finding was that no student, regardless of language background, had had the opportunity to teach more than two 75-minute classes during the course of their practicum placements in the AU's IEP. Because of the IEP's reluctance to accept NNES student teachers and its reluctance to let any practicum student gain significant teaching experience, it was decided that the TESOL practicum would be reorganized to better meet its student teachers' needs. The reorganization of the TESOL practicum course included two phases, a "cognitive phase" and an "affective phase." The two sections that follow describe the changes made in each of the two phases.

Phase I: The "Cognitive Phase"

This first phase in the reorganization of the practicum course has been characterized as "cognitive" because its focus was on improving students' learning opportunities. Although a primary impetus for this reorganization was to find practicum placements where our NNES student teachers would be welcome, the cognitive phase was instituted to respond to the overall MA in TESOL student audience and did not specifically address potential concerns of NNES student teachers.

Some of the changes made included the following:

1. Transferring the instructional duties for the practicum seminar from the IEP instructor to a seminar instructor, an adjunct professor familiar with the values and curriculum of the TESOL program.
2. Hiring a practicum placement supervisor responsible for locating and supervising practicum placements, consulting with host instructors, helping student teachers plan the lessons they teach, consulting with student teachers and host instructors on at least

a biweekly basis, communicating with the seminar instructor regularly to report on developments in the practicum placement, serving as a sounding board for student teachers and host instructors if concerns arise, observing the student teachers' teaching, and ensuring that student teachers and host instructors complete all requirements for the placement, thus relieving the seminar instructor of these obligations.

3. Developing a practicum seminar syllabus focused on providing student teachers with the skills they need for practicum teaching. For example, some of the topics examined in the fall 2001 offering of the seminar included: assessing student learning styles and abilities, creating effective learning environments, giving instructions and eliciting student participation, correcting errors and providing feedback, structuring group and pair work, etc.

4. Requiring that student teachers participate in the host classroom for a minimum of 30 hours during the placement.

5. Increasing the minimum number of classes to be wholly taught by the student teachers to at least five classes.

6. Placing student teachers in institutions other than the AU IEP, often based on the reputation of the host instructor's teaching and mentoring skills.

7. Trying to place student teachers in classrooms that represent as closely as possible the student teachers' intended student audiences. (E.g., those who want to work with primary level learners are placed in elementary schools.)

These changes were well received by students (Brady, 2001), and the faculty members were satisfied with the results. However, some of the placements were not as successful as we had hoped. In one instance, the TESOL program's most promising NNES student teacher was placed at a local community college with a host instructor who was highly recommended by her director. We expected this to be a model placement. However, the result was disastrous. Both individuals were utterly and vocally disappointed with the other, and neither participant's expectations for the practicum placement were met. For example, the host instructor complained that the student teacher was unwilling to take initiative, that her attitude at times seemed sullen and hostile. Conversely, the student teacher felt the host instructor was cold and uncooperative, that the host instructor was never available to discuss the classes, and that consequently she could not respond to the host instructor's expectations because she didn't know them (Brady, 2001). Given that both the host instructor and the student teacher were people of goodwill, successful in their respective roles, and excited about the new opportunity of cross-institutional practicum, their dissatisfaction with one another was unexpected. It was likely that their frustration was due to cultural misunderstanding (Archer, 1986). To respond to such socio-affective issues, the AU TESOL practicum entered the second phase of evaluation and development.

Phase II: The "Affective Phase"

This second phase of modification to the AU TESOL practicum could be called "affective" in orientation in that our primary concern was to improve understanding between host instructors and student teachers, especially NNES student teachers. To have better insight into the nature of previous problems, we conducted focus group sessions with seven recent NNES graduates who had participated in practicum placements (see Munby, Lock, Hutchinson, Whitehead, & Martin, 1999, on using focus groups to evaluate teaching practica). Two assumptions guided our inquiry:

1. Practica and student teaching placements are, in the best of circumstances, stressful and potentially threatening for both the host instructor and the student teacher (Brady, 2002; Johnson, 1996; McGregor, 1991; Richards & Lockhart, 1994). Placements are threatening because they involve mutual observation and evaluation. The threat posed by this mutual observation tends to be intensified by the nature of the teaching profession: we do not regularly carry out teaching in the presence of other teachers.

2. When the host instructors and student teachers come from different cultural/educational backgrounds, the potential for misunderstanding can be increased, because each participant is bringing different expectations to the practicum experience. The resulting tension can be all the more painful, because, typically, both parties are operating with goodwill and the best of intentions. Consequently, they do not anticipate misunderstanding. They assume that they are participating in the same discourse system. This assumption may actually heighten misunderstanding, because it causes both parties to assume similarity, thereby overlooking subtle differences in educational values and beliefs, in notions of effective classroom practices, and in appropriate mentor-apprentice interactions (Barna, 1985; Scollon & Scollon, 2001).

   Results of the focus group sessions. On the whole, the students' concerns about the practicum tended to be administrative and procedural (e.g., assignment criteria were not clear enough; the practicum placement experiences and the practicum seminar curriculum were not sufficiently integrated).

NNES student teachers, naturally enough, did not want special accommodation, or treatment different from that received by their NES peers. This desire for equal treatment caused them to reject a proposal to specifically place NNES student teachers with NNES host instructors so that the NNES host instructors could be explicit models and mentors.

NNES student teachers felt that their greatest difficulty during their practicum placements was knowing when and how to approach their practicum host instructors. Reasons for approaching the host instructor included requests to take a more active role in the class, requests for clarification on instructions and assignments, and requests to receive feedback. Many said that they had expected the host instructors to take more initiative in these interactions. Student teachers had also expected host instructors to provide more time for feedback and debriefing.

Although the focus group students explicitly denied any insecurity due to their language proficiency, other comments suggested that their English was sometimes a concern. For example, students generally expressed discomfort about being asked by the host instructor to participate in class activities without advance warning. They wanted to be notified so they could prepare in advance and avoid "not having the language ready" (Brady, 2001, p. 1).

Although impressions were mixed (some focus group participants felt they had been very well received because they were nonnative English speakers like their ESL students; others felt that ESL students had shown a lack of respect for them as teachers because they were nonnative English speakers), all focus group participants were concerned about how they were perceived by students in the ESL classes in which they had been placed.

Focus group participants felt that the notion of a practicum was a relatively new one to them and that not having a clear idea of what they would be doing hampered the effectiveness of the placements. They were unsure of the purpose of the placement, its relationship to the weekly practicum seminar, their role in the host classroom, the host instructor's expectations for them, and the perceptions that host classroom students would have of NNES student teachers.

Affective phase modifications. Drawing on the results of the focus group sessions, we proceeded to make eight modifications. Following is a description of the changes made in response to the feedback received. First, to provide the NNES student teachers with a good nonnative English speaker model while respecting their desire to be treated in the same manner as their NES counterparts, we sought a seminar instructor whose experience and reputation made her admirably qualified to teach the course and who was also a nonnative English speaker. This was the best of both worlds: a nonnative English speaker model, someone who could share her experience and support, was available, yet this guidance would not be seen as some sort of special accommodation needed for NNES student teachers only.

Second, to provide students with the skills they needed for practicum teaching, the practicum seminar needed to include a strong element concerning "practical pedagogy"—that is, dealing with classroom and program constraints, providing lesson plan review, and giving feedback on the classroom placement experience. In the practicum placement, students are continually confronted with the reality of curricula imposed by the school; textbook choices made by others; standardized tests that students must pass; and the practices of the host instructor, which they need to respect. A goal of the practicum seminar was to communicate to student teachers that the practicum experience was not about the negative or positive aspects of teaching at a certain institution but was more concerned with how they could learn to cope with the realities of their particular teaching situations.

Thus, the seminar was redesigned to provide students with both instruction and practice on how to adapt to these circumstances by finding a balance between all they had learned in their teacher education classes and the constraints of their particular practicum classrooms. Through this process, student teachers gained experience in how to structure their specific classroom environments in order to make them more conducive to learning (Gebhard, 1990).

Third, to benefit both NES and NNES student teachers, one class session of the seminar was to be explicitly devoted to issues related to NNES professionals (e.g., the strengths that NNES professionals typically bring to the language classroom and examples of discrimination in hiring and employment). This helped support NNES student teachers and enhanced NES student teachers' awareness of issues related to NNES professionals. The most important of these issues for NNES student teachers was that of the job search. To address this issue, the seminar instructor introduced proactive interview strategies concerning perceptions of NNES professionals in the roles of teachers, colleagues, and subordinates (Flynn & Gulikers, 2001).

Fourth, comprehensive pre-placement counseling sessions involving the placement supervisor, the host instructor, and the student teacher were scheduled. The purpose was to have all parties reflect on their expectations for the practicum and discuss ways to most effectively meet these expectations before the placement began. In some instances we were also able to have the host instructor's program director attend these sessions. This was the optimal briefing arrangement because we could address the expectations of the student teacher, host instructor, host director, and placement supervisor with all parties present.

The counseling sessions had two primary purposes:

1. Dealing with affective issues common in practicum placements and emphasizing that some anxiety was natural for both parties. When the placement was for NNES student teachers, we explicitly addressed all parties' possible concerns about language proficiency, not because any NNES student teacher's individual language proficiency was necessarily a concern, but simply to bring attitudes and concerns about language into the open.
2. Discussing the general characteristics of action research—involving teacher-initiated classroom investigations that seek to increase the teacher's understanding of classroom teaching and learning and to bring about change in classroom practices (Richards, 1998)—and encouraging both the teacher and the student teacher to see the practicum placement as an opportunity where, together, they could learn more about language teaching. It was felt that this emphasis on collaboration would lessen the tendency of either party to feel judged by the other and would encourage a more positive, collegial relationship.

Fifth, the placement supervisor attempted to follow up with all student teachers and host instructors on a biweekly basis, so as to address possible questions or misunderstandings as soon as they came up. Emphasis was on the placement supervisor being a sounding board to let concerns come out.

Sixth, to foster ESL student acceptance of student teachers, we encouraged host instructors to introduce student teachers not as a "student teachers" but as "visiting teachers," and student teachers were encouraged to look for small ways to participate in the classroom from the very start, so that the ESL students would view them engaged in teaching behaviors and therefore identify them as teachers.

Seventh, we encouraged the host instructors and student teachers to approach the five observation reports required of the student teachers as informal action research opportunities; that is, the host instructors were asked to identify components of their classrooms that they would like to investigate, then they and the student teachers together would devise methods for observing these components and collecting data on them. The intention was to make the practicum experience more collaborative, more mutually beneficial, and more collegial. Some examples of action research opportunities carried out by MA in TESOL students in host classrooms included (a) looking at transitions between small-group work and unified class activities to make the transitions more fluid and to create a full sense of closure and (b) examining small-group interactions to find ways to have all students participate more actively.

Finally, individual post-practicum debriefing sessions were instituted for both the student teacher and the host instructor, to address complaints, to praise success, and to help both parties reflect on what they had learned from the practicum placement experience.

Recommendations

In this section, we present several recommendations that should be considered when redesigning a practicum course. The section presents recommendations concerning the overall practicum course, the practicum seminar, and the practicum placement.

Concerning the Practicum Overall

(1) Make changes in the practicum to respond to the needs of NNES student teachers and you will benefit all student teachers. Making the goals of the practicum clear is particularly important to NNES student teachers because they may be unfamiliar with such learning experiences. However, making practicum goals clearer also makes the practicum more meaningful for all students. In addition, reading about and discussing issues related to NNES professionals is obviously a benefit to our NNES student teachers, and the experience has value for our NES student teachers as well. For example, in our case, after a discussion on issues related to NNES professionals, one NES student teacher remarked, "I'd been lulled into thinking I didn't need to worry about my intercultural sensitivity, but I learned there was a lot I'd never even thought of before." Similarly, initial counseling sessions on expectations were introduced as a direct response to unsatisfactory experiences in placing some NNES student teachers due to cross-cultural misunderstandings. However, we soon discovered that these initial counseling sessions improved practicum placements for all students (native and nonnative English speakers alike), because all parties' expectations were being explicitly discussed before the practicum placement began.

(2) Provide student teachers with the means to respond to classroom constraints. If classroom constraints are not addressed, student teachers, confounded with the "ideal" that they have learned about in teacher education classes and the "reality" of the host class-

room, may conclude that the twain shall never meet and that their teacher education courses have been impractical and unrealistic. They may feel ready to abandon theory altogether and try to get by on intuition alone (see Johnson, 1996, on typical student teacher frustrations). This frustration can be addressed at two levels. First, in the seminar classroom, the seminar instructor can discuss classroom constraints and general ways to respond to them. Then, the placement supervisor can help the student teachers discover and address the constraints of their particular placement classrooms (especially when planning lessons the students will teach). Thus, both instructors can model how the principles of their program's methodology classes can be used to improve lessons and teaching, even within the constraints of particular classes and curricula.

(3) Have realistic expectations about the time needed to ensure a successful practicum. Practica make significant time demands on seminar instructors, who must continually listen to the needs and frustrations of student teachers and respond to them in the seminar course content. Practica also make significant demands on placement supervisors, since they must regularly consult with both student teachers and host instructors. Moreover, placement supervisors must walk both student teachers and host instructors through what is often a new experience and must be available to help student teachers through multiple drafts of each of their lesson plans). In desiring to do the right thing, it is easy to underestimate just how much time can be involved.

Concerning the Practicum Seminar

(1) Enlist a qualified NNES professional as a seminar instructor whenever possible. A NNES seminar instructor will be sensitive to the NNES student teachers' needs, will be a model they can relate to, and can help both NES and NNES student teachers understand their career through the eyes of a nonnative English speaker. However, in cases where a NNES seminar instructor/model is not available, providing the NNES professional perspective and building sensitivity toward NNES student teachers' concerns can still be achieved by emphasizing the following points in the practicum seminar:

   a. Encouraging discussion of common assumptions and attitudes about NNES professionals and about how they can affect learner, peer, and administrative reactions to NNES professionals.
   b. Respecting NNES student teachers' knowledge of their chosen field and the positive practices they bring to teaching, especially those that come from their language learning experience.

c. Recognizing NNES student teachers' need to practice the discourse of the TESOL field and enhance their language proficiency.

d. Striving to improve students' confidence in their teaching abilities and developing their reflective capacities, while de-emphasizing counterproductive concerns, such as trying to achieve perfect pronunciation.

(2) Don't neglect issues related to language proficiency. For NNES student teachers, we must often assume that language proficiency is an issue. Medgyes (1999) advances four hypotheses addressing differences between NES and NNES professionals:

Hypothesis 1: they differ in terms of their language proficiency
Hypothesis 2: they differ in terms of their teaching behavior
Hypothesis 3: the discrepancy in language proficiency accounts for most of the difference found in their teaching behavior
Hypothesis 4: they can be equally good teachers in their own terms. (p. 25)

Medgyes' thesis is that, to some extent, our teaching behaviors respond to our language proficiency. Helping student teachers see how their proficiency affects their teaching is a necessary component of practicum instruction. There are two elements of instruction that need to be addressed in this regard. The first is in-depth exploration of the language structures (and possible variants) that the NNES student teachers will frequently use in teaching, along with developing strategies that they can use to continue expanding their classroom discourse repertoire on their own (Spratt, 1994). The second is providing an assessment and feedback component to help NNES student teachers see how effectively they are managing classroom discourse. This will help NNES student teachers build confidence and self-esteem, which in turn will effect changes in their teaching behavior. Each of these components will reinforce the other and will lead not only to closing language proficiency gaps (between NES and NNES professionals) but also to giving students a better understanding of all the components of classroom discourse (which include interpersonal relations, beliefs and values about learning, and conventional classroom practices).

Thus, a major part of the NNES student teachers' training should include exploring the educational discourse of the practicum host institution to avoid misunderstandings, particularly between host instructors and student teachers. We cannot assume that the NNES student teachers are familiar with the full range of educational discourse outside their MA in TESOL program. By introducing them to this discourse, the NNES student teachers will learn how to engage in useful practices, such as appropriate ways to approach their host instructor with requests for clarification and feedback. As a result, NNES student teachers will recognize that they are becoming more acculturated to the classroom culture of the host institution and, consequently, will grow in confidence in their teaching ability.

In the practicum seminar, NES student teachers can participate in this process by sharing their school experiences with their NNES counterparts. In turn, by learning what is new to their NNES counterparts, the NES student teachers can develop a better understanding of the complexities of the student-teacher interdiscourse system (Scollon & Scollon, 2001).

(3) Help all student teachers, especially NNES student teachers, attend to their students' educational cultures. Both NES and NNES student teachers will benefit from exploring and understanding their classroom students' home cultures and attitudes toward education (Ovando & Collier, 1998). However, it may be particularly important to help NNES student teachers respond to these differences, for although NNES student teachers will know from experience that the educational cultures of the home culture and the host country will differ, NNES student teachers may have difficulty helping their own students through that transition. Where the NES student teachers can help their students acculturate to the local educational culture by sharing their extensive knowledge of that culture, their NNES counterparts may not feel that they are sufficiently acculturated themselves to respond effectively to their students cross-cultural needs. In addition, all student teachers (native and nonnative English speakers alike) need to be regularly reminded that different classroom behaviors may (or may not) be acceptable in different educational cultures (e.g., engaging in sidebar talk in class, "helping" others during exams, interrupting the teacher), and that teachers need to be careful about judging these behaviors for they may, in fact, be perfectly acceptable in the students' home country educational culture.

(4) Give students the tools for spotting performance gaps. Teacher education course work alone, even in the best teacher education programs, is unlikely to produce superlative student teaching during the practicum placement. Concepts that students successfully discuss or implement in their teacher education program assignments often fail to make the perilous crossing to the student teachers' practicum classroom teaching, despite the students' belief in them (James, 2001; Richards & Lockhart, 1994; Wallace, 1991). For example, in some cases, student teachers may sometimes lapse into teaching as they were taught (as students in their earlier education), not as they have learned to teach in teacher education courses (Gor-

such, 2000; Richards & Lockhart, 1994). Therefore, a key element of practicum seminar instruction should be activities designed to help student teachers work through the performance gap—that is, the difference between the practices that teachers feel they believe in and the practices in which they actually engage in their classrooms. Teaching videos, if properly introduced, can be an excellent vehicle for bridging performance gaps and can include activities such as (a) viewing models of good teaching, (b) studying displays of ineffective techniques intentionally modeled by teacher trainers (Schwartz, 2002), and (c) having student teachers reflect on their videos.

(5) Encourage and promote student teacher reflection, especially for NNES student teachers. The primary reason for encouraging reflective practice is the need to build self-esteem and self-confidence. Many NNES teachers have solid self-images with healthy reserves of self-esteem, but others, particularly young professionals or those still in training, lack self-confidence and are often very self-conscious about their own language abilities (Kamhi-Stein, 1999, 2000). Having such teachers reflect on all that they have learned about English and teaching and asking them to honestly assess what they can and cannot do will give them the confidence they need both to provide effective teaching to their students and to try out new techniques that they may encounter in their teaching careers.

Second, professional self-discovery is a particularly helpful process for NNES professionals; while NES professionals may need to learn what their relationship is to teaching (and their sense of self), they (for better or worse) don't have to explore the relationship of English to their identity—English being the medium of their primary discourse. For NNES professionals, English is, by definition, the medium of a secondary discourse, a discourse that one has had to acculturate into and in which one is likely not a full member—and in which one might have very good reasons for *not* choosing to be a full member (Medgyes, 1999; Wong, 1993). Therefore, the relationship between English and the NNES professional is much more complicated than it is for many native English speakers, and part of being a more effective teacher of English will almost surely involve coming to terms with how English relates to one's identity.

One way to implement such reflection is to ask NNES student teachers to meet regularly with their advisor to explicitly explore their knowledge of how they teach English, their intellectual and professional growth, and, most important, the relationship between English and their identities. In this way, when they complete their MA in TESOL program, they will have a sense of themselves as TESOL instructors who have a well developed sense of their own professional identities (Braine, 1999; Kamhi-Stein, 1999, 2000).

*(6) Help NNES student teachers from non-NABA settings identify
and respond to the teaching practices of their home countries.* For
NNES student teachers planning to return to their home countries to
teach English, it may be desirable to build in supplemental advising
sessions and to help student teachers identify differences between the
educational cultures they have encountered in their teacher education
program and the educational culture they will be returning to. If the
advisor and NNES student teachers can collaboratively identify some
of these differences and formulate strategies for responding to them,
student teachers will be much better equipped to face the realities of
the teaching situations they will encounter after graduating (Burnaby
& Sun, 1989; Li, 1998; Wheeler & Boak, 1992).

*(7) Ensure that practicum assignments respond to the chal-
lenges of the practicum placement.* Course assignments for the
practicum must be reconsidered to ensure that they genuinely support
teacher development. For example, traditional observation reports
(i.e., reports that describe whatever classroom elements student
teachers decide to observe without any specified, prior focus) may
do little more than establish that student teachers were present in
the host classroom and that they kept themselves busy (see Munby
et al., 1999, for student reactions to traditional practicum assignments).
More relevant assignments could include some of the following:

   a. Analyzing the host classroom discourse system.
   b. Tracking student errors and classroom language that host class-
      room students could benefit from noticing. (See Lewis, 1997, on
      "noticing" language.)
   c. Observing host instructors and consulting with them to report on
      their teaching beliefs, values, and regular classroom practices.
   d. Identifying the constraints of the host classrooms and possible
      responses.
   e. Engaging in action research with the host instructor, using ob-
      servation as a means for collecting data.

Concerning the Practicum Placement

*(1) Acknowledge that practicum placements are logistically
complicated.* Teaching practica, regardless of the field of teaching,
are by nature messy, complicated, and prone to disorder. Full-time
master's students are busy, host instructors work hard to do a good
job teaching their classes (and if they are part-timers, they may be
working at more than one institution), and seminar instructors and
placement supervisors have many duties beyond those associated
with the practicum. In addition to these challenges, there are trans-

portation problems, scheduling problems, family emergencies and obligations, and other problems that are not directly related to the practicum or classroom placements (e.g., the terrorist attacks on the United States on September 11, 2001, occurred as we were still trying to find placements for some of our fall 2001 student teachers).

While a solid administrative structure and thorough preparation may lessen some of these tensions, it is unrealistic to suppose that they could be consistently eliminated. Therefore, from the moment they enter the practicum experience, student teachers and host instructors need to be made aware that with so many parties, so many institutions, and so many schedules involved, practica can at times be aggravating, complicated, and hard to manage. However, if all parties keep this in mind, the difficulties can be overcome and the learning potential of the practicum placement can be maximized.

(2) Pay attention to how language proficiency affects classroom communication and cooperation. In addition to responding to language proficiency issues of NNES student teachers in the practicum seminar, we must also be prepared to address how these issues can impede communication and cooperation in the practicum placement. At times in placements, host classroom students have complained that they often could not understand NNES student teachers (not unlike complaints well documented with international teaching assistants) (for discussions on the topic, see Anderson-Hsieh & Koehler, 1988; Tyler, 1992). We have observed classes where a NNES student teacher made regular errors using the target language feature of the lesson itself. We have seen cases, especially in ESL classrooms, where student teachers, while clearly being highly proficient in English, did not have the same fluency in English as their young charges.

Problems such as these can lead to high anxiety and insecurity on the part of the NNES student teacher, confusion on the part of classroom students, and perhaps hesitation on the part of the classroom instructor to give the NNES student teacher as much classroom autonomy as one might give to a NES student teacher. Such mistrust may, in turn, be exacerbated if NNES student teachers and host instructors do not carry out adequate discussion of classroom matters because one party or both believe that the NNES student teacher's proficiency makes such communication too difficult. This is not uncommon in native-nonnative English speaker interactions (Levine, Baxter, & McNulty, 1987; Roberts, 1998).

It is the placement supervisor who is probably best placed to address the issue of language proficiency in the context of the classroom placement. The placement supervisor can carefully (but regularly) probe potential concerns about language proficiency with the student teacher and the host instructor individually. If host classroom students complain that the NNES student teacher is difficult to understand, it is very important to remind the classroom students that learning an international language like English implies the need to understand a variety of accents. If a NNES student teacher's oral production is indeed problematic, one approach for responding is to provide the student teacher with brief, controlled, and carefully prepared lesson activities; gradually, the student teacher and the classroom students will become accustomed to one another's communication patterns. Finally, it is important that the placement supervisor regularly remind all parties of the benefits that NNES professionals can bring to the classroom (for discussion of this topic, see J. Liu, 1999; Medgyes, 1999; Samimy & Brutt-Griffler, 1999).

(3) Scaffold host instructor and student teacher collaborative research efforts during the practicum placement. Having a commitment to action research and encouraging student teachers to structure observation assignments on an action research model will not guarantee that host instructor and student teacher collaborative research activities occur in the practicum placement classroom. There may be a variety of reasons for this lack of follow-through. For example, the student teacher and the host instructor simply may not have a good understanding of what action research entails. Some host instructors may not have the habit of reflecting on classroom practices, and even if they do, they may feel that indicating any uncertainty about their teaching may seem tantamount to admitting they have teaching problems. Therefore, the placement supervisor should remind the host instructor and student teacher of the potential value of collaborative classroom research, suggest to them how such research might be carried out in their shared classroom, and communicate with the host instructor privately to identify some areas of research that the student teacher might consider in her observations. Examples of collaborative research activities include, but are not limited to, shared curriculum or lesson revisions, discussions on classroom practices, and monthly "teaching tips" presentations (where each teacher in the group presents a teaching technique that has been found useful).

(4) Make learner needs analysis part of the classroom placement experience. Student teachers should be encouraged to familiarize themselves with the students in the class and with the cultural perspectives and expectations that those students may bring to class. As Johnson (1996) points out, not having time to learn the specific needs of students in the host classroom causes student teachers to feel tension and a lack of control. More generally, while NNES student teachers may have mastered the nuances of classroom behavior in the NABA setting during their MA in TESOL program, they may be unprepared for ESL student behaviors that are completely conven-

tional and appropriate in the students' home educational cultures (Faltis, 2001). Thus, at the beginning of the practicum placement, once the student teacher has begun to associate names and faces, it is beneficial for the host instructor to provide a short thumbnail briefing on each student's background, achievement, and behaviors. As to helping NNES student teachers gain more general knowledge of the different cultures represented in the classroom, it may be useful to look at descriptions such as those found in *Teaching Language Minority Students in the Multicultural Classroom* (Scarcella, 1990)—for example, descriptions of cross-cultural differences in how students interpret teacher feedback, descriptions of parental expectations about schooling across common U.S. language minority groups, and general descriptions of the cultures and histories of major U.S. language minority groups.

(5) Familiarize students with practicum classroom discourse systems to reduce learning curves. TESOL practica (indeed, all practicum placements) should be viewed as full-fledged discourse systems—that is, systems of communication with their unique values and beliefs, their unique ways of identifying individuals as members, their own ways of learning to become a member, and their unique roles and relationships (Scollon & Scollon, 2001). As is the case with any discourse system, there is inevitably a learning curve to be experienced when entering a practicum placement classroom (Scollon & Scollon, 2001). Obviously, the more the practicum resembles other discourse systems that a student teacher has experienced, the shorter the learning curve will be. This may be why NES student teachers are often able to "get by" with less explicit support than some NNES student teachers. The "interdiscourse distance" between their primary discourse and the discourse of the placement classroom is relatively small. However, because no classroom is identical to another, there is always some sort of learning curve. Host instructors have their own beliefs and practices, each class its particular group of students, and each class its distinct curriculum. Learning curves can be reduced by discussing expectations before the practicum placement, by knowing the curriculum and institutional expectations for the class, and by sharing with the student teacher the host instructors' beliefs and values about teaching.

In this context, host instructor values and beliefs about teaching are of primary concern, particularly if they seem to be in conflict with the practices or beliefs fostered by the teacher education program. For example, if the host instructor is observed engaging in practices that the teacher education program feels are not particularly communicative, the placement supervisor must comment in a respectful and nonjudgmental manner and must prepare the student teacher to do likewise. In the spirit of cultural relativism, we need to avoid characterizing host classrooms as good or bad or right or wrong. We should simply accept them as different. Host classroom practices must be evaluated in context, and the student teacher needs to realize that there are no ubiquitous best practices or perfect teachers. To provide such context, the placement supervisor should meet with the host instructor before the practicum begins, to mutually explore the beliefs, values, and practices of both the host instructor and the teacher education program. It is equally necessary to consider the host classroom curriculum (which may often impose its own values and practices). By starting off this way, differences can be considered from a perspective of mutual respect, parties will feel more open about discussing differences, and if the student teacher does raise questions about the host instructor's practices, the placement supervisor has a means for contextualizing those practices.

Such efforts may be of particular value for NNES student teachers, who, knowing their own educational cultures best, may unconsciously use their cultural assumptions to interpret teacher and student roles, appropriacy of classroom activities, or the nature of a relationship between a mentor and an apprentice (Bardovi-Harlig & Hartford, 1993; Brady & Cho, 2000; Brinton, 1989; Jin & Cortazzi, 1998). Therefore, just as we need to familiarize ourselves with host instructor values, beliefs, and practices, so, too, we should come to know those held and practiced by student teachers, especially if they are NNES student teachers. By knowing the discourse system that student teachers are coming from and knowing well the classroom discourse they will be entering, we can facilitate their intercultural (and interdiscourse) transition and make for a more enriching practicum placement experience.

(6) Develop awareness of teaching values by engaging in multiple, overlapping dialogues. TESOL practica should provide student teachers opportunities to develop reflective teaching practices (Chamberlin, 2000). For example, in preparation for teaching a lesson, the host instructor may discuss the lesson with the placement supervisor to explain the goals of the lesson and to ensure that the lesson will be in accordance with the teacher education program's expectations. Obviously, the host instructor will also discuss the lesson with the student teacher; in turn, the student teacher will discuss the lesson with the placement supervisor. Afterward, the placement supervisor may again contact the host instructor to share some of the planning decisions that went into the lesson. This ongoing round-robin dialogue ensures respect and guarantees a collaborative atmosphere.

Conclusion

NABA teacher education programs have been reasonably effective in providing the knowledge and skills needed for their students to become good TESOL instructors. Where these programs may need to become more effective is in creating contexts to bring such skills and knowledge into the individual student teacher's classroom practice. If we have not been so successful in bringing knowledge into practice, it is possibly because our assumptions about classroom discourse have become self-evident—we may have forgotten that they might need to be explicitly introduced to our MA in TESOL students. We may have fallen into this trap of self-evidence because we have typically had the luxury of working primarily with students from our own educational culture (i.e., students from our particular NABA setting)—an educational culture so similar to our NES student teachers' primary discourse that they may have managed to "get by" using their primary discourse to "teach well enough" without our having provided the teacher development needed to help them "teach well."

Thankfully, as NNES student teachers join our teacher education programs, they help us see the extent to which learning to teach is not self-evident. For NNES student teachers to succeed, we need to make the practicum experience more transparent, we need to make our practicum expectations explicit, and we need to explore the value systems and interpersonal relationships in play.

If we fail to respond to lessons that our NNES student teachers can teach us, we may set up conditions where our NES student teachers are able to cope but where, conversely, our NNES student teachers may sometimes fail. We may create situations where our NES student teachers can carry out the classroom practices we expect without prior instruction, while their equally intelligent and capable NNES counterparts are left trying to fathom our intentions. We may, at times, find ourselves having to watch as native English speakers with dubious teaching skills are accepted without hesitation for employment, while more skilled and better-equipped nonnative English speakers are kept at arm's length.

Our sense of fairness and a genuine commitment to providing our students with the most meaningful instruction possible should cause us to restructure our teacher education programs so that they respond to the needs of our NNES student teachers at least as well as they have responded to the needs of our NES student teachers (Kamhi-Stein, 2000). This will typically cause us to focus on cross-cultural perceptions of teaching and classrooms and on the need to make these perceptions explicit.

What we have learned in the process of restructuring the AU's MA in TESOL practicum course is that the transition from being a student to being a teacher is a process of interdiscourse adaptation for all student teachers, both native and nonnative English speakers. In responding to the cross-cultural needs of our NNES student teachers by making the purpose and the structure of our practicum clearer and by creating contexts where students can explore educational beliefs and expectations, we have not only benefited our NNES student teachers; we have benefited all our students.

Note

1. The matter of what constitutes "significant teaching experience" (which would allow a student to be waived from the practicum requirement) varies greatly. Lía D. Kamhi-Stein reports (personal communication, 2002) on one program that requires three years of documented full-time teaching experience for students to be waived from its practicum course. For the American University TESOL program, because the practicum requirement is a one-semester course, we have decided to define "significant teaching experience" as one semester of full-time teaching. We have further defined "full-time teaching" as 12 to 15 contact hours per week (this being based on the university's requirement for minimum contact hours per week for three-credit internship experiences). By implication, 6 to 8 teaching contact hours per week over two semesters, or 3 to 4 contact hours per week over 12 months would also typically constitute "significant teaching experience."

References

Amin, N. (1997). Race and the identity of the nonnative ESL teacher. *TESOL Quarterly, 31*(3), 580–583.

Anderson-Hsieh, J., & Koehler, K. (1988). The effect of foreign accent and speaking rate on native speaker comprehension. *Language Learning, 38*(4), 561–613.

Archer, C. M. (1986). Culture bump and beyond. In J. M. Valdes (Ed.), *Culture bound: Bridging the cultural gap in language teaching* (pp. 170–178). Cambridge: Cambridge University Press.

Bardovi-Harlig, K., & Hartford, B. S. (1993). Learning the rules of academic talk: A longitudinal study of pragmatic change. *Studies in Second Language Acquisition, 15*(3), 279–304.

Barna, L. (1985). Stumbling blocks in intercultural communication. In L. A. Samovar & R. E. Porter (Eds.), *Intercultural communication: A reader* (4th ed., pp. 330–337). Belmont, CA: Wadsworth.

Brady, B. (2001, March). Making teacher education practica more valuable for nonnative English-speaking students. In L. D. Kamhi-Stein (Organizer), *NNES teachers-in-preparation in practicum courses.* Colloquium conducted at the 35th annual meeting of Teachers of English to Speakers of Other Languages, St. Louis, MO.

Brady, B. (2002, April). *Restructuring evaluative observations to improve teaching performance*. Paper presented at the 36th annual meeting of Teachers of English to Speakers of Other Languages, Salt Lake City, UT.

Brady, B., & Cho, Y. M. (2000, October). *International students and classroom participation: Matching expectations and reality*. Paper presented at the annual meeting of the Washington Area Teachers of English to Speakers of Other Languages, Fairfax, VA.

Braine, G. (1999). From the periphery to the center: One teacher's journey. In G. Braine (Ed.), *Non-native educators in English language teaching* (pp. 15–28). Mahwah, NJ: Erlbaum.

Brinton, D. M. (1989). What novice teachers focus on: The practicum in TESL. *TESOL Quarterly, 23*(2), 343–350.

Burnaby, B., & Sun, Y. (1989). Chinese teachers' views of Western language teaching: Context informs paradigms. *TESOL Quarterly, 23*(2), 219–238.

Chamberlin, C. R. (2000). TESL degree candidates' perceptions of trust in supervisors. *TESOL Quarterly, 34*(4), 653–673.

ELI Strategic Plan Committee. (1999). *A strategic plan for American University's English Language Institute*. Washington, DC: American University, College of Arts and Sciences.

Faltis, C. (2001). *Joinfostering: Teaching and learning in multilingual classroom* (3rd ed.). Upper Saddle River, NJ: Merrill.

Flowerdew, J. (1999). The practicum in L2 teacher education: A Hong Kong case study. *TESOL Quarterly, 33*(1), 141–144.

Flynn, K. F., & Gulikers, G. (2001). Issues in hiring nonnative English-speaking professionals to teach English as a second langauge. *CATESOL Journal, 13*(1), 151–160.

Freeman, D. (1982). Observing teachers: Three approaches to in-service training and development. *TESOL Quarterly, 16*(1), 21–28.

Freeman, D. (1989). Teacher training, development, and decision making: A model of teaching and related strategies for language teacher education. *TESOL Quarterly, 23*(1), 27–45.

Gebhard, J. C. (1990). Interaction in a teaching practicum. In J. C. Richards & D. Nunan (Eds.), *Second language teacher education* (pp. 118–131). Cambridge: Cambridge University Press.

Gee, J. P. (1996). *Social linguistics and literacies: Ideology in discourses* (2nd ed.). London: Taylor & Francis.

Gorsuch, G. J. (2000). EFL educational policies and educational cultures: Influences on teachers' approval of communicative activities. *TESOL Quarterly, 34*(4), 675–710.

Govardhan, A. K., Nayar, B., & Sheorey, R. (1999). Do U.S. MATESOL programs prepare students to teach abroad? *TESOL Quarterly, 33*(1), 114–125.

James, P. (2001). *Teachers in action: Tasks for in-service language teacher education and development*. New York: Cambridge University Press.

Jin, L., & Cortazzi, M. (1998). The culture the learner brings: A bridge or a barrier? In M. Byram & M. P. Fleming (Eds.), *Language learning in intercultural perspective: Approaches through drama and ethnography* (pp. 98–118). New York: Cambridge University Press.

Johnson, K. E. (1996). The vision versus the reality: The tensions of the TESOL practicum. In D. Freeman & J. C. Richards (Eds.), *Teacher learning in language teaching* (pp. 30–49). New York: Cambridge University Press.

Kamhi-Stein, L. D. (1999). Preparing non-native professionals in TESOL: Implications for teacher education programs. In G. Braine (Ed.), *Non-native educators in English language teaching* (pp. 145–158). Mahwah, NJ: Erlbaum.

Kamhi-Stein, L. D. (2000). Adapting U.S.-based TESOL education to meet the needs of nonnative English speakers. *TESOL Journal, 9*(3), 10–14.

Levine, D. R., Baxter, J., & McNulty, P. (1987). *The culture puzzle: Cross-cultural communication for English as a second language*. Englewood Cliffs, NJ: Prentice-Hall.

Lewis, M. (1997). *Implementing the lexical approach: Putting theory into practice*. Hove, England: Language Teaching Publications.

Li, D. (1998). "It's always more difficult than you plan and imagine": Teachers' perceived difficulties in introducing the Communicative Approach in South Korea. *TESOL Quarterly, 32*(4), 677–703.

Liu, D. (1999). Training non-native TESOL students: Challenges for TESOL teacher education in the West. In G. Braine (Ed.), *Non-native educators in English language teaching* (pp. 197–210). Mahwah, NJ: Erlbaum.

Liu, J. (1999). From their own perspectives: The impact of non-native ESL professionals on their students. In G. Braine (Ed.) *Non-native educators in English language teaching* (pp. 159–176). Mahwah, NJ: Erlbaum.

MacNaughton, G., & Clyde, M. (1990, June). *Staffing the practicum: Towards a new set of basics through clarifying roles*. Paper presented at the National Workshop on Early Childhood Practicum, Victoria, Australia. (ERIC Document Reproduction Service No. ED338365)

McGregor, A. L. (1991). The development of self assessment skills in TESOL teacher preparation. In S. Anivan (Ed.), *Issues in language programme evaluation in the 1990's* (Anthology Series No. 27, pp. 72–83). (ERIC Documentation Reproduction Service No. ED367154)

Medgyes, P. (1999). *The non-native teacher*. Ismaning, Germany: Hueber.

Munby, H., Lock, C., Hutchinson, N. L., Whitehead, L., & Martin, A. (1999). Evaluation by teacher candidates of a field-based teacher education program: An introduction. *Teacher Education Quarterly, 26*(2), 35–50.

Ovando, C. J., & Collier, V. P. (1998). *Bilingual and ESL classrooms: Teaching in multicultural contexts* (2nd ed.). Boston: McGraw-Hill.

Richards, J. C. (1998). *Beyond training: Perspectives on language teacher education*. New York: Cambridge University Press.

Richards, J. C., & Crookes, G. (1988). The practicum in TESOL. *TESOL Quarterly, 22*(1), 9–27.

Richards, J. C., & Lockhart, C. (1994). *Reflective teaching in second language classrooms*. New York: Cambridge University Press.

Roberts, C. (1998). Awareness in intercultural communication. *Language Awareness, 7*(2/3), 109–127.

Samimy, K. K., & Brutt-Griffler J. (1999). To be a native or non-native speaker: Perceptions of "non-native" students in a graduate TESOL program. In G. Braine (Ed.), *Non-native educators in English language teaching* (pp. 127–144). Mahwah, NJ: Erlbaum.

Scarcella, R. C. (1990). *Teaching language minority students in the multicultural classroom*. Englewood Cliffs, NJ: Prentice-Hall.

Schwartz, R. (2002, July). Evaluating your teacher training program. In B. Brady (Director), *Designing EFL teacher training programs*. Workshop conducted at the meeting of the American University TESOL Program, Washington, DC.

Scollon, R., & Scollon, S. W. (2001). *Intercultural communication: A discourse approach* (2nd ed.). Malden, MA: Blackwell.

Spratt, M. (1994). *English for the teacher: A language development course*. New York: Cambridge University Press.

Tang, C. (1997). On the power and status of nonnative ESL teachers. *TESOL Quarterly, 31*(3), 577–580.

Tyler, A. (1992). Discourse structure and the perception of incoherence in international teaching assistants' spoken discourse. *TESOL Quarterly, 26*(4), 713–729.

Wallace, M. J. (1991). *Training foreign language teachers: A reflective approach*. New York: Cambridge University Press.

Wheeler, A. E., & Boak, R. T. (1992, February). *Cross-cultural collaboration in teacher education: A case study*. Paper presented at the annual meeting of the American Association of Colleges for Teacher Education, San Antonio, TX. (ERIC Documentation Reproduction Service No. ED348344)

Wong, R. (1993). Pronunciation myths and facts. *English Teaching Forum, 31*(4), 45.

Preparing Nonnative
English Speakers for EFL
Teaching in Hong Kong

Icy Lee
Hong Kong Baptist University

In recent years, nonnative English-speaking teachers (NNESTs) in the field of teaching English to speakers of other languages (TESOL) have become more and more vocal in expressing their concerns and visions. As a result, there has been a concomitant growth in research focusing on nonnative English-speaking professionals. While a lot has been said about the problems and challenges NNESTs face in teaching English as a second or foreign language (see, e.g., Amin, 1999; Lee, 2000; Thomas, 1999), not much has been written to discuss how NNESTs can be helped to cope with their problems and challenges. Since NNESTs face challenges unique to their own teaching context, it is imperative that teacher preparation programs be geared toward helping them cope with the specific problems they are confronted with.

In this chapter, I set out to explore how teacher education programs in Hong Kong can prepare NNESTs enrolled in a pre-service program for teaching English as a foreign language (EFL) in secondary schools (i.e., grades 7–13). First I outline the background of English language teaching in Hong Kong with specific reference to the power imbalance between native English-speaking teachers (NESTs) and NNESTs to highlight the challenges faced by NNESTs in Hong Kong. Then I go on to delineate the strategies I have used in a pre-service teacher education program to prepare a group of NNESTs for EFL teaching in Hong Kong. The aim of the chapter is to underline the need for a pre-service teacher preparation program that sensitizes NNESTs to their specific needs and strengths and prepares them for the challenges they are going to encounter.

Power Imbalance: NESTs versus NNESTs

In Hong Kong, although the majority of English teachers are nonnative speakers, the power relationship between NESTs and NNESTs is one of imbalance. This can be reflected in the public's shaken faith in NNESTs' ability to teach English, on the one hand, and the increasing importance attached to the roles of NESTs, on the other.

Eroding Confidence in NNESTs

In recent years, there have been increasing complaints about the falling level of proficiency of NNESTs, which is said to cause a decline in students' English proficiency. In 1996, as a result of mounting public concern about the falling level of proficiency of teachers of English, the Hong Kong government decided to investigate the establishment of language benchmarks for all teachers in Hong Kong. After some preliminary investigations, the government formally announced the launching of a benchmarking test in 2000, an initiative to set the standards of language proficiency expected of English teachers. The objective of language benchmarking is to make sure that all English teachers possess at least the minimum level of proficiency needed to teach English (i.e., a level 3 on a scale of 5) and to encourage them to strive for higher levels of language proficiency (i.e., levels 4 and 5) (see "Background," Hong Kong Education Department, n.d.a). Exemption is granted to teachers with an English degree (e.g., English studies, literature, translation) and relevant teacher training (i.e., training with specialization in English and supervised teaching practice). Those who are not exempt can opt for either taking the benchmarking test or attending authorized language proficiency training programs organized by institutes in and outside Hong Kong (currently there are eight providers altogether). The courses, designed for teachers at different levels of proficiency, are aimed at helping them meet and exceed the language proficiency requirements set by the government.

The benchmarking test for English teachers, which is held annually, consists of five components: speaking, listening, reading, writing, and classroom language. Here are the requirements of each of the components:

- Reading: (1) completing a multiple-choice cloze and (2) reading comprehension and answering open-ended questions

- Writing: (1) writing expository text and (2) correcting and explaining errors/problems in a student's composition
- Listening: listening to a 30-minute text and answering 20 questions of different types
- Speaking: (1) (a) reading a poem aloud; (b) reading a prose passage aloud; (c) telling a story, recounting an experience, and presenting arguments; and (2) engaging in a group discussion
- Classroom language: having two live periods observed on two school days, with assessment focusing on (1) grammatical accuracy; (2) pronunciation, stress, and intonation; and (3) language of interaction

In order to be benchmarked, teachers are expected to attain level 3 in all components, but not necessarily in one and the same assessment. It is expected that by 2005, all practicing language teachers will have met the benchmarks. NESTs hired by the government are likely to be exempt since they should already possess an English degree plus the relevant training.

The consequence of English teachers not reaching the language proficiency required by the government is not explicitly stated in the official document. However, in the "Question and Answer" section of the online document *Language Proficiency Requirement for Teachers* (Hong Kong Education Department, n.d.b), the Education Department does underline the importance of English teachers attaining the language proficiency requirement: "for the sake of the students and the public, schools have the responsibility to ensure that their teachers' performance is up to a minimum acceptable level, and language teachers should have a minimum acceptable level in language proficiency" (para. 21). Some schools have in fact already added into their contracts of employment a term that requires English teachers to meet the language proficiency requirements.

It is clear from the preceding that the government has put a high premium on English teachers' language proficiency. Unfortunately, the results of the first two territory-wide benchmarking tests held in 2001 and 2002 are far from satisfactory. In the first test, given in 2001, only 33% of the test takers passed the writing component, and only 50% passed the speaking component (Hong Kong Examinations Authority, 2001). There were even lower passing rates in the writing component (less than 30%) and listening component (less than 40%) in the second test in 2002 (Hong Kong Examinations Authority, 2002). The media have been quick in their attempt to smear NNESTs, emphasizing their low level of English proficiency and in particular trying to ridicule those who do not make the grade. In an editorial entitled "English Lesson" in the local English newspaper *South China*

Morning Post (July 3, 2001, p. 17), the editor–as evidenced in the following criticisms quoted from the editorial–was relentless in carping at English teachers' language competence:

> By far the greater number [of NNESTs] are opposed to benchmarking because they doubt their ability to pass. . . . Last week's disappointing test results show what critics have claimed all along; namely that the poor quality of English teaching is the prime reason for the falling standard of English among the young. . . . However, it is no good blaming pupils for lacking English skills when many of their tutors are not much better.

In reality, however, it is not certain how much generalization one can make about the results of the first two benchmarking tests. One problem is that the background of the test takers is unknown. In the first test, for instance, it was said in local newspapers that only 34% of the test takers were practicing teachers, while the rest were believed to be teachers-in-preparation.

Given the situation that NNESTs are faced with, it is understandable that many of them feel frustrated and demoralized, not to mention the fact that they are facing many other problems, such as excessive workload and the need to cope with ongoing language education reforms proposed by the Education Department. One big challenge NNESTs are facing is, therefore, how to salvage the public's eroding confidence in their ability to teach English and how to boost their own confidence.

Increasing Importance of NESTs

In response to teachers' falling English proficiency and in order to enhance the quality of English language teaching, in 1997 the government started recruiting NESTs (both locally and overseas) to teach in secondary schools. Locally, these NESTs, appointed under Native-speaking English Teacher (NET) Schemes (Hong Kong Education and Manpower Bureau, 2003), are referred to as NETs. The main aim of the NET Schemes is to upgrade students' English language proficiency. Now each secondary school has one NET recruited by the government (or more hired by schools of their own accord). In 2000, 20 NETs were recruited to help implement the Primary Schools English Development Pilot Project in 40 primary schools. In September 2002, the NET Scheme was extended to all primary schools in Hong Kong, with two of them sharing one NET.

In secondary schools, NETs are seen as performing very important functions in the teaching of English. Their roles, as defined by the Education Department, include the following:

- to be responsible for classroom teaching and assessment;
- to provide support to the English Panel Chairperson, including assisting in curriculum development and preparation of teaching materials;
- to assist in conducting extra-curricular activities related to the English language, e.g., speech, drama, debate, choral speaking and extensive reading;
- to assist in running oral activities for students after school;
- to assist in setting up an English corner in the school where students can come together to practice oral English and read English books under their guidance; and
- to act as an English language resource person for other teachers in the school. (Hong Kong Education and Manpower Bureau, 2003, *NET Scheme in Secondary Schools*, para. 1)

The NET Scheme in primary schools, on the other hand, is seen to fulfill the aim of supporting and strengthening English language teaching and learning by

- providing an authentic environment for children to learn English;
- developing children's interest in learning English, helping them build the confidence for near-native communication, cultivating a lasting interest in, and establishing the foundation for, life-long learning of the language;
- helping local teachers develop innovative teaching and learning methods, materials, curricula and activities suited to the needs of local children; and
- disseminating good practices in language teaching and learning developed within the scheme through regional teacher development programmes such as experience-sharing seminars/workshops and networking activities. (Hong Kong Education and Manpower Bureau, 2003, *NET and ELTA Scheme in Primary Schools,* "Objectives," para. 2)

In primary schools, the roles of NETs are defined by the Education Department as follows:

- undertake teaching duties and try out good teaching models/practices related to the learning, teaching and assessment of English;
- provide support for the English panel, including contributing to school-based curriculum development and professional development of fellow teachers as well as developing and preparing learning/teaching materials;

- organize and conduct extra-curricular activities related to English learning and teaching such as plays/skit performances, school-based English camps, English language games (day), story-telling activities, songs and dances, verse speaking, and extensive reading; and, if applicable, to contribute to other extra-curricular activities such as IT, art and craft activities and sports; and
- act as an advisor on language teaching and learning for the principal and teachers in the school. (Hong Kong Education and Manpower Bureau, para. 2)

From the preceding descriptions of the NET scheme and the duties of NETs, it is clear that NETs are expected to play a central and somewhat leading role in the English department in both primary and secondary schools—namely, to act as English language resource persons or advisors for teachers, to assist the panel in curriculum and materials development, and to play a leading role in school-based development. For those NETs who have no or little firsthand teaching experience in Hong Kong, it is in fact doubtful that they can live up to the expectations of the Education department. It is also questionable—especially for those new to the Hong Kong context—whether or not they can design materials and activities suited to the needs of local students. Instead of inculcating the idea that all the English teachers within the English department, including the NNESTs, have different things to offer, NETs are singled out and elevated to the status of more knowledgeable and more resourceful—and hence more powerful.

In terms of teaching, some NETs are given differential treatment. Currently, the normal practice of secondary schools is to ask English teachers to teach three classes of English where they focus on the training of all language skills. However, a number of schools ask the NETs to teach oral English skills exclusively to all students in the school. The sociopolitical implication of such a lopsided practice, put simply, is that NNESTs are not competent enough or are less competent than NESTs in teaching oral English. However, by virtue of the fact that NNESTs speak the same mother tongue as their students, they may well be in a more advantageous position to teach oral English, since they understand the particular difficulties their students face in learning to speak EFL.

While it is true that NESTs can enrich the English-speaking environment and have a positive impact on English language teaching in secondary schools, their contribution tends to be overrated. As a result, some NNESTs feel that their work is undermined and that they are overshadowed by NESTs. In the first session of my full-time teacher preparation program at my previous university (Chinese University of Hong Kong) in 2001–2002, where all the pre-service teachers were nonnative speakers with hardly any full-time teaching experience, I asked my pre-service teachers to think about the challenges English teachers in Hong Kong face. One group of pre-service teachers came up with the following:

> The public doubts teachers' ability, especially teachers whose mother tongue is not English.

In our follow-up discussion, a pre-service teacher said that one major problem NNESTs face is that they don't speak with a "good" accent, which lessens their credibility and the public's trust in their ability as English teachers. These views show that NNESTs enrolled in pre-service teacher preparation programs are very much aware of the power imbalance between NESTs and NNESTs. Somehow, my pre-service teachers felt that because they are nonnative speakers, it takes extra effort for them to convince the public of their competence to teach English (e.g., that their knowledge of the English language is as good as that of their nonnative speaker counterparts). Also, given the public's eroding confidence in NNESTs, my pre-service teachers felt that they were going to encounter many more difficulties and challenges in English language teaching than their native speaker counterparts.

Preparing NNESTs: How?

In what ways can teacher preparation address the specific needs of NNESTs? In this section, I examine some strategies that I have used to assist my pre-service teachers from a nonnative English-speaking background in order to prepare them for EFL teaching in Hong Kong. My main purpose is to sensitize the NNESTs to professional issues (particularly those related to nonnative speakers), encourage reflection, make them aware of the advantages possessed by nonnative speakers in teaching English, and boost their confidence by helping them develop their strengths.

The strategies I describe draw on my experience as a teacher educator in the full-time Postgraduate Diploma in Education (PGDE) Program at the Chinese University of Hong Kong (CUHK). In the teacher preparation program, in 2001–2002, I taught a compulsory course called "Subject Curriculum Teaching" (SCT), which prepares pre-service teachers for EFL teaching in secondary schools in Hong Kong. I had 18 pre-service teachers in my group, all native speakers of Cantonese, whose ages ranged from 21 to 26. Of all the 18 pre-service teachers, 13 of them had an English-related degree. None had teaching experience in a secondary school, and only one of them had taught in a primary school (for one year). The SCT class seeks to equip prospective teachers of English with the skills necessary for English language teaching and for future self-development in the face of changing theories of language and changing theories of teaching and learning by offering a foundation in both areas. The topics covered include learning theories, language teaching methodology, second language acquisition, lesson planning and evaluation, grammar, vocabulary, assessment, and the teaching of the four language skills.

In the SCT course, I met my pre-service teachers two times a week for a total of 100 hours in two semesters. Therefore, I had plenty of opportunities to interact with them in class and to help them become more aware of professional issues related to native speakers and nonnative speakers. In the following sections, I discuss four main strategies that can be used to prepare nonnative English-speaking pre-service teachers: (1) encouraging reflection; (2) capitalizing on nonnative speakers' strengths; (3) reinforcing the need for ongoing language improvement; and (4) using the nonnative English-speaking teacher educator as a role model.

Encouraging Reflection

Reflection is crucial to teacher development and an effective tool of teacher empowerment (Bailey, Curtis, & Nunan, 2001). In my teacher preparation program, to encourage my pre-service teachers to engage in reflection, particularly reflection that sensitized them to issues related to NNESTs, I made use of an electronic forum and e-mail dialogue journals. The electronic forum, which was set up by the university, enabled me to post questions for discussion with my pre-service teachers as a group. Through the forum, my pre-service teachers not only responded to my questions but also discussed relevant issues with their peers. In e-mail dialogue journals, my pre-service teachers initiated discussions as they themselves came up with issues they were interested in.

To give an example of the topics discussed on the forum, the first discussion question I posted arose from the issue of "accent" raised by a pre-service teacher in class. The pre-service teacher said that since NNESTs of Hong Kong do not have a "good" accent, their credibility as English teachers is easily challenged. Capitalizing on the perfect opportunity to stimulate thinking on the issue of accent in relation to NNESTs, I asked pre-service teachers to read an article authored by myself and available online and to share their views on the topic. In the article (Lee, 2000), I shared my experience as an ESL teacher in Canada where my nonnative accent was challenged. I also outlined

the advantages NNESTs have over their native English-speaking counterparts. The message I wrote to my pre-service teachers follows:

> A very interesting point about challenges faced by English teachers came
> up in our first session yesterday, and I'd like to follow it up by sharing with
> you an article I've written for *TESOL Matters* (published in 2000). The title
> of the article is "Can a Nonnative Speaker Be a Good English Teacher?" To
> give you some background, I have become very interested in the nonnative
> speaker issue in TESOL/TESL thanks to my Canadian teaching experience.
> One main reason is that I was the only nonnative speaker in my two work-
> places (Douglas College and Simon Fraser University). As you may be aware,
> international students normally wish to be taught by native speakers of
> English. . . . If you're interested in my story, please read my article. And do
> give me your feedback.

All 18 pre-service teachers in my class responded to my message
and engaged in an active online discussion. Overall, they expressed
very positive views about NNESTs; for example, they acknowledged
their strengths and pointed out specific ways in which nonnative
English speakers can help students. I extract here some verbatim
quotations from the forum. One pre-service teacher, Jack,[1] added
other characteristics of nonnative English speakers to support what
is said in my article:

> Having the advantage of speaking the students' mother tongue, we can
> sometimes use the experiences that we learn Chinese language to help
> students relate their new learning experiences in English with that in their
> mother tongue. For example, when we teach students how to write letters
> to friends in English, we may activate their previous knowledge of writing
> to friends in Chinese letters or e-mail. This can give English learners greater
> access to contact knowledge and to their own prior knowledge and experi-
> ences, offer opportunities for interaction, and support the development of
> their English language skills as well as their self-esteem. Rapport from the
> teachers is also shown to the students.

On another occasion, pre-service teachers were discussing the topic
of error correction in the writing classroom. Most of my pre-service
teachers felt that NESTs tend to de-emphasize students' errors in
writing and do not provide the kind of help that EFL learners need. I
asked my pre-service teachers to read an article authored by myself
on error correction in the writing classroom (Lee, 1997) and to express
on the forum their views on the thorny issue of error feedback. The
exchanges turned out to be extremely rich. They raised meaningful
questions about the topic—for example, whether teachers should

implement detailed marking or selective marking techniques, how to use selective marking, the use of model essays, how to change student perceptions about error correction, and how to use error codes effectively. They also shared different ideas about error treatment—for example, linking error correction with grammar instruction, organizing post-writing workshops on specific errors, and drawing students' attention to the way first language interference might result in faulty sentence constructions. All these issues are directly relevant to the teaching of EFL writing. The point I emphasized to my pre-service teachers throughout the forum discussions is that as NNESTs and EFL learners themselves, they were in an advantageous position to understand students' difficulties in correcting errors and to try out different ways to help them cope with their problems.

On the whole, my pre-service teachers appreciated the opportunities provided for them to share ideas through the forum. One pre-service teacher wrote in her evaluation of the forum:

> The forum allows me to think deeply before expressing my ideas to other classmates. Their various opinions, on the other hand, strengthen my self-reflections. As a result, I have become more aware of my own views that are different from others.

Another pre-service teacher commented:

> Different questions and suggestions come out through forum discussions. All these help build my knowledge and raise my awareness of the essence of teaching and learning—to teach and motivate students to think and learn actively rather than to test their ability.

As I noted earlier, the other channel of communication I used to encourage reflection was e-mail dialogue journal writing. I asked my pre-service teachers to send me e-mail dialogue journals on a weekly basis. I did not specify the topic for each week; instead, I told them to pick up on issues discussed in class. Unlike the electronic forum, in e-mail dialogue journals, my pre-service teachers initiated the discussion as they themselves selected the topics they were interested in. Also, e-mail dialogue journals differed from the forum in that the dialogue, which was between the individual pre-service teachers and myself, was more personal and more catered to individual needs.

A myriad of professional issues were raised in the dialogue journals, ranging from language policy in the classroom and classroom management and discipline to the teaching of language skills like reading, speaking, listening, and writing. The majority of these issues are pertinent to my pre-service teachers' understanding of their unique role as NNESTs. For instance, quite a lot has been said on the topic of the medium of instruction in the English classroom—that is, whether English teachers should use their first language (L1) to assist classroom instructions. One pre-service teacher, Nancy, discussed this issue in her dialogue journal:

> I would like to raise the issue of whether one should use Cantonese to explain in an English lesson. I agree that we should try our best to explain in English, but it is easy to do so with students who are good at it and are motivated. However, I am a little concerned when students are very weak at English. They may have a sense of hopelessness regarding their own ability and might have already given up trying. They have perhaps switched off to English language completely. If they have still got a little bit of motivation left, wouldn't it be better to encourage them by making it easier for them? Still, it is a controversial issue because if you start giving in, then your students would expect Chinese explanations from then on. However, if one insists on speaking in English all the time without considering the ability of the students, some of them may give up altogether. I guess the question here is more about motivating students with learning difficulties, especially when the students are very weak at listening. I think this is a real problem for English teachers. Perhaps it may be relieved by some of the methods that were brought up in our lessons, such as using group work, task-based activities and simple communicative language games. Still, I do agree that students should become active learners and we should set up the environment for them to learn actively. I agree that this is not an easy task at all. However, we can strive to do our best and not to give up hope in the face of difficulties, right?

Through engaging in reflection, Nancy became more cognizant of her unique role as a nonnative English-speaking professional in helping her students learn English in a language-rich environment in the EFL classroom. In my response, I showed my understanding of the difficulties NNESTs encounter in trying to formulate their language policy in the EFL classroom and yet reinforce the importance of adhering to the "use-English-as-much-as-possible" principle so as to maximize comprehensible input for students:

> My position is very simple. Broad principle: use as much English as possible, even though it means spending more time (but comprehensible input is provided, so it's not a waste of time). In lower-band schools and/or situations where using lots of English may spoil the teacher-ss relationship, etc.—tell students clearly your expectations and let them know what is going to happen in your class—e.g. 50% of L1 in the first month, then 60% in second month, etc. etc. The principle behind: use of L1 initially but with

strategies to WEAN IT OFF GRADUALLY. (In reality, almost all teachers end up using more and more L1, so it's important to be aware of this. Also, let ss know very clearly that there will be more and more L2 and less and less L1.) You're right—we should motivate students. Explain to students your "good" intention behind the language policy, stand firm and don't budge easily. I'm sure your enthusiasm and concern for their improvement are quite sufficient factors to motivate them.

On another occasion, another pre-service teacher, named Karen, shared her views of the NET Scheme in one of her dialogue entries. Karen wrote:

Employing NET teachers is quite a fast possible means to encourage them to practise spoken English. However the gloomy picture is that most do not account the fact that nonnative speakers have knowledge of a second language learner that the NET teachers usually lack. There are times when NET teachers face grammatical issues coming from their intuitions without explanations. Nonnative speakers encountered similar language experiences as their students, understand their problems and solve them more easily. The devaluation of local teachers strengths and efforts weaken their morale towards teaching. I would consider inculcating the belief that both NET teachers and local teachers have their own strengths and drawbacks that are irreplaceable but complementary to each other. Local teachers can have near native language knowledge, understand their students' more easily with regard to their own learning path and instill learning skills as a second language learner.

In my response to Karen's dialogue journal entry, I reiterated my view about the importance of ongoing professional development as key to the empowerment of NNESTs:

Ongoing professional development should be encouraged, and local teachers should actively take part in different professional development activities. . . . If NNS teachers don't keep upgrading themselves professionally, they may be replaced by their native speaker colleagues.

Overall, the pre-service teachers' feedback on the value of dialogue journals was very positive. In the last e-mail dialogue journal discussion, I asked them to give some evaluative comments on dialogue journal writing. All those who responded gave overwhelmingly positive comments. For instance, one pre-service teacher wrote:

Dialogue journal writing made me reflect on what I had learnt. Every week, I had to submit a piece to the teacher. Where did I get the idea? Mainly from re-thinking about what I had learnt in the lessons. In other words, dialogue journal writing helped consolidate what I had learnt. Besides, I can raise individualized and personal questions in the journal. Since the pace of the lessons was a bit fast, it is difficult for me to think thoroughly and ask for details for further understanding, or my questions were so minor that talking about them in the lessons was a waste of time. With the journal writing, I could ask questions that I could not ask in the lessons. Also, I could ask questions based on my own circumstances and get "tailor-made" response from the teacher. . . . . Also, it can help building rapport between teachers and students.

According to my pre-service teachers, reading my responses helped them become more reflective. One pre-service teacher remarked:

You are a very good listener. I can learn something from your responses. You are very resourceful and you give me some very good and useful advice. You stimulate me to think more and sometimes inspire me to think from other angles.

Through reflecting on different professional issues, my pre-service teachers learned to be more autonomous learners, "using the knowledge acquired as a basis for further development" (Richards, 1990, p. 15).

Capitalizing on the Strengths of NNESTs

NNESTs possess some obvious advantages over NESTs (see Gill & Rebrova, 2001; Kamhi-Stein, Lee, & Lee, 1999; Lee, 2000), and these strengths have to be recognized and reinforced. In my teacher preparation program, I often made a conscious attempt to draw my pre-service teachers' attention to their own strengths as nonnative speakers. Grammar teaching was one of the areas I worked on.

Although it is rather well known in the literature that nonnative speakers are perceived to be more knowledgeable than native speakers in grammar teaching (Kamhi-Stein et al., 1999), there is research indicating that novice teachers tend to avoid grammar teaching due to their own sense of inadequacy (Numrich, 1996; Richards, Ho, & Giblin, 1996). When asked about their concerns in grammar teaching, my pre-service teachers told me that they felt inadequate because they did not possess native speaker intuitions of English grammar. In my classroom activities, I aimed to show my pre-service teachers that they in fact had acquired a good understanding of English grammar, which was not necessarily inferior to that of the native speakers.

An example of this point is how my pre-service teachers and I worked on the passive voice. I used an inductive approach and asked them to read a number of sentences using the passive voice, identify unacceptable sentences, and then identify with some rules regarding the use of passives. The outcome of the activity was not surprising. First, almost all the pre-service teachers were able to identify the inappropriate sentences. Second, at the end of the group discussion, my pre-service teachers were able to articulate several rules as to when passives are inappropriate. For instance, they pointed out that a passive could not be formed with an intransitive verb, as in "My brother was died by my mother." They also recognized that certain verbs (e.g., *contain* and *have*) were quite limited in their ability to form a passive. However, my pre-service teachers found it difficult to explain why "The station was left by the train ten minutes ago" is inappropriate. I showed them a similar sentence—"The child was left by the mother five minutes ago"—and asked them to discuss why the second sentence is acceptable. With some prompting, my pre-service teachers were able to articulate a plausible explanation—that is, it is generally inappropriate to put the least important information at the beginning of a sentence. The activities focusing on the passive voice showed my pre-service teachers that though they were not native speakers of English, they possessed a good understanding of the English grammar—that is, they were able to analyze the sentences and come up with rules that govern the use of passives, a feat that a lot of native speakers are unable to do (see Gill & Rebrova, 2001).

Through grammar activities that raise pre-service teachers' awareness of the language, they can become more confident of their own knowledge about grammar. Borg (2001) believes that it is important that teachers develop a positive attitude toward their knowledge about language. For nonnative speakers, it is particularly important that teacher education programs provide them with opportunities to develop and refine their knowledge of grammar so that they become more perceptive of the difficulties EFL students face during the learning process.

Another skill area I made use of to reinforce the NNESTs' strengths is pronunciation. When NNESTs share the same native language with their students, they are in an advantageous position to anticipate and prevent students' language difficulties (Medgyes, 2001). In one of my speaking lessons, I asked my pre-service teachers to analyze some pronunciation difficulties that Cantonese speakers of English may have and to identify the potential problems, mainly the sounds they themselves found difficult to pronounce or sounds that they thought were commonly mispronounced by Cantonese speakers of English. In this awareness-raising exercise, my pre-service teachers were asked to refer back to their mother tongue and discover the reasons why some English sounds may pose difficulties for Cantonese-speaking students. They also discussed ways to teach the difficult sounds to help their students better understand how these sounds are articulated. For example, a lot of Cantonese speakers of English have difficulty pronouncing nasal sounds and tend to confuse /n/ with /l/. They also tend to confuse /r/ with /w/, and they find it difficult to pronounce consonant clusters like /pl/ and /kl/. Different ideas about how students can be helped in pronouncing these difficult sounds were discussed in class—for example, (1) putting a finger beneath the nose when pronouncing /n/ and /l/ and feeling the air that escapes through the nose for /n/ but not /l/ or (2) drawing attention to the difference in the shape of the tongue in pronouncing /r/ and /w/.

As a result of the language awareness activities, my pre-service teachers said that their awareness of common pronunciation difficulties for Cantonese speakers was greatly enhanced. With sharpened awareness of why and how some sounds are particularly difficult for Cantonese speakers, nonnative speakers are better equipped to teach pronunciation. They do not just work on correcting students' pronunciation mistakes; more important, they can anticipate and prevent the mistakes. In light of Medgyes' (2001) point of view that teacher education should focus more on strategies for preventing than correcting errors, it can be said that nonnative speakers, given their knowledge of the EFL students' L1, are in a better position to prevent errors than are their native English-speaking counterparts.

Reinforcing the Need for Ongoing Language Improvement

The public's criticism of NNESTs' declining English proficiency was a matter of real concern for my pre-service teachers. Many of them felt that they did not have a very good command of the English language and said that they enrolled in the PGDE Program partly to upgrade their English skills. Aside from equipping these pre-service teachers with the skills necessary for EFL teaching, I deemed it extremely important to provide them with opportunities for language enhancement and to reinforce the need for ongoing language improvement. Medgyes (1999) has rightly pointed out that in order for NNESTs to be "effective, self-confident and satisfied" (p. 179), they have to be near-native speakers of English.

At CUHK, optional language courses designed to enhance proficiency in English are provided for pre-service teachers who major in English. All my 18 pre-service teachers were motivated learners of English, so they all opted to join these language courses. Outside these courses, I constantly reminded my pre-service teachers of the importance to engage in lifelong learning that focuses on language improvement. To this end, I involved my pre-service teachers in activities of different kinds to enhance their language awareness, so that they would be better equipped to implement strategies designed to help them improve their English language skills as part of their ongoing professional development. For example, I gave my pre-service teachers questionnaires to help them analyze their learning styles and learning strategies to find out what kind of language learners they are (see Cohen, Oxford, & Chi., n.d.a, n.d.b). I also showed them the range of language learning strategies available for EFL learners (see Johnson, 2001; Nunan, 1999; Oxford, 1990) and made them aware of their strengths and limitations in the use of language strategies. For example, some EFL learners are particularly weak in the use of social strategies (i.e., interacting with others), and some may not be aware of how communication strategies (e.g., using paraphrases and circumlocution) can be used to cope with communication breakdown.

Also, through writing dialogue journals on a weekly basis, my pre-service teachers came to realize the value of ongoing writing practice from the perspective of a learner. As noted by one of them:

> Writing a short piece each week could help keeping or even polishing my writing skills.

My pre-service teachers appreciated the fact that through writing practice, they could improve their writing. At the same time, by way of tailor-made responses to different questions raised in dialogue journals regarding ways to upgrade their English language skills, I reiterated the importance of ongoing language improvement. For instance, I encouraged extensive reading, by recommending English books for leisure reading; and I underlined the importance of becoming more "language aware," by suggesting grammar books (e.g., *Collins COBUILD English Grammar* [1990] and Michael Swan's *Practical English Usage* [1995]) that my pre-service teachers could read and refer to in order to brush up on their grammar.

Furthermore, through encouraging pre-service teachers to raise language issues both inside and outside class (e.g., in dialogue journals), I emphasized that it is crucial to play the role of teacher and learner at the same time and to adopt a spirit of inquiry, constantly asking questions and trying to find answers to problems, including language problems like grammar and pronunciation. For example, questions such as how to pronounce foreign words in the English lexicon (e.g., *croissant*) and whether both "I suggested he did it" and "I suggested he do it" are correct, have been raised and discussed in and outside class. All in all, using a variety of techniques, I helped my pre-service teachers become more aware of the need to engage in ongoing language improvement so as to keep upgrading their English proficiency to native or near-native competence.

Using the Nonnative English-Speaking Teacher Educator as a Role Model

The preceding strategies, I believe, are best implemented by nonnative English-speaking teacher educators, who can serve as effective role models for NNESTs. Having gone through a similar process of teacher training, nonnative English-speaking teacher educators are more likely to understand the problems faced by pre-service teachers from a nonnative English-speaking background. Besides, nonnative English-speaking teacher educators are in a good position to demonstrate different strengths specifically possessed by NNESTs. For instance, by analyzing Cantonese-speaking students' problems in learning English pronunciation, I demonstrated the inside knowledge nonnative speakers possess about students' pronunciation difficulties. By helping NNESTs enhance their grammatical awareness of the use of the passive voice in English, I modeled a technique of grammatical analysis that NNESTs can confidently use with their explicit knowledge of grammar. Last but not least, nonnative English-speaking teacher educators can serve as good role models in emphasizing the notion that successful language teaching does not primarily depend on L1 background or accent but, instead, relies considerably on the enthusiasm and eagerness of the practitioners to self-reflect, to learn, and to enhance their instructional practices accordingly. All these qualities, if possessed and manifested by a nonnative English-speaking teacher educator, are more likely to make an impression on NNESTs enrolled in pre-service programs, because the NNESTs themselves can easily identify with such a teacher educator. These ideas are reflected in the following end-of-course comments made by my pre-service teachers. One pre-service teacher commented:

Your enthusiasm in teaching is my role model.

Another pre-service teacher commented in a similar fashion:

Your enthusiasm in teaching and learning can be one of our examples.

As their teacher, I honestly felt that my pre-service teachers were imbued with strength and power when they left my course. One pre-service teacher wrote in the comments:

I will always remember the way you teach when I teach my students.

Another wrote:

> I've learnt a lot and would try to use some new teaching methods that you've shown to me.

I am not suggesting that a native English-speaking teacher educator could not have made a similar impact on my pre-service teachers. One thing I am rather sure of, though, is that since I am a nonnative speaker, my pre-service teachers were able to connect with me easily. They probably felt that what I could accomplish as a nonnative speaker is something manageable and achievable for themselves, too.

Conclusion

Using the case of Hong Kong, I have discussed how teacher preparation programs can aid in the process of empowering NNESTs to prepare them for EFL teaching. Through electronic forum discussions and e-mail dialogue journal writing, I have provided prospective teachers with opportunities to examine professional issues related to NNESTs, to express their voice, and to engage in reflection regarding issues particularly pertinent to NNESTs. I have also underlined the specific strengths possessed by nonnative speakers and encouraged my prospective teachers to capitalize on their strengths to benefit their teaching—for example, in teaching specific skills such as grammar and pronunciation. Throughout the course, I have reiterated the importance for NNESTs to keep upgrading their English language skills in order to attain native or near-native competence. The techniques I have used, I believe, are applicable in other EFL teacher education contexts, especially when the teacher educators, like myself, are nonnative speakers of English who speak the same mother tongue as their teacher trainees.

Nonnative English-speaking teacher educators, with firsthand knowledge of the pre-service teachers' native language, can identify the potential strengths of the trainees as well as areas in which they lack confidence. Apart from further developing their strengths and helping them meet their needs in specific areas, nonnative English-speaking teacher educators can promote reflection by engaging teacher trainees in discussions (through group forum discussions and e-mail dialogue journals) pertinent to their local context. What's more, nonnative English-speaking teacher educators understand better the needs of their nonnative English-speaking teacher trainees as language learners, and hence they can point their pre-service teachers in the right direction regarding ongoing language enrichment and other professional development activities. Indeed, as a nonnative

English-speaking teacher educator myself, I strongly believe that nonnative English-speaking teacher educators, like their nonnative English-speaking pre-service teachers, have a most significant role to play in bringing about positive change in English language teaching. They can take small steps toward empowering NNESTs for the most challenging task of English language teaching. These small steps, when taken together, can represent milestones for nonnative English-speaking pre-service teachers.

Note

1. Pseudonyms are used to protect the participants' identities.

References

Amin, N. (1999). Minority women teachers of ESL: Negotiating white English. In G. Braine (Ed.), *Non-native educators in English language teaching* (pp. 93–104). Mahwah, NJ: Erlbaum.

Bailey, K. M., Curtis, A., & Nunan, D. (2001). *Pursuing professional development: The self as source.* Boston: Heinle & Heinle.

Borg, S. (2001). Self-perception and practice in teaching grammar. *ELT Journal, 55*(1), 21–29.

Cohen, A. D., Oxford, R. L., & Chi, J. C. (n.d.a). *Language strategy use survey.* Retrieved May 8, 2003, from *http://carla.acad.umn.edu/profiles/CohenPapers/ Lg_Strat_Srvy.html*

Cohen, A. D., Oxford, R. L., & Chi, J. C. (n.d.b). *Learning style survey: Assessing your own learning styles.* Retrieved May 8, 2003, from *http://carla.acad.umn. edu/profiles/CohenPapers/LearningStylesSurvey.pdf*

Collins COBUILD English grammar. (1990). London: HarperCollins.

English lesson (2001, July 3). *South China Morning Post,* p. 17.

Gill, S., & Rebrova, A. (2001, March). Native and non-native: Together we're worth more. *ELT Newsletter.* Retrieved March 25, 2002, from *http://www.eltnewsletter. com/back/March2001/art522001.htm*

Hong Kong Education and Manpower Bureau. (2003). *Native-speaking English teacher (NET) schemes.* Retrieved May 8, 2003, from *http://www.emb.gov.hk/ chi/highlights.asp?sid=16&cid=71*

Hong Kong Education Department. (n.d.a). *Language proficiency requirement for teachers: Background.* Retrieved May 8, 2003, from *http://www.emb.gov. hk/lpa/english/teacher/background.htm*

Hong Kong Education Department. (n.d.b). *Language proficiency requirement for teachers: Q & A.* Retrieved May 8, 2003, from *http://www.emb.gov.hk/aid/chi- nese/english%20v/link/teacher/qa.htm*

Hong Kong Examinations Authority. (2001). *Language proficiency assessment for teachers (English language) 2001: Assessment report.* Retrieved May 8, 2003, from *http://www.emb.gov.hk/aid/chinese/english%20v/link/teacher/appendix/ AssessmentReport(ENG)2001.pdf*

Hong Kong Examinations Authority. (2002). *Language proficiency assessment for teachers (English language) 2002: Assessment report.* Retrieved May 8, 2003, from *http://www.emb.gov.hk/aid/chinese/english%20v/link/teacher/appendix/ 2002AssessmentReport(English).pdf*

Johnson, K. (2001). *An introduction to foreign language learning and teaching.* Harlow, England: Longman.

Kamhi-Stein, L. D., Lee, E., & Lee, C. (1999, August/September). How TESOL programs can enhance the preparation of nonnative English speakers. *TESOL Matters, 9*(4), 1, 5.

Lee, I. (1997). ESL learners' performance in error correction in writing: Some implications for teaching. *System, 25*(4), 465–477.

Lee, I. (2000, February/March). Can a nonnative speaker be a good English teacher? *TESOL Matters, 10*(1), 19.

Medgyes, P. (1999). Language training: A neglected area in teacher education. In G. Braine (Ed.), *Non-native educators in English language teaching* (pp. 177–195). Mahwah, NJ: Erlbaum.

Medgyes, P. (2001). When the teacher is a non-native speaker. In M. Celce-Murcia (Ed.), *Teaching English as a second or foreign language* (3rd ed., pp. 429–442). Boston: Heinle & Heinle.

Numrich, C. (1996). On becoming a language teacher: Insights from diary studies. *TESOL Quarterly, 30*(1), 131–153.

Nunan, D. (1999). *Second language teaching and learning.* New York: Heinle & Heinle.

Oxford, R. L. (1990). *Language learning strategies: What every teacher should know.* Boston: Newbury House.

Richards, J. C. (1990). The dilemma of teacher education in second language teaching. In J. C. Richards & D. Nunan (Eds.), *Second language teacher education* (pp. 3–15). Cambridge: Cambridge University Press.

Richards, J. C., Ho, B., & Giblin, K. (1996). Learning how to teach in the RSA Cert. In D. Freeman & J. C. Richards (Eds.), *Teacher learning in language teaching* (pp. 242–259). Cambridge: Cambridge University Press.

Swan, M. (1995). *Practical English usage* (2nd ed.). Oxford: Oxford University Press.

Thomas, J. (1999). Voices from the periphery: Non-native teachers and issues of credibility. In G. Braine (Ed.), *Non-native educators in English language teaching* (pp. 5–13). Mahwah, NJ: Erlbaum.

Questions for Reflection

1. In their chapter, Pasternak and Bailey argue that language proficiency and professionalism should be viewed as continua. In contrast, Medgyes (1994) argues that NES and NNES professionals exhibit distinctly different characteristics in terms of their proficiency and teaching behaviors. Which of the two positions do you support? Why?

2. In their chapter, Pasternak and Bailey argue that "language teacher preparation programs can do a great deal to ensure that their students have the opportunities they need in order to feel more confident and prepared when they graduate." They also describe a variety of activities that language teacher preparation programs can implement in order to improve the confidence and preparation of their graduates. Analyze a language teacher preparation program with which you are familiar. What are some of the activities described by Pasternak and Bailey that are implemented in the program? What other activities would you suggest that the program implement?

3. In their chapter, Matsuda and Matsuda argue that teacher preparation programs should implement a collaborative model of teacher preparation, and they describe an online journal sharing project drawing on native and nonnative English speaker collaboration. What are the implications of Matsuda and Matsuda's ideas for the organization of language teacher education programs? What are some examples of collaborative activities, other than the project described by Matsuda and Matsuda, that could be implemented in language teacher preparation programs?

4. In her diary study, Brinton found that some factors that affect NNES student teachers are similar to those that affect all novice teachers, regardless of their language status. According to Brinton, other factors affecting NNES student teachers "seem to be

unique to the student teachers' backgrounds as L2 speakers of English." How might practicum supervisors deal with these two different sets of factors in the practicum course?

5. Brinton suggests having native and nonnative English speakers team teach. What conditions are necessary for team teaching to succeed? What factors would threaten the success of team teaching?

6. In their chapter, Brady and Gulikers suggest encouraging host instructors (also known as "mentor teachers" or "master teachers") to engage in action research projects. What kinds of benefits can result from the implementation of action research projects? What problems, if any, could be associated with the implementation of action research projects in practicum courses? What should the role of the student teacher be in classrooms where action research projects are implemented?

7. Brady and Gulikers suggest familiarizing student teachers with the discourse systems of the classrooms in which they complete their practice teaching. In what ways can this idea be implemented in the practicum course? In what ways can this idea be implemented in language teacher education programs?

8. The chapter by Pasternak and Bailey and that by Lee agree that language teacher preparation programs must create opportunities to help teachers-in-preparation improve their English language skills. What is your position on this issue? What role, if any, should language teacher preparation programs have in helping NNES student teachers develop their English language skills?

9. Drawing on the notion of "language enhancement" proposed by Pasternak and Bailey and by Lee, examine a teacher preparation program with which you are familiar. How would you modify the program to integrate a language enhancement component?

Section 4
Focus on the Classroom

Section 4 complements the previous three sections by discussing the implications of theory, research, and language teacher preparation initiatives for the instructional practices of NNES professionals teaching in ESL and EFL settings. In the first chapter, "From Japan to the U.S. and Back: Co-Constructing Perspectives on English as a Foreign Language Education in Japan through Teacher Education in the U.S.," Elza Magalhães Major, a teacher educator from a nonnative English-speaking background, and Ayako Yamashiro, a U.S.-trained EFL professional, reflect on their reconstructed views about FL education and teacher preparation. The chapter offers some suggestions for adapting Western ESL instructional practices to the realities of the Japanese classrooms.

In the following chapter, "The Nonnative English-Speaking Teacher as an Intercultural Speaker," Carmen Velasco-Martin argues that in the European Union, the figure of the "intercultural speaker"—referring to both language teachers and language students—leaves no place for the issue of native speaker versus nonnative speaker. Velasco-Martin describes a variety of classroom projects in which she uses her skills and knowledge as an intercultural speaker to help her EFL students become intercultural speakers, develop a better understanding of their own culture, strengthen their cultural identity, thereby contributing to their overall education.

The final two chapters in the book emphasize the value of native and nonnative English speaker collaboration. Despite extensive discussions focusing on the importance of native and nonnative English speaker collaboration, there has been limited documentation illustrating examples of collaborative projects. The last two chapters in the book are designed to fill this gap in the literature. In the chapter "Collaboration between Native and Nonnative English-Speaking Educators," Luciana C. de Oliveira and Sally Richardson argue that although most educators recognize the benefits of collaboration with other colleagues generally, many may not be aware of the numerous benefits attained by collaboration between native and nonnative-speaking educators in particular. In their chapter, the authors discuss these benefits, beginning with a history of their own collaborative relationship that began in graduate school and has continued for several years. They discuss their individual differences and similarities and how both have contributed to their relationship and enhanced their understanding of their students, of their ability to teach more effectively, and of their professional lives. The authors conclude with recommendations for how professionals can establish and maintain a lasting collaborative relationship.

In the last chapter, "The Development of EFL Standards in Egypt: Collaboration among Native and Nonnative English-Speaking Professionals," Marguerite Ann Snow, Maysoun Omar, and Anne M. Katz describe a collaborative project in which native and nonnative English-speaking professionals produced standards for EFL teachers, in-service teacher trainers, educational leaders, and in-service training courses in Egypt. Central to the project were the notions that collaboration would benefit all professionals, regardless of their language background, and that collaboration would also result in substantive contributions from both the native and the nonnative English speakers working on the standards project. In their chapter, Snow et al. describe the steps followed in developing the standards and the lessons learned from the collaboration. The chapter concludes with the authors' reflection on their shared growth as professionals.

From Japan to the U.S. and Back: Co-constructing Perspectives on English as a Foreign Language Education in Japan through Teacher Education in the U.S.

Elza Magalhães Major
University of Nevada, Reno

Ayako Yamashiro
Okinawa International University, Okinawa Christian Junior College, and University of Okinawa

Beginning at the End of the Journey

At the end of the 2002 conference of the TESOL organization, Ayako, a nonnative English-speaking (NNES) student from Japan about to graduate from a U.S.-based master's program in teaching English to speakers of other languages, and Elza, her professor and advisor at the University of Nevada, Reno, took a trolley ride together through Salt Lake City to kill time before a flight back to Reno. The destination of the trip seemed unimportant. Ayako and Elza chatted, taking inventory of the most significant conference events for the novice TESOL professional. Ayako had successfully presented a paper at the Graduate Student Forum and a second paper in a colloquium that Elza had organized. Buying books and collecting free ones at the TESOL publisher's exhibit had also been exhilarating for Ayako. Seeing in person keynote speakers whose work she had to read and critique in her courses (e.g., J. Cummins, T. Skutnabb-Kangas, and D. Nunan) had also been an exciting experience.

Ayako began to thank Elza for having encouraged her to experience the TESOL conference as a novice TESOL professional and for two years of mentoring through her graduate studies. Elza deflected the gratitude by reminiscing on Ayako's many academic and personal accomplishments since her initial journey from Japan to the U.S. a few years earlier to improve her English and earn a master's degree in teaching English to speakers of other languages. Together, Elza and Ayako traced the milestones along Ayako's sojourn: her research projects on bilingual education of Amerasian children in Okinawa, on attitudes toward the English and the Japanese languages among the Japanese in Japan, and on the changing policies and practices in language education in Japan; her conference presentations; her interest in sociopolitical concerns of NNES professionals in the field of teaching English to speakers of other languages; her recent position on appropriate methodologies for English as a foreign language (EFL) teaching in Japan. Elza pointed out that she had also gained insight into language education in Japan through Ayako, as professors often expand their own knowledge through their students' projects and discoveries. The conversation turned to the collaborative project on which Elza and Ayako were soon to embark: a chapter for this book. What should the book chapter be about?

As a teacher educator and a mentor of native English-speaking (NES) and NNES graduate students at the University of Nevada, Reno, Elza is concerned with the impact of her master's program on the preparedness of NNES graduate students when they return to their countries to teach EFL. On that aimless ride in Salt Lake City, Elza realized it was important to share Ayako's reconstructed beliefs with the TESOL community. This particular NNES graduate embodies the perspectives of NNES graduate students from countries where the presence of English in society and English language teaching are reflections and agents of sociolinguistic and educational changes. The spread of English as the world's de facto lingua franca has been described as linguistic imperialism (Phillipson, 1992), and its diffusion in countries where it is not a native language (e.g., Japan) is described as a sociocultural phenomenon responsible for first language (L1) loss and linguistic changes (Kachru, 1985). Ayako's perspectives on English education in her country testify to the influence of English in Japan, the attitudes of the Japanese people toward EFL teaching and learning, and the struggles and inconsistencies among educators and government agencies to regulate and reform English instruction in Japan. What occurs in EFL classrooms in Japan today is an amalgam of many elements that were brought to light during Ayako's graduate studies. Other Japanese and Asian graduate students in the same program corroborated and shared her insightful perspectives on the impact of English on their countries, both in the EFL classroom and in society in general.

In Salt Lake City, Elza and Ayako disembarked from the trolley at the same station where they had departed two hours earlier. On the ride with no destination, they became aware of the discoveries both student and mentor had experienced along the paths they had traveled together for two years. Ayako had reconstructed her views about English instruction in Japan and on her own intellectual and professional abilities as a future teacher of EFL in her home country. She referred to her own milestones: a newly found identity as a NNES professional; a sense of social consciousness and concern for educational and sociopolitical issues of her homeland (Okinawa); an understanding of EFL methodologies as choices to be made by the teachers in their instructional settings; and a sense of urgency in advocating for educational reforms at home. Elza certainly had gained a better understanding of the sociocultural impact of the English language in Japanese society and in Japanese language classrooms. She was also witnessing the result of insightful reflectivity by one of the students in her program.

The product of Ayako and Elza's collaborative reflections, this chapter focuses on the many aspects of EFL education in Japan. The chapter begins with brief descriptions of Ayako and Elza's backgrounds and of the graduate program where they met and interacted for two years. Next, the chapter describes the attitudes of the Japanese toward English and the current EFL education system in Japan. In the subsequent section, Ayako reveals her reconstructed perspectives on EFL education in Japan—perspectives that surfaced during her graduate studies in the U.S. and after her return home. In the final section, Elza discusses the implications of their merged ideas for teacher educators of NNES graduate students enrolled in master's programs in teaching English to speakers of other languages.

The Collaborators

Ayako, the Student

Born in Okinawa to a trilingual father—who speaks Okinawan, Japanese, and English—and a monolingual Japanese mother, Ayako never learned to speak Okinawan at home or in school. Thus, she had difficulty communicating with her grandmother who only spoke Okinawan. Probably for this reason, she has always been interested in sociolinguistic issues related to the people of Okinawa. One of the first courses she took in her master's program in the U.S. was "Bilingual Education." She felt encouraged to delve into her own Okinawan background. She conducted research on the educational, linguistic, and political factors involved in the language loss of Okinawans. She also analyzed the social status, discriminatory treatment, and educational plight of the Amerasian children of U.S. military men and Okinawan women who live in and around the U.S. military base in Okinawa. At that point, she came to the realization that the neglect of Amerasian children in Okinawa by the local schools was just one instance of discriminatory treatment of linguistic minorities in Japan. She saw the need for Japanese society and educational institutions to consider bilingual education for the children of aboriginal (Okinawans, Ainus) and imported (Koreans, Chinese, Brazilians) linguistic minorities in Japan, in order to raise their social status and integrate them into the Japanese society.

For most aspiring Japanese teachers of EFL, studying in an English-dominant country is desirable. Their hopes are usually twofold: to improve communicative skills in English and to gain exposure to the culture, customs, educational practices, and current English as a second language (ESL) and EFL methodologies. EFL teachers in Japan see several advantages to studying in master's programs (in teaching English to speakers of other languages) in English-dominant countries. First, future EFL teachers in Japan usually gain content knowledge about language, rather than experience with teaching strategies, during teacher training; therefore, they greatly benefit from field experiences and from learning about instructional strategies, methods, and materials in graduate programs outside of Japan. Furthermore, because there are very few graduate programs that train teachers in second language (L2) classroom strategies in Japan, students who earn a degree (in teaching English to speakers of other languages) in the U.S. will be able to contribute to the improvement of EFL teacher training programs in Japan. Another advantage is that the cross-cultural experience in an English-dominant country can be shared with Japanese students of English. For instance, after living in the U.S., a Japanese teacher of English would be able to arouse the curiosity and interest of the students by sharing personal stories from experiencing celebrations such as Thanksgiving, the Fourth of July, or Memorial Day. The teacher's insights into cultural practices of daily living, home life, shopping, traveling, leisure, work, and school activities among people in the U.S. can certainly enliven a language class and assist in the L2 acquisition process. To this end, both the Japanese Ministry of Education, Culture, Sports, Science, and Technology (MEXT) and the local boards of education currently encourage Japanese-born teachers of EFL to pursue professional development overseas.

Ayako's professional training as an EFL teacher began in Okinawa with a bachelor's degree in European and American studies. She took additional courses at the university to earn a license to teach junior and senior high school English. After teaching middle and high school students and adult EFL in Okinawa for three years, she decided to travel to the U.S. in 1998 to improve her English language skills at a college in Maryland and at an intensive English program (IEP) in Nevada, before seeking admission to the master's program in teaching English to speakers of other languages. During her studies in the master's program, she worked hard to improve her written and spoken competence. Her professors often praised the quality of her academic work in terms of insightfulness and depth of critical analysis. As a result, she earned an outstanding international graduate student award from the university and a travel grant to present two papers at the TESOL 2002 conference. She also had a chance to present at a California TESOL's regional conference, with support from her academic advisor. Now that she is back in Japan, she believes she did the right thing. Her linguistic competence improved, and she earned a highly regarded graduate degree from a U.S. university. She knows she is better prepared now for the challenges of the EFL classroom, and her experience and graduate degree from a U.S. institution are valued by her employers, her colleagues, and her students.

Elza, the Professor

Elza first came to the U.S. as an international student because she wanted to work on a bachelor's degree and a master's degree. Upon return to her home country, Brazil, she taught EFL to children and adult learners for four years. A second trip to the U.S. in the mid-1970s, as a young immigrant wife and mother, was for permanent residence. At that time, a NNES teacher of English could not find employment teaching ESL very easily, despite linguistic competence and academic and professional qualifications to do so. Elza was repeatedly told by program administrators that their policy was to hire only native speakers of English as ESL teachers, regardless of the level of fluency or proficiency in English of the nonnative speaker applicant. Years later, a high demand for ESL teachers to work with large numbers of Southeast Asian refugees made it possible for Elza to find employment in adult ESL programs and other school settings (adult basic ESL programs, community colleges, and IEPs). But the feeling and the reminders of being a "second-class" professional—not quite a native speaker—were always there.

Elza's own awakening to the fact that being a NNES bilingual and bicultural professional was actually an asset in her line of work only occurred after two decades of teaching, when she returned to graduate school to work on a doctorate degree in education and was exposed to social constructivism and critical pedagogy. Social constructivism (Johnson, 2000; Vygotsky, 1978) proposes that learning is socially constructed by students and teachers in a community of learners, through negotiation of meaning. When working with graduate students from diverse backgrounds—native and nonnative speakers of English—the co-construction of knowledge is further enriched by the diverse worldviews that students bring into the classroom community. When they become teachers, their experience with social construction of knowledge and negotiation of meaning can be implemented in their own classrooms. In teacher education, critical pedagogy is a vehicle for critical thinking and reflectivity for personal and social transformation toward the development of critical social consciousness (see Freire, 1973, Giroux, 1988; Wink 2000). Critical pedagogy supports the view that teachers are moral agents, whether they choose to maintain the status quo or to engage in supporting changes where changes are needed for the benefit of their students. To Elza, the intersection of social constructivism and critical pedagogy promotes awareness of sociopolitical issues in L2 teaching. Through shared knowledge in the community of learners, students often conclude that language teaching—or any teaching—does not occur in a value-neutral vacuum: it is always a political act with educational and social consequences. Toward this goal, Elza and her students explore sociopolitical issues and advocacy concerns related to L2 teaching and learning globally and locally.

A teacher educator in a college of education since 1997, Elza currently teaches courses in bilingual education, L2 acquisition, ESL theory and methods, and language assessment to graduate and undergraduate education majors at the University of Nevada, Reno. She also supervises the master's program practicum students and heads a grant-sponsored professional development program for K–12 teachers of English language learners in northern Nevada. She sits on the board of an elementary charter school[1] that offers a dual language curriculum. Her conference presentations, research, and publications reflect an interest in the professional preparation of NES and NNES teachers and in the development of critical social consciousness among pre-service and practicing teachers of L2 learners.

Ayako's Professional Training in the U.S.

The master's program where Ayako studied in the U.S. is described on its web page as follows: "it is an interdisciplinary program designed for both native and non-native speakers of English who wish to teach ESL or EFL. The degree prepares the candidates for employment as teachers, program directors, curriculum consultants, or materials developers" (Teaching English to Speakers of Other Languages, 2003, "About the Program," para. 1). Admission requirements are a 3.0 grade point average, graduation from an accredited institution, a score of 550 or above on the Test of English as a Foreign Language (TOEFL) for NNES students, and competence in two languages (English plus one other) for both native and nonnative speakers of English. Like most graduate programs in teaching English to speakers of other languages, it offers basic course work that includes "Introduction to Linguistics," "Descriptive Grammar," "Second Language Acquisition," "Second Language Methods and Materials," "Curriculum Development," and "Language Assessment." In addition, students take "Bilingual Education," "Sociolinguistics," "Sociocultural Concerns in Education," and various cross-departmental electives (including, but not limited to, such courses as "World Englishes"). Local ESL instruction programs—IEPs, community colleges and adult basic ESL programs, K–12 schools, a bilingual charter school, family resource centers, and professional trade unions—are available sites for practica and internships.

Among its more than 40 students, ranging in age from 23 to over 60, the program enrolls three types of students: NNES international students (primarily from Asia and Latin America), NES elementary and secondary school teachers, and NES students with various academic and professional backgrounds who are interested in domestic careers in ESL teaching or in overseas EFL teaching positions. Very few NES students have not had much cross-cultural or crosslinguistic experience. Faculty members in the program have Ph.D.'s in TESOL education or applied linguistics. The program embraces the notion of social constructivism (Richardson, 1997; Vygotsky, 1978), reflectivity (Dewey, 1933; Richards & Lockhart, 1994), and critical social consciousness (Freire, 1973; Giroux, 1988, 1997; Wink, 2000), highlighting the sociopolitical role of ESL/EFL teachers in their classrooms and in their communities (Freeman & Johnson, 1998; Major & Celedon-Pattichis, 2001). Courses also draw attention to the localized EFL or ESL contexts in which the graduate students are teaching or plan to teach (Freeman, 2000, 2001); that is, the students engage in curriculum design and instructional practices suitable for their targeted student population and school setting. Faculty address the differing professional interests of the three types of students in the program as an asset; that is, both NES and NNES students benefit from student-centered pedagogies and multiple ways of approaching L2 teaching.

Understanding EFL Education in Japan

Ayako's Deconstruction of Sociopolitical and Linguistic Issues in Japan

Before plunging into a discussion of EFL education in Japan, it is important to understand what are often seen as paradoxical views about the role of English in Japanese society and the attitudes of the Japanese toward English. This section addresses the attitudes of the Japanese toward English, manifested through conflicting views (Anglomania and "English allergy"), which are perceived by Japanese scholars and others as a result of linguistic imperialism (with English as the world's lingua franca) in Japan. Elza and Ayako see a connection between public attitudes toward English and the paradoxes of EFL teaching and learning in Japan.

Attitudes toward English in Japan can be summarized within three realms: (1) English as the gate to internationalization (Kubota, 1998), (2) linguistic hegemony or imperialism (Phillipson, 1992; Tsuda, 1997), and (3) the paradox of Anglomania and "English allergy" (Clark, 1998; Tsuda, 1997). This section will briefly elaborate on each of these points because they permeate EFL teaching and learning in Japan.

It is undeniable that English is the gate to the internationalization of most English-dominant nations. Economic globalization is a necessity and a reality in most non-English-dominant countries, with English as the lingua franca. The Japanese believe that the English language is the first step toward the internationalization of Japan. The use of English loanwords (e.g., *table, building, computer*) is seen as "cool" by youngsters and a sign of internationalization by others (Kubota, 1998). Nakamura (as quoted in Kubota, 1998, p. 303) refers to an advertisement for an English language school in a Tokyo subway that said, "If you have a dream in English, you are *kokusaijin* (international person)," with the implication that students of English at that school would be able to dream in English and become international. The Japanese also tend to believe that the English language is a language of prestige because of its role in global communication. The L2 becomes a vehicle for the Japanese to identify themselves with Westerners (Kubota, 1998). Similarly, Japanese attitudes toward other languages and cultures (e.g., other Asians) are not as positive, with a tendency to look down upon other languages and cultures, including those of language minorities within Japan (Kubota, 1998).

As noted earlier, attitudes toward English in Japan can also be summarized within the realm of linguistic hegemony or cultural imperialism. Phillipson (1992) and others have addressed the worldwide impact of English as a force of linguistic imperialism or "Coca colonization, McDonaldization, or colonization of the mind" (Tsuda,

1997, p. 23). According to Tsuda (1997), a prolific writer about English as a dominant power in Japan, the Japanese in general, as well as EFL teachers and students, are unaware of the concept of linguistic hegemony and its influence on attitudes toward the native language and English. The equation becomes more complicated when the national obsession among the Japanese for learning English and using loanwords is driving families to encourage their young children to acquire English in nursery schools. These parents display pride in the fact that their children are able to speak better English than Japanese (Tsuda, 1997). Some Japanese people may have indeed developed a complex of linguistic inferiority in relation to the value of their native language.

When we add to this scenario the paradox of EFL instruction in schools as preparation for entrance and graduation examinations, the result is usually very frustrated students who take pride in years of dedication to English studies but can never reach the elusive "native-like" level of proficiency. This frustration has been defined by Clark (1998) as "English allergy," or an "internalized aversion to the product of the pursuit of competence in a language that represents admission to the global society and the avenue to professional success" (p. 46). The Japanese students end up with negative feelings, or "allergy," toward the English language. These feelings erode their self-confidence and motivation to improve their oral proficiency.

Ranging from Anglomania to English allergy, against a backdrop of linguistic hegemony, attitudes toward the English language and English instruction in Japan are problematic and paradoxical (this issue will be addressed later in this chapter, when EFL practices in Japan are discussed). The next section describes the new Japanese national standards for language instruction, Japanese teacher preparation programs, teacher certification procedures, and EFL instructional practices.

Japanese National Standards and Policies for EFL Instruction

Under the Japanese educational system, from middle school on, students must study a foreign language, which for most means English. EFL educational policy in Japan has been drastically and rapidly changing in recent years through MEXT's efforts.

The educational system in Japan is tightly controlled by MEXT, with respect to curriculum standards, textbooks, and teacher guidelines. MEXT has ordered implementation, beginning in 2002, of EFL instruction in elementary schools during a class period called "Integrated Study." This class is designed to offer Japanese schoolchildren opportunities to interact with fluent speakers of English and develop communicative abilities. The purpose of such early exposure to EFL is to promote not only linguistic competence in English but also awareness of and positive attitudes toward foreign cultures and worldviews. Ultimately, MEXT hopes to instill an early commitment to internationalization among Japanese schoolchildren.

It is significant to note that the introduction of English in elementary schools places the burden of EFL instruction of elementary schoolchildren on their regular teachers, who have not been trained or certified to teach EFL. With the introduction of English in elementary schools, support and assistance by local people who are fluent in English are being sought and will be needed in order to lead this challenge to success.

According to MEXT, the goals of high school EFL education in Japan are "to develop students' basic practical communication abilities such as listening and speaking, deepening the understanding of language and culture, and fostering a positive attitude toward communication through foreign languages" (Ministry of Education, Culture, Sports, Science, and Technology, 2003, "The Course of Study for Lower Secondary School," para. 1). Therefore, the overall goal of the national standards, or guidelines, set by MEXT is to implement English education in ways that students can conduct daily conversations and communicate effectively in English. To achieve this goal, the following initiatives are in place:

- *Super English Language High Schools*—To offer advanced English education exclusively at selected high schools that design new curricula for advanced Japanese learners of English.
- *Foreign Studies Program*—To encourage teachers to expand their knowledge and experience in English education by pursuing advanced degrees in such countries as England and the U.S.
- *Domestic Studies Program*—To encourage teachers to share with their peers knowledge and information gained in advanced degrees within Japan.
- *Assistant Language Teacher (ALT) Program*—To hire native speakers of English from the U.S., Canada, Great Britain, or Australia with undergraduate bachelor's degrees in any field. Their job is to serve as native English speaker resources and teachers' aides at assigned schools in Japan. Recruitment and training is conducted through the Japanese embassies and the Japan Exchange and Teaching (JET) Program. According to the Consulate General of Japan in San Francisco (2003), of the 6,200 participants placed in Japanese schools in 2002, nearly 50% were from the U.S.

Teacher Preparation, Certification, and EFL Instructional Practices

Teacher certification in Japan for K–12 teaching is multitiered and depends on the degree earned at a junior college or university. Once Japanese students pass the general entrance exam and are admitted to a college or university, those who plan to enter the teaching profession simply take teacher preparation classes in addition to the regular college or university core curriculum. There are no specific levels of linguistic proficiency in a L2 or additional requirements for admission into the teaching program. Teacher preparation at a two-year (junior) college or a four-year university must offer the required course work set by MEXT. Among the teacher preparation courses are "Educational Principles," "Educational Psychology," "English Teaching Methods," and "Practicum in Public Schools." Students intending to teach EFL also take "English Linguistics," "American and British Literature," "English Communication," "Comparative Cultures and Languages," and so forth. A brief practicum or internship requires students to practice teaching at a school for about two to four weeks (depending on the grade level at which the teachers will teach) under the supervision of a teacher at the school, who usually determines what and how the teacher candidate will teach. Overall, the initial preparation of EFL teachers in Japan is primarily generic and theoretical, with little exposure to (or knowledge of) field-related teaching methodologies or classroom management.

Upon graduation from a college or university and completion of the teacher preparation course work, the aspiring Japanese teacher of EFL applies to the local school board for a teaching certificate. There are three levels of teaching certificates, depending on the university or college degree obtained: the advanced certificate, the first-class certificate, and the second-class certificate. The advanced certificate is given to teachers with a master's degree or higher, the first-class certificate is for teachers with a bachelor's degree from a four-year university, and the second-class certificate is for junior college graduates. The level of education achieved and the type of teaching certificate teachers earn determine the types of teaching jobs and rank of schools at which they will be eligible to apply. After receiving a teaching certificate from the local board of education, the candidates must pass the content-area (English language and literature) national examination. Only then they can be hired to teach within their local district.

The guidelines issued by MEXT for all schools in Japan are the foundation for the content and design of EFL curricula. Individual schools can design their own EFL courses and set the number of instructional hours, but they must demonstrate compliance with the national guidelines. Despite a perception that the guidelines are limiting and cumbersome, teachers must find a balance between those guidelines and their desired curriculum. Since instructional methodology is not addressed in-depth in teacher preparation programs in Japan, novice teachers are left to fend for themselves professionally. Once hired, in addition to their regular teaching load (an average of 30 contact hours per week), EFL teachers are required, as are all other Japanese teachers, to conduct student counseling, attend faculty meetings, and participate in after-school club activities. This scenario poses a challenge for EFL teachers who have difficulty finding time for standards-based curriculum planning and professional development outside of school obligations. It is far easier to replicate the teaching methodologies they experienced as EFL students themselves in Japanese schools.

It is often pointed out that the instructional practices in EFL teaching in Japan have been ineffective for most students despite six years of required language instruction starting in middle school. The curriculum is teacher-centered and taught from grammar-translation, skills-based, audio-lingual approaches in large classrooms with approximately 40 or more students. EFL instruction is approached by EFL teachers and students as a required school subject that is tested on university entrance exams. Because of this focus, student motivation is low, and communicative competence is weak. Under this paradigm, students cannot develop either fluency or communicative abilities, because of lack of opportunities to apply the grammar and vocabulary knowledge they may have gained through the study of English grammar and translation. Japanese-born EFL teachers are themselves the products of the educational system in Japan (Takada, 2000). For the most part, they feel linguistically and methodologically unprepared to teach EFL right after graduation from a university, because they were not able or required to achieve linguistic proficiency as students and did not gain pedagogical knowledge on or experience in how to teach a L2. In short, EFL teacher training and the development of appropriate instructional curricula in Japan still leave a lot to be desired, despite efforts to improve instruction through MEXT. Implementing the changes envisioned by MEXT will require concerted efforts in two arenas: better preparation of new EFL teachers and massive retraining of current teachers, an endeavor that will take great amounts of time, energy, and funding.

Ayako's Reconstructed Perspectives on EFL Education in Japan

It is an understatement to say that EFL education in Japan is different from ESL instruction in the U.S. Throughout her graduate studies in the U.S., Ayako often pondered how she would adapt the knowledge and experience she was acquiring in the U.S. to the Japanese school setting. In this section, Ayako addresses theoretical concepts and instructional methodologies that are reflected in Japanese educational practices, as well as individual and sociocultural factors that affect learning but are not addressed in the classrooms. She also offers some suggestions for adapting Western ESL instructional practices to the realities of the Japanese classrooms.

First, through her studies of theories of L2 acquisition, Ayako began to see the influence of a belief among Japanese educational policy-makers in the Critical Period Hypothesis. According to Brown (2000), the Critical Period Hypothesis claims that there is a biological period (which ends during adolescence) when ideal language acquisition takes place. This hypothesis has been widely discredited in recent years, through empirical evidence that supports the notion that adult learners can and do acquire L2 competence. When MEXT decided to implement EFL teaching at the elementary level to overcome the insufficient level of competence at the high school and college levels after years of EFL instruction, it seemed to subscribe to the Critical Period Hypothesis. Policymakers seem to have believed that earlier exposure to the L2 would in fact promote a higher level of communicative competence and linguistic proficiency. Yet this political decision reveals that three other significant factors that influence L2 acquisition were not considered: (1) the exclusive focus on grammar-translation, audio-lingual methodologies used in schools for the purpose of preparing students to pass entrance examinations; (2) the importance of individual differences in L2 acquisition; and (3) the sociocultural implications of the paradoxical attitudes of the Japanese toward English. Each of these factors is discussed next.

Japanese students' lack of communicative competence in English can be directly linked to classroom instructional practices. The fact that middle and high school students must pass entrance examinations that test their knowledge of English grammar poses a serious dilemma for teachers and students. While MEXT wants to promote positive attitudes toward and oral fluency in English among Japanese students (as part of a national concern with globalization through national guidelines for EFL instruction), the reality is that students are tested on English vocabulary, grammar, and translation on high-stakes standardized exams that determine their academic and professional future. Thus, middle and high school EFL curricula continue to focus on test preparation via the traditional grammar-translation and audio-lingual methods. Nevertheless, too much focus on form (grammar and translation) results in lack of communicative competence. Finding a balance between form-focused instruction and meaningful communication in the classroom is a challenge that Japanese teachers of EFL can overcome with creative adaptation of new ways of teaching EFL in order to promote the development of fluency and accuracy. The communicative approach can be applied to encourage Japanese EFL students to use English in meaningful and realistic situations in the classroom. The first step for methodological changes is to reform the teacher preparation curricula so that instructional methodologies are addressed before teachers graduate from a college or university. If knowledge of EFL pedagogical practices does not become a requirement for teacher preparation and certification in Japan, the onus of curriculum reform will rest solely on the novice EFL teachers, an unrealistic expectation (as discussed earlier in this chapter).

In Japanese EFL classes, common classroom practices usually rely on a lecture format, with teachers transmitting information and students taking notes or filling out work sheets. In her studies as an ESL learner and a graduate student in the U.S., Ayako noticed that in ESL classrooms there is often an emphasis on student-centered activities, meaningful interactions, and paired work and group projects, with students working with their peers to discuss topics, role-play, problem solve, conduct research outside of class, and give follow-up presentations in class. In order to emphasize communicative competence in Japanese classrooms, teachers can encourage students to interact with one another in pairs or groups, engage actively in actual and meaningful conversation, and give and receive peer feedback as appropriate (see the chapter by Liu in this book, for examples of how he uses his own experiences as a NNES professional in the peer review process). These communicative interactions in the classroom enable students to realize that they are the center of the learning that is taking place, and they are also responsible for applying learning strategies and practicing the language in the classroom. These activities motivate students to become speakers of English in the classroom, while providing a comfortable environment for them to converse in English regardless of level of fluency.

Although it is often the case that Japanese EFL students expect grammar explanations and translation practice in order to prepare for exams, Japanese EFL teachers can be prepared to accomplish both. For example, in English for academic purposes classes in IEPs in the U.S., instruction often combines both form (grammar) and meaning (interactive written or oral communication). In order to merge form with communication in the Japanese classroom context, classroom time can be reorganized to address academic reading and writing and oral communication in more meaningful ways. For example, writers' workshops, individual portfolios, and journal writing can be used to develop language awareness and practice of form, while providing the teacher with individual progress records. These activities can be used for group work, in-class discussions, and presentations in English, so that students learn through the four language modes (reading, writing, listening, and speaking). These adaptive modifications have the potential to make the EFL classroom in Japan student-centered, enabling students to be more active in using English in the classroom.

While seemingly an idealistic proposition and a challenge for Japanese EFL teachers and students because of the traditional classroom practices in Japan, this paradigm shift in classroom instruction is necessary to meet the globalization and internationalization goals set by MEXT. The first step is to bring forth understanding that the teachers' role is not to lecture or transmit knowledge about a foreign language but to facilitate and guide meaningful student interactions in the classroom. Finally, emphasizing the communicative aspects of language leads students to realize that learning a foreign language is important, not only because it is a school requirement that is tested on exams, but also because it provides them an opportunity to understand other worldviews through active verbal exchanges, which is further related to learning about other cultures. Only in this way will the Japanese be able to meet MEXT's goal of helping students develop "a positive attitude toward communication through foreign languages" (Ministry of Education, Culture, Sports, Science, and Technology, 2003, "The Course on Study for Lower Secondary School," para. 1).

One obstacle to adapting Western ESL classroom practices in Japan is the number of students in the classrooms. There are usually more than 40 students in Japanese EFL classes. If EFL teachers in Japan want to change the size of the classes for pedagogical reasons, they are not allowed to do so, because class size is a policy decision under MEXT's control. That is not to say that it will remain impossible for EFL teachers to play a more active role in getting involved with the reform movement of English education currently taking place in Japan. They can do so by contributing the experiences and knowledge they have acquired in graduate programs overseas. For example, one contribution may be to modify the initial lesson presentation format through the implementation of a holistic approach to lesson presentation, involving the use of games, pictures, or holistic samples of language use in audio, visual, or printed format, in order to contextualize language use and draw students' attention to meaningful uses of the language (Shrum & Glisan, 2000). In this approach to instruction, the lesson begins with student interaction and participation in authentic and contextual uses of the language before moving on to skills-based activities that focus on form. Form-focused instruction with meaningful communication involves a number of classroom practices that would be welcomed by Japanese students because they are motivating and meaningful.

Another way for EFL teachers with degrees from U.S. graduate programs to implement their new knowledge in Japanese EFL classrooms is to model reflectivity and explore storytelling (starting with narratives of their experiences outside Japan) and then involve students in their own reflectivity and storytelling of experiences with other cultures and languages (see the chapter by Velasco-Martin, this volume, for examples of how reflectivity can be used in the EFL classroom). Through the experience gained through graduate work in overseas programs in teaching English to speakers of other languages, Japanese EFL teachers have a broadened understanding of pedagogical choices for EFL instruction; that is, methods, materials, and classroom activities can be selectively used to meet both the national concern with communicative fluency in English and the required preparation for entrance examination needs of their students.

As mentioned earlier, Japanese-born EFL teachers are usually not very proficient in oral communication in English, due to the traditional grammar-based instruction under which they first learned English. One important result of studying outside Japan in programs in teaching English to speakers of other languages is that Japanese EFL teachers do improve their linguistic proficiency and gain self-confidence in using English in daily life and in the classroom. This can greatly benefit the Japanese EFL classroom. EFL teachers with overseas experience can promote communicative interactions in English among their students by acting as linguistic models and facilitators. By referring to their personal experiences as English language learners themselves, EFL teachers with overseas educational experience and improved confidence in their linguistic abilities can truly motivate students to engage in authentic communication in the classroom and disregard worries about imperfect accents or use of inappropriate vocabulary or sentence structures. They can clarify to students that linguistic errors are a common characteristic of the developmental acquisition of a L2.

The Japanese school practice of keeping students quiet in class has to be addressed differently in the EFL classroom from a communicative perspective; simply stated, in order to improve oral communicative competence, students must engage in oral communication in the classroom. In the U.S., Ayako witnessed and participated in ESL classroom group activities with Japanese and other Asian students with very positive results. For these reasons, she believes that shy or hesitant Japanese students would greatly benefit from working in groups in the EFL classroom under the guidance of teachers. Another way to promote student interaction in English is through e-mail and web-based discussions, as is often done in language programs and universities in the U.S. In Japan, the implementation of in-class group work or web-based class activities would promote communicative competence of Japanese students.

In summary, the classroom practices and methods of L2 instruction learned in overseas programs in teaching English to speakers of other languages can be adapted to English education in Japan. However, it would take joint efforts by EFL teachers in the same schools, in the same prefectures, and nationwide (through support from MEXT) for significant changes to occur beyond one or two individual classrooms. Toward this goal, there must be a concerted national effort to promote changes in methodologies both within individual classrooms and within the entire structure of English education nationwide, in addition to revised curricula for teacher preparation. Since MEXT has taken the leadership in redesigning language education in Japan, it is imperative that those with experience and degrees inside and outside of Japan in teaching English to speakers of other languages be asked to contribute to discussions of pedagogical reform of English instruction in order to explore realistic implementation of new ways of teaching English to Japanese students.

A second factor (in addition to instructional practices) affecting the L2 acquisition process is individual differences, including, but not limited to, students' levels of inhibition, anxiety, and motivation; the degree to which students take risks; and so on. These differences were a new concept to Ayako during her studies in the U.S., and they need to be part of teacher knowledge about EFL teaching in Japan. Once teachers understand that individual differences play a role in the L2 classroom, class activities can be designed toward facilitating learning by all students. In the U.S., one of the classroom practices that Ayako saw as appropriate for assisting shy or hesitant Japanese students in participating in class without fear of humiliation or embarrassment were collaborative learning and student-centered group and paired activities described earlier. Other practices are the use of culturally relevant materials with high interest for preteens and teenagers (e.g., films, songs, TV programs, novels, magazines), variety of lesson presentation modes and language practice activities (e.g., Total Physical Response, storytelling, problem solving, information gap, task completion, research and presentation projects). The more interesting, varied, and relevant the lesson materials are, the easier it is to attract and maintain the students' interest and motivation, thus lessening the level of anxiety and fear of failure. Although teacher preparation in Japan has limitations (as discussed earlier), student individual differences must be addressed as part of the basic course work required of those who want to become teachers. Undoubtedly, it will take time and energy for all or any of these ideas to be implemented in Japan and for EFL students and teachers to gain familiarity with and acceptance of them.

A third factor identified in the beginning of this section as significant to EFL learning—but not addressed by the directives issued by MEXT regarding English language competence—is the sociocultural implication of the paradoxical attitudes of the Japanese toward English (Anglomania and English allergy). Because of the implications of attitudes toward languages in Japanese society and among Japanese EFL learners, it is crucial for EFL teachers in Japan to be aware of the impact of the English language in Japanese society and of the attitudes people display toward their own native language compared with the value of English for internationalization of Japan. The Japanese language is sometimes viewed by the Japanese as less prestigious than English because of the economic and cultural power of English as the world's lingua franca. The misconception that English is more prestigious than Japanese is perpetuated in the classroom, not because EFL teachers are agents of English dominance or imperialism, but because they may lack knowledge and understanding of linguistics concepts such as language universals and sociolinguistics (Tanaka, 1995). Thus, it becomes the EFL teachers' responsibility to develop legitimate sensitivity toward language equality and neutrality among Japanese students. EFL students need exposure to the cultural, social, and political aspects of L2 learning—perhaps through readings and in-class discussions, in either English or Japanese, about the causes of positive or negative attitudes the Japanese may hold toward the Japanese and the English languages. A lack of awareness of these concepts can be detrimental to the development of self-confidence among Japanese students pursuing linguistic competence in a L2 toward which they may feel ambivalent. The emotional conflicts that arise from the conflicting views and feelings about English that exist in Japanese society must be explored in the EFL classroom.

View from the Mentor's Desk: Implications for Teacher Educators

Through her collaboration with Ayako, Elza has certainly expanded her understanding of current educational and sociopolitical issues related to L2 education in Japan, and she hopes the readers have, too. The collaborative-shared knowledge that resulted from two years of interactions between mentor and student has validated Elza's approach to L2 teacher education, particularly in relation to her concern with the education of NNES graduate students in English-dominant countries. On the trolley ride in Salt Lake City described in the opening of this chapter, Elza realized that the conference experience had been a turning point for Ayako—the end of her academic program and the beginning of her professional journey. Her early engagement in the profession, in seeking answers and participating in scholarly endeavors and advocacy, are evidence of one student's response to social constructivism, critical pedagogy, and reflectivity in teacher education.

This final section addresses the preparation of NNES teachers in English-dominant countries within four arenas: (1) interdisciplinary course work in teaching English to speakers of other languages programs, (2) paradigm shift in teacher education, (3) ways to reconcile apparent differences between NES and NNES graduate students, and (4) induction of teacher candidates into professional organizations and activities.

First of all, the span of Ayako's reconstructed perspectives on language issues in her country presents evidence that a broad interdisciplinary approach to teacher education is important for the education of all aspiring L2 teachers, native and nonnative English speakers alike. In addition to taking the traditional courses such as L2 acquisition, theory and methods of teaching English to speakers of other languages, curriculum development, assessment, and so forth, Ayako had opportunities to explore linguistic and sociopolitical issues that were relevant to her world, in courses such as "World Englishes," "Bilingual Education," "Sociolinguistics," and "Sociocultural Concerns in Education." By exploring sociopolitical issues such as language rights of linguistic minorities, language varieties, linguistic imperialism, the politics of bilingual education, identity theories, and TESOL's position on nondiscriminatory employment around the world, Ayako has applied critical thinking to her examination of educational issues in Japan from a wide, cross-disciplinary framework.

A concern with sociopolitical issues and critical social consciousness in L2 education is the watermark of a paradigm shift in the TESOL field that has been taking place over the past two decades. This paradigm shift means that teacher educators today stress reflectivity (Zeichner & Liston, 1996), encourage action research—a form of classroom-based reflective investigation of student learning—among practitioners (Auerbach, 1994; Nunan, 2001), and foster positive dispositions toward linguistic differences and multiculturalism in addition to acquisition of knowledge and skills (Major & Brock, 2003; Zeichner, 1996). Field experiences (practica and internships) are collaborative and reflective (Johnson, 2000). Courses on methods and instructional materials explore a gamut of teaching contexts, multimedia delivery formats, implementation of standards and performance-based assessment, and creative teaching, rather than delivering packaged traditional ESL methodologies (Kumaravadivelu, 2001; Nunan, 1999; Richards & Renandya, 2002). In addition, teacher educators in many TESOL graduate programs in English-dominant countries aim to reconcile the differing interests and backgrounds of NES and NNES students

(Braine, 1999; Govardhan, Nayar, & Sheorey, 1999; Kamhi-Stein, 2000; Matsuda & Matsuda, this volume; Tajino & Tajino, 2000).

Ayako and her NNES peers, alongside their NES peers, were part of a graduate program that integrates and highlights the differences between EFL and ESL, between native and nonnative English speakers. This is accomplished by building a community of reflective learners who, together and individually, deconstruct and reconstruct knowledge about L2 teaching and learning globally. Students take the responsibility for the learning, and the teacher educator orchestrates, facilitates, and redirects. Teacher educators today model the collaborative and interactive nature of learning they hope their graduates will implement in their own classrooms.

To this end, teacher educators who are concerned with the education of NNES teacher candidates disseminate professional information and encourage those students in particular (and all graduate students in general) to join professional organizations, stay abreast of the professional trends and scholarly publications, attend conferences, present papers, submit articles or book reviews for publication, and become advocates for their own students. The teacher educator's most lasting influence is to demonstrate by example that the intellectual growth of every educator is part of a lifelong engagement in reflectivity and professional development. Ayako seems to be well on her way along that path. She also personifies the reflective and socially conscious NNES professional in the TESOL field who teacher educators hope to see leave their graduate programs.

Note

1. A charter school is a public school that is given autonomy to make decisions about its structure and curriculum.

References

Auerbach, E. (1994). Participatory action research. *TESOL Quarterly, 28*(4), 693–697.

Braine, G. (Ed.). (1999). *Non-native educators in English language teaching.* Mahwah, NJ: Erlbaum.

Brown, H. D. (2000). *Principles of language learning and teaching* (4th ed.). White Plains, NY: Addison Wesley Longman.

Clark, G. (1998). Overcoming Japan's English allergy. *Japan Quarterly, 45*(2), 46–53.

Consulate General of Japan in San Francisco. (2003, March). *The Japan Exchange and Teaching Program.* Retrieved November 15, 2002, from *http://www.cgjsf. org/jet*

Dewey, J. (1933). *How we think: A restatement of the relation of reflective thinking to the educative process.* Boston: D. C. Heath.

Freeman, D. (2000, October/November). Imported theories/local understandings, part 1. *TESOL Matters, 10*(4). Retrieved November 15, 2002, from *http://www.tesol.org/pubs/articles/2000/tm0010-01.html*

Freeman, D. (2001, December/January). Imported theories/local understandings, part 2. *TESOL Matters, 11*(1). Retrieved November 15, 2002, from *http://www.tesol.org/pubs/articles/2000/tm0012-03.html*

Freeman, D., & Johnson, K. E. (1998). Reconceptualizing the knowledge-base of language teacher education. *TESOL Quarterly, 32*(3), 397–417.

Freire, P. (1973). *Education for critical consciousness.* New York: Seabury.

Giroux, H. A. (1988). *Teachers as intellectuals: Toward a critical pedagogy of learning.* Granby, MA: Bergin & Garvey.

Giroux, H. A. (1997). *Pedagogy and the politics of hope: Theory, culture, and schooling: A critical reader.* Boulder, CO: Westview.

Govardhan, A. K., Nayar, B., & Sheorey, R. (1999). Do U.S. MATESOL programs prepare students to teach abroad? *TESOL Quarterly, 33*(1), 114–125.

Johnson, K. E. (2000). Innovations in TESOL teacher education: A quiet revolution. In K. E. Johnson (Ed.), *Teacher education* (pp. 1–7). Alexandria, VA: TESOL.

Kachru, B. B. (1985). Standards, codification, and sociolinguistics realism: The English language in the outer circle. In R. Quirk & H. G. Widdowson (Eds.), *English in the world: Teaching and learning the language and literatures* (pp. 11–30). Cambridge: Cambridge University Press.

Kamhi-Stein, L. D. (2000). Adapting US-based TESOL teacher education to meet the needs of nonnative English speakers. *TESOL Journal, 9*(3), 10–14.

Kubota, R. (1998). Ideologies of English in Japan. *World Englishes, 17*(3), 295–306.

Kumaravadivelu, B. (2001). Toward a postmethod pedagogy. *TESOL Quarterly, 35*(4), 537–560.

Major, E. M., & Brock, C. (2003). Fostering positive dispositions towards diversity: Dialogical explorations of a moral dilemma. *Teacher Education Quarterly, 30*(4), 7–26.

Major, E. M., & Celedon-Pattichis, S. (2001). Integrating sociopolitical awareness into a teacher education curriculum. *TESOL Journal, 10*(1), 21–26.

Ministry of Education, Culture, Sports, Science, and Technology. (2003, March). *The course of study for lower secondary school: Foreign languages.* Retrieved November 15, 2002, from Ministry of Education, Culture, Sports, Science, and Technology, Elementary and Secondary Education website: *http://www.mext.go.jp/english/shotou/030301.htm*

Nunan, D. (1999). *Second language teaching and learning.* Boston: Heinle & Heinle.

Nunan, D. (2001). Action research in language education. In D. R. Hall & A. Hewings, *Innovation in English language teaching* (pp. 197–207). New York: Routledge.

Phillipson, R. (1992). *Linguistic imperialism.* Oxford: Oxford University Press.

Richards, J. C., & Lockhart, C. (1994). *Reflective teaching in second language classrooms.* Cambridge: Cambridge University Press.

Richards, J. C., & Renandya, A. (Eds.). (2002). *Methodology in language teaching: An anthology of current practice.* Cambridge: Cambridge University Press.

Richardson, V. (Ed.). (1997). *Constructivist teacher education: Building new understandings.* London: Falmer.

Shrum, J. L., & Glisan, E. W. (2000). *Teacher's handbook: Contextualized language instruction* (2nd ed.). Boston: Heinle & Heinle.

Tajino, A., & Tajino, Y. (2000). Native and non-native: What can they offer? *ELT Journal, 54*(1), 3–11.

Takada, T. (2000, August/September). The social status of L1 Japanese EFL teachers. *TESOL Matters, 10*(3). Retrieved March 25, 2002, from *http://www.tesol.org/pubs/articles/2000/tm0008-04.html*

Tanaka, S. O. (1995). Japanese media in English. *World Englishes, 14*(1), 37–53.

Teaching English to Speakers of Other Languages. (2003). *Programs of study.* Retrieved October 25, 2002, from University of Nevada, Reno, TESOL Program website: *http://www.unr.edu/tesl/program.htm*

Tsuda, Y. (1997). Hegemony of English vs. ecology of language: Building equality in international communication. In L. E. Smith & M. L. Forman (Eds.), *World Englishes 2000* (pp. 21–31). Honolulu: University of Hawaii Press.

Vygotsky, L. S. (1978). *Mind in society.* Cambridge: Harvard University Press.

Wink, J. (2000). *Critical pedagogy: Notes from the real world.* New York: Longman.

Zeichner, K. (1996). Educating teachers for cultural diversity. In K. Zeichner, S. Melnick, & M. Gomez (Eds.), *Currents of reform in preservice teacher education* (pp. 133–175). New York: Teachers College Press.

Zeichner, K., & Liston, D. P. (1996). *Reflective teaching: An introduction.* Mahwah, NJ: Erlbaum.

The Nonnative English-Speaking Teacher as an Intercultural Speaker

Carmen Velasco-Martin
University of Barcelona and Embassy of Spain, Washington, DC

It is widely accepted that people from different cultures maintain different beliefs, values, and norms, all of which contribute to different expressions of reality. Cultural differences can provoke communication conflicts that are not merely linguistic in nature but related to questions of cultural knowledge, attitudes, and ideologies (van Dijk, Ting-Toomey, Smitherman, & Troutman, 1997). Communication is not only a matter of exchanging information and ideas; it involves interaction with other people and an understanding of their way of life, of their beliefs and values, and of their behaviors. Learning foreign languages and their corresponding cultures is of great importance to the facilitation of communication. It has the potential to foster mutual understanding and acceptance between different cultures. Students need to acquire alternative perspectives of the world and to critically reflect on themselves and their society in order to communicate and interact effectively (Byram & Tost Planet, 2000). The learning of at least one foreign language (FL) and the corresponding culture(s) will help students to acquire the skills they need to become intercultural speakers and will ultimately facilitate intercultural communication itself. FL teachers play a very important role in helping to reduce the stereotypes and preconceived ideas about an FL culture and, therefore, in promoting a more accurate understanding of the culture studied. Investing in learning foreign languages and cultures may also contribute to and potentially result in global understanding and economic and technological advantages (Hadley, 1993).

Intercultural communication and the figure of the FL teacher as an intercultural speaker are the focus of this chapter. After a brief introduction to the notions of intercultural communication competence and the intercultural speaker (and its relation to the native/nonnative speaker notions), I provide examples of how I construct my FL classroom to create a bridge between the target culture and the students' culture. In this chapter, I also explain how I draw on the notion of intercultural awareness to promote FL students' intercultural and intracultural understanding. Finally, I describe two kinds of classroom projects: one geared toward developing connections between cultures and one aimed at promoting intercultural respect and critical thinking.

Intercultural Communication

Intercultural communication generally refers to interactions among people of different cultures (Jandt, 2000; Novinger, 2001). The importance of intercultural communication has been widely discussed not only in the fields of applied linguistics and TESOL but also in other disciplines, such as sociology, anthropology, ethnography, psychology, and linguistics. Intercultural communication competence (ICC) is the ability to understand and relate to people from other countries and cultures (Byram, 1997b). ICC involves an understanding of and respect for other cultures and their differences from one's own. Martin (1993) agrees that ICC needs to include cultural membership beyond one's own national borders and that it should also consider the relationship between "interactants" (i.e., people from different cultures who interact with each other). Effective intercultural communication can help to achieve cooperation and understanding on a global level (Young, 1996).

Learning an FL can contribute to the development of ICC. In this view, FL teaching is regarded as a process of helping students "attain competence in intercultural communication through learning a language and its relationship to the cultural practices and identities interlocutors bring to an interaction" (Byram, 1997b, p. 47). As such, FL teaching involves enabling students to react linguistically and culturally in an appropriate manner in communication situations that require them to apply general cultural and linguistic competence, not only in the FL and its corresponding culture, but also in their own (Fenner, 2001). The focus of FL instruction, then, is the teaching of a language and its culture, out of which should arise critical awareness.

The acquisition of intercultural competence involves the students' ability to recognize the relativity of cultural practices, values, and beliefs, including their own. Intercultural competence is not learned through a body of knowledge; it is acquired by developing attitudes of openness and respect for otherness and by establishing relationships between one's native culture and at least one foreign culture. In this view, the responsibility of the teacher is not to transmit a body of minimal knowledge but, rather, to ensure that students have the means of independently acquiring knowledge and understanding. All this requires pedagogical and didactic skills and knowledge on the part of the teacher.

The question of language and culture teaching has become particularly prominent in the last few years in Europe. This is reflected in a number of Council of Europe publications that emphasize that language learning must have a cultural dimension (see, e.g., Byram, 1997b; Byram & Zarate, 1997a, 1997b; Council of Europe, 1997; Fenner, 2001; Trim, 1997) and is clearly exemplified in the development of the "Common European Framework for Languages," in which an emphasis is placed on the sociocultural and sociolinguistic dimensions in FL teaching and learning. Byram and Zarate (1997a) view sociocultural competence as part of ICC. Sociocultural competence, or what others call "intercultural competence" (Byram, 1997b; Byram & Zarate, 1997a), is considered an important component of language teaching and learning, as is recognized not only in the European Community but also in countries outside the European Union (EU), including the U.S. (see, e.g., American Association of Teachers of French, 1996; American Council on the Teaching of Foreign Languages et al., 2003).

The Intercultural Speaker

Byram and Zarate (1997a) challenge the assumption that in order to be able to reach communicative competence in a second language (L2), students should conform to the rules and norms of native speakers and should be assimilated into their target culture (i.e., that they should give up cultural attitudes and ways of life that have nurtured them, in order to adopt the FL culture). On the contrary, they argue that students should not be "trained" as native speakers but, rather, need to develop an intercultural personality that can relate to both cultures—and that in so doing, they become more mature, complex people. Byram and Zarate suggest that students be described as "intercultural speakers," ones who play the role of cultural intermediaries between the two or more cultures that they relate to. In the same line of thought, Trim (1997) defends the idea that language learners are not some form of new recruit to the community of native users of the language and that cultural assimilation is no longer considered an indispensable aspect of linguistic proficiency. The intercultural speaker, in this view, is "somebody who crosses frontiers, and who is to some extent a specialist in the transit of cultural property and symbolic values" (Zarate, 1997, p. 11). Trim explains that intercultural speakers—in their role as mediators between cultures—should be able to identify, explain, and resolve conflicts between two given communities. Byram and Zarate (1997b) have developed the concept of "interculturality" as an educational objective. They explain that by using an FL in a way that shows an understanding of the culture behind it, students will develop a more complex personality that will enable them to bridge the cultural gap and to become intercultural speakers. Byram and Zarate (1997a) also explain that to reach the "interculturality" objective, instruction must include situations of contact and exchange with native speakers so that language learners are given the opportunity to play the role of cultural intermediaries.

FL teachers themselves should be intercultural speakers (Byram, 1997b), positioned between the foreign language and culture and their own. As such, FL teachers allow language learners to compare languages and cultures, and in the process they can better understand their own culture and strengthen their own cultural identity. The intercultural dimension extends the FL teachers' traditional role and invites them to take on new responsibilities—such as addressing ethnocentric attitudes, openness to others, and reflection on the native culture, all of which may be activated through experiencing cultural differences (Byram, 1997a).

Competent intercultural speakers boast intercultural skills and knowledge that can deal with the issue of cultural difference (Byram & Zarate, 1997a, 1997b). In order to become intercultural mediators, intercultural speakers should be able to create stable relationships between their own culture and the foreign one, by way of acquiring knowledge about the FL culture and using that knowledge to reflect on both cultures.

In the EU, the figure of the "intercultural speaker"—referring to both language teachers and language learners—leaves no place for the issue of *native speaker* versus *nonnative speaker*. The Council of Europe supports the idea that the knowledge of languages will improve communication among its citizens, will result in mutual understanding and cooperation, and will help overcome prejudice and discrimination. Europe is a multilingual, multicultural community that has a very strong policy of support for the learning of foreign languages. The objective of the language policy of the EU and its member states is that all European citizens be able to communicate in at least two foreign languages in addition to their mother tongue. The "Common European Framework for Languages" (Consejo de Europa, 2002) provides a theoretical basis for teaching, learning, and evaluating languages. It fully integrates the sociocultural and sociolinguistic components of language learning. It also describes standards for language learning and language teaching and has become the basis for course design, materials development, and staff development.

The Spanish Context

English as a Foreign Language Instruction in Catalonia

Education is compulsory in Spain for everybody between 6 and 16 years old. Learning at least one FL is obligatory throughout this compulsory period and throughout the *bachillerato* (post-compulsory education leading to university studies) and/or some post-compulsory education vocational studies. The FL class meets three times a week, for an hour each session. Students choose the FL they want to learn from those offered at their school. English is the most widely FL offered, sometimes the only one, as is the case with most elementary schools (grades K–6). All high schools offer at least two foreign languages. High school students learn a second FL starting their third year, unless they belong to a special program or live in a bilingual community. In bilingual communities such as Catalonia, where both Catalan and Spanish are official languages, both languages are taught in school from kindergarten through *bachillerato,* and high school students study only one FL (usually English)—although a second FL is optional for students in their third year of high school.

FL curricula guidelines are developed by the Ministerio de Educación y Ciencia (MEC, the equivalent to the Department of Education in the U.S.). This is the very first level of specification and includes minimum basic competencies, the likes of which should also be locally developed by the FL department in every school, thereby constituting a second level of specification. A third level of specification, in the form of a class syllabus, is developed by the FL teacher. Curricula guidelines provide a framework for FL instruction but give teachers freedom to develop their own units or projects and/or restrict themselves to a textbook.

The MEC curricula guidelines hold that learning an FL means acquiring communicative competence, which includes grammar competence, discourse competence, sociolinguistic competence, strategic competence, and sociocultural competence. These guidelines also highlight the educational function of the FL, asserting that learning an FL helps students to know other ways of understanding reality, enriches their cultural world, favors the development of attitudes of tolerance and respect, and puts into perspective the importance of the students' ways of viewing the world (Ministerio de Educación y Ciencia, 1995).

The MEC guidelines are divided into three categories: general objectives, contents (i.e., facts, concepts, and conceptual systems; procedures; values, norms, and attitudes) and final objectives. Table 1 shows an example of how the sociocultural component is developed

TABLE 1. Levels of Curricula Development

	General Objectives	Contents	Final Objectives
First level	• Recognize the importance of knowing an FL as a means of better understanding one's own language and culture and as a language of international communication and understanding in an intercultural world.	*Facts and concepts* • Habits, traditions, and ways of thinking, living, and relating in the different linguistic communities studied; correspondences with the student's own culture. • Social, institutional, geographical, historical, and scientific points of reference, especially those that help one understand the complexity of the present world. *Attitudes and values* • Acceptance of otherness and difference. • Value one's own cultural identity with respect to others. • Overcome prejudices and stereotypes about cultures and peoples.	• Observe in the FL common and distinctive aspects in relation to one's own language, and reflect on how languages work. • Value the variety in human communication. • Value unknown or unusual things, other ways of living or thinking, and the differences among peoples.

Second level	*Facts and concepts* • Habits and cultures in other countries. • Democratic rights and freedom in the world. • Cooperation and solidarity with minority cultures. *Attitudes and values* • Respect toward the aspects of other cultures that are different from one's own. • Value diversity as an enriching factor. • Value the knowledge of other languages as a means of personal growth, at the social and individual level.	• Reflect on the importance of language in the communication among people of different cultures. • Reflect on the cultural similarities and differences among different countries.
Third level	• Culture shock: living abroad. • Families and homes: cultural differences. • Alternative medicines. • Fighting for ideals: Nelson Mandela.	• Reflect on a variety of social questions: racism and human diversity, ideologies and ideals, education, etc. • Show a critical attitude toward one's own and other ways of living and thinking.

within each of these three categories for the three different levels of guideline specification.

School departments normally choose textbooks from those that are approved by MEC; the selected books are not to be biased with respect to gender, ethnicity, religion, and so on, and are adapted to the Spanish/Catalan reality. These FL textbooks foster understanding and respect for different cultures and languages. They usually showcase not only native English speakers but also nonnative English speakers from different countries and cultures that communicate in English and have different accents, different opinions, and different points of view. The textbooks explore not only the target language culture but also topics that are of interest to teenagers—such as music, traveling, ecology, and art—and help to introduce and compare different cultures, including the native culture. Beyond contributing to the total education of the student, the FL class plays a very special role in exposing students to other cultures and peoples and in making connections and comparisons among the native culture, the target culture, and even other cultures. In fact, it seems only natural that intercultural education is a goal of the FL classroom. Keeping in line with this idea are the directions that the MEC gives for FL teaching; when speaking of the approach language learning should follow, it states that a language reflects a culture and that FL instruction should introduce students to the cultural contexts of the language under study. By doing this, students will develop positive attitudes toward other cultures (Ministerio de Educación y Ciencia, 1995).

FL teachers often serve as a link between the native culture and the target culture. FL teachers have undergone the process of learning an FL and, to different extents, have been immersed in the FL and first language (L1) cultures. FL teachers have multiple opportunities for immersion in the FL culture. For example, while doing undergraduate studies, FL teacher trainees are given the opportunity to participate in a variety of EU-sponsored programs designed to enhance their FL and intercultural skills (e.g., Socrates, Lingua). Once they have completed their undergraduate studies, FL teachers are also given the opportunity to participate in short-term programs (e.g., summer courses sponsored by regional education authorities) or long-term exchange programs organized by the Spanish central government (e.g., the Assistant Teachers Program in the EU, the U.S., Canada, and so on; the Visiting Teachers Program in the U.S. and Canada).

In order to qualify to teach in the public school system, all FL teachers—including native speakers of the target language—need to demonstrate their proficiency not only in the FL but also in the L1 of the community (if it happens to be a bilingual community like Catalonia, then proficiency must be demonstrated in both L1s of the community).

Additionally, the proficiency of FL teachers must extend beyond that of the languages in question and must encompass that of the cultures in question, too. Taking advantage of the aforementioned opportunities of immersion in the FL and its corresponding culture, FL teachers can develop sociolinguistic competence as defined by Byram and Zarate (1997a); if they do so, they become intercultural speakers who can play the role of intermediaries between the FL and the L1.

Intercultural Communication in the FL Classroom

The English as a foreign language (EFL) classes that I describe in this section take place in a high school in the city of Badalona, which has approximately 300,000 inhabitants and is located near the industrial area of Barcelona, Spain. The city underwent significant development in the 1960s due to an industrial boom. At that time it received immigration from other regions of the country, especially from the province of Andalusia. It now receives immigration from countries in and outside the EU. The school is located close to the city center, in a neighborhood populated basically by the first and second generations of immigrants already mentioned. The school now has approximately 500 students of various backgrounds, from middle-class to working-class, from the university-bound to those who will pursue vocational studies and even those with special needs.

I teach EFL to different levels of high school students: compulsory education students (third and fourth years) and *bachillerato* students (i.e., those preparing to enter a university). In my classes, I have always tried to create a connection between the target language culture and the students' culture. When I speak of the target language culture, I do not refer to the culture of any particular English-dominant country. In teaching EFL, my goal is not only that my students learn the FL and use it as a means of communication both within and outside the FL classroom but also that they understand the culture behind the language; in other words, that they acquire sociocultural competence and become sensitive to social conventions that affect language communication between people of different cultures; in short, that they eventually play the role of intercultural speakers themselves. In order to attain this objective, I do my best to encourage my students to acquaint themselves with and respect other cultures. I do so basically by acting as a cultural intermediary between the FL culture and the L1 culture, by incorporating the perspectives of both the native speaker and the FL speaker on all issues, by comparing cultural references, and by promoting attitudes and values that show openness and interest to foreign cultures and their people. My lifelong process as an FL learner facilitates this task. I have gone through the experience of learning an FL, of getting to know its culture, of relating the FL culture to mine, and of understanding the differences and similarities between both cultures. The ways in which I try to provide my students with opportunities to get acquainted with the FL culture include the following:

- *Meeting English-speaking people.* I invite friends of mine who are visiting or live in the area to come to my school and chat with my students; I provide my students with contacts for visiting groups of foreign students, who initiate communication with my students through written correspondence and then get to meet them when they visit Barcelona. In the last five years, five different groups of my students have exchanged correspondence with groups of English-speaking students. In three instances they were native speakers of English, and in the other two they were English language learners from other countries in the EU. On three occasions, they have met in person in Barcelona. Also, native and nonnative English speakers from the U.S. have visited my class and chatted with my students. Teaching assistants from Great Britain and Canada, who have developed activities focusing on the culture of their countries in relation to the Catalan/Spanish culture, have met with my students on a weekly basis for extended period of times.
- *Experiencing an English-dominant country.* This can be a virtual experience, a trip done through research, or a real-study trip. The autonomous government of Catalonia, through its Ministerio de Educación y Ciencia, offers scholarships to groups of high school students (for years 2–4 and for post-compulsory education) to visit a foreign country whose official language is one that the students are learning. In order to receive the scholarships, students have to develop a project in their FL classroom and outline a plan for the visit. If they are awarded the scholarship, they are required to develop a second project that focuses on their trip once the visit is completed. So far, my students have received scholarships every time they have applied—twice in the last five years—and have traveled to Great Britain and to the Republic of Ireland, accompanied by at least two teachers, one of them being their FL teacher. Furthermore, my students, in collaboration with students in other EU countries, have participated in a SIMULAB project, an international web-based communication project centered around a specific problem or "simulation" (see Nielsen & Hever, 1998, for details on how a simulation is organized). Working in collaboration with other EFL learners, my students designed an imaginary town in Ireland and created the infrastructure to attract tourism to it.

In my classes, I usually assign a project that students work on for a full term. Throughout the years, I have had my students work on two kinds of projects. The first project consists of helping students to develop cultural understanding about an English-dominant country, with the goal of eventually visiting it. The second project, designed to help students develop intracultural awareness, is centered on a topic of interest to the students or one that is linked to the general education curriculum, such as ecology, human values, and so on.

Project one: Developing cultural understanding. This project is designed to develop intercultural understanding by becoming acquainted with a city or country. The project requires students to work in small groups and plan, develop, and publish the projects. Since this kind of project is quite complex, each group of students first divides the work into various manageable parts and eventually reintegrates them to complete the project, the results of which must be shared with the whole class.

Barcelona 4 You, a project developed by first-year *bachillerato* students, had the dual goal of creating a tourist resource guide about Barcelona—including a brochure and a web page for a group of foreign students visiting the school and city—and applying for a scholarship to travel to London. To meet the first goal, students did research on Barcelona. Specifically, they obtained general tourist information (e.g., how to move around the city, where to go, what places to visit, and where to eat) through available sources—(e.g., books, encyclopedias, brochures from travel agencies, and the web) and through personal experience (e.g., discos and cafes students had been to). Since students had to show the city to foreign students of their own age, they needed to bear in mind not only the age factor but also the visitors' cultural background. In order to accomplish this, students had to develop sociolinguistic competence so that they would avoid conflict with the foreign students' social conventions and so that the foreign students would become familiar with Spanish conventions. Students prepared and published a guide of Barcelona for teenagers, accompanied by a videotape and an audiotape showcasing the most representative monument in the city, the Temple of the Sacred Family, designed by Gaudí.

The students submitted the project to the MEC and obtained a scholarship to spend two weeks in London. In order to prepare for their visit, students did some research on London and learned very basic information such as how to get around or how some British habits differ from Spanish habits (e.g., eating times and driving). Students also read and discussed the book *How to Be an Alien*, by George Mikes (2000), which deals with preconceptions about British people. Once in London, students stayed with British families, attended a language school, and began preparing the project that they had to develop once they returned to Spain, which they called *The London Experience*. The project consisted of a guide of London, containing information on the students' visits, a collective diary, and a videotape of their visit.

The *Barcelona 4 You* project contributed to the students' intercultural education in that they had to reflect on their own culture. By doing research on Barcelona, a city with which they were very familiar, they had to reflect on their own reality, habits, and beliefs and compare them with the ones of their prospective audience, a group of foreign students, so that they could create a connection with them, share their way of living, avoid possible misunderstandings, and so on. *The London Experience* was the result of authentic foreign culture learning and reflected the students' thoughts, points of view, and experiences in a foreign country. This project was very motivating for the students, not only because they met foreign people of their own age, but also because it was the result of the scholarship they had earned. The project was also quite easy to plan and develop, since the information needed was accessible through many sources.

Another project of this type, designed to develop intercultural understanding, involved getting to know the history of a country—in this case, Ireland—through a variety of resources, with an initial emphasis on movies. The reason for choosing Ireland was that students would be able to relate Ireland's struggle for independence to the history of Catalonia and its relationship with the government of Spain. This project was titled *Let's Go to Ireland* and was developed by fourth-year students in the Compulsory Education Program. In this particular case, the project was a joint venture of two teachers from two different departments in the school, the FL department and the social science department. The teachers' responsibilities involved identifying the projects' components, selecting the movies, and supervising the project. The movies viewed were *The Quiet Man, Innisfree, Michel Collins, In the Name of the Father, Some Mother's Son*, and *The Commitments*. The history teacher was in charge of introducing the students to the historical events that appeared in every film before their viewing, of clarifying doubts related to historical events, and of helping students with the content of the project. After viewing the film, students did additional research on its historical context, using such sources as web pages, encyclopedias, reference books, and history books. The English teacher was in charge of teaching language skills, sociolinguistic awareness, and the reading texts. The result of the project was a web page focusing on the history of Ireland and a videotape showing how the students prepared for and celebrated Saint Patrick's Day, which ultimately familiarized the school population with Saint Patrick's Day traditions. This project was also awarded a scholarship to go to Dublin for two weeks. Just as the students who went to London did, the Ireland-bound students prepared for their trip before departing, in order to develop an understanding of the Irish way of life. Once in Dublin, students stayed with Irish families, visited the main monuments of the city, and attended a language school, where they began to prepare the project that they would have to develop once they returned to Spain. The project, which the students titled *A Walk through Dublin*, consisted of a PowerPoint presentation showcasing a day-by-day account of their stay in Dublin as recorded by different students, a short guide of Dublin with in-depth tourist information, and a collective diary.

This project had the benefit of integrating a strong listening component, since students had to watch the original versions of the films with subtitles. Also, movies, if well chosen, can provide a very good picture of the foreign country and its culture. On the other hand, teachers may have a difficult time finding films that are appropriate for the topic being researched and/or for the age of the students concerned.

Project two: Looking into the students' own reality. This second kind of project completed in my class is not directly related to any foreign country but, rather, is anchored in the general (as opposed to FL) school curriculum. In this type of project, the objective is to develop intracultural understanding, which involves helping students overcome cultural differences in the perceptions, thinking modes, and values that influence intracultural communication. Even though the project is not designed to focus on a particular aspect of an FL culture, the project incorporates materials and presents examples of such. Students have focused on various topics, depending on their self-perceived needs or interests. These topics have ranged from advertising to movies, from visual art to music, from literature to comic strips—but always with a bent toward their role in society.

Advertising, a successful classroom project completed by *bachillerato* students, focused on the role of ads in society. The project's objective was to have students look at advertising with a critical eye, to decode the messages ads transmit. To meet this objective, students analyzed and classified ads that had appeared in various types of English-speaking media (e.g., magazines, TV, newspapers), paying attention to such components as the mode of language use (oral and/or visual), the type of audience to which ads were addressed, and the information they presented. Although the ads selected had been published in English-speaking media, they were chosen in particular because their message was universal and not tied to any single culture; in fact, a few of the ads studied had also been released in Spanish and/or Catalan in Spain. After analyzing the ads, students worked in small groups to create their own ads. Since students used different media, the ads were produced in different forms (video, photography, posters, brochures, etc.). Then students presented their ads, designed either as a parody of a real ad or as a serious attempt to showcase a product to their peers. The resulting ads were accompanied by a written paper in which students explained their ads in terms of their target audience, the language used, the ad script, and so on. The written paper also included an analysis of other ads they had reviewed in the course of completing their project.

As already noted, this project was designed in order to help students develop critical-thinking skills, in that they had to reflect on the role of advertising in our modern society. By studying ads coming from English-dominant countries, students were able to compare them with the ones they usually see in the various media of their L1. They came to the conclusion that beyond its language of transmission, advertising may well use a universal language, given that a number of ads are created to appear in the media of several different countries.

Another project anchored in the general school curriculum was a term project sponsored by the MEC of Catalonia and designed to educate students in values such as respect for people and cultures different from their own, respect for nature, and respect for cultural expressions. This project, named *Computers in the English Classroom,* was carried out by students with learning difficulties, and was developed entirely in a computer lab.

In this project, students became computer literate by learning how to use different computer tools, ranging from a word processor to a web page composer. They also learned how to use e-mail, surf the web, and participate in an Internet chat. The teacher designed the materials using existing web pages, some originally in English and some translated into English from Catalan or Spanish, and adapted the materials to the students' level of content knowledge and level of proficiency in English. The teacher-developed materials consisted of four units:

1. The introduction unit presented different computer tools. It was designed to teach students to use a word processor, to use computer-mediated communication tools (e.g., e-mail and chats), and to create web pages. While carrying out the tasks in this unit, students opened e-mail accounts and created their first web page, in which they introduced themselves, their families, and their friends.

2. The first unit focused on Europe. It provided information about the EU, its official languages, and its new common currency. It also provided information about immigration and immigrants, the

New Europeans, and so on. Drawing on the information learned, students created a web page about the country of origin of one of the students at the school.

3. The second unit dealt with the environment and how people can contribute to preserve it. It focused on recycling, particularly everyday waste, and on alternative sources of energy. Students created a web page designed to raise people's awareness of how they can contribute to save the planet.

4. The third unit focused on art works displayed in the students' cities or towns, particularly on the buildings and sculptures that form the urban landscape. It was presented as a guided walk around Barcelona. Students created a web page about Gaudí, the renowned Catalan architect, and his work. They designed a PowerPoint presentation about the sculptures found on the streets of a Barcelona neighborhood of their choice.

Of the four units developed, only the first unit offered a perspective of cultures beyond that of the students', and the topics covered focused on different ways of viewing reality—different beliefs, attitudes, and values not always shared by different cultures. For example, in the first unit, students learned about the cultures of the "new European immigrants," who hail from countries so different as Morocco, China, Colombia, or Belarus; and they were able to compare them to people from their own culture. Students followed the teacher-made materials, did the exercises required, and created their own materials in English, using different formats (e.g., web pages, PowerPoint presentations, and drawings) depending on the task at hand.

Students enjoyed the experience of acquiring computer skills in the EFL class and, at the same time, grappled with issues that made them more responsible citizens. They became more aware of the importance of knowing what is around them, of respecting other people's facts and opinions, of acting in a responsible way to care for the earth, and of respecting the artwork around them.

Conclusion

In this chapter, FL teaching has been presented as a means of achieving ICC, involving teaching a language and its culture, and promoting critical awareness. This requires that teachers have the skills and knowledge of the intercultural speaker so that they can act as cultural intermediaries. FL teachers, in this view, provide students with opportunities of interacting with peers from the target language, through the use of computer-mediated communication tools, through face-to-face communication, or through actual experience in another cultural and linguistic environment. I have also described how these three types of interactions are made available in my EFL classroom.

In this chapter, I have argued that FL students need to develop an intercultural personality, play the role of cultural intermediaries between the cultures they are related with, and become intercultural speakers who foster understanding between the FL culture and their own by comparing and establishing relationships between them. This will lead to a better understanding of the students' own culture, a development of their critical awareness, and a strengthening of their cultural identity, thereby contributing to their overall education. For this to happen, the FL students' use of the target language must include situations of contact and exchange with native speakers, in which they must be able to play the role of cultural intermediaries. My EFL class plays a central role in helping students to accomplish this.

References

American Association of Teachers of French. (1996). AATF National Commission on Cultural Competence: *Understanding culture: Indicators of competence.* Retrieved February 12, 2003, from *http://www.siu.edu/~aatf/underste.html*

American Council on the Teaching of Foreign Languages et al. (2003). *National standards for foreign language education: A collaborative project of ACTFL, AATF, AATG, AATI, AATSP, ACL, ACTR, CLASS, and NCJLT-ATJ.* Retrieved February 12, 2003, from *http://www.actfl.org/public/articles/details.cfm?id=33*

Byram, M. (1997a). The intercultural dimension in "language learning for European citizenship." In M. Byram and G. Zarate (Eds.), *The sociocultural and intercultural dimension of language learning and teaching.* Strasbourg, France: Council of Europe.

Byram, M. (1997b). *Teaching and assessing intercultural communicative competence.* Clevedon, England: Multilingual Matters.

Byram, M., & Tost Planet, M. (Eds.). (2000). *Social identity and the European dimension: Intercultural competence through foreign language learning.* Strasbourg, France: Council of Europe.

Byram, M., & Zarate, G. (1997a). Definitions, objectives, and assessment of sociocultural competence. In M. Byram, G. Zarate, & G. Neuner (Eds.), *Sociocultural competence in language learning and teaching: Studies towards a common European framework of reference for language learning and teaching* (pp. 9–43). Strasbourg, France: Council of Europe.

Byram, M., & Zarate, G. (Eds.). (1997b). *The sociocultural and intercultural dimension of language learning and teaching.* Strasbourg, France: Council of Europe.

Consejo de Europa. (2002). *Marco común europeo de referencia para las lenguas: Aprendizaje, enseñanza, evaluación.* Madrid: MECD-Anaya.

Council of Europe (1997). *Language learning for European citizenship: Final report of the project*. Strasbourg, France: Council of Europe.

Fenner, A.-B. (Ed.). (2001). *Cultural awareness and language awareness based on dialogic interaction with texts in foreign language learning*. Strasbourg, France: Council of Europe.

Hadley, A. O. (1993). *Teaching language in context*. Boston: Heinle & Heinle.

Jandt, F. E. (2000). *Intercultural communication: An introduction* (3rd ed.). Thousand Oaks, CA: Sage.

Martin, J. N. (1993). Intercultural communication competence: A review. In R. L. Wiseman & J. Koester (Eds.), *Intercultural communication competence. International and intercultural communication annual* (17, pp. 16–29). Newbury Park, CA: Sage.

Mikes, G. (2000). *How to be an alien*. London: Pearson Education.

Ministerio de Educación y Ciencia. (1995). *Secundaria obligatoria. Lenguas extranjeras*. Madrid: Author.

Nielsen, G., & Hever, B. (Eds.). (1998). *Collaborative tasks for language learning in the web*. Oslo, Norway: Statens ressurs of voksenopplæringssenter.

Novinger, T. (2001). *Intercultural communication: A practical guide*. Austin: University of Texas Press.

Trim, J. (1997). *Apprentissage des langues et citoyenneté européenne: Rapport final du groupe de project (1989–1996)*. Strasbourg, France: Éditions du Conseil de l'Europe.

van Dijk, T. A., Ting-Toomey, S., Smitherman, G., & Troutman, D. (1997). Discourse, ethnicity, culture, and racism. In T. A. Van Dijk (Ed.), *Discourse studies: A multidisciplinary introduction: Vol. 2. Discourse as social interaction* (pp. 144–180). London: Sage.

Young, R. (1996). *Intercultural communication: Pragmatics, genealogy, deconstruction*. Philadelphia: Multilingual Matters.

Zarate, G. (1997). Cultural issues in a changing Europe. In M. Byram & G. Zarate (Eds.), *The sociocultural and intercultural dimension of language learning and teaching*. Strasbourg, France: Council of Europe.

Collaboration between Native and Nonnative English-Speaking Educators

Luciana C. de Oliveira
University of California, Davis

Sally Richardson
California State University, Hayward

A collaborative relationship is a partnership consciously entered into by the people involved, the team members. It is a relationship that is purposely pursued in order to achieve a common goal and to provide the team members with support. Saltiel (1998) defines collaboration as a partnership between two or more people who work together on a common goal and, together, accomplish and learn more than they could if they were working alone. Wildavshy (1986) states that the essence of the collaborative process is when "the participants make use of each other's talents to do what they either could not have done at all or as well alone" (p. 237). Baldwin and Austin (1995) contend that in order for a collaborative relationship to be successful, the team members must build their collaborative relationship on mutual trust, respect, and even affection.

In recent years, the advantages of collaboration among teachers have become evident in many contexts (Hargreaves, 1994; Little, 1990). Many educators have worked collaboratively on research projects, on books, on curriculum development, and in team teaching. Through such collaboration, these educators have not only accomplished more than they would have accomplished alone; they have also expanded their knowledge and honed their skills. There are, however, unique benefits when native English-speaking and nonnative English-speaking educators form a collaborative relationship. In this chapter, the co-authors describe the benefits that they (i.e., Luciana C. de Oliveira, a nonnative English-speaking educator, and Sally Richardson, a native English-speaking educator) have gained from such a collaborative relationship. They also explain how and why their relationship benefited not only themselves but their students as well. Finally, they provide suggestions for how other educators might initiate and maintain such a collaborative relationship.

The Authors' Paths as Educators

Luciana was born and raised in Brazil, attending Brazilian schools from kindergarten through college. She started to study English as a foreign language (EFL) at the age of 12 and knew relatively early that she wanted to be an English teacher. She began her teaching career at a private school in Araraquara, São Paulo, in 1993, where she taught beginning, intermediate, and advanced EFL to children, adolescents, and adults. Luciana received her bachelor of arts degree and teaching credential in languages, English and Portuguese, from the State University of São Paulo in January 1997. In the same year, she was admitted to the master of arts (MA) program in TESOL option at California State University, Hayward (CSUH), where she subsequently earned her MA degree in 1999. Then, she was hired as a lecturer for the English Department at CSUH, teaching developmental and upper-division English composition to native and nonnative speakers for one year. Luciana is now a doctoral candidate in education at the University of California, Davis.

In 1976, Sally received her bachelor of arts degree in art with an emphasis in drawing and painting from San Francisco State University, where she also earned her clear single-subject teaching credential in art. She taught art and dance part-time at the high school level for a year but left the field of education to operate her own graphics business for over ten years. In 1994, she decided to return to teaching and entered the MA program in English with the TESOL option at CSUH. While in the process of completing her MA degree, she also obtained the Cultural and Linguistic Academic Development (CLAD) certificate. She earned her MA degree in 1999 and was hired as a lecturer at CSUH, where she continues to teach developmental and upper-division English composition to native and nonnative English speakers.

The History of the Collaborative Association

Luciana and Sally first met in 1997 when they were both graduate students at CSUH. New to the U.S., Luciana felt somewhat overwhelmed by the amount of reading she would have to do in a second language. Although Luciana had many questions about the language and the culture around her, she would not approach other graduate students at first, because she felt uncertain about her abilities. This dilemma continued until she told herself that she needed to take advantage of the opportunity of being in the U.S. Luciana started to pay more attention to her peers in the graduate program and to consider which ones she felt comfortable interacting with. Sally, one such student, seemed open and talked to Luciana, asking her questions about her experiences in the U.S. In fact, she seemed to understand the difficulties faced by a nonnative speaker new to the U.S. academic culture. After a while, Luciana started to ask Sally questions such as the importance of Thanksgiving in the U.S. and the meaning of some words her professors were using. Becoming friends with Sally played an important role in Luciana's development as a graduate student and in her future as a teacher of English as a second language (ESL). It was her friendship with Sally that led her to participate more actively in many classes and, therefore, to practice her language skills.

Sally was also drawn to Luciana. She found Luciana open and approachable and noticed that Luciana was an experienced EFL teacher. Although Sally had some teaching experience, it had been many years since she had taught. Moreover, she had never taught ESL or EFL, so she felt that working with someone who had experience in teaching English would greatly benefit her.

The manner in which Luciana and Sally's collaboration began is typical of how many collaborative partners begin such a relationship—they select each other almost by instinct (Sgroi & Saltiel, 1998). In other words, the two individuals sense a camaraderie or meeting of the minds, prompting them to select each other. Such collaborative relationships, according to Sgroi and Saltiel (1998), often become more than mere professional relationships. This was the case with Sally and Luciana's relationship while graduate students. It began as a friendship, then blossomed into a collaborative relationship, which in turn strengthened the friendship.

When Luciana and Sally started teaching at CSUH as part of their MA practicum, they felt that collaborating would benefit both of them. They therefore decided to meet twice a month during their six-month practicum, to share ideas and materials, talk about their students and their academic needs, discuss their teaching experiences, and assist each other as needed. This beginning stage in their collaborative relationship was fundamental to their professional development because they were able to receive regular supportive feedback from each other. As Little (1987) states, teachers who work together are able to "build program coherence, expand individual resources, and reduce individual burdens for planning and preparation" (p. 504). This is essentially what Sally and Luciana were accomplishing with their collaboration.

Richards and Lockhart (1994) state that critical reflection is essential as a basis for evaluation and decision making and fosters a deeper understanding of teaching. During their practicum, Luciana and Sally reflected collaboration by discussing the classes they taught, their students' reactions, and the strategies each used to present new content and vocabulary. After graduation, they continued this reflection by sharing ideas, handouts, and class materials and by giving each other supportive feedback. This collaboration also extended to conference presentations and the co-authorship of articles and chapters.

Making the Collaborative Relationship Work

How do Luciana and Sally make their collaborative relationship work? And why does it work so well for them? Although they have a lot in common, such as their teaching approaches, they also differ in many ways. In addition to their differences in background (e.g., education, culture, and native language), they also have different cognitive styles. Luciana is a linear/mathematical thinker, while Sally, who comes from an art background, tends to be a global thinker. But it is precisely these differences that make their collaboration work. According to Shannon and Meath-Lang (1992), successful collaboration is built on recognizing and appreciating the different gifts, skills, and expertise of the other person. Furthermore, it is built on the abilities of the collaborators to appreciate their respective differences without feeling less competent themselves. These conditions are both met in Sally and Luciana's collaborative relationship. Because of their different perspectives and abilities, they often need to provide each other with detailed explanations, in the process arriving at a clearer understanding of their own opinions.

Riordan and da Costa (1996) refer to this process of discovering more of what one thinks while discussing ideas with a collaborative partner as "double-thinking." They add that this thinking out loud often leads to a refinement of ideas and an incorporation of new ideas. For example, Sally and Luciana had each designed a peer review activity. In Sally's activity, students had to summarize their peer reviewers' comments. In Luciana's activity, students had to write a revision plan based on the peer review. In one of their collaborative meetings, Luciana and Sally decided to combine their ideas into one activity. This is just one of the types of cumulative effects that collaboration fosters.

Another example of Luciana and Sally's process of collaboration is a reading-writing journal[1] assignment that they co-designed. The assignment required students to pick out key ideas from a chapter, summarize them, and respond to them. To facilitate the completion of the task, students were provided with a sample reading-writing journal entry handout with three columns labeled "key idea," "summary," and "response." Sally decided to provide the first example for the students. She chose an academic textbook chapter to analyze and picked the term *thesis statement* as her key idea. In the sample handout, she put "thesis statement" in the "key idea" column; in the "summary" column, she summarized what a thesis statement is; and in the "response" column, she supplied a response to the idea of a "thesis statement" in the way she thought a student might respond. Sally shared the sample handout with Luciana, who, as a nonnative speaker, said she thought that ESL students might become confused by the example. She explained to Sally that ESL students may not understand that the term *thesis statement* was only being used as an example of a key idea. Sally and Luciana revised the handout together and wrote a new example that would not be open to misinterpretation.

A further example of Luciana and Sally's collaboration is their process of preparing for presentations at professional conferences. First, they discuss ideas and then mull them over for a week or two. They next meet again to brainstorm, devise a plan, and discuss their individual roles for each aspect of the presentation. After that, they work individually on their tasks and meet at least three more times to put materials and handouts together and to rehearse. Central to Luciana and Sally's presentations is the spirit of cooperation that is the foundation of their collaborative relationship.

As in any relationship, collaborative academic relationships have certain dynamics in terms of decision making and roles. According to Baldwin and Austin (1995), these roles are negotiated and developed over time. Furthermore, Baldwin and Austin state that different relationships vary along a continuum in terms of the degree of flexibility in the partners' roles. At one end of the continuum are partnerships that initially set forth specific roles that remain the same regardless of the type of project. At the other end of the continuum are partnerships where the rules and roles of the relationship are unspoken and shift, depending on the type of project the collaborators are working on. Luciana and Sally's collaborative relationship falls in different places on this continuum, depending on the task. When collaborating on presentations, Sally is usually the note-taker, while Luciana compiles the materials to create the master handout that will be given at the presentation. Although neither of them articulated their specific roles, each role developed because of their complementary, yet different, skills and interests. Today, they each automatically assume these roles. However, on other projects, such as the writing of this chapter, they adjust their individual roles as the need arises. Sometimes these roles are determined by who has more time to do a certain task; at other times the roles are determined by their individual preferences and talents.

Luciana and Sally are able to make their collaboration work well because they manage not to have power struggles in their relationship, instead handling all decisions with communication and compromise. Lasley, Matczynski, and Williams (1992) explain that "in collaborative partnerships, power is shared, and goals are set by consensus" (p. 257). Because of their mutual respect, neither Luciana nor Sally has any energy invested in being "right" or in being the one to make all the decisions. Such mutual respect is paramount if such a collaborative relationship is going to work, whether the two people involved are native-speaking or nonnative-speaking educators. Clark and Watson (1998) state that in order for a collaborative relationship to work, it is essential that the people involved let go of being the one always in power or always in the limelight. Shannon and Meath-Lang (1992) state this even more strongly when they recommend that if one is interested in selecting a partner for collaboration, people who are controlling or have the need to be a "prima donna" should be avoided.

Luciana and Sally handle the process of decision making by always beginning any new task—be it designing a classroom activity, planning a presentation, or even writing this chapter—with brainstorming to discover what they think or what they know. Then, whichever one comes up with an idea first makes a suggestion. If the other sees a problem, she suggests an alternative that they then discuss again. This process of back-and-forth discussion, suggestions, and alternatives results in either a combination of ideas, a compromise, or an acquiescence by one party. But at the core of this is the knowledge that each person is bringing her own particular talents and knowledge to the situation. The respect that they each feel for each other and each other's uniqueness has never yet made any decision wholly the work of one or a problem for either.

All collaborative relationships might not, however, work as smoothly as Luciana and Sally's. Even if some conflicts or challenges arise, collaboration should still be pursued, as many of these conflicts can be overcome, especially if the partners are willing and able to work through their differences. Baldwin and Austin (1995) interviewed many collaborators and asked them to give metaphors for their collaborative relationships. Some of the words mentioned were "marriage," "sisterhood," "partnership," "teammates," "buddy," and "friendship." As with any successful, close relationship, there needs to be deep mutual respect and the process of give-and-take. If those seeking to collaborate remember to keep these qualities paramount in their relationship, conflicts should be able to be resolved and the relationship maintained.

Perceived Benefits of Collaborating

When two people work toward a common goal, a synergy tends to occur. Often just the process of exchanging ideas with another stimulates new ideas. Similarly, when one person shares a classroom activity or handout with another person, that person often elaborates on and improves upon the original. The intellectual stimulation that occurred as a result of their collaboration became clear to Sally and Luciana only after they began working together. This is the true value of collaboration, which tends to be heightened when it involves a native speaker and a nonnative speaker.

Benefits for the Nonnative English-Speaking Professional

Luciana's association with Sally has enabled her to acquire idioms, vocabulary, and pronunciation as well as to gain sociolinguistic competence (i.e., the knowledge of when to appropriately use specific words or phrases). Learning new idioms tends to be difficult even if one has a fairly good knowledge of vocabulary. For instance, in Portuguese the idiom "kick the bucket" means "make a mistake," prompting Luciana (until otherwise informed by Sally) to assume this same meaning when hearing the phrase uttered in English. Sally also helped Luciana learn how to pronounce words that were difficult for her (e.g., *managed* and *damaged*) by allowing her to watch her mouth as she pronounced each word and by teaching her how to break the words into syllables and pronounce the sounds separately—an effective technique that Luciana has since shared with her students. Nonnative speakers face situations that require not only knowledge of vocabulary, idioms, and pronunciation but also sociolinguistic competence. For instance, when Luciana arrived in the U.S., she did not know how to answer the greeting "What's up?" as she had never learned this greeting in Brazil. She therefore asked Sally what it meant and how to respond to it. As a result, she now not only interacts appropriately when encountering this phrase but has also taught it to her Brazilian colleagues. For Luciana, having a native English-speaking colleague assist her with these nuances of American English has made her a more knowledgeable, confident teacher.

Benefits for the Native English-Speaking Professional

By collaborating with Luciana, Sally has become better able to understand the process of learning ESL and EFL. It is one thing to study the theory of second language acquisition that is taught in graduate classes but another to actually know someone who has gone through the process and be able to ask them questions. In turn, Luciana shared strategies that she used to learn English, many of which Sally has subsequently suggested to her students. For example, Luciana makes lists of new vocabulary words and verb forms that she needs to memorize and posts them on her bathroom mirror so that every time she looks at the mirror, she sees the words. While this strategy may seem odd, it has worked very well for Luciana. Sally shared this strategy as well as others with her students, who responded favorably because they were actual strategies used by a successful English language learner.

Additionally, when a native speaker has a collaborative relationship with a nonnative speaker, she is able to gain an in-depth knowledge about another culture and, in the process, to gain more insight into the cultural needs of students studying in the U.S. The term *culture shock* takes on a new meaning and a greater significance when one can discuss it in detail with someone who has actually experienced it. The insight that the native speaker gains can make the native speaker more aware of what her students are going through and, consequently, more sensitive to her students' needs.

Although Sally and Luciana did not keep a formal diary of their collaborative relationship, they were required to keep a self-reflective teaching journal while they were in the graduate program. The following journal entry by Sally exemplifies the value gained by a native English speaker who has the input of a nonnative English-speaking professional:

> I spoke to Luciana about a grammar activity on identifying subjects and verbs that I did in class last week which did not seem to go over very well. She gave me some great advice. She said that as a second language learner herself, she had always found it helpful to identify the verb first before identifying the subject, and then to ask *who did whatever the action of the verb is.* So when I reviewed this part of grammar with my students, this is the strategy that I suggested. This time around the students did much better at identifying subjects. Thank-you, Luciana! (November 1, 1998)

Moreover, Luciana's experience as a learner of verb tenses in English specifically aided Sally in effectively teaching verb tense to ESL students—an arduous lesson for ESL and EFL students. As a former

English language learner, Luciana had many good recommendations for helping language learners to grasp the concept of verb tense in English. For instance, she recommended grouping certain tenses together so that they could be better contrasted and, therefore, perhaps, easier for many students to learn.

Finally, collaborating with Luciana helped Sally become aware of the importance of using language modification strategies in the language classroom. In the course of their conversations, Sally used many idioms and vocabulary terms with which Luciana was not familiar. Since Luciana asked the meaning of these items, the necessity of always defining unfamiliar lexical items to students became apparent to Sally, leading her to incorporate this awareness into her day-to-day teaching. Even though the necessity of defining unfamiliar vocabulary is mentioned in ESL methods classes and textbooks, it is only through the experience of working with a nonnative colleague (who *will* question the meaning of unknown lexical items, unlike many ESL students) that this awareness becomes internalized.

As a native speaker, one can only have theoretical knowledge of what it is like to learn English as a second language. A nonnative English-speaking professional who has actually gone through the process knows firsthand what it is like and can illuminate the process for the native English-speaking educator.

Benefits for Students

Luciana and Sally's students benefit from the enhanced cultural and linguistic awareness that results from these educators' collaborative relationship. For example, Luciana now knows more about U.S. culture and can share this information with her students. Sally, on the other hand, now has insights into what it is like for an English language learner to be in a different culture and to get along with different people. She is able to use Luciana as a model for her students, sharing Luciana's experiences and strategies and inspiring them in their study of English. Hearing about the success of a nonnative speaker now working in the U.S. as an English teacher makes the goal of fluency seem more achievable and motivates Sally's learners to work hard to achieve their own individual goals.

Additional Benefits

Complementing the benefits to their students are the practical and professional benefits that both Luciana and Sally have reaped from their association. As teachers, their collaboration has helped reduce preparation time, since they have been able to share class handouts and even course curricula. For example, Luciana had taught the first-tier writing course (for students who fail the university's writing skills test) four times before Sally was assigned to teach that particular class. Luciana was therefore able to provide Sally with copies of all her class materials and handouts, drastically reducing Sally's preparation time. Sally reciprocated by sharing her class materials for the second-tier writing course, one she had taught 10 different times before Luciana was assigned to teach that class. This helped Luciana better understand the curriculum that followed hers. As a result, she was better able to prepare her first-tier students for this course. She was also able to save the course materials for future use in other teaching situations. Little (1987) mentions that when colleagues "work in concert," they not only reduce their individual planning time but also increase their ideas and materials. Sally and Luciana's collaboration provides clear support for Little's claim.

In addition to benefiting their teaching, their collaboration has helped them both grow as professionals. Luciana had done numerous presentations while she was in Brazil, but Sally had not done any before she graduated from the MA program. Since Luciana had experience and was comfortable presenting at professional conferences, she suggested to Sally that they co-present. This offer is essentially what prompted Sally to start doing conference presentations. Being able to collaborate makes the presentation process easier because colleagues can inspire one another, generate numerous ideas by brainstorming, and share the workload—important advantages when one is teaching full-time and time is limited. Professional presentations not only help Sally and Luciana grow as professionals but also enhance their development as language educators. Their co-presentations allow them to share some of the things they are doing in their classes with other professionals and to receive feedback and suggestions. Also, preparing the presentations and writing chapters such as this one help Sally and Luciana to become better teachers because of their continual reflection about what they are doing in their classrooms.

Conclusion

If Sally and Luciana had known what benefits could accrue from native and nonnative English-speaking educator collaboration, they would probably have formed such an association sooner. Through their experience, they have come to recognize the specific benefits unique to collaboration between native and nonnative English-speaking educators. They not only intend to continue sharing teaching ideas and co-presenting; they are even discussing collaborating on a book.

Despite the current research on teacher collaboration (DiPardo, 1999; Riordan & da Costa, 1996), not much research has been done on collaborative relationships between native English-speaking and nonnative English-speaking educators. Further research in this area would be of great value to the community of TESOL educators, as would further literature on the specific benefits of native and nonnative collaboration. Both these efforts might help encourage this type of collaboration.

Furthermore, such collaboration could also be built into graduate programs where directors of such programs would encourage, recommend, and even require students in the program to experiment with the act of collaboration. Such collaboration could take the form of team teaching or partnership work as part of the practicum experience, as in Luciana and Sally's case. Although not required to form a partnership, they have both gained so much from their association that they feel others might also benefit from such a relationship. Kamhi-Stein (1999) describes how she has implemented collaborative projects in the classes she teaches in the MA TESOL program at California State University, Los Angeles, suggesting the importance of encouraging collaboration between native and nonnative teachers. If such collaborative experiences were systematically built into graduate programs, more successful collaborative relationships might be established. At the very least, the participants would be able to use their resulting knowledge of collaboration when assigning collaborative tasks to their students. Requiring this type of collaboration could even span different graduate programs; for example, students in MA TESOL programs could be asked to collaborate with graduate students majoring in literature. Given the diversity of the student population in most U.S. colleges and universities today, anyone teaching English will, most probably, have nonnative speakers in their classrooms and could benefit from the input of a nonnative educator.

For nonnative English-speaking educators, the benefits of collaboration with a native speaker tend to be apparent. For example, several nonnative speakers in the MA program in English at CSUH have asked Luciana how they might start such collaboration. Luciana advised them to pay close attention to other students in the program who might want to develop such a relationship and who seem committed to spending time discussing aspects of their teaching.

Because of the many benefits that can be gained from such an association, Sally and Luciana recommend that future and practicing native and nonnative English-speaking teachers actively pursue a collaborative relationship. The following suggestions stem from their own experience:

1. The key step involves approaching another individual and expressing the wish to collaborate.
2. Those wishing to collaborate should use the opportunities that present themselves to scope out possible collaborators. (Graduate students taking classes together or educators serving on the same committee or attending the same meetings can use these opportunities to identify individuals who seem compatible.)
3. Successful collaborations tend to involve a blend of personalities.
4. Collaborators must work at getting along well and learn to respect one another.
5. Both parties must recognize how much they can gain from the collaboration. A native English-speaking educator will gain just as much as a nonnative in this type of collaboration.

When one finds another professional with whom to collaborate, the way to maintain such a relationship is to have mutual respect, appreciate each other's differences, let go of any investment in being the one who has to always "run the show," and utilize each person's individual strengths. There is so much to be gained by this type of collaborative relationship that the opportunity should not be missed.

Note

1. The idea for this type of journal was inspired by an unpublished handout produced by Joyce Podevyn (March 1999) based on the Cornell note-taking system.

References

Baldwin, R. G., & Austin, A. R. (1995). Toward a greater understanding of faculty research collaboration. *Review of Higher Education, 19*(1), 45–70.

Clark, M. C., & Watson, D. B. (1998). Women's experience of academic collaboration. In I. M. Saltiel, A. Sgroi, & R. Brockett (Eds.), *The power and potential of collaborative learning partnerships* (pp. 5–11). San Francisco: Jossey-Bass.

DiPardo, A. (1999). *Teaching in common: Challenges to joint work in classrooms and schools.* New York: Teachers College Press.

Hargreaves, A. (1994). *Changing teachers, changing times: Teachers' work and culture in the postmodern age.* New York: Teachers College Press.

Kamhi-Stein, L. D. (1999). Preparing nonnative professionals in TESOL: Implications for teacher education programs. In G. Braine (Ed.), *Non-native educators in English language teaching* (pp. 145–158). Mahwah, NJ: Erlbaum.

Lasley, T. J., Matczynski, T. J., & Williams, J. A. (1992). Collaborative and noncollaborative partnership structures in teacher education. *Journal of Teacher Education, 43*(4), 257–261.

Little, J. W. (1987). Teachers as colleagues. In V. Richardson-Koehler (Ed.), *Educator's handbook: A research perspective* (pp. 491–518). New York: Longman.

Little, J. W. (1990). The persistency of privacy: Autonomy and initiative in teachers' professional relations. *Teachers College Record, 91*(4), 509–536.

Richards, J. C., & Lockhart, C. (1994). *Reflective teaching in second language classrooms.* Cambridge: Cambridge University Press.

Riordan, G. P., & da Costa, J. L. (1996). *Self-initiated high school teacher collaboration.* Paper presented at the annual meeting of the American Educational Research Association, New York. (ERIC Document Reproduction Service No. ED398638)

Saltiel, I. M. (1998). Defining collaborative partnerships. In I. M. Saltiel, A. Sgroi, & R. Brockett (Eds.), *The power and potential of collaborative learning partnerships* (pp. 5–11). San Francisco: Jossey-Bass.

Sgroi, A., & Saltiel, I. M. (1998). Human connections. In I. M. Saltiel, A. Sgroi, & R. Brockett (Eds.), *The power and potential of collaborative learning partnerships* (pp. 87–92). San Francisco: Jossey-Bass.

Shannon, N. B., & Meath-Lang, B. (1992). Collaborative language teaching: A co-investigation. In D. Nunan (Ed.), *Collaborative language learning and teaching* (pp. 120–140). New York: Cambridge University Press.

Wildavshy, A. (1986). On collaboration. *Political Science and Politics, 19,* 237–248.

The Development of EFL Standards in Egypt: Collaboration among Native and Nonnative English-Speaking Professionals

Marguerite Ann Snow
California State University, Los Angeles

Maysoun Omar
Alexandria University

Anne M. Katz
School for International Training

The backdrop for this chapter is a project to develop standards for the English as a foreign language (EFL) setting in Egypt. The project, called "Pharos" after the famous lighthouse that safeguarded the harbor in Alexandria at the time of Alexander the Great, is ambitious—to illuminate a new direction for the professional development of English teachers. To achieve this goal, groups of professionals in the teaching English to speakers of other languages (TESOL) field, both native and nonnative speakers representing many different positions and settings, have collaborated to produce four sets of standards for the Egyptian context—for English teachers, in-service teacher trainers, educational leaders, and in-service training courses.[1]

Throughout this chapter, we refer to a project model that includes native and nonnative speakers of English collaborating to do the work of standards development in Egypt. Because our focus is on the particular qualifications each of us brings to the project, the language status (i.e., native or nonnative proficiency in English) of the participants has not defined or stratified our respective roles in the project. The two native speakers contributed their expertise in standards development, while the nonnative speakers brought their local knowledge and understanding of the Egyptian educational system. In other words, the key criteria for identifying participants were the various types of expertise and experiences we each contributed to the project.

The chapter begins with a brief background on standards-based educational reform as an international movement and then provides an overview of the Pharos project. The heart of the chapter is concerned with three components of the project as examples of the volume's theme of native and nonnative professionals learning and teaching from experience.

Standards-Based Educational Reform

Brief Background on Standards-Based Reform in the United States

A major effort to improve the education of primary and secondary students across curriculum areas has centered on the use of standards to ensure the delivery of quality education (Marzano & Kendall, 1998). This reform movement is based on the premise that all students can and should achieve high standards of learning in challenging content areas. Standards describe what learning should look like and how learning should be provided in order to increase student achievement. Content standards, for example, describe what students should know and be able to do. Performance standards specify how well students must do in achieving those standards. In addition, standards-based reform efforts are designed to maximize students' potential for success and restore public confidence in education.

While much of the work in standards over the past 15 years or so has focused on describing the academic content (across the curriculum) that students should know and be able to use (cf. Gomez, 2000), that focus is shifting to the skills and knowledge that teachers need to have in order to implement a standards-based curriculum (Kuhlman & Murray, 2000; TESOL, 2002). What do teachers need to know and be able to do as they guide students to achieve to high content standards? To create standards-based change in schools, educators have identified the following teacher competencies:

- Teachers need to be able to adapt existing instruction to incorporate new pedagogical strategies;

- they need to be able to develop multiple approaches to content knowledge;
- they need to feel comfortable using a range of instructional resources;
- they need to be able to create a sense of community in the classroom;
- they need to understand how to implement a range of assessment tools to document student learning. (Cloud, 2000)

For teachers to develop these competencies so that they are effective and successful in standards-based schools, teacher preparation and professional development programs need to change both how and what they teach. National certification boards for teacher education programs have developed standards to guide reform efforts to improve the quality of teacher education programs (cf. National Council for the Accreditation of Teacher Education, 1995; National Board for Professional Teaching Standards, 1998; TESOL, 2002). These standards are based on conceptual frameworks informed by research, theory, and best practices, and they represent a shared and coherent vision of effective teaching.

Brief Background on Standards-Based Reform in Egypt

Standards reform efforts in education are not solely a U.S.-based phenomenon. English as a second language (ESL) standards, for example, have been developed in Australia, Canada, and England (McKay, 2000; McKay et al., 2001a; McKay et al., 2001b). Fujimoto (2000), in discussing the feasibility of EFL standards, reported results of a survey showing that 82% of respondents felt there was a need for standards in their respective countries, and as we write this chapter, we know of standards projects starting in places as diverse as China, Italy, and Qatar. In Egypt, the former Ministry of Education has shown a keen interest in standards-based reform of educational practices. In a 1999 videoconference broadcast to teachers in Egypt and the U.S., Dr. Hussein Kamel Bahaa Eldine, Egypt's then minister of education, highlighted the importance of reform when he told his audience, "Educational reform is the greatest national project of Egypt . . . [and] teachers are the pillars of educational reform" (Monem, El-Sokkary, Haddaway, & Bickel, 2001, p. 26).

Perhaps we might say that another pillar for the reform effort is improving the teaching and learning of English, since English is perceived as an "essential" course of study for Egyptian schoolchildren. As the lingua franca of commerce, English provides an important avenue to economic development within the country and with its commercial partners. Thus, it is not surprising that English is the main foreign language taught in Egyptian schools. To increase the number of English-proficient Egyptians, the Ministry of Education has undertaken efforts to bolster English language programs. In 1994, the ministry lowered the starting age for beginning the study of English in public schools from the sixth year of primary school to the fourth year, and plans currently call for lowering the start of English instruction to the first year of school. Students who complete the secondary level will have taken 10 or more years of instruction in English as a subject area. However, there is wide dissatisfaction with students' ability to *use* English, especially for the kinds of purposes targeted by the ministry.

The lack of proficiency in English has been attributed to a shortage of "qualified" teachers and supervisors (El Naggar et al., 2001). With the increased need for English teachers at the primary level, it has become apparent that many English teachers have neither sufficient training in creating effective classroom environments, especially for young learners, nor much experience in using communicative English language methods. In addition, our Egyptian counterparts noted that teachers' own English skills are often inadequate for modeling proficient and communicative language use—an issue further impacted by regional variation in skill level and available training resources. The development of standards for English teachers, in-service teacher trainers, educational leaders, and in-service training courses has been strongly supported by the ministry, which views the improvement of English teaching and learning as an educational priority.

The Pharos Project

Overview of the Project

The Pharos project is taking place under the auspices of the Integrated English Language Program II (IELP-II), a United States Agency for International Development (USAID) project, which has actively worked in English language teaching in Egypt for about 15 years. While IELP has been offering in-service training programs to improve the delivery of English language education for many years, it was only recently that staff determined the need for consistent criteria in measuring the effectiveness of these programs. The standards project was initiated as a way to create a coherent base for evaluation and planning of project programs. Consonant with IELP-II's overall objective to increase the number of qualified English teachers in both the public and private sectors, the goals of the Pharos project are to develop standards that will:

- lead to improvement in English classroom instruction and teacher education systems;
- provide a framework to support training and technical assistance;
- offer a set of consistent criteria to evaluate the effectiveness of such technical assistance; and
- ultimately serve as a model for other content areas, such as mathematics, science, Arabic, and foreign languages such as French and German.

The project commenced in June 2001 with a team of four, two U.S. TESOL professionals and two Egyptian professionals. The makeup of the team reflected complementary roles and expertise. The U.S. consultants had experience with various components of TESOL's U.S.-based standards projects, and the Egyptian consultants were very knowledgeable about the pre-service and in-service needs of English teachers in the Egyptian setting. The first activity consisted of a review of existing standards documents developed by associations and agencies for both language and subject-area teaching, to get a sense of the scope, formats, and categories previously used in other large-scale standards projects.

Out of these extensive discussions, the team designed a framework that could be applied to all four sets of target standards. The framework entailed three conceptual levels. The first level, "domain," was defined as general, overreaching or crosscutting areas broad enough to account for the various audiences and settings involved in English language teaching in Egypt, but narrow enough to be useful in developing a complete system of standards. The team selected seven domains that, we felt, covered the needs of the four settings in which we planned to develop standards. The seven domains and their definitions are listed in Figure 1.

With the draft conceptual framework in place, we devoted the next six months to developing standards for each domain. Each consultant took responsibility for preparing a draft of one set of standards. When the four drafts were ready, we exchanged the sets of standards and commented extensively on one another's drafts. By January 2002, the first draft of the four sets of standards was produced, incorporating feedback from all four consultants. The first draft also contained some sample indicators, defined as assessable, observable behaviors or activities that educators or programs may perform to show progress toward meeting a particular standard. Figure 2 presents sample standards for Domain 1 (Vision and Advocacy) for the four sets of standards.

DOMAINS	DEFINITIONS
DOMAIN 1	**Vision and Advocacy** are defined as the beliefs and directions for learning shared and supported by stakeholders who are committed to acting as agents for excellence in English education and training.
DOMAIN 2	**Language Proficiency** is defined as the level of English language competence that enables educators to perform their tasks and duties.
DOMAIN 3	**Professional Knowledge Base** is defined as the core principles and methods of the professional disciplines that underlie effective instructional programs for the teaching of English or the training of English teachers.
DOMAIN 4	**Planning and Management of Learning** are defined as the setting up and delivery of appropriate learning and teaching experiences to achieve instructional objectives in English teaching and training.
DOMAIN 5	**Assessment and Evaluation** are defined as the systematic process of planning, collection, analysis, and use of data to make decisions to improve English teaching and learning.
DOMAIN 6	**Learning Community and Environment** are defined as settings where learning takes place. All members of the learning community—students, educators, parents—are respected regardless of differences and encouraged to actively participate throughout the learning environment.
DOMAIN 7	**Professionalism** is defined as modeling ethical professional conduct, engaging in reflective practice, and pursuing lifelong professional growth and career opportunities.

FIG. 1.   Seven domains of Pharos project standards

Field Discussions with Egyptian Partners

Once the four sets of draft standards were complete, we embarked on the next phase—namely, introducing them to the field and seeking feedback from Egyptian professionals. This phase provided another facet of the collaborative process between native and nonnative professionals and reflected a bidirectional approach in which the designated team of U.S. and Egyptian consultants wrote the draft standards and then shared them with Egyptian partners. This approach ensured feedback from the field, adding concrete input to the document from those most knowledgeable of the target settings. In this vein, we appreciate Widdowson's (1994) point that the nonnative speaker (in our minds, best labeled the "Egyptian English-teaching professional") is in the "better position to know what is appropriate in the contexts of

English Teacher Standards
Standard 1: The English teacher contributes to the development of the school's vision and goals for English teaching.
Indicator A: The English teacher participates in the establishment of the schools' beliefs, mission, and goals that take into consideration the interests and concerns of stakeholders.
Teacher Trainer Standards
Standard 1: The teacher trainer understands and supports the training program's vision and goals.
Indicator A: The teacher trainer explains the program's vision and goals to colleagues and other professionals.
Educational Leader Standards
Standard 1: The educational leader facilitates the development, articulation, implementation, and stewardship of a vision of English language learning that is shared and supported by a range of stakeholders.
Indicator A: Leaders provide resources to staff so they can meet to develop a shared vision of effective English language learning.
In-Service Training Program Standards
Standard 1: The program is guided by a clearly articulated vision, philosophy, and set of goals for English in-service education, developed in collaboration with key stakeholders and reflecting the pursuit of high-quality training for teachers.
Indicator A: The program has a mission statement describing its philosophy and goals.

FIG. 2. Sample standards for Domain 1

language learning" (p. 387). The bidirectional approach (illustrated in Figure 3) included top-to-bottom and bottom-to-top elements to achieve two goals: (1) dissemination of the draft standards to the field through focus group discussions, meetings, and conferences; and (2) review, from the field, of the draft standards and indicators, as well as development of additional standards and indicators. The next section describes in more detail the content of the field discussions.

A series of workshops was held with stakeholders representing the English language teaching community. Referred to as "partners," they included English teachers, supervisors, teacher trainers, training course designers and monitors, educational leaders, representatives from the Ministry of Education, professors from university faculties of education, and staff members of IELP-II. Most were "specialists" in English teaching; that is, they had graduated from faculties of art or education where they both studied the English language and took education courses. The workshops sought to familiarize the invited partners with the background of standards-based educational reform, to introduce and discuss the terminology associated with standards-based instruction and assessment, to discuss challenges and strate-

FIG. 3. Bidirectional approach to standards development

gies for implementing standards in Egypt, and to review and critique the domains and standards contained in the draft standards document. The partners were also asked to write additional standards and indicators as a way to involve them more actively in the development of the standards and to ensure that the standards and indicators truly reflected the needs and conditions of the Egyptian context. While the development of the first draft of the domains and standards was a top-to-bottom process, the development of indicators was primarily a bottom-to-top process.

The process of reviewing and critiquing the draft standards included considerations of *content* (in terms of the full coverage of knowledge, skills, and attitudes within each domain) and *language* (in terms of clarity and comprehensibility). Participants were asked to consider the following criteria in analyzing the standards: (1) importance (Is the standard a critical and necessary component of English language teaching?); (2) relevance (Does it help focus efforts to improve English teaching and learning?); (3) reality (Is it attainable and consistent with what is necessary and expected?); (4) consistency with the Egyptian educational context (Is it linked to Egyptian educational goals?); (5) understandability (Does it use the language of the educational field while communicating clearly?); and (6) focus (Does it say exactly which specific actions and results are expected?).

The extensive feedback from the workshops was incorporated into the draft document, and a second draft was prepared in June 2002. The second draft contained finalized domains, revised standards, and some indicators for the four sets. This draft was subsequently disseminated to selected partners to be reviewed again in light of the criteria already described—that is, importance for English teaching and learning, relevance for English language learning in the Egyptian context, and comprehensibility/use of straightforward language.

This bidirectional approach to standards and indicators development followed three cycles: draft, feedback, and review. During each cycle, "veteran" partners were consulted, and new partners were added. In retrospect, we can now see that the first introduction of the Pharos project to the Egyptian English teaching community was like throwing a stone in water. The first encounter was a shock that brought a wave of alertness to the first group of partners. The more they were exposed to and involved in discussions, the more they became aware of the importance of standards for educational reform. At the same time, involving new partners expanded dissemination of the concept of standards and created a wider circle, both numerically and geographically, of field discussions.

We learned a lot about what to expect in the feedback cycles. With each new group of partners, defining the key terms *standards* and *indicators* was the first step in the awareness raising. Although the draft document provided these definitions, there was typically confusion about the terminology and the rationale behind the choice of terms. Furthermore, it became clear to us that presenting and discussing all four sets of standards further contributed to the confusion. At this point, we made the decision to concentrate on the English teacher and teacher trainer standards, both to create a tighter focus for the field discussions and because of their more immediate application to IELP-II's objectives.

In the indicators development workshops, we concentrated on defining the term *indicator,* critiquing sample indicators, and developing (as a group) criteria for good performance indicators. A good indicator, for example, should:

- cover all aspects of the standards
- show more specifically what the standard "looks like"
- contain action verbs
- demonstrate assessable or observable behaviors or actions
- be limited in scope
- use straightforward language
- (perhaps) include examples
- be specific to the context (e.g., the classroom, the in-service training course)

The procedures for writing new indicators followed a vertical approach, going from standard to indicator. Participating partners analyzed each standard by main task or function and main components: knowledge, skill, or attitudes. We here present examples of the kinds of discussions that took place in these sessions, to illustrate the process.

Figure 4 provides a visual representation of the analysis for Domain 2 (Language Proficiency), Standard 1: ***"The English teacher uses oral and written English language appropriately and fluently."***

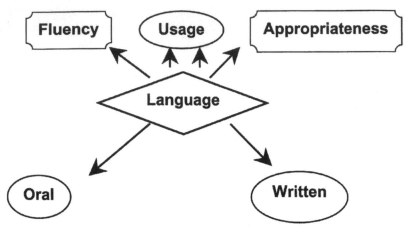

FIG. 4. Sample analysis of Domain 2, Standard 1

After analyzing Standard 1, participants developed the following new indicators:

> **Indicator A:** *The English teacher adapts his or her language usage to fit a variety of student abilities.*
>
> **Indicator B:** *The English teacher models both accuracy and fluency.*
>
> **Indicator C:** *The English teacher demonstrates language proficiency through scores on tests, oral interviews, or interacting with competent language specialists.*
>
> **Indicator D:** *The English teacher demonstrates good reading and writing skills and strategies.*

This analytical approach, however, did not prove to be equally effective for all the standards. Some concepts were so abstract that the participants had difficulty developing appropriate indicators. This was the case with Domain 7 (Professionalism), Standard 2: *"The English teacher exhibits a genuine commitment to meeting the requirements of the job and is fair and tolerant."*

In the workshops, the participants were asked to develop indicators for teacher commitment. This presented a challenge for participants. They were asked to reflect on and then find answers to at least one of the following questions:

When you say, "This teacher is really committed":

- what do you see?
- why do you say it?
- what in his/her behavior makes you say that?

This reflective approach proved to be very effective in helping participants to brainstorm and develop indicators for some of the more abstract concepts in the standards. They produced the following indicators showing how to meet the commitment standard in observable and assessable ways:

Indicator A: *The English teacher works for personal gratification not for rewards.*

Indicator B: *The English teacher mentors young teachers.*

Indicator C: *The English teacher reacts appropriately and quickly to problematic situations.*

Indicator D: *The English teacher volunteers for school activities.*

Indicator E: *The English teacher takes part in administrative issues.*

Indicator F: *The English teacher completes tasks in a timely manner.*

Indicator G: *The English teacher is punctual and strives to achieve a 100% teacher attendance rate.*

The approach used to develop indicators for the trainer standards followed another strategy. It built on the participants' previous experience as trainers and trainees. The starting point was to come up with a profile of a good trainer. The participants developed a list of qualities and characteristics of a good trainer. The participants described the good trainer in terms of "what he/she is," "what he/she has," and "what he/she uses." The good trainer, according to the profile generated by the participants, is *active, charismatic, convincing, creative, decisive, democratic, experienced, flexible, focused, knowledgeable, motivated, motivating, open-minded, self-confident, tolerant, and trainee-centered.* He/she presents an appropriate appearance, has legible handwriting and an audible voice, and possesses good presentation skills and problem-solving techniques and strategies. He/she uses appropriate body language and eye contact and uses modern technology when possible.

The participants were then asked to review the trainer standards. They had to review and comment on the standards under each domain in light of the domain definitions and the indicators under each standard. These discussions and comments contributed to the development of a new draft of the trainer standards based on the profile the participants had developed of effective trainers, thus ensuring that the profile of an effective trainer is based on the model represented by experienced Egyptian teachers in the field and reinforcing our conviction that the Egyptian teachers were in a better position to know what is appropriate in the context of local training (cf. Widdowson, 1994). The field discussion also led to another output. The trainer profile established criteria for the selection of trainers for the "Communicative Reflective Methodology" course described in the next section.

Piloting the Teacher Standards: The "Communicative Reflective Methodology" Course

With the draft of the English teacher standards revised, the Pharos project added another dimension to standards development by addressing the issue of how to apply the standards to practice. This first application involved using the standards to revise an existing teacher training course offered by IELP-II, entitled "Communicative Reflective Methodology" (CRM). To IELP-II staff, the CRM course seemed to be a natural "fit" for the emerging standards, since its course design focused on developing many of the competencies targeted in the English teacher standards. Reviewing the course involved examining the existing course in light of the standards to determine just how close that fit was—were all standards represented, or were some neglected (and if so, which ones)? The result of the analysis would then guide revision of course elements to create a standards-based CRM course.

The task of developing a standards-based CRM course required several distinct steps. First, using a rating scale to show the degree of congruence of specific course tasks to the standards indicators, a team of Egyptian partners worked in small groups to analyze all of the tasks included in the 16 units of *Tasks for Teacher Education* (Tanner & Green, 1998), the course book that formed the foundation of the CRM course. *Tasks for Teacher Education* utilizes a task-based approach and is based on a set of assumptions about teaching and learning that includes, for example, drawing on existing experience and knowledge, reflecting on one's own beliefs and attitudes, and assuming responsibility for one's own learning.

Preliminary results of the task analysis revealed that the tasks in *Tasks for Teacher Education* effectively covered Domain 4 (Planning and Management of Learning) of the teacher standards with the exception of the technology standard. A separate assessment component in the CRM course covered Domain 5 (Assessment and Evaluation). Since not all of the tasks could be included in the standards-based syllabus for the CRM course due to time constraints, the U.S. consultants analyzed the results task by task to determine which tasks best covered the standards. Tasks that were considered to "fully cover" the standard as rated by the Egyptian partners were selected for inclusion in the CRM course.

With the ratings and resulting analysis completed, a new group of Egyptian partners made up of senior supervisors, veteran CRM trainers, and the U.S. consultants reviewed the first draft of the CRM syllabus. Based on their experiences as trainers or their knowledge of the teaching context, including Egyptian teachers' typical strengths and weaknesses, the partners engaged in an extended discussion, weighing coverage of the targeted standards against such issues as allotted time, topical sequencing of units, and the needs of teachers in the field. In the end, recommendations were made for revision of the draft course syllabus. The major changes to the syllabus were resequencing some of the units, adding additional tasks, developing journal prompts for units that did not have suggested entries or prompts that better corresponded to the session's topic or activities, and reorganizing the task sequences and time allotments to better fit the three-hour (after-school) sessions of the CRM course.

In response to trainers' concerns about the effectiveness of the assessment component developed for the last offering of the CRM course, a set of seven assessment units was developed, each designed to be delivered in 60-minute sessions throughout the CRM course. The development process drew on the feedback of experienced CRM trainers and involved collaboration between the U.S. and Egyptian consultants. Each unit consisted of a series of activities around some aspect of assessment. Like *Tasks for Teacher Education,* the assessment tasks were designed so that teachers reflect on their own experiences and engage in learning activities as a means of gaining a greater understanding of assessment theory and practice. Each unit also included handouts with supplemental information that trainers could present during class time or assign for homework. Most important, they aligned with the standards of Domain 5 (Assessment and Evaluation).

Awareness-Raising Seminars

Another aspect of the plan for the Pharos project was to gradually involve a larger pool of Egyptian EFL specialists with a view toward project sustainability. To inform teachers, teacher trainers, and supervisors about the role of standards in educational improvement and reform in Egypt, IELP II supported a series of awareness-raising seminars in four Egyptian governorates. Prior to the seminars, a four-day training-of-trainers (TOT) workshop was held to assist the selected Egyptian seminar trainers in designing seminars that would be appropriate for and relevant to the needs of their respective governorates. The TOT was designed to provide the participants with hands-on working sessions in which they could design the agendas and develop materials and activities for each seminar. It had eight overall objectives: (1) identify the audience for the four awareness-raising seminars; (2) develop procedures for assessing the needs of the audience; (3) determine the general theme or topic for each seminar; (4) write overall objectives for the four seminars and for each individual seminar; (5) determine the schedule for the four seminars; (6) identify equipment, materials, and facilities needed and develop a budget that takes into consideration these needs; (7) design an agenda for each seminar that specifies the activities to be covered and the trainer who will be responsible for each activity; and (8) create or assemble materials needed for each seminar.

The four awareness-raising seminars took place over a four-month period in the four governorates. To determine the effectiveness of the seminars, we designed an observation checklist using many of the characteristics of effective trainers that the experienced Egyptian trainers had developed for the CRM course described previously. Preliminary analysis revealed that, in general, the seminars were quite successful. The Egyptian trainers, especially the supervisors with a lot of training experience, were very adept at seminar planning, especially at planning interactive agendas and developing relevant interactive tasks and activities that took into account their designated audiences and their needs (primary and secondary English teachers and supervisors). Trainers were also effective in imparting the theme that standards should be seen as a blueprint for individual professional development. Most important, the seminars, conducted entirely by local Egyptian colleagues, were grounded in the needs and concerns of the teachers and settings in which they were conducted.

Conclusion

In planning the Pharos project, the immediate aim was to design a set of standards that would provide guidance and criteria for internal management of and decision making about IELP-II's training program for English teachers. At that time, some thought was given to the possible further applicability of such standards to the national context, but project staff primarily envisioned disseminating the Pharos project as a model for the Ministry of Education to consider in designing its own standards for teaching. It appears that these efforts have had the hoped-for broader impact. Just recently the Ministry of Education has formed the National Committee on Standards, several members of which are IELP-II staff members who have worked closely with the Pharos project. The committee is charged with designing standards that would apply to *all* teachers in Egypt. The implications for such a project include using such standards, instead of seniority, as a basis for promotion; requiring professional development throughout a teacher's career; and upgrading the status of teachers. In a clear indication of impact, the committee has chosen the Pharos teacher standards as the template from which to begin their work.

As the Pharos project winds down, it is appropriate to ask ourselves how, from our vantage point, our work might affect EFL teaching in Egypt and what effect it has had on its participants. The establishment of the National Committee on Standards offers promise for improved professionalism of teachers across the country. Perhaps more important, however, the standards developed both by Pharos and ultimately by the National Committee on Standards can provide short-term and long-term goals for individual teachers. English teachers will be able to visualize the pathway toward professional competence; they can assess where they currently are on this path and seek out opportunities for professional growth. Moreover, the standards offer multiple avenues for professional development—from indicators for improving levels of English language proficiency to expanded knowledge of principles of assessment and evaluation. Just as Pasternak and Bailey (this volume) offer a framework for improving language proficiency and professional preparation, the Pharos standards offer a road map for teachers as they progress through their careers. In addition, while the Pharos project focuses on in-service teachers, another project, STEPS (standards for teachers of English at pre-service), focuses on teachers-in-training and newly qualified teachers of up to three years—offering a comprehensive plan for improving the knowledge, skills, and attitudes of English teachers in Egypt. One of our last steps involves the training of English supervisors in understanding and using standards in their daily duties of observing teachers and designing professional development activities in their assigned primary and secondary schools.

The design of the project reflected a collaborative approach to standards development that enriched the key participants, the feedback processes that were established, and the products that ensued. Working in conjunction, the U.S. and Egyptian consultants brought expertise to the project; we benefited as well from the opportunity to grow professionally ourselves within a project that offered many challenges. We also developed enduring professional relationships of the same kind described by de Oliveira and Richardson (this volume). The field discussions extended the collaboration between native and nonnative English-speaking professionals into an extended circle of partners. They not only succeeded in raising awareness of standards across the Egyptian English teaching community but also led to significant and substantive contributions to the four sets of standards, reinforcing our belief that extensive collaboration is essential for any standards development project. The closer the participants are to the teaching and learning setting, the greater the chance is for meaningful insights and contributions and for buy-in by those who will ultimately be most affected by the educational reforms. Moreover, sustainability is more likely to occur when credible local professionals are charged with the design and implementation of such reforms. It also further reinforced our belief in the positive outcomes that can result when native and nonnative English-speaking professionals collaborate in an educational endeavor.

Note

1. The authors wish to thank the Integrated English Language Program II for the tremendous support in carrying out the Pharos project, with special appreciation to Amal Nasralla and Lorraine Denakpo.

References

Cloud, N. (2000). Incorporating ESL standards into teacher education: Ideas for teacher educators. In M. A. Snow (Ed.), *Implementing the ESL standards for pre-K–12 students through teacher education* (pp. 1–32). Alexandria, VA: TESOL.

El Naggar, Z., Hana, R., Haggar, K. A., Sahakian, S., El Baz, A. R., & Ibrahim, M. (2001). *Proposal for project to set performance standards for English language majors at faculties of education.* Cairo, Egypt: Ain Shams University, Center for Developing English Language Teaching.

Fujimoto, D. (2000, February/March). Looking ahead to international standards. *TESOL Matters, 10*(1). Retrieved June 1, 2003, from *http://www.tesol.org/pubs/ articles/2000/tm0002-04.html*

Gomez, E. L. (2000). A history of the ESL standards for pre-K–12 students. In M. A. Snow (Ed.), *Implementing the ESL standards for pre-K–12 students through teacher education* (pp. 49–74). Alexandria, VA: TESOL.

Kuhlman, N., & Murray, D. E. (2000). Changing populations, changing needs in teacher preparation. In M. A. Snow (Ed.), *Implementing the ESL standards for pre-K-12 students through teacher education* (pp. 33–48). Alexandria, VA: TESOL.

Marzano, R. J., & Kendall, J. S. (1998). *Implementing standards-based education.* Washington, DC: National Education Association.

McKay, P. (2000). On ESL standards for school-age learners. *Language Testing, 17*(2), 185–214.

McKay, P., Coppari, P., Cumming, A., Graves, K., Lopriore, L., & Short, D. (2001a, March/April/May). Language standards: An international perspective, part 1. *TESOL Matters, 11*(2), 1, 4.

McKay, P., Coppari, P., Cumming, A., Graves, K., Lopriore, L., & Short, D. (2001b, June/July/August). Language standards: An international perspective, part 2. *TESOL Matters, 11*(3), 11, 15.

Monem, D. A., El-Sokkary, W., Haddaway, C., & Bickel, B. (2001, November/December). English teaching in Egypt: At the crossroads of global communication. *ESL Magazine, 4*(6), 26–28.

National Board for Professional Teaching Standards. (1998). *English as a new language standards for national board certification.* Southfield, MI: Author.

National Council for the Accreditation of Teacher Education. (1995). *Standards, procedures, and policies for the accreditation of professional education units.* Washington, DC: Author.

Tanner, R., & Green, C. (1998). *Tasks for teacher education: A reflective approach.* Harlow, England: Addison Wesley Longman.

TESOL. (2002). *Standards for P–12 ESL teacher education programs.* Washington, DC: Author.

Widdowson, H. G. (1994). The ownership of English. *TESOL Quarterly, 28*(2), 377–389.

Questions for Reflection

1. In the chapter by Major and Yamashiro, the authors offer some suggestions for adapting Western ESL instructional practices to the realities of the Japanese classroom. Select a classroom in a setting with which you are familiar. Given the students' objectives for learning English, what adaptations, other than those described by Major and Yamashiro, would you suggest implementing?

2. In her chapter, Velasco-Martin suggests that the figure of the "intercultural speaker" should replace the figure of the "nonnative speaker." Do you agree? In what ways does the notion of the "intercultural speaker" differ from the figure of the "nonnative speaker"?

3. Velasco-Martin describes a variety of projects in which she uses her skills and knowledge as an intercultural speaker in an EFL setting. Describe how a NNES professional with whom you are familiar could implement the notion of the intercultural speaker in a setting other than the one described by Velasco-Martin.

4. The chapter by de Oliveira and Richardson describes the benefits of native and nonnative English speaker collaboration. It also describes how de Oliveira and Richardson make their collaborative relationship work. What conditions, other than those described in the chapter, are necessary for the collaborative process to succeed? What factors would threaten the success of collaborative relationships?

5. The chapter by Snow, Omar, and Katz describes a collaborative project in which native and nonnative English speakers produced standards for the Egyptian context. What implications might the approach to collaboration described in the chapter have for other settings?

Contributors

Annette Aagard currently teaches ESL at Palomar College and National University in San Diego, California. She received a master's degree in TESOL from California State University, Los Angeles.

Nuzhat Amin received her Ph.D. from the Ontario Institute for Studies in Education of the University of Toronto (OISE/UT). Her research interests are interdisciplinary, focusing on minority women, language, and power. She has published in *TESOL Quarterly, TESOL Matters, CATESOL Journal, Contact,* and the feminist journals *Canadian Woman Studies* and *Resources for Feminist Research.* She is co-editor of *Canadian Woman Studies: An Introductory Reader* (1999) and volume 2 of *Feminism and Education: A Canadian Perspective* (1994). She has taught English, ESL, and EFL in Canada, Pakistan, and Poland. At present, she is assistant professor in the School of Education at Long Island University, where she teaches in the Department of Curriculum and Instruction.

Kathleen M. Bailey received her Ph.D. in Applied Linguistics from the University of California, Los Angeles. Since 1981 she has worked at the Monterey Institute of International Studies, where she has been the head of the TESOL-TFL MA program and the director of the intensive English program. She is currently the faculty advisor to the Language Program Administration certificate students and the Peace Corps Masters Internationalist candidates. Her research and teaching interests include language assessment, teacher education and supervision, the teaching of speaking and listening, and research methodology. In 1998–1999 she was the president of the international TESOL association.

Brock Brady is coordinator of TESOL programs at American University and past president of the Washington Area TESOL affiliate. He has taught in the U.S., Africa, Central America, Europe, and Asia and has directed English teaching programs for the State Department. His research interests include teacher training methodology, cross-cultural discourse analysis, and teaching pronunciation. His wife, Kyongsook, is a nonnative English-speaking teacher.

George Braine is associate professor of English at the Chinese University of Hong Kong. His research interests are in second language writing and academic literacy. He was the first chair of the Nonnative English Speakers Caucus in the TESOL organization and is the co-editor of the *Asian Journal of English Language Teaching.*

Donna M. Brinton serves as a lecturer in Applied Linguistics and TESL at the University of California, Los Angeles, and as academic coordinator of the university's courses for matriculated students. She teaches graduate courses in TESL methodology and for over 20 years has supervised the TESOL field practicum. Her research interests focus on novice teacher development—in particular, the special challenges faced by nonnative English-speaking graduate students who enroll in North American TESOL programs. She is the past co-editor of the *CATESOL Journal* and has co-written or co-edited several teacher resource books as well as numerous articles in the field.

Luciana C. de Oliveira is a doctoral candidate in education (language, literacy, and culture; second language acquisition) at the University of California, Davis (UCD). She is the English language research coordinator for the Area 3 History and Cultures project at UCD. Her research interests include academic literacy development and nonnative English-speaking teachers in the TESOL field.

Angelica Ching is a candidate for the master's degree in TESOL at California State University, Los Angeles. She is currently working on her thesis, which focuses on nonnative English-speaking professionals teaching ESL classes. Her areas of interest include nonnative English-speaking teachers and the use of technology in the classroom. She is originally from Panama and is literate in both Spanish and Cantonese.

Goedele Gulikers is associate professor in the Language Studies Department at Prince George's Community College in Largo, Maryland. She has been a language teacher for 20 years. She earned a master of arts degree in Slavic philology in her native Belgium and taught in Moscow for five years. She then earned an M.Ed. in TESOL in the U.S. and taught in intensive English programs in Virginia and

Maryland. Prior to her current position, she served as the ESL curriculum coordinator at Anne Arundel Community College, where she ran the adult and higher education programs.

Jette G. Hansen is assistant professor of English Language/Linguistics and Second Language Acquisition and Teaching (SLAT) at the University of Arizona. She was born in Denmark and began learning English at age 10, when her family immigrated to the United States. Her research interests stem from her family's experiences in learning English and include the acquisition of a second language phonology, gender and second language acquisition, and peer response. She has published in *Applied Linguistics, TESOL Quarterly, TESOL Journal,* and *Written Communication* and is the co-author of *Peer Response in Second Language Writing Classrooms* (2002).

Beverly S. Hartford is professor of Applied Linguistics at Indiana University. Her research areas include world Englishes, interlanguage pragmatics, and nonnative English-speaking teachers. She teaches courses in sociolinguistics, pragmatics, world Englishes, and applied English grammar. In addition she has been a trainer of ESL/EFL teachers for 33 years, teaching and developing methods and material courses. She has taught and conducted teacher training in a large number of places around the world, including Nepal, Poland, and Venezuela.

Lía D. Kamhi-Stein is associate professor at California State University, Los Angeles, where she teaches in the MA TESOL program. Her research interests are academic literacy, the integration of computer-mediated communication tools in TESOL teacher preparation, and nonnative English-speaking professionals. She was a co-founding member of the Nonnative English Speakers in TESOL Caucus and of the Nonnative Language Educators' Issues Interest Group in the California TESOL affiliate. She was the first NNEST Caucus newsletter editor and served as caucus chair. In 2002–2003, she served as CATESOL president. She is currently on the TESOL Board of Directors serving as Director-at-Large (2004–2007). She has published in *TESOL Quarterly, TESOL Journal, TEXT, The Journal of Adolescent and Adult Literacy,* and *Lectura y Vida,* as well as in other journals and in edited volumes.

Anne M. Katz received her Ph.D. in second language education from Stanford University in 1988. She has worked for over 20 years as a researcher and evaluator with educational projects involving linguistically and culturally diverse students. As a lecturer at the School for International Training in Brattleboro, Vermont, she teaches courses in curriculum, assessment, and evaluation. She has also worked as a teacher educator in Brazil and Egypt. She led the TESOL-sponsored team that developed assessment guidelines for the pre-K–12 ESL standards, and her most recent publications focus on standards-based assessment systems. In her work, she promotes linkages between research and the classroom to support student learning and teacher development.

Icy Lee is assistant professor in the Department of Education Studies at Hong Kong Baptist University. She has teaching experience at the secondary, undergraduate, and postgraduate levels in Hong Kong. She also has ESL teaching experience in Vancouver. Her articles have appeared in the *Journal of Second Language Writing, System,* and other publications. Her main research interests include ESL writing and ESL teacher education. She was the winner of the 1999 TESOL Award for Excellence in the Development of Pedagogical Materials.

Jun Liu is associate professor of English at the University of Arizona. His research interests include sociocultural and sociopolitical aspects of second language learning and teaching in both ESL and EFL contexts, classroom-oriented research methodology, and L2 writing. He has published in *TESOL Quarterly, ELT Journal,* the *Journal of Asian Pacific Communication,* and *Educational Research Quarterly.* He has authored *Asian Students' Classroom Communication Patterns in U.S. Universities* (2001) and co-authored *Peer Response* (2002). A recipient of the 1999 TESOL Newbury House Award for Excellence in Teaching and past chairperson of the Nonnative English Speakers in TESOL Caucus, Jun Liu served on the TESOL Board of Directors as Director-at-Large (2001–2004).

Ahmar Mahboob is assistant professor of Linguistics and TESL at East Carolina University. Born in Karachi, Pakistan, he has taught English in a number of countries, including Pakistan, the United Arab Emirates, South Korea, and the United States. He has presented and published on diverse linguistics and TESOL issues, including world Englishes, pidgin and creole languages, language policy and planning, minority language studies, and nonnative English-speaking professionals. He has served as the president and vice president of Indiana TESOL (INTESOL). He is the founding editor of *INTESOL Journal.* He is currently serving as the chair of the Nonnative English Speakers in TESOL Caucus.

Elza Magalhães Major, a nonnative English speaker, is assistant professor of TESOL in the Department of Educational Specialties, College of Education, at the University of Nevada, Reno. Before earning a Ph.D. in education, she taught secondary and adult ESL and EFL in a variety of school settings in the U.S. and in Brazil. Her areas of interest are the cultural and linguistic mismatch between K–12 teachers and their language minority students, critical social consciousness in teacher education, and nonnative English-speaking professionals in the TESOL field.

Aya Matsuda is assistant professor of Applied Linguistics at the University of New Hampshire, where she teaches undergraduate and graduate courses in TESL and linguistics. Her research interests include world Englishes, teaching English as an international language, and international teaching assistants.

Paul Kei Matsuda is assistant professor of English and associate director of composition at the University of New Hampshire. He teaches various writing courses, as well as graduate courses in composition studies and applied linguistics. Founding chair of the Symposium on Second Language Writing, he has edited *On Second Language Writing* (2001) and *Landmark Essays on ESL Writing* (2001).

Karen L. Newman is project manager for the Interdisciplinary Collaborative Program, a professional development program for content and ESL teachers, at Indiana University's School of Education. She is pursuing doctoral studies in language education, with a minor in TESOL/applied linguistics. She currently teaches foreign language and ESL/bilingual methods courses for pre-service and in-service teachers. She has also taught learning skills courses, as well as college-level German. Previously, she taught EFL in Austria and Germany. Her research interests include language teaching methodology, nonnative English-speaking teachers, aesthetic and social reform movements, and alternative education.

Maysoun Omar is associate professor in the Faculty of Education at Alexandria University, Egypt. She followed her studies in French language and foreign language education in Egypt, France, and Canada. She is trilingual and teaches and conducts research and training in the fields of language education in Arabic, French, and English. She collaborated in the English department reform project and the development of standards for quality training in the Institute of Public Administration in Saudi Arabia. She is currently consulting for the U.S.

Agency for International Development in Egypt on an EFL standards project for the Egyptian context and on an educational reform project in Alexandria.

Myoung-Soon Ashley Paik is an English language development teacher at Los Altos High School in La Puente Hacienda Unified School District. She is also an instructional technology assistant in Academic Technological Support (ATS) at California State University, Los Angeles. Her research interests include content-based instruction, language testing, and the use of the World Wide Web as a communication tool.

Mindy Pasternak earned her master's degree in TESOL from the Monterey Institute of International Studies. She is currently working with executive and foreign language programs at the same institution and is a board member and curriculum designer for TravelingEd.org, an educational nonprofit organization. Prior to beginning her graduate studies, she taught English to elementary- and secondary-aged students in Seville, Spain. More recently, she taught English to Chinese middle school English teachers in Jiangxi Province, China, and has taught academic and business English in California. It was her work with Chinese English teachers that fueled her interest in issues regarding nonnative English-speaking professionals.

Sally Richardson is a lecturer at California State University, Hayward (CSUH), where she teaches upper-division composition to native and nonnative speakers for both the English Department and the School of Science. She also teaches occasional classes in the master's in TESOL program at CSUH. Her areas of interest include teacher collaboration, teacher training, and technology-enhanced teaching and learning.

Linda Sasser is the English language development (ELD) program specialist for the Alhambra School District, where she develops ELD curriculum and content-based materials for elementary and high school programs and conducts staff development and training for teachers in ELD and in Specially Designed Academic Instruction in English. She serves on the UCLA Writing Project Advisory Board and teaches ESL at Pasadena City College. In 1999–2000, she served as president of the California TESOL affiliate.

Marguerite Ann Snow received her Ph.D. in Applied Linguistics from the University of California, Los Angeles, in 1985. She is professor in the Charter College of Education at California State University, Los Angeles, where she teaches in the TESOL MA program. She is co-author of *Content-Based Second Language Instruction* (2003), co-editor of *The Multicultural Classroom: Readings for Content-Area Teachers* (1992) and *The Content-Based Classroom: Perspectives on Integrating Language and Content* (1997), and editor of *Implementing the ESL Standards for Pre-K–12–Students in Teacher Education* (2000). She has published in *TESOL Quarterly, Applied Linguistics,* and *The Modern Language Journal.* She had a Fulbright fellowship in Hong Kong (1985–1986), and in 1989 she received, along with her co-authors, the Pimsleur Award from ACTFL for the best research study in foreign language education. She was given the Outstanding Professor award at California State University, Los Angeles, in 1999. In addition to working closely with local public school teachers, she has trained EFL teachers worldwide. She is currently consulting on a project for the U.S. Agency for International Development in Egypt to develop EFL standards.

Karl Uhrig is a Ph.D. candidate in language education at Indiana University (IU), Bloomington. He has been teaching ESL at the Intensive English Program at IU since 1995. Currently, he is also teaching foreign language and ESL/bilingual teaching methods for pre-service and in-service teachers. His research focuses on language learning strategies. He has presented several papers on this topic, as well as on nonnative English speaker issues.

Carmen Velasco-Martin holds a master's degree in TESOL from California State University, Los Angeles, and is a Ph.D. candidate at the University of Barcelona, Spain. Her academic interests are testing and evaluation, sociolinguistics, and second language acquisition. She was an EFL teacher in Spain and a bilingual education teacher in California for many years. As an EFL teacher trainer, she specializes in the use of information and communication technologies in the language classroom. She is presently an education advisor at the Embassy of Spain in Washington, DC.

Ayako Yamashiro received her master's degree in TESOL from the University of Nevada, Reno, in 2002. She has presented papers focusing on bilingual education and EFL instruction at California TESOL and international TESOL conferences. She worked at the Ministry of Foreign Affairs in Japan. Currently, she teaches English grammar and reading classes at Okinawa International University, Okinawa Christian Junior College, and the University of Okinawa in Japan.

Subject Index

academic skills, 45, 48
accents, 10, 11, 19, 20, 21, 45, 46, 53,
  65, 70, 102, 108, 110, 111, 127,
  128, 141, 168, 222, 236, 237, 270,
  284
  American (American English), 21,
    40, 47, 49, 76
  Australian, 21
  British, 21, 76
  Canadian, 71, 76
  Danish, 47
  Hong Kong, 21
  Inner Circle, 77
  Pakistani, 62, 77
  teachers', 169
  white, 65, 71
accented(ness), 159, 168
acculturation, 29, 37, 49
accuracy, 157, 166, 168, 199, 202,
  268, 316. See also fluency
  areas of, 166
  grammatical, 159, 232
  segmental, 168
advocacy, 260, 273, 312
Amerasian children, 256, 258
Anglomania, 262, 263, 272. See also
  English allergy
assessment, 35, 173, 184, 217, 232,
  234, 237, 273, 319
  aural discrimination, 168
  and evaluation, 312, 318
  language, 260, 261
  needs, 171

performance-based, 273
principles of, 321
self-, 197
speaking, 169
standards-based, 273, 313
attitudes
  about English language, 141, 256,
    257, 262–263
  ethnocentric, 280
  toward international teaching
    assistants, 184
  about language, 214
  perceived, 81
  of students toward nonnative
    English-speaking teachers, 4,
    19–21, 59, 60, 65–67, 122–144,
    169
attrition, 47
avoidance, 51

Basic Interpersonal Communicative
  Skills (BICS), 45, 48
beliefs, 28, 31, 76, 122, 223, 278
  Asian, 28
  educational, 152, 211
  reconstructed, 256, 257, 266
  about teaching, 20, 198–199, 220,
    223–224, 312, 318
bilingual community, 281, 284

Canada, 4, 53, 59, 61, 62, 63, 65, 66,
  67, 68, 69, 70, 76, 77, 78, 101,
  160, 167, 237, 264, 284, 286, 309

335

Author Index